Memoirs of Khalilullah Khalili

An Afghan Philosopher Poet
A Conversation with his Daughter, Marie

By Afzal Nasiri & Marie Khalili

Published by:
Afzal Nasiri & Marie Khalili
Virginia

ISBN 978-0615889726

Table of Contents

Dedication

To all those who languished
under the oppressive rule
of former Afghan leaders.

To the brave nation of Afghanistan.

Acknowledgements

To adequately thank everyone who helped Marie and I with this project is almost impossible.

Our special thanks to Mr. Qavi Koshan of Omaid weekly for his relentless pursuit of the facts and skills in listening and putting the Persian (Dari) words on paper from radio cassettes. His diligent work is commendable.

We must thank Dr. Wassey Latifi, an Afghan Scholar and Academician (in Virginia) who read the Dari text and offered us his literary expertise on many occasions.

Our sincere thanks to Dr. Rawan Farhadi, Afghan scholar and a former Ambassador and Deputy Foreign Minister of Afghanistan (During the time of King Zaher Shah), for his useful tips and advice.

We should also thank Cindy Brookshire, a writer and blogger who lives in Prince William County (VA), for her extra-ordinary patience, prudent advice, and sincere assistance in putting the English translation together and give it the current form. She helped us proofread several times.

Thanks are due to Stacia D. Kelly, PhD, an author living in Prince William County (VA) who helped us with the format of the book and editing of the text, making it simple to read and understand.

Thank you to Katherine Gotthardt for helping establish the website: MemoirsofKhalili.com. She has graciously updated the site whenever we needed to add new contents.

Thanks are due to Prof. Wassef Bakhtari (also CA), who in spite of being under the weather, helped read the Persian proof and forwarded some very enlightening suggestions and corrections of dates.

And last but not least, Heidi Sutherlin, from My Creative Pursuits, for the beautiful cover design.

Testimonials

"This book should be read by all those who are the fans of late Ustad Khalili and also those who are interested in the history of Afghanistan in the 20th century. It is a very interesting book. Before the second edition comes out with any changes, reading the first edition is a must…"
~ *Dr. Rawan Farhadi, Linguist and senior Afghan Diplomat (California)*

"The child at whose birth the ruler of the time bestows name on him, and during the rule of that king's son - who defeated the Great Empire and won independence for his country - that child becomes an orphan and tends sheep to earn living… that is Ustad Khalili…"
~*Dr. Inayat Ullah Shahrani, Afghan intellectual and scholar living in California.*

"This is an adventurous and eventful story of the life of Ustad. It takes one through the old traditions and forgotten customs. The reader will travel through the dark days of history in Afghanistan. The revered Ustad goes through a period in life where he is saved from the clutches of gallows and later rises to become the Advisor to the king of his time. He had a very viable memory and talks in details about the episodes in his life…"
~ *Sayed Faqir Alavi, Former Afghan journalist an scholar – Canada.*

"This book is an original phenomena, a collection of stories of a national figure of our country. The narration has been written on paper from tapes and documents and published without tampering with the original and is being presented to the people interested in his life…"
~ *Dr Wassey Latifi, an Afghan scholar in Virginia.*

Preface

Dear Readers,

Marie Khalili

These are the memoirs of my father Ustad (Professor) Khalilullah Khalili, who was born in 1907 to a powerful and renowned family in the Jahan Ara gardens in Kabul. He died on May 4, 1987 in Islamabad, Pakistan among the Mujahideen and refugees of Afghanistan.

Incidentally, Ustad Khalil's father, Mustufi-Mumalik (Chief Accountant equivalent to Minister of Finance) Mohammad Husain Khan also died on May 4, 1919. (King Amanullah executed him for telling King Habibullah that Amanullah was conspiring to murder him.)

We have published these memoirs as told by the Ustad keeping in tact the authenticity of his words and whatever the poet said about the ups and downs in his life. My father used to say:

The eyes of the Gazelles taught me the poetry
The attack of the lions taught me how to fight

Ustad Khalili was buried around sundown in Peshawar, in the Cemetery of Afghan Mujahideen, near the border of Afghanistan, according to his will.

My husband, Afzal Nasiri, recorded these memoirs. Part of it he had written in English and I have translated that into Persian. These memoirs have not been tampered with, and have been published the way he narrated them. There may be some gaps, in some parts it does not flow smooth: however, we did not want to change the original or add or subtract. We have tried our best to keep the story flowing.

Ustad Khalili willed we delay the publication of these memoirs, at least 20 years after his death.

I was very close to my father. My siblings always accused me of being his favorite. Whenever my father would write new poetry he would read it to me and ask my opinion. It was an honor for me. I must confess I am neither a poet nor a scholar. I was only 15 or 16 years old when my father read to me his fresh poetry and sought my reaction. He had just recuperated from a heart attack and wrote a piece called " Images I saw"… He dedicated it to me.

> *I opened my eyes I saw the world*
> *I saw the face of beloved Marie*
> *Her tears were falling down my cheeks*
> *She was kissing my hand and arms*
> *I said the day will soon come*
> *your pearls (tears) will be needed*
> *Then use this treasure (her tears)*
> *as a sacrifice to my casket*
> *and offer them as souvenirs.*

Unfortunately, my father's sudden death in Pakistan did not give me an opportunity to even cry next to him and drop a few tears on his casket.

I vividly remember a hot summer day in New Jersey. We had read the news about Soviet bombardment of Afghan villages and indiscriminate killing of Afghan Mujahideen (freedom fighters) and ordinary people. This news made my father very uncomfortable. My husband, Afzal, and I insisted to drive him towards Hudson River in New York. Upon returning to New Jersey I asked him, "Did you like visiting Hudson River?" With tearful eyes and on the spot he made this couplet:

> *Hudson River does not intoxicate me because*
> *I am Crazy about the roaring waves of another River*

After reaching New Jersey he completed this poem, which is part of his collection.

The last gift my father gave to me was in 1978. The communists had just taken over the country with the help of the Soviet Union. My father's books and library in Kabul

had been confiscated. The doors of our country were opened to the outsiders. Amid this tumultuous ordeal I gave birth to my eldest son on May 23, 1978. My father wrote an ode for him and named him "Khalil". He named him after himself, which was the greatest gift to me. I wish he was alive today to see him as a successful attorney in Northern Virginia.

Marie Khalili Nasiri
Spring 2009, Manassas, Virginia
USA

On May 23, 2012, coinciding with my son Khalil's birthday, Khalili's remains were brought back to Afghanistan from his original resting place in Pakistan and buried near the University of Kabul, close to Jamaluddin Afghani's mausoleum (an Afghan intellectual of the early 20th century). Afghan academicians, intellectuals, and scholars attended his re-burial ceremony. This was against my wife Marie's personal wishes.

Afzal Nasiri

شعر خلیل به قلم استاد

بسم الله الرحمن الرحیم

Persian Text of Khalili's poem in his own handwriting on the birth of our son Khalil. For a clear copy please check the website MemoirsofKhalili.com.

Introduction

These are the memoirs of Ustad Khalilullah Khalili, the eminent historian, poet, philosopher, and statesman of Afghanistan, which were written in Maywood, New Jersey, between 1983 and 1986 while he was in exile in the United States, during the Soviet occupation of his country. Looking for the end of the Soviet Afghan War (1978-92) and with a view to returning to his beloved Afghanistan, Ustad Khalili moved to Pakistan in 1986. Unfortunately, he did not realize his hopes and died in Islamabad, Pakistan on May 4, 1987. The end of the Soviet invasion of Afghanistan would not come for another five years.

Khalili authored more than 70 works of poetry, fiction, histories, and Sufi studies. His booklet, *From Balkh to Konya*, on the 13th century mystic poet Jalaluddin Balkhi-Rumi, is highly regarded across the Persian-speaking world as well as India and Pakistan. His most notable work was published after the invasion of Afghanistan by the Soviet Union in 1979. His themes were vastly patriotic, having been influenced by the popular struggle against the communist regime and military occupation. His work provided inspiration to the resistance and its freedom fighters.

Khalili stands out in modern Persian poetry and is among the few contemporary Afghan poets to gain a following in Iran. His rubaiyats (couplets) have been translated into English and Arabic by several scholars. Khalili's rubaiyats are often compared to those of the 11th century Persian poet, Omar Khayyam. In reference to his *Quatrains of Khalilullah Khalili*, published in English by Idris Shah, Professor Aljubouri of Al Mustansiriyah University of Baghdad writes:

> *Like his famous predecessor, Professor Khalili's scope is very wide and he covers a variety of topics. These embody, above all, the poet's spiritual unrest in search of eternal truth as well as deep concern for the enigma of creation of life and death. In his rubaiyats we can clearly discern Khalili's evident*

enjoyment of life, its pleasures and beauties.

Khalili is best remembered for his quatrains. His literary influence (according to him) includes Nezami, Rumi, Saadi, and the tranquility inspired by Hafez.

As his son-in-law, I had the rare opportunity to join him while he lived in humble accommodations in Maywood. Marie and I began compiling notes, tapes, and even video of his memories of Afghanistan, of his friends, and the history of the country during his time there. I also accompanied him on a visit to Princeton University in 1984. While there, Khalili was shocked to see the well-maintained collections of his work, where students of Persian literature study it.

As the husband of his eldest daughter, Marie Khalili, my father-in-law always showed a special affection toward me, or so he made me feel when I was in his company. After a hard day's work, we would all gather in his Maywood apartment. We came to the U.S. as political refugees from Afghanistan after the Soviet invasion and occupation in 1979.

Marie and I arrived in the U.S. with our son, Khalil, on January 12, 1981 and joined my father-in law's family in New Jersey the next day. Ustad Khalili left his post as Afghanistan's Ambassador to Iraq and eventually sought political asylum in the U.S., where he ended up in Maywood. (He was a good judge of character: upon quitting his post as Afghan Ambassador to Iraq after the communist coup in Afghanistan, he was offered a job at Baghdad University by Saddam Hussain, then President of Iraq. Khalili refused the offer and went on to the U.S. via Germany.) Our evening routine was to visit him and his wife, Fauzia. We would sit around the modest apartment and talk about days gone by.

He lived in a small, two-bedroom garden-style apartment with barely enough room to accommodate all his guests who would find their way to him from around the country. In the summers we carried folding chairs outside to one corner of the apartment building lawn. There we would gather and continue our conversations about

Afghanistan and his life. Our neighbors would watch us with curiosity, but were always very polite and accommodating.

He would often muse that he had lived many chapters of history and was privy to many conversations with the kings, generals, and ministers who steered it. "But, alas! I have not written any of it down!" he said. As we listened to his stories and his memories, it became clear to Marie and I we needed to record this oral history for posterity. At first he hesitated, but soon acquiesced to the will of his beloved daughter. I realized the cultural and historical value of this opportunity.

My father, Ghulam Qadir Nasiri, had fled to British India at age 12 after his father (my grandfather, Malik Zaman Nasiri of Farza-Kohdaman, a supporter of Habibullah Khan Kalakani) was brutally murdered by the forces of Nadir Shah following the overthrow of Habibullah Kalakani. Having grown up in India, my educational career was entirely in English, culminating in a Master's degree in Political Science from India's Aligarh University. I moved to Afghanistan in 1972, where I began to improve my Persian. While there, I was a young journalist working as a member of the editorial board of the Kabul Times, the only English language daily newspaper of Afghanistan, and the place where I would later meet my wife.

We began recording Ustad Khalili's memoirs one evening in May 1983. While my initial notes on Khalili's memoirs were in Persian, I soon switched to English, a language with which I was professionally fluent. The task of documenting and translating our notes into Persian was taken on by my wife, Marie, who is herself an accomplished journalist and recognized figure in Persian literary circles.

I continued taking notes at the pace set by Khalili himself. His memory served him well, and despite not having his journals and notes, he recounted every detail, name, and place to us over the course of multiple evenings. In some instances, he could not recall the exact dates of an event. In those cases, we tried carefully to recreate a

timeline and identify an accurate date.

We purchased a tape recorder to speed up our progress to ensure the accuracy of our notes. After two years working on the project he announced he was moving to Pakistan at the invitation of Zia-ul-Haq, then President of Pakistan. He never listened to the tape recordings and as a result, never had the opportunity to tie together disparate stories or correct apparent conflicts regarding dates.

Over the course of this project, Marie and I assembled the memoirs together from our notes, tapes, and memories of those conversations with great care, deferring to his spoken word as much as possible. Our goal is to honor the integrity of his words, keep his thoughts intact, and preserve his stories and voice for future generations. His memoirs are a living history of Afghanistan. He was an eyewitness to the rule of five of its kings and its first president.

Khalili spent sleepless nights tormented by the invasion of Afghanistan by the Soviets. He longed for the day when the country would be free of brutal occupation. Knowing Khalili, I know the rule of Taliban and the role played by them, and other terrorist organizations in Afghanistan would have tormented him as equally as Soviet rule, as would the current occupation by the American and NATO forces. The first part of Khalili's memoirs cover the time from his birth in Kabul in 1907 to the Soviet occupation. Khalili was the eldest son of Mustufi-ul-Momalik Mohammad Hussain, the Minister of Finance to Habibullah Khan, father of Amanullah Khan. Amanullah Khan executed Mustufi Mohammad Hussain for speaking out about Amanullah's involvement in the assassination of his own father, Habibullah.

The second part of his memoirs include political developments from the rise of Mohammad Nadir in 1929, his assassination, and the rise of Zahir Shah until the time of Khalili's resignation as Afghan Ambassador to Iraq in 1978. It further details eight years of struggle he waged through his pen against the Soviet occupation. Khalili's work was instrumental in uniting the diverse bands of freedom fighters in their resistance to the occupation.

Ustad Khalili left for Pakistan in 1986, before we could complete his memoirs. He promised to complete this project when he returned; however, his illness and death were sudden, and it was a promise he was unable to keep. The final chapter, therefore, has been left incomplete. His passing triggered an immense outpouring of grief in Afghanistan and among its diaspora.

This book is the final result of the project. I am currently working with my son Khalil Nasiri, an attorney in Virginia, upon whom Ustad bestowed his name, to translate and edit the English version. Our hope is that this book will serve as the testimony of an eyewitness account to eight decades of Afghan history for future generations. Ustad Khalilullah Khalili died in Islamabad, Pakistan in 1987 and was buried in Peshawar, Pakistan, next to the tomb of Pashto poet Rahman Baba, near the Afghan border, according to his wishes. On May 23, 2013, he was re-buried at Kabul Univeristy campus.

Afzal Nasiri
October 2013
Manassas, VA
Afzal.nasiri@gmail.com

Editor's Note: The English translation is not verbatim. We have kept the contents and the spirit of what Ustad Khalili wanted to convey, intact.

Section One

My Life, My Memoirs

Here is to you my sweet daughter Marie.

In October 1983, I visited Pakistan and was once again amid my fellow countrymen living in exile in the suburbs of Peshawar and inside parts of the motherland. The visit enabled me to meet the freedom fighters in the backdrop of the towering and majestic Khaiber Mountains. I could talk to the stars shining in the skies over Afghanistan, my beloved country. The soothing Khaiber breeze brought news of the death of my countrymen, reminding me of their sorry plight. The sight of orphans and widows full of sorrow penetrated my flesh, deep into the bone marrow. I witnessed young people endure blindness, facial scars, amputated limbs, and burnt bodies. Both Afghan and Pakistani doctors were present, but had limited resources. A doctor without medicine was as good as no doctor at all.

I cannot forget the moment I observed a mother whose only son's leg was amputated. The doctor advised him to wait until he could be fitted with an artificial limb. Her son wanted to go back to the front, however, to fight the infidel Soviet invaders. Neither I, nor the doctor, could convince him not to go. The youth took leave with his mother's blessing and returned to the front where bravery, guns, and death were waiting to welcome him.

During the last 15 years under the monarchy, during Sardar Mohammad Daoud Khan's time, my campaign against communism was curtailed by pressure groups inside the court and government. I was Afghanistan's ambassador in Baghdad when Daoud Khan was overthrown by a lightning quick and bloody coup d'état (April 1978). As soon as the news broke, I resigned from my post, leaving Iraq for West Germany for a brief stay to recuperate from the initial shock of the communist coup. There, I studied my country's situation and received the medical attention I needed for my active and nagging stomach ulcer.

While my ulcer was still active, I came to the U.S.,

seeking political asylum to continue necessary medication (1979). Disease and homelessness were not the only factors that brought me to the U.S. New York City is the home of the world, and the American nation is known for its support of human rights. I felt I could, at the same time, better serve the cause of my country and people by raising the voice of the Afghans here, and muster world opinion for the liberation of my country against the communist invaders. To me, a Jehad (Holy War) through the pen or with a gun is equally honorable, as long as the goal is the same.

From the day I landed in the U.S., I started my Jehad of bringing Afghans closer and keeping in touch with them. I made concerted efforts to launch my crusade through my pen so my voice could reach the peace and freedom loving people of the world. In spite of my financial limitations, I continued my medical treatment. As soon as conditions improved, I traveled to Pakistan in October 1983.

In Pakistan, I met leaders of the freedom fighters. My efforts were three-dimensional:

1. To campaign through my pen for the continuation of the Jehad,
2. To bringing unity of thought among the mujahideen (freedom fighters), and
3. To unify the mujahideen on the war front.

Some mujahideen groups printed, published, and distributed my writings and poems inside Afghanistan, as well as the outside world. Among them was my book, *Matemsera (Hall of Sorrow)*, which was printed and distributed by the Society of Afghan Writers. My booklet, *Yare-Ashna (Old Friend)*, which reflects Dr. Mohammad Iqbal's love and relationship to Afghanistan was published in both Persian and Urdu by Professor Burhanuddin Rabbani, a leader of the Jamiate Islami. Similarly, a pamphlet, *Gulgoon Kafanan (The Martyrs)* and a translation of *Gita-Anjali (Devotion to Songs)* by Rabindranath Tagore were published by Jamiate Islami. *Zam-Zam-e-Ashk* (Zam-Zam - The Sacred Water Fountain in Mecca; Ashk means tears) was published by the popular freedom fighter Maulavi Khalis. The printing of *Ghausul Azam (The Great Saint of Islam)*, in Urdu and Persian, was taken care of by another leading freedom fighter, Sayed Ahmad Gailani.

In this journey, I met the President of Pakistan, General Mohammad Zia-ul-Haq, twice informally. In spite of being bedridden, I spent 10 months in Pakistan and continued meeting the commanders of the freedom fighters who were returning from the front for supplies. The basis of all our talks was the continuation of the Jehad until the expulsion of the Soviet forces from Afghanistan and founding of a national government. I repeatedly told them the leader of Afghanistan should come from among the people, and the succeeding regime should be people oriented, especially from among those who sacrificed in the success of the Jehad.

What made me most proud was the true belief of these people in their Jehad. Their stories were very touching and full of pain, which will affect the hardest of hearts.

General Zia-ul-Haq asked me to tell him whatever I had on my heart. I told him, "I have two things to say, one concerning me, and the other concerning you."

"For you," I told him, "Victory in your strife and wiping of the tears of the Afghan refugees. For me, just two meters of land."

He nodded his head in approval, but asked, "What would you do with two meters of land?"

I told him, "If I die before the freedom of my country, grant me two meters of land near Khaiber Pass so I may be buried there and the winds blowing from Afghanistan may caress my grave."

While addressing public meetings in Pakistan I always drew the attention of the audience to the fact we – Afghanistan and Pakistan – are two nations with common religion, culture, and history.

"No plot, subversion or threat has separated us or will be able to do so," I said. "Twenty years ago I was passing through Pakistan when the political relations between the two governments were strained, instigated by the common enemy. In spite of this, the University of Panjab invited me to speak. I underlined in my speech that no matter how many times Pakistani and Afghan governments recall their ambassadors from each other's capitals, the bond of friendship between the two nations remains as strong as ever."

"For a thousand years the flag of the ambassador of the people of Afghanistan is flying high and fluttering here," I added. "That is the flag of Dada Ganj Baksh, Ali Ibne Usman Hajuveri Ghaznavi. The grave of his mother is in Ghazni, now being trampled under the feet of the Soviet invaders. I told them if the Kabul River brings red water into Atak River, it would redden the Atak; if it brings white water it would whiten the Atak."

"We committed a mistake," I concluded. "I hope you will not repeat the same."

My Father

My father, Mirza Mohammad Hussain Khan, belonged to the Safi tribe of Sayed Khel village in Parwan province. Sayed Khel is approximately 50 kilometers north of Kabul. It is in the vicinity of the Jabal Seraj citadel. His early education was in Kabul and Parwan. During the rule of Amir Habibullah Khan (1872-1919) he rose to hold high posts in the court. He is the founder of the first bookkeeping and accounting system in Afghanistan and was decorated with the Diamond Award by the Amir. His literary and scientific abilities are explained well by Ustad Salahuddin Saljoqi in his introduction to my first volume of poetry published in Tehran, Iran.

My father was appointed as the Minister of Finance of Amir Habibullah with the title of Mustufi-ul-Momalik. In 1901, Amir Habibullah also conferred upon him the honorary title of Naib Salar (Vice-Commander, Civil and Military, in Charge of Frontier Affairs and Khan of the Northern Region). He served in this capacity for 18 years.

In 1324 AH Qamari (1905 AD), Amir Habibullah Khan began his journey around Afghanistan to take in a firsthand account of the state of affairs and people. This sojourn took him from Kabul to Ghazni, Kandahar, Herat, Maimana,

Mazar-i-Sharif, Kataghan, Panjsher, Parwan, and back to Kabul. He traveled on horseback through the rough and tough terrain of the countryside.

The people of Parwan and Panjsher appointed my father to head the welcome committee. Mustufi cleared Khawak Pass and built a citadel in Panjsher for people and caravans. Two months after the arrival of the king in Kabul, Mustufi invited the king for a dinner at his house. The house, located on the Kabul River, was later confiscated and after the execution of my father at the hands of King Amanullah, it became the Soviet embassy in Kabul. (It is now the Russian Embassy.)

After evening prayers, as the king, dressed in all his glamour and glory, entered the gates, a humble poet was born to Mustufi: That was me (1907).

My father had no other children and this night for him was a celebration of two events: One, the arrival of the king, and the other, my birth. The Amir himself spoke the words of the Holy Koran in my ears and named me Khalilullah. He ordered the shawl of his ancestor, Amir Dost Mohammad, be put on my cradle (a traditional act). Amir Dost Mohammad had many children and all of them achieved long lives. Was it due to the shawl or my own luck that I have lived a long life? In all these years, however, the light of success has never dawned on me.

My Mother

My mother belonged to the Safi tribe from the Mahmud Iraqi village. This village is located 60 kilometers north of Kabul. Why the village is called Mahmud Iraqi, no one knows.

The saying goes, "In Ghazni, on a stone in an ancient graveyard, from the time of Mahmud Ghaznavi, I have read the name Mahmud Iraqi."

My mother was the daughter of Abdul Qadir Khan, who was a renowned Khan in that region. He was well revered and popular for his hospitality.

One of the sons of Abdul Qadir Khan was Abdul Rahim Khan, later to be Governor of Herat, Minister of Public

Works and Deputy Prime Minister. The story of the bravery of Abdul Rahim Khan in Herat needs a separate book. My mother died at an early age in Kabul. I was seven years old at that time. My mother is buried at Shah-e-do Shamshera, a shrine in downtown Kabul.

Hanoz garm bood jai bosai ke nehad
Ba royem wa chashmem wa sarem madere malik seerem

I can still feel the warmth where she kissed
My forehead and my eyes – my angel-faced mother.

I started school at age five. Habibiya and Harbia were two schools newly opened in Kabul. My father, meanwhile, opened a branch of Habibiya in our own compound. This is referred to in the *Serajul Akhbar*, a weekly paper published in Kabul. My father donated a fixed amount to the Habibiya school fund.

The branch school had 22 students. The subjects taught included math, geography, history, and literature, as well as theology and the Holy Koran. The teacher of the Persian language class was a very strict and disciplined gentleman. His consistent pressure helped me to learn the Persian alphabet, and I started reading in six months' time.

My father also had a small hospital in our compound. Dr. Mohammad Hayat Khan of Punjab was hired to run the hospital. My father wanted the Indian doctor to teach us English but the religious priest forbade this. I have had a stammering problem since childhood that restricts my ability to learn other languages. During after dinner gatherings at my home, usually attended by Khans (nobles) and learned people, my father always made me read selections from *Mathnavi* by Maulana Jalaluddin Balkhi-Rumi in Persian.

Four years passed and my teacher continued his concerted efforts to teach me all he could. By summer, I went to our home in Hussain Kot, north of Kabul. The area was formerly called Qalai Murad Beg. Nadir Shah (1929-30) named Hussain Kot after my father. The area has pleasant weather, very much like Paghman.

It was here that I became friends with nature. The cold

water springs sprouting from the heart of the land and the shade of the dense and aged trees impressed me profoundly. I slept many a night on the roof of the house. My governess, who was from Hazarajat, taught me the names of different stars. She had a tale for every one of the ones she knew by name. Some of these tales were horrifyingly dreadful and some, of course, pleased and intrigued me.

On many occasions in the middle of the night, the cooing of a bird would awaken me from deep sleep. My governess told me this bird, which is called the "Bird of Right" (Murghe-Haq), does not have a nest. It keeps flying around aimlessly all through the day. In the night, it hangs itself by a branch of a tree and keeps cooing until dawn, "Right, right, right...." In the morning it drops a drop of blood from its beak and continues flying again.

The evenings at Hussain Kot were eventful. We always went out horseback riding. My father had a large stable with expensive stallions. In Kabul, every evening, either in our garden or in the Babar Shah gardens, we participated in local sports. The game I cherished most was Mir Badakan, which resembles American baseball. Goal was also popular sport and was played in Chaman (Pakistan). The Amir, more often than not, participated in this game. Some of our Indian friends taught us how to play cricket. One of these friends was Maulana Obadullah Sindhi, an Indian intellectual.

My father also owned an automobile – the only person other than the Amir to do so. I can still recall while driving up to Jabal Seraj (70 kilometers from Kabul) we stopped the car at least three times to change the thermostat water or engine coolant. Every winter we would go from Kabul to Jalalabad, which is much warmer and pleasant during winters. In those days Kabul to Jalalabad, a distance of 140 kilometers, was divided into seven equi-distances, each requiring one day to travel on horseback or on foot.

Habibullah Khan Seraj (Father of Amanullah Khan) 1901-1919

The first time I saw the Amir, he was a guest of my father at Hussain Kot, and I remember seeing him in 1334 AH (1915 AD). It was the year when the Dilkusha (palace) was completed, and according to Afghan custom, my father sent gifts to the Amir as a token of good luck on moving into the new palace. I accompanied the gifts and when the Amir saw my pale complexion, he decreed the pressure of education be eased.

"Even if Mustufi's children are unable to pursue higher education they will not remain unemployed in my kingdom," he said.

In the summer of 1338 AH (1919 AD), my father, as a routine, accompanied Amir Habibullah Khan to Jalalabad. That year the weather was mild and very pleasant, and our garden in Jalalabad was full of blooming shabboo flowers (gillyflowers or wallflowers). One hot evening my father was entertaining his friends with evening tea. I was busy playing with my school friends. Suddenly, the Amir's car appeared from behind the boundary wall of the garden. The sound of the auto horn and my father's voice made the gatekeeper dash for the gates quickly. The Amir entered the garden in his car.

When my father went to open the door, the Amir said, "What a beautiful blooming carpet of flowers you have," and continued, "I will only leave the car if you promise to accompany me to Kalagosh for a hunting expedition."

My father whispered something in his ear. Neither others nor I understood anything. I distinctly remember the Amir, who was smiling until now, quickly appeared disturbed.

The Amir answered in a low but sharp voice to my father: "You are always admonishing me."

Instead of stepping out of his car, he ordered the driver to turn back. My father, astonished with the sullen reaction of the Amir, sank into his chair. After a few minutes of silence he addressed Maulavi Obaidullah Sindhi, who was with him:

Choon qaza ayed Tabib abla shawad
Aan dawa dar naffe khud gumrah shawad

When the time comes, the Tabib becomes ignorant;
He fails to recognize his own cure.

In reply, Maulavi suggested my father give the Amir
something in writing so a document of what he told the
Amir would remain.

This was the last time I saw the Amir.

The same day the Amir had gone on his hunting
expedition, Mustufi sent a personal letter to him. The
messenger was instructed to deliver the letter to the Amir in
person. The messenger wore a black garb and his horse was
also black. This was done deliberately to catch the Amir's
attention. The Amir's car reached Darunta the following
morning and the messenger delivered the letter. The Amir
took the letter and stuck it in his pocket to read later. This
small act would change the destinies of thousands. If the
Amir had read that message, possibly the future of
Afghanistan would have been different.

The letter fell into the hands of those plotting his
assassination and who were part of entourage of the Amir.
The day passed in fishing and hunting. As night fell, the
Amir was himself hunted. The sound of gunshots from the
tent of the Amir broke the silence of the dark night. The
brother and the eldest son of the Amir, along with others,
rushed to his tent. The assassin escaped under the shield of
darkness.

It is 1985, and in the more than 64 years that have
passed since this episode, the assassin remains anonymous.
There are different stories circulating, however. This story,
which I repeat here, was told by two of the Amir's
bodyguards.

According to the guards, the standard practice was that
a group of seven soldiers from four different regiments
were appointed every night to guard the four corners of the

Amir's tent. Two soldiers from Saros regiment were always at the door of the tent. The two guards who told their story to me were from Saros.

The Amir would sleep on a cot in the tent facing west. Each night, a storyteller would narrate stories to him while two servants massaged his legs. A red lamp with a small flame flickered on the stool in the corner. As soon as the Amir went to sleep, Farah Bashi (his aide-de-camp) would enter the tent and turn off the lamp. The storyteller and the two servants were then allowed to leave. The guards further said that on this night, as soon as the lamp was turned off and the servants left, they were the first ones to hear the gunshots. It seemed the assassin had snuck in earlier and hid inside the tent. The assassin put the barrel of the gun into the ear of the Amir, so the sound did not travel too far. The bullet struck the Amir's brain. Colonel Shah Ali Raza, son of General Sayed Shah Khan from the Hazara tribe, caught hold of the assassin's wrist; however, as soon as the Amir's brother, son and Commander-in-chief Mohammad Nadir, and others entered on the order of the Commander, the assassin was let go.

The Amir was young – about 47 years old. His body was rushed to Jalalabad immediately and reached there at 10 o'clock in the morning. According to the custom, when the Amir went to Jalalabad during the first half of his stay, one of his sons was appointed as Regent in Kabul. Amanullah completed his tenure of 1-1/2 months. He was due in Jalalabad and Hayatullah; the elder brother, was supposed to go to Kabul.

Hayatullah fell sick on his way to Kabul and stayed at Nimlah Garden. His journey was delayed by one day and according to the well-hatched plan, the Amir was assassinated that night. Kabul was left to Amanullah, third son of the Amir. The elders were summoned for advice.

Mustufi, before anybody else, recommended the body of the Amir be transferred to Kabul and a new king be elected by a majority vote.

Nasrullah, brother of the Amir, did not agree to it. His reasoning was very weak. He stressed that late Amir Habibullah would not have wanted his dead body transferred from one city to the other. Possibly, Nasrullah Khan was under the impression Amanullah would support him as the king, because two years previously an abortive attempt on the life of the late Amir was traced to Amanullah. At the time, the angry Amir wanted his son blinded; however, it is believed Nasrullah Khan came to the rescue, chiding Amanullah and letting him off the hook. He forced Amanullah to sign a pledge on the Holy Koran to never contest for the throne.

Mustufi supported Inayatullah (Moinus Saltana), the eldest son of the late Amir and heir apparent. Inayatullah's mother was the daughter of Amir Mohammad Khan-Tagavi of the Safi tribe. Amir Mohammad Khan was brother of Usman Khan who was martyred during his successive assault on the British position in the Asmai Heights during the Second Anglo-Afghan War (1878-1880).

Mustufi also belonged to the Safi tribe. Moinus Saltana, however, with his eyes full of tears and out of respect for his father, said: "I would be blinded if I sit on the throne of my father."

Amir Habibullah Khan was laid to rest in the garden where he played golf.

Strange enough, Farah Bashi Shujaudaula made a lightning visit to Kabul and informed Amanullah of the assassination. Amanullah in Kabul and Nasrullah in Jalalabad both proclaimed accession to the throne. Amanullah, while crowning himself King, vowed that unless and until he found the killers he would not place his sword back in its case. Nasrullah, weak and isolated, resigned from the throne.

The military regiments in Jalalabad, at the instigation of Amanullah, staged a coup and arrested all top government officials, including Commander Mohammad Nadir and Mustufi, and took them to Kabul. A little known low-ranking officer, Sarwar, who was from Herat, staged the coup. Sarwar was later appointed Magistrate of Panjsher Valley. It was a reward for his petty deed. He would hardly complete three months in his post when, on the order of Amanullah, he was choked to death while sleeping.

Poor Shah Ali Reza, who caught hold of the assassin of

Amir Habibullah, was brought to Kabul in chains. Amanullah gave his sword to Mahmud Sami, an alien from Iraq, who used it to slash his mouth and then, with a heavy stroke, slew Ali Reza's body in two. Amanullah, according to himself, said he saw his father in the dream revealing the assassin's name. Sayed Shah Khan, father of young Ali Reza, took the slashed and bloodied body of his son, and placed him in a grave opposite Eid Gah Mosque in Kabul.

After the fall of Amanullah Khan, people lit candles and lamps on Ali Reza's grave, considering him to be a martyr.

The Effects of Habibullah Khan Seraj's Assassination on the Foreign Policy

The assassination of Amir Habibullah took place on February 20, 1919, toward the end of World War I. The British Empire was under pressure to announce the independence of Afghanistan and related territories. The Soviets were preparing to attack Bokhara. A stable and powerful regime in Kabul was not in the best interest of the two big powers of the time. The question still looms: Which of these two powers precipitated the assassination of Amir Habibullah? These facts can best be explained in the political archives of Moscow and London.

Amanullah Khan declared war on the British. He dispatched aging Abdul Quddus Khan to Kandahar at the head of a strong force. Abdul Quddus, who boasted he could conquer London with 313 men (emulating the 313 men with whom Prophet Mohammad, PBUH, won the Battle of Badr in Arabia in 2 AH or 624 AD). Abdul Quddus Khan put on the same garb Prophet Mohammad (PBUH) wore during the Battle of Badr. The only thing he abstained from doing was calling himself Prophet (PBUH). He could not move even an inch out from the city of Kandahar.

Saleh Mohammad, newly promoted by Amanullah Khan as Sepahsalar-Commanding Officer, left for Khaiber commanding a sizable force. He won this title and position

because he kept the Kabul garrison loyal to Amanullah Khan. Saleh Mohammad, on his way to Khaiber, was attacked by air and returned to the capital in despair. Amanullah Khan was angered and ordered him to break his own sword (a traditional humiliation for an Afghan soldier).

Amanullah Khan released Mohammad Nadir from jail and sent him with his two brothers, General Shah Mahmud and General Shah Wali, along with General Abdul Wakil Nooristani, Brigadier Mohammad Alam Kohistani and General Panin Beg toward Gardez. Well-known Babrak Khan Jadrani, out of enthusiasm for martyrdom, traveled on foot the full distance. Two Mojaddadis, also known as Hazrat of Shor Bazar, accompanied them too. Mohammad Nadir won the battle against the British with his soldiers' bravery and the help of the people. The defeat of Saleh Mohammad and Abdul Quddus forced Amanullah to consider moving his capital from Kabul to Bamiyan. British bombers also attacked some parts of Kabul. After the victory of Nadir in Gardez, Mahmud Tarzi, along with other generals of the army and elders of different tribes, prevailed upon Amanullah Khan not to leave Kabul for Bamiyan.

Execution of My Father and A Fall from Grace

While the war against the British continued, at this time about 10,000 people from Kohistan, Kohdaman and Panjsher came to Kabul and presented a memorandum to Amanullah Khan, asking for the release of Mustufi and permission to go to Jehad against the British under his leadership. Nasrullah was still alive and in jail. Amanullah Khan promised the people he would release Mustufi within three days. They believed him and left Kabul for their homes. The very next day, on the fifth day of Shahban 1338 AH Qamari (1919 AD) my father was executed in the Arg (palace) without a formal trial. His body was buried secretly in Sherpur. No one was allowed to mourn or cry in

public for my father's death.

All of his property in Kabul, Kohistan and Jalalabad, which had been confiscated as soon as my father was arrested, was taken from us. Three hundred soldiers surrounded our home in downtown Kabul. After sunset on the day of my father's execution, our family – including my two brothers, my sister and me – were led to a barn where we were housed for some time to come. I was a little over eleven years old at that time. Except for one old rug and a few kitchen utensils, we were not allowed to take anything. A woman from the Hazara tribe managed to come and live with us. She was as kind as a mother could be.

The barn was next to the house of my paternal uncle, Mohammad Hassan Khan. Because he was bedridden and could not be jailed, he was put under house arrest. No visitors or medical personnel were allowed. My poor uncle was dying of his sickness, and the death of my father was kept secret from him. His last wish was to see me before his death. I was led into the house from the roof. My uncle waved me near him. He noticed my wet eyes and kissed me on the forehead. My step-grandmother, the stepmother of Mustufi, was weeping. She was from a renowned family of Farah. I was watching my uncle's face in the candlelight (the Jabal Seraj power station, installed by Amir Habibullah, was not commissioned yet). It was my first time watching someone die.

Suddenly, a soldier entered the house without permission carrying arms. He kicked my dying uncle and said, "I have brought some good news for you." While he was being given a reward, I was wrapped in a blanket to avoid being spotted. The soldier continued, "Congratulations, your brother was executed two days ago, and orders have been given for your execution, too." My uncle bade him farewell by weakly waving his hand. The soldier turned and left, saying, "I have delivered the Amir's message to you."

Mohammad Hassan Khan's face turned pale. His breathing was getting shallower. I started reading verses from the Holy Koran. He breathed his last breath in a few minutes. After two days we were allowed to bury him in the dark of the night.

When Ramadan (the month of fasting) came we were still in the barn isolated from others. No one was allowed in or out. In those days, the advent of Ramadan was announced by the firing of a cannon. Iftar (breaking of fast at sundown) and Saher (start of fasting at dawn) were also announced this way. One night the cannon was fired eleven times. Later we learned it announced the death of the eleven confidants of Nasrullah Khan who tried to ambush Amanullah Khan's car in Kargha. Nasrullah Khan was also executed later in the tower of Haram Sarai, and he was buried secretly in Qola Chakan near Asmai Heights. During the time of Nadir Khan, a tomb was erected in that place.

We remained in the barn for 18 months. Amanullah Khan ordered us exiled to Logar, but on the recommendation of Ghulam Mohammad Khan, Minister of Commerce from Wardhak and Shujaudaula, now Minister of Security, we were exiled in Mahmud Iraqi. We heard the full story of the arrest and execution of my father from Ghulam Mujtaba Khan, Deputy Minister of Finance, Sadduddin Khan Logari and Ahmad Ali Khan, Chief of Staff. All three were present when my father was executed. All three had the same version.

According to them, Amanullah Khan was in the Ministry of Foreign Affairs, which was to the west of the palace, and was called Stor Palace. It was about the time of evening prayers and the month of Saur (May). Some trees still had blossoms. They brought my father to him with both of his hands tied at the back. The noise of his shackles could be heard from far away.

He was wearing a white Kandahari turban and Kurk Chapan of Herat. He still had on his gold framed eyeglasses. He looked at the Amir with great anger and contempt. He and the Amir exchanged a few words. It all boiled down to the same letter my father had sent to the Amir in Jalalabad. Until the end they could not find a single convincing reason for the arrest of Mustufi. Consequently, he was hanged in the Arg garden. Mustufi uttered the following verses before he breathed his last. While walking toward the gallows, he kept repeating in a loud voice, "God

is great – Allah-o-Akbar."

> *Mara kushti wa*
> *Taqseer na gufti;*
> *Ajab kafir dile*
> *Allah-o-Akbar*

> *You killed me not telling,*
> *What sin I committed*
> *What an infidel hearted,*
> *God is Great.*

When he brought down the ropes of the gallows, the hangman's hands were shaking.

Mustufi said, "Strange, they are hanging me, and you are shivering."

The hangman requested Mustufi put the rope around his own neck, however, Mustufi said, "Come and put the rope around my neck and say on the order of Amanullah Khan."

He was buried in an unknown place (Sherpur).

Exile to Mahmud Iraqi

My maternal uncle, Abdul Qasim Khan, died while we were exiled to Mahmud Iraqi, which was my mother's birthplace. My other uncle, Abdul Salam Khan, who was a military colonel in the garrison of Herat, was transferred to a civilian job and sent to Kataghan. His brother Abdul Rahim Khan was a colonel in the Herat garrison. My grandmother was still living in Mahmud Iraqi. The government ordered that no one be allowed to meet us. We were to live isolated in Sidquabad. Qalai Sidquabad was built by Abdul Qadir Khan, my maternal grandfather. It was in a secluded place away from population. Its walls were 14 meters high and for us, it was a fortified prison.

After six months my grandmother left us and went to Herat to live with her son. Meanwhile someone falsely reported to the authorities that Mustufi's children had

precious jewels. One night armed men broke into the fort and destroyed everything looking for jewels. My grandmother's property was destroyed also.

My Introduction to Mahmud Tarzi's Work

My former governess, somehow or another, was able to find us two sheep. To keep ourselves busy, we started tending the sheep. One day, in the storeroom of my grandmother, I happened to see an old wooden box that contained some books and a few volumes of *Serajul Akhbar*, the weekly newspaper. It was the first time I read the work of Ustad Mahmud Tarzi. (Born in 1865 in Ghazni, his father, Ghulam Mohammad Tarzi was exiled by Amir Abdur Rahman Khan to Damascus, 1886-1990, and grew up there, returning to Afghanistan in 1902). My father advised me to read his books after the completion of my studies. The books included four by the French novelist Jules Verne – *The Mysterious Island, Around the World in Eighty Days, Twenty Thousand Leagues under the Sea,* and *A Journey to the Skies* – which Mahmud Beg translated from Turkish into Persian.

Another book in the box was *Az Har Dahan Sokhan e wa az Har Chaman Saman e (From Every Mouth an Expression and from Every Grass, a Greener Meadow of Jasmine).* This book was a collection of articles and stories. Some of them were translations, and some were written by Mahmud Beg. Another book in the box was a collection of Mahmud Beg's poems *Adab Dar Fan (Literature in Art).* Another book was *Journey to Three Continents,* in which Mahmud Beg wrote about his journey to Asia, Europe, and Africa with his father.

I studied Persian and Arabic during the time of my father. The poetry and literary work of Mahmud Beg astonished me. His literary ability was of high caliber. The same night I read his translation of *The Mysterious Island,* I also went through the other books. Mahmud Beg's poetry was completely different from Maulana Saadi and Hafez.

Mahmud Beg's poetry spoke of nationalism, independence, motherland, telephone, telegraph, coal, etc., contrary to his predecessors, who spoke of wine, love, philosophy, mysticism, and social behaviors. For example Mahmud Beg's poetry was as follows:

The telegraph has brought news from East and West,
The message and the messenger are history now.
This is the time of rail, car and electricity,
The steps of camels are a thing of the past.
or
This is the time when gun and dagger are necessary,
The world is of the guns and the time is of the daggers.

or
They are martyrs of foreign oppression,
They are dipped in the blood of the country.

Mahmud Beg's books delivered me from the anxiety and monotony of my solitude, and inspired me to write poetry of my own. It was here I launched my poetic career.

I would sit night after night under the dim light of the oil lamp and write. There was no one to edit or guide me in writing. A year and a few months passed. A modern school was opened in Mahmud Iraqi about three kilometers from Sidqahad and located in Deh Bale. I longed to go when I saw the other youth heading there. I sent an application to Ghulam Mohammad Khan through my faithful governess. It took her four days to travel from Mahmud Iraqi to Kabul. Ghulam Mohammad Khan pleaded to Amanullah Khan on our behalf to let us join the school.

Permission to Attend School

At that time Kohistan, Panjsher, Najrab, and Tagab had one commissioner. The commissioner was Mohammad Aman Khan of Shighnan. He assured Amanullah Khan of our character. Amanullah Khan decreed that we should be allowed to go to school.

Everyone thought it to be a great favor. What a happy

day it was! We entered the society from solitude.

The school had four grades, 120 students and five teachers. My brother, Najibullah, and I were promoted from first grade to fourth grade. I remember very well that in math, literature, and writing I surpassed the teacher. On days when the teacher was absent, I would teach the second and third grades.

The top student of the fourth grade was known as the captain. The current captain was the son of the rich Khan of Kohistan, Abdul Wahab. My brother and I went to school mostly barefoot and hungry. I was appointed as the captain within a month. On the day of Eid, the students of the school were taken to the mosque for prayers. I was asked to speak before the congregation, and my speech prepared in advance by the teacher.

The son of the Khan of Kohistan was first in line, and I was fourth. The strict advice of my governess was that I should not speak. She was afraid the government might get rid of me. My persistence prevailed over my governess. She gave in, but not before making sure I wore old and tattered clothes so the king's men wouldn't get the wrong impression. We still have the jewels that belonged to my father.

My speech consisted of a few verses from the Holy Koran and some couplets from Saadi's Bostan relating to an orphan. More than 5,000 people were in the congregation. The Khan and his relatives applauded for their son. After my speech, some people took me into their arms and wept.

I came home scared. I passed the whole day of Eid in fear. My governess was also upset, but nothing happened to me. I completed the fourth grade at the school in Mahmud Iraqi and placed first in my class.

Kohdaman

Ahmad Ali Khan Lodin was appointed governor at Charekar. According to organization at that time, Qalai Murad Beg up to Panjsher, Tagab and Bamiyan were ruled from Charekar, and it was known as Hukumate Kalan (big).

The commissioner was called Hakim Kalan. Again, fate was on my side. Ahmad Ali's wife, after years of marriage, gave birth to a son. The local Hakim was Shamsuddin. He was a graduate of Habibiya High School and was our neighbor in Kabul. One day he came to the school. He requested the teachers write something on the occasion of the birth of Hakim Kalan's son and send a bright student to Jabal Seraj to read it in front of the Hakim on behalf of all other students.

The teachers got together in a corner and talked for some time, finally coming up with a draft and reading it to Shamsuddin. The article was full of heavy Arabic words and compound sentences. He did not like it. He asked them to rewrite it. They went to the farthest corner of the garden, then called me and asked me to write it. I wrote a few lines and this verse of Hafez in the beginning:

> *Bar kash ai murgh sahar*
> *Naghmai daoudi ra*
> *Keh sulaiman gul*
> *Az tarafe hava baz amad*

> *Follow, oh morning bird*
> *The beautiful voice of Daoud (Prophet)*
> *King Sulaiman (Prophet)*
> *Has appeared in the air*

The teachers did not think my article would be liked. I learned to write "beautifully" when my father was still alive. The teachers took the article to the Hakim. I was watching and listening to them from the side of a tree. I was afraid. The Hakim liked and appreciated it. He asked who wrote it. They kept quiet. The Hakim's clerk heard my name and whispered to the Hakim. I was taken to him. The Hakim was a faithful man to Amanullah. I remembered the words of my governess, and thought I would be thrown into prison. On the contrary, upon seeing me scared and in old clothing, the Hakim's eyes were filled with tears. I thought this might be out of contempt or anger. The Hakim took me in his arms and comforted me.

Comforting an orphan is an act of generosity and humility. He took me to Jabal Seraj himself. One of the Khans of Kohistan who had enmity with my uncle went to the Hakim and told him in my presence, "This enemy of the king is not allowed to leave Kohistan. You might get into trouble."

The Hakim replied, "Honor and dishonor is in God's hands. What can this orphan do?"

We reached Jabal Seraj before sunset. Hundreds of people were standing ready to fire guns in the air as an Afghan tradition to congratulate Hakim Kalan on the birth of his son. I was supposed to read the article before the crowd before the gun-firing ceremony, on behalf of the students and people of Kohistan. God is witness that I did not like this one bit. Ahmad Ali Khan came out of the Qalai Sarwar Khan. Two men accompanying him started sobbing as soon as they saw me.

"Did my son die?" Ahmad Ali worriedly inquired.

"No," they answered, "But his father died."

Both of them were eminent men of Kohdaman and were close to my father. The people were watching this, spellbound. Shamsuddin stepped forward and said, "Khalilullah has come to read an article before you."

One of the two men replied, "No, Khalilullah Jan is the orphan of Mustufi."

The circle of the gun-wielding people closed. Ahmad Ali pulled me near him and kissed me on the forehead.

Holding my hand he went toward Jabal Seraj power station. This power station is mentioned in A.C. Jewett's book on Afghanistan. Jewett was a visiting engineer from the U.S. and helped build some of the projects (1911-1919).

Realizing the delicacy of the moment, Ahmad Ali said, "Tell the people this is not the time of merry-making. Let them go home."

We had dinner with the Hakim.

Tutumdara

With the permission of Hakim Ahmad Ali, I left for Tutumdara. Alone, in the dark night, afraid of thieves and dogs, I found Abdul Rasul outside. We went to school together. He was from Panjsher and was two years older than me. He was as kind as a brother. I asked Abdul Rasul to accompany me to Mohammad Afzal Khan's house. He had walked all the way from Kohistan to Jabal Seraj. Tutumdara is about five kilometers from Jabal Seraj. When we reached Tutumdara, the doors to Mohammad Afzal Khan's qala were locked. The daughter of this Khan was engaged to me at the age of seven by my parents. The Khan, son of Jalandar Khan, belonged to a very renowned family of the region. He was an elite landowner and very famous. I went there not because I was his future son-in-law, but because I wanted to spend the night there and leave in the morning for Kohistan. Abdul Rasul kept on bugging me the whole way to turn back and sleep in a mosque and go home in the morning. He thought the Khan might not let us in for fear of the Amir.

We knocked on the door. A big Turkish dog was tied to a chain, and the old durban asked us who we were. The durban rested against the wall and was quiet for a couple of minutes. He then invited us to his room. He said, "I'll go and inform the Khan. Afzal Khan is lion-hearted and a gentleman. He will not throw you out of the house, and if he does, I will take you to my house."
Within five minutes he came back and took us into the qala. They were still awake. Under the light of the kerosene lamp I saw some women and children. The Khan was resting with pillows under his arms, and an old man was playing the robab, a short-necked lute made of wood, in the other corner. The man was Peer Mohammad Khan, Khan of Parwan, and a friend of my father. He was playing this theme on the robab:

Man lazzate dared ba darman na farosham

I don't want a cure for this sweet pain...

The Khan took me for his nephew and asked about my father. I realized the Khan had mistaken me for someone else. I stammered and told him who I was, and that my father had been killed. Peer Mohammad Khan stopped the robab abruptly and called out my name. I was welcomed amid hugs and warm tears. The women and girls hid themselves from my sight. The Khan showed great courage in welcoming me. The next day he discussed my situation with Ahmad Ali Khan without any fear and asked him to approach the Amir for forgiveness.

Those who saw me in the Khan's house were filled with remorse that I was an orphan, but also feared Amanullah Khan's wrath on the Khan.

For the first time since the death of my father, I was given new clothes. The Khan did not mention anything about my being his future son-in-law; however, and I, for my part, did not see myself in a position of being his son-in-law.

Meeting Amanullah Khan

I returned to Kohistan and waited three months for a word from Ahmad Ali, but nothing came through. Dejected and depressed, I kept on going to school. One morning, news came to school that I was to go to see Ahmad Ali Khan with my brother. Ahmad Ali Khan sent us to Salang. There, by order of Amanullah Khan, a road was cut from Jabal Seraj to the foot of Salang Pass, and he and Queen Soraya were to come and officially open the road. The road was dirt with wooden bridges.

At Salang Pass, the royal camp was set up so the king could have lunch with the people. My brother and I waited near the camp under a tree while the king opened the road near Jabal Seraj. We waited in fear of the unexpected. We thought, "Here is the king who killed our father – what will he do to us? He might order our deaths, and have us thrown from the mountain or drowned in the river."

We prayed to God to put mercy in his heart. Our governess told us, "When you come face to face with Amanullah Khan, do not be afraid. Remember God."

Finally, Amir's caravan reached the camp. The king and queen stepped out. My brother and I hid behind the tree. The gathering made me think of my father, how he used to hold banquets in honor of the king's father. The feasting lasted three hours. The tempting smells of exotic foods reminded us of our good days. Every minute we counted, expecting to be invited. No one paid any attention to us. Finally, we heard the gunning of the car and smelled exhaust smoke in the air. We were losing an opportunity to meet the king. At the last moment Ahmad Ali Khan called my name, and I ran toward him.

I had seen the king many times and recognized him, but this time, the eyes of an orphan met the eyes of a strong king; the eyes of the murderer of my father met mine. I presented my application with shaking hands. Before reading the application, the king gave me a cursory look. With every line he read, he stared at me. I feared he was becoming infuriated I was still alive.

In the end, he asked, "Who wrote this application?"

Ahmad Ali Khan answered, "Khalilullah Jan wrote it."

Again, the king repeated, "Who wrote this application?" Ahmad Ali repeated my name.

The king faced the sky, hesitated, and said, "If I return all of your father's confiscated property, you will become lazy and a glutton."

Then he consented.

"For every class in school you finish, part of your father's property will be returned to you," he pronounced.

In the end, he pledged, "It is my promise."

I saw Moinus Saltana sitting in the rear seat, watching me. The king ordered I should go home in a carriage and then, he left in his car.

I was very happy. After so long a time, I was free. My friends would not hate me or be afraid of me. I could study freely now. No one would kill me because of my father, I thought. I wanted to reach home as soon as I could, to break the good news to my sister and my governess.

Ironically, after about four months, a big landslide would wash away most of the road at Salang Pass. But the king's word was law, and the law took its course.

After three months, 13 jerib of land and three small vineyards in Sarai Khuja were returned to me. I completed the fifth grade in the primary school of Sarai Khuja and was placed first in my class. After the final exams, Ali Mohammad Khan, who was president of the Education Department and later became Minister of Foreign Affairs, visited the graduating class of the primary school. Sherjan, the Minister of Court of Habibullah Khan Kalakani, who was Hakim of the area, also visited.

I was fortunate both these important and learned men were present during my exam. I stood first among the primary schools of the region. I was given a medal and a certificate of distinction.

I was still a student when Mohammad Afzal Khan invited me in Tutumdara and showed me a document that stated, "Mohammad Afzal's daughter is engaged to Khalilullah, son of Mustufi."

Mohammad Afzal wrote to Amanullah asking his approval for marriage. Amanullah Khan wrote him back, saying, "It is in your interest not to marry your daughter to Mustufi's son."

The Khan asked me, "What should I do?"

I replied, "I can say nothing against the king's order."

The Khan said, "You should know until the time of Mustufi's death, my daughter was engaged to you. Now that Amanullah is against this, consider my daughter to be your maid and servant. You should continue your studies. I will take care of your marriage and will bear all the expenses."

Later, I became a teacher at the same school. My salary was 30 afghanis per month. As time went by, I became the principal of the school.

Amanullah Khan (1919 AD)

Gradually, Amanullah Khan's popularity began to erode. The regime of Bokhara had already crumbled. The king, Sayed Ali, took refuge in Afghanistan. The Bolshevics overran Bokhara. Thousands of people – men, women and children – followed him across the border into Afghanistan. Most of them came to Kabul – tired, hungry, and defeated. In every mosque they went to, the elite and elders of the area called upon the people to help the refugees. The elders emphasized the conditions forcing the people of Bokhara to leave their homeland. They urged the people to treat the refugees as guests and reminded them, according to the Holy Koran, these people had a right to live in Afghanistan in line with the Afghan traditions.

Wherever refugees passed through, the people of the area provided them with food and shelter and listened as they told their stories about the persecutions under communism. I taught my students to welcome the refugees by reciting verses from the Holy Koran. It should not be left unsaid the people of Afghanistan were close to the people of Bokhara. They called it Bokhara Sharif (Sacred Bokhara) because Imam Abu Ismail, who collected the sayings (Hadis) of Imam Bokhari, is buried there, as is Bahauddin Naqshband Bukhari, founder of Naqshband (Golden Chain) school of thought.

Afghanistan had thousands of followers of the Naqshband school of thought. Most of the Ulama (Mashaekh) of Afghanistan from Kabul, Herat, Balkh, and Ghazni traveled to Bokhara for higher learning. Until the fall of Bokhara, many of the students from Afghanistan received higher education in the Diwan Begi religious school in Bokhara.

The commercial ties between the people of Afghanistan and Bokhara were very strong. The courts of Afghanistan and Bokhara had close ties. Haji Abdul Qayoum Zargar, renowned visionary of Afghanistan, always traveled to Bokhara. My father would send personal letters and gifts to the king of Bokhara, who also always exchanged gifts with the eminent people of Afghanistan. Once, the king of Bokhara sent a golden knife and belt to me.

After the death of my father, Haji Qayoum told me he used to carry reports from Bokhara to the court of Habibullah Khan. The king of Bokhara came to Gulbahar through Darqat port, Khanabad and Panjsher on horseback. Amanullah Khan ordered people not to communicate with the overthrown king of Bokhara. Hussain Kot, the place of my father, was vacated for him. From Gulbahar to Hussain Kot he traveled by car. If he had traveled on horseback, it would have taken him at least two weeks to reach Hussain

Kot, passing through throngs of well wishers.

In spite of tight security and a security escort for the king of Bokhara, the people met him secretly in Hussain Kot. The people even wanted to raise an army and accompany the king via Mazar-i-Sharif to Bokhara.

As soon as the government came to know about this, it sent him south of Kabul to Qalai Fatu Chardehi and reduced his pension from 12,000 to 4,000 afghanis. No doubt, in the beginning, Amanullah Khan dispatched a strong force to help the king of Bokhara, but as soon as Bokhara fell, Amanullah Khan was tricked by the empty and cunning talks of Lenin, and he signed an agreement of neutrality with him. Amanullah Khan expanded his ties with the Soviets and moved the king of Bokhara from Qalai Fatu to downtown Kabul, into an old house.

Opposition to Amanullah Khan

With the passage of time, opposition to Amanullah Khan became very visible. The people of Paktia under the leadership of Mullah Abdullah, known as Mullah Lang (disabled), marched toward Kabul and came close to the city. During the ensuing fight thousands of people from both sides were killed. Mullah Lang declared his Holy War against Amanullah Khan on the basis of religion. Mullah Lang's campaign was picking up strength and was close to igniting a fire all over the country.

Soon the fire was contained and movement curtailed. A man named Abdul Karim, who was related to Amir Yaqub Khan, came to Paktia from India. Suddenly, the religious uprising of Mullah Lang took a political turn. The fire ignited by the Mullah died down and failed to light anywhere else. Abdul Karim was instrumental. Who sent this Abdul Karim to Paktia – the British, the Soviets, or both? Mullah Lang gave himself up to the state. He was guaranteed safe conduct by Amanullah on the Holy Koran. Soon after that, Mullah Lang was executed in Kabul with 21 others. Abdul Karim went back to India and was later murdered.

Nadir Shah during his reign built a tomb for Mullah

Lang. In Kohdaman and Kohistan, unrest began. The people started grouping into small units to oppose the king through small and isolated incidents.

Not a day or night passed without an attack in both urban and rural areas. The caravans were also attacked. Two underground guerrilla groups were organized in Kohdaman under Shah Mohammad and Wali. The government could not arrest them because the people supported them. Consequently, Shujaudaula was recalled from London, where he was Ambassador of Afghanistan. He was appointed governor of the troubled sectors. The first thing Shujaudaula did was to extend amnesty to both leaders of the movement. One day he invited them to a dinner at his residence and had them killed.

There were people in government who had contacts with the underground forces. The people of Dari-Khel, Jadran rose against the regime. The government defeated, arrested, and killed many of them and a number of them, including men, women, and children, were exiled to the north. These actions and similar ones backfired in the face of Amanullah Khan. The king created more enemies than friends with his oppressive attitude toward unrest.

From wherever the afflicted people of Jadran passed, Amanullah had new enemies. The king, unaware of his actions, was busy modernizing and westernizing education and social systems. Numerous new schools were built along the countryside and in Kabul. Amania School was built on the French pattern of education, and French teachers were hired. Nejat School was built by German aid, and the German language was taught. The higher education army school, civil servants school, office employee school, language school, and fine arts schools were also built. Amanullah himself used to go to different schools.

Amanullah Khan's Reforms

Land taxation was also an important step Amanullah Khan took at that time. During the Amani period, tax

collection changed from barter of grain to currency, and tax was collected twice annually. He reformed office work and created different ministries. The minister was known as Nazir and later was called Minister.

Amanullah Khan called a meeting in Kabul. Those invited to this meeting were appointed through decrees of the king, and were mostly members of the royal family or former government employees. The goal of this meeting was to produce a Nizamnama (ruling document) instead of a constitution because the members were not elected. Nizamnamas drafted by this group were signed by the king. The basic ruling documents were called Maliya, Gumruk, Civil Nizamnamas, etc.

The king reformed the courts and organized them along modern lines. He created Tamiz, Murafeha, and Ibtedaia. Tamiz was the high court and held sessions in Kabul, Murafeha, and sessions in Ibtedaia were held in every province. The primary court was in every governorate. Afghanistan was divided at that time into five provinces and four Hukumate Alas.

The five provinces were Kabul, Kandahar, Herat, Turkistan and Kataghan, and Badakhshan. The four Alas were Mashriqi, Junubi, Maimana, and Farah.

Hukumate Kalan was part of a province or Hukumate Ala. Hukumate Kalan constituted a number of small units. Some of these units were further broken down into Alaqadaris. In Naibul Hukumate and Hukumate Ala, the military commander was called Firqa Misher. Every unit had a Judge Superior, Primary Judge, Commander of Kotwali (Police), Director of Education, Director of Drafting, and a Mustufi, who ran the government.

Amanullah Khan called for a Jirgah, a general meeting, for the first time. The representatives of the people were selected on the recommendation of the people and review of the Hakim. Members of the council, religious leaders, ministers, directors of departments, and members of the royalty participated in the Jirgah. The king presided over the Jirgah. A difference of opinion did appear between the people and the king in the first Jirgah. Important decisions were made. The Islamic Khilafat was also discussed.

People were free to speak their opinions during the proceedings of the Jirgah.

Every year at the end of the month of Sunbula (September), the Jashen (Independence Day) was celebrated in Paghman. The entrance to the Jashen cost one afghani. The king himself inaugurated the Jashen every year.

Gradually, the emancipation of women took root. Girls' schools opened in Kabul. Amid all these activities; however, lawlessness thrived. Bribery, theft, and insecurity became the order of the day. Amanullah Khan sent groups of students for higher studies to the Soviet Union, Europe, and Turkey.

Foreign affairs policy was based on enmity of the British and friendship with the USSR. It was at this time a gap was created between the people and the state. No one told the facts to the king. The king's attention was riveted on modernization or lifting the face of the country and the expansion of education. In the mosques, the clergy embarked on a concerted propaganda campaign against the king. The majority of the teachers came from religious schools, and they joined hands with the clergy.

I was still at Sarai Khurga School. Every day, students came to my house after school to study literature. Reading the Holy Koran correctly was also introduced in the school, and the local people asked me to lead the prayers as Imam. Many people brought their court papers to me to be corrected and rewritten. In spite of my youth, most of the people accepted my mediation in solving their petty differences and quarrels. All this helped build their confidence in me.

I was married at this time. The daughter of Afzal Khan, who had a basic education at her father's house, helped me a great deal. My financial condition deteriorated with the increase in my social contacts, presence of innumerable guests every day, and the birth of my children. I did not accept any compensation for teaching the students or resolving the disputes. Nights and days passed in affliction and hunger.

I was very supportive of Amanullah Khan's attention to educational development. I visited Kabul without the permission of government and met Ustad Saljoqi by chance near the Kabul River. He was very kind to me. We talked for a while, and he read a few verses from *Khaqani*. Saljoqi was a teacher at Habibiya School. He was the first intellectual from Herat I met. I still remember the deep effect of that conversation on me. We talked about Sufi poet Abdul Haq Betab. He was also a teacher in Habibiya School. Betab's sister was my father's first wife, who had no children.

I would stay for days at my stepmother's house. It was here I came to know Betab. Like a very kind teacher, he corrected my poems. My stepmother stitched Arakhcheen Zari and sold the garments to buy me books. I would walk to Kabul all the way from Sarai Khuja. My father's friends would feel pity for me, but could do nothing for fear of the government.

Faiz Mohammad Khan, the Minister of Education, knew my father. Finding me capable, he appointed me as principal of the school. I will never forget the moment I took over that job. The pleasure of that moment is unforgettable. I never matched the pleasure again, even when I became an advisor to the king, a minister, and an ambassador.

Habibullah Khan Kalakani (1929)

Habibullah Kalakani was becoming a popular name those days in Kohdaman. I knew him from the time when he was a gardener at my father's estate in Hussain Kot. During the afterhours, in school, in the markets and also in my house, the topic of discussion was Habibullah. His story was like the stories of Amir Hamza and Abu Muslim (legendary figures in Islamic history). He had become a legend, a folk hero.

In spite of the fact I held no grudge against the government and was busy in school doing my job, I was blamed for anti-government activities and ousted from

Kohdaman. I said goodbye to my students and took my wife and children to Kabul. I went to Faiz Mohammad Khan directly. He made his earnest efforts to help me, but all in vain. Amanullah Khan did not throw me in prison, however. I was appointed as a clerk in the Ministry of Finance through a decree.

Most of the ministries were located inside the Arg. The Ministry of Finance was very familiar because my father had been the Minister of Finance. The new job as clerk was contrary to my taste. Mirza Mir Hashim, a friend of my father, was the Minister of Finance at that time. He was very helpful, and I was appointed to the Herat desk at the ministry. At the end of every month the work of every province was sent to the Ministry of Finance. I was appointed as primary clerk for 60 afghanis per month and became a proficient accountant very quickly. Most of the officials of the Ministry of Finance had worked under my father and were very kind to me. Some adversaries of my father never liked my proficiency and popularity.

It was at the Ministry of Finance I made a number of Herati friends. Many of them were intellectuals and men of letters, and their accents were different from Kabul. They would talk to me about the historical places of Herat, like the tomb of Khwaja Abdullah Ansari, and about Maulavi Jami. They told stories about the congregation mosque of Herat, and about the abundance and affluence of their province. They recited poems of Haji Ismail Siyah. My love for Herat peaked.

The Heratis knew my father well. Sometimes they brought gifts of pista, kurk, and qanavez (a kind of silk cloth produced in Herat), and I always did my best to help them. I talked to them about the tombs of Kabul, and they told me of the tombs of Herat. Heratis always had an upper hand.

In those days, the distance between Kabul and Herat was covered in one month in winter and 20 days in summer. The shortest route to Herat was through Bamiyan and Chaghcharan, through Hazarajat. The other route was via Mazar-i-Sharif, Maimana, and Murghab. The third route was via Ghazni, Kandahar, and Farah. All three routes were traversed by caravans, camels, and horses. It was for this reason people of Herat were not aware of the happenings and developments of Kabul and vice-a-versa. Telephone and telegraph connections were not yet installed between Kabul and Herat.

My financial condition deteriorated further. My salary was insufficient to meet my expenses. At home, I had my wife, children, brothers, and sisters and, above all, innumerable guests. I rented a small house for eight afghanis per month. My house had two rooms. We slept in one room and the other room was for guests. I missed the free water, fruit, and clean air of Kohdaman.

During six months of the year, working hours were 8 a.m. to 4:30 p.m., and the other six months, from 9 a.m. to 3:30 p.m. If one was late without an excuse, a day's salary was deducted. I wore the same clothes day in and day out. After a great effort, I was able to find a job for my brother Najibullah. In spite of my busy schedule, I would go to Deh Mulla Arab, an eminent intellectual from Mazar-i-Sharif and Abdul Rehman Khan Shaheed Peghmani to study Arabic grammar and logic.

The ministries moved to Paghman during three months of summer. Paghman was like Kohdaman to me. During the first year none of my friends wanted to share their room with me in Paghman, because they were afraid of the government. I rented a house in Chandalbai, for three afghanis a month. I cooked my own meals. I always made time to go to the mountains and sit in seclusion, working on my poetry. Night after night I would go to the public park and sit in a corner reading my books under the park lights. At night, under clear skies, the fresh air of Paghman was always a source of inspiration to me. In summer, I would send my family to Kohdaman and visit them twice a month.

Going from Paghman to Kohdaman on foot was not an easy task. Thieves and vagabonds crossed my path many times, but as soon as they recognized me, they left me alone.

Amanullah Khan Visits to Europe

Three years passed. In December 1927 Amanullah Khan decided to go to Europe. He embarked on his journey accompanied by the queen. Mahmud Tarzi was Ambassador to Paris, and Ghulam Siddique, son of the Commander-in-chief Cherkhi, was the Minister of Foreign Affairs.

According to the letters of Mahmud Tarzi, which I read later, he was against Amanullah Khan's journey to Europe. Nadir Khan was the Afghan envoy to Paris before Mahmud Tarzi and resigned on medical grounds. Nadir Khan was appointed in Paris by the Ministry of Defense. Earlier, Nadir sent arms and ammunition to Ghazi Anwar Beg during the Bokhara expedition against the Soviets. The Soviets protested to Amanullah Khan. Some people say Nadir was against the government because Amanullah Khan paid the military with food instead of money and because soldiers complained officials stole even from that. Therefore, Amanullah Khan sent him to Paris. Nadir resigned amid controversy from the Paris post. One story was that Amanullah Khan considered Mullah Lang to have been instigated by Nadir's family. However, Nadir had the confidence of the people, and his family was highly respected.

In early 1928, Amanullah Khan became the first king of Afghanistan to travel to Europe. His entourage included the queen with three women royalty, and also Ghulam Siddique Khan, Minister of Foreign Affairs, Sardar Sher Ahmad, President of the Assembly, Ali Ahmad Khan, Governor of Kabul, and other officials also traveled with them.

Mohammad Wali Khan

Amanullah Khan appointed Mohammad Wali as regent. He was from Darwaz and grew up in Amir Abdur Rahman's court. Amir Abdur Rahman had two kinds of Ghulam Bachas (court servants). Ghulam Bache-Khas and Ghulam Bacha Aam (main and general servants). Ghulam

Bache-Khas received their education in private and higher schools wore golden belts, and some of them wore emerald and diamond earrings. They were masters of etiquette and taught horseback riding and court manners. All these servants hailed from highly respected families. Wali Khan was in charge of Ghulam Bache-Khas. He was well cultured and mannered and a very respected person.

Most of these Bache-Khas were appointed to important and high positions during the time of Amir Abdur Rahman, Amir Habibullah, Amir Amanullah, Mohammad Nadir, and Mohammad Zahir. For example, Abdul Ahad Khan Wardhaki, in the beginning of Amanullah's rule, was imprisoned on charges of taking part in his father's assassination, and was exiled to Bokhara. Later he received amnesty and became Minister of Interior and accompanied Amanullah Khan to Europe. In Nadir Shah's and Zahir Shah's times he was appointed President of the Assembly seven times. While he was President of the Assembly he also attended cabinet meetings.

Mohammad Wali Khan also headed the committee on western and Asian countries to introduce Afghanistan when Amanullah Khan assumed power. He successfully returned home from his trip and was then appointed Minister of Foreign Affairs. Later, he was appointed Minister of Defense in place of Mohammad Nadir. It was from here the two families drifted apart.

Nadir's family thought Wali Khan, who played a pivotal role in the defeat of Mullah Lang, told King Amanullah that Mullah Lang was instigated by Nadir. Amanullah Khan awarded Wali Khan the Elmar Ala, highest decoration, and lands of my father in Hussain Kot. Wali Khan, in respect of friendship with my father, one day invited me to Hussain Kot. He was so kind and courteous to me I completely forgot the bitterness of the murder of my father and confiscation of these very lands.

He said, "Until you and other inheritors of this land permit me, it would be unlawful for me to till this land or even say prayers here."

Malik Ghulam Nabi Istalifi, Shahnawaz Khan of Qala Murad Beg, and Mohammad Karim Khan were also present during this conversation. As soon as they recognized me they expressed their disillusion over Amanullah Khan's decision to execute my father. Every time Amanullah Khan left Kabul for the countryside, Mohammad Wali was the regent.

When Amanullah Khan returned from Europe, he started emulating a western lifestyle. Mohammad Wali Khan realized the whole nation was against this and advised Amanullah Khan to stop, but he did not listen. Anticipating danger to the country, Wali Khan resigned. At the time of Habibullah Kalakani, Mohammad Wali Khan remained in his house and was not disturbed. As soon as Nadir took over power, he imprisoned Wali Khan on charges of opposition to Amanullah Khan and complicity with Habibullah Kalakani.

Wali Khan was sentenced to death, but on the interference of some friendly countries, the death sentence was commuted to eight years in jail. I can swear to God Mohammad Wali had nothing to do with Habibullah Kalakani. He was framed. When Mohammad Wali met Habibullah Kalakani, he did not know him. Others introduced him to Habibullah.

Mohammad Wali remained in the palace jail for four or five years and during the first year of Zahir Shah, he was executed on the order of Prime Minister Mohammad Hashim Khan, along with Khwaja Hidayatullah and Ghulam Jailani, brothers of Ghulam Nabi Charkhi and Mohammad Mehdi, a learned youth of the Qizelbash tribe. A few days before their execution took place, Mohammad Kabir, the young son of Munshi Nasir, went to the British Embassy to kill the British envoy. He failed in his attempt and instead killed two or three guards of the embassy. Prime Minister Hashim thought Mohammad Wali instigated the attack, although he had been in isolation for over four years.

When Amanullah Khan went to Europe, he left behind a country in chaos. Once a week a newsreel about his journey was screened in the Kabul cinema. Showing the bare faces of the queen and other women of royalty before foreigners further fueled the fire of antagonism and hatred against Amanullah Khan. If they drank water or juice, people took it as alcohol and lamb kebab as pork kebab. Rumors ran like fire from one point of the country to the other that the king of the Islamic country had turned into an infidel. Religious leaders contributed immensely toward the campaign.

Amanullah Khan predicted this himself. I remember when he was leaving for Europe, he invited officials to the Dilkusha garden before dawn to bid farewell. In his speech, he said, "I am going. I am not afraid of the foreign enemy. I'm afraid of the enemy from within, especially these mullahs who might deceive you during my absence and tell you the old and rotten things. Do not fall prey to their magic."

In the end he added, "My proud nation, remember what I have said. I may be dead, and you may be alive."

I also recall some elder officials said the king became an infidel even before his journey. At the call for prayer, people walked to the mosque for prayers.

Return of Amanullah Khan from Europe

Amanullah Khan returned to Kabul via Iran, passing through Herat, Kandahar, and Ghazni. The road from Herat to Kandahar was newly laid. He was warmly welcomed from Herat to Kabul. But every time he stopped and spoke, the warmth of the welcome tended to lessen. Amanullah Khan did not have a great regard for the customs and traditions of the people. For example, in Herat he said the lands in trust at Khwaja Abdullah Ansari tomb would be sold to the people and Basti Khwaja Abdullah Ansari in Gazargah would be broken. It was a custom that anyone who took refuge in the tomb, a criminal or a saint, was not to be arrested.

He did the same thing in Kandahar at the Khirqa Sharif, a holy tomb where some personal effects of Hazrat Mohammad are placed. He told the people Khirqa is an old

dress, and Khwaja Abdi is just a bunch of decayed bones.

Amanullah Khan returned to Kabul. Every ministry and organization built welcome gates for him. From Qalai Qazi to Kabul men and women lined the streets. At every welcome gate slogans and poems were posted. A transport company built one gate next to the Taimur Shah tomb. This company employed political figures such as Mir Sayed Qasim Sar Munshi, Faiz Mohammad Khan Nasiri and Abdul Aziz Hussain. They always opposed the government through their pens. Mohammad Anwar Khan Baburi, the representative from Jalalabad who was a good friend of mine, requested I write something for this gate. My former governess also advised me. My relatives from Kohistan and Kohdaman were surprised they were not afraid of writing my poem on the gate. My poem was on the forefront. The verses were written in golden letters on velvet surrounded by light bulbs. The glamour of the gate attracted people to it.

The motorcade of the king and queen was coming from Darul Aman to the Dilkusha. Government officials gathered on the lawns of the palace to welcome the royal party. Amid the groups of welcome-wishers, students from the school were in the first row.

Ustad Salahuddin Saljoqi rode with the king's motorcade. The air was filled with the firing of cannons, the singing of songs and the shouting of slogans. On one of the gates Amanullah Khan was called Rabbunnau, god of luck and happiness. The bare face of the queen; however, was not liked by many people who were conservative and strictly religious. It was a day of celebrations. Amanullah Khan delivered his famous speech on the lawn of the Dilkusha. The whole city was lit as part of the celebration. I remained confined to my house with my family. My relatives from Kohdaman and Kohistan who were invited to welcome of the king were, ironically, my guests.

My house was about 500 meters south of the Arg in a place called Guzare Khiyaban. It was a place where my grandfather's servants once lived. It was a lonely place. On the morning of the celebration, at about 8 o'clock, Ustad Saljoqi came to see me. He was exuberant, and said, "The king read your poem on the gate and was pleased. He stopped the car to read it again. When he read your name at the end of the poem, he asked me, 'Who is Khalilullah?' I introduced you, though afraid of the repercussions. The king said he wants to see you and thank you. He has promised to send you to Europe for higher studies."

Though a little scared in the beginning, I was thrilled, and the first thing I did was reveal this to my wife and then to my former governess. As I went to the Ministry of Finance, Minister Mir Hashim congratulated me. It seemed Ustad Saljoqi told everybody.

Effect of European Visit on Amanullah Khan's Government

Amanullah Khan started translating his reforms into action. He invited government officials every evening to the Ministry of Foreign Affairs in the Stor Palace, and narrated to them the episodes of his journey. One evening Saljoqi took me with him. I was becoming very bold. I thought Amanullah Khan did not hate me any more after the poem I wrote in his praise. When we entered the room the king was speaking about his journey to London. He was ridiculing King George V and praising the Soviets for their hospitality. All foreign envoys were present as usual. The people applauded approvingly and laughed at the king's jokes.

At the end, one of my friends asked me, "What are you doing here?"

I said, "I have written a poem, and the king has pardoned me and will send me to Europe."

He whispered to me, "You must be kidding. Saretu boi qorma mei dehad." This is an Afghan proverb, meaning roughly, "I can smell your cooked head."

"Go to Kohdaman and listen to what the people are saying," he added. "This regime is not going to last long." Even before he could finish, I left the place, scared to death. Every day a decree was proclaimed.

As the summer approached the ministries moved to

Paghman, and the Assembly also convened there. This year my financial condition improved a little. Faqir Mohammad Khan, a renowned businessman of Kabul known as Shere-arti, became my acquaintance through Mirza Bedil. Often he invited me to read Bedil's poems together. He allowed me to live rent-free in his house near Paghman Mosque.

In the past two years, none of my colleagues shared rooms with me. But this year, as a result of Saljoqi's efforts in promoting me and also partly due to this big house given free for me to live in, it seemed everybody wanted to share space with me. I rented out the first and third floors of the building. My tenants included three members of the Assembly from Mazar, Herat, and Nangarhar. I came to know of the latest political developments through them.

The assemblyman from Nangarhar, Mohammad Anwar of the Baburi tribe, was a great gentleman. His family was highly educated and had good relations with my father. The Assembly still convened on the old lines. Amanullah Khan chaired the Loya Jirgah in Paghman. This Jirgah, which lasted five days, included new representatives along with the ministers, high-ranking government officials and members of the old Assembly. The major topics discussed were the Purdah system, sending girls to foreign countries for education, the marriage age, and cash fines for crimes. The highlight of the Jirgah was the establishment of a national assembly on enfranchisement.

There were two important actions. First, the king repealed the veil. Queen Soraya entered the assembly hall bare faced, thus officially lifting the veil. Second, Prince Rahmatullah was named heir to the throne.

The Jirgah members accepted the king's actions as fate accompli, including members from Kohdaman and Kohistan who were my friends.

"We and others accepted the actions tentatively," they explained. "Once we return to our homes, we will discuss it with religious leaders, and then decide what to do."

The government ordered the deposit of all outstanding government dues from past years in Kohistan, Kohdaman, Herat, etc. Efforts were being made to expand the education system. Groups of students – boys and girls –

were sent to Europe and Turkey for higher education.

The government also ordered the removal of the veil from women's faces in public. According to another decree, Thursday was declared as weekend instead of Friday. Also, no one was to be seen in Kabul and Paghman without western dress and a felt hat, or they would be fined. It was also decreed that instead of the Imam, a government minister should lead the Friday prayers.

There remained no choice for people but to accept what Amanullah Khan liked. Whatever economic assistance promises made by the foreign governments did not materialize.

Bribery and insecurity became the order of the day. Every day caravans were attacked and people looted.

The Independence Day celebrations were held in Paghman. The conservatives and religious-minded people who participated in the celebrations saw with their own eyes the new laws in practice, that is, women without veils and western lifestyle.

Rumors were ripe throughout the country that the king had turned infidel. The king's actions certified the rumors. For example, he ordered women wearing the Chaderi (long garb with a veil) should be stopped and their veil be scissored from their face. One day the people of Kohdaman invited the king to Istalif. In the evening when the call for prayers was given, the king reacted sharply, saying, "Wherever I go, I cannot get rid of this screeching voice."

The king's words had a bad impact on his hosts. They said they made a mistake by inviting this infidel for a feast. The elders earlier asked me to write a welcome address in honor of the king. I questioned, "Did you mention my name to the king?"

They said, "No. Before leaving, the king took a copy of the address with him. We did not want to mention your name to the infidel."

Before the arrival of the king all the walls adjacent to the king's routes were demolished. Amanullah Khan's words about the call for prayers traveled like fire throughout Kohdaman and Kohistan, adding more fuel to the already burning flames of hatred against the king.

Habibullah Kalakani

Habibullah was a young man from Kalakan, a small village in Kohdaman, about 20 kilometers north of Kabul and lying parallel to the main road running from Kabul to Jabal Seraj. Kalakan is one of the six villages in that area, and it is one of the most populous villages of Afghanistan. Kalakan is overwhelmingly populated by Tajiks who own vineyards.

Habibullah's father was a water-carrier to the Afghan freedom fighters battling against the British troops at Bala Hissar (Fort) during the Second Anglo-Afghan War. He was called Baba Saqao. Habibullah in his youth worked on my father's farm in Hussain Kot. During the Amani period he was drafted in military. At this time two highway robbers were increasingly active, disturbing the peace. The Amani government had a price on their heads and wanted them dead or alive. One day Habibullah, while coming back home from Kabul, was confronted by these two robbers, who wanted his gun. Habibullah killed both of them. Instead of commending Habibullah, the Magistrate of Kalakan apprehended him and put him in jail.

Habibullah escaped from prison and took to the mountain as an outlaw, opening a new chapter in his life. News of Habibullah's apprehension and escape traveled far and wide. The people of Kohdaman who were tired of the government's high-handedness came around him. Some government officials corroborated with him. Even some of Amanullah Khan's family members backed Habibullah.

Amanullah Khan's overtures on religion fell short of people's historic desire. They preferred Habibullah to deliver them.

One day while traveling from Kabul to Kohdaman, I saw Habibullah. A friend of mine from Panjsher accompanied me. We were on foot. Habibullah was well armed. His friends wanted to arrest us; however, Habibullah, as soon as he heard my name, respected me. I asked him what was going on.

"God wants me to overthrow Amanullah Khan," he

said. "The religious leaders have given me their blessing. I have received messages from different tribes of the country."

"You will see the results pretty soon," he added.

He left with his friends, and I walked away with mine.

Habibullah's claims seemed like a folk tale at that time. I could not believe a king who is the son of a king, who helped gain freedom, brought education to illiterates, is recognized by world leaders, and has at least 100,000 soldiers at his command boasting of cannons and planes – could be overthrown by a young, unknown, poor man, illiterate, and wearing simple clothes. Every passing day, however, brought more authenticity to Habibullah's words.

Start of Insurrection

The Shinwar and Momand tribes rebelled against Amanullah Khan's government. Whatever aid was sent from Kabul was ineffective as government soldiers either defected or returned without fighting. The magistrate of Charekar, who wanted to arrest Habibullah, was killed in a roadside encounter. The government appointed Ahmad Ali Khan as administrator of Kohdaman and Kohistan in Charekar. In fact, the conflict took the shape of a battle between crown and religion, proving people follow the cry of religion and not the crown.

A rumor prevailed that Ahmad Ali Khan reached an understanding with Habibullah and convinced him to take up arms against the Shinwar rebellion. Ahmad Ali Khan told Habibullah he would seek Amanullah Khan's permission that night on the telephone and let Habibullah know. In those days one could not direct dial a telephone in Afghanistan. Ahmad Ali had to contact Jabal Seraj first to get to Amanullah Khan.

By chance of luck the operator at Jabal Seraj was a very conservative Muslim and a friend of Habibullah. He sent a message to Habibullah to come to Jabal Seraj and listen to the conversation between Amanullah Khan and Ahmad Ali Khan. Habibullah, with one of his aides, went to the telephone station at Jabal Seraj. It is said Amanullah Khan told Ahmad Ali to wrap a book in a cloth and deceive this illiterate robber into thinking it was the Holy Koran. Ahmad Ali was to send him and his friends to Kabul to receive military supplies, and was told Amanullah would do the rest. Habibullah went to Ahmad Ali in the morning. There he was presented the king's message on a book wrapped in cloth as if it was the Holy Koran. Habibullah left for Kabul with 100 to 150 men to get arms.

At the time of his departure to Kabul, some elders and religious leaders who were told of the conversation of the king with Ahmad Ali came to Habibullah. They gave a Fatwah that the Jihad against Amanullah Khan is legal. A large portion of Amanullah Khan's army was busy suppressing the rebellion in Shinwar.

Habibullah said, "I will go to Kabul with God's blessing. Either death will embrace me, or the crown will fall at my feet."

The religious leaders, who included Hazrat Mojaddadi of Kohdaman, Buzurgjan, prayed for his success. One of the Khans of Kohdaman who had religious influence, too, presented his precious white horse to Habibullah so he could ride it when leading the caravan.

Habibullah turned his face toward Qibla and called out, "God is great, Allah-o-Akbar."

All this took place in the Laghmani village of Charekar.

One or two months before this Hazrat Mohammad Sadiq Mojaddadi with Masoom Jan, his nephew, had gone to Paktia, and declared Jihad against Amanullah Khan. But they were arrested and brought to Kabul.

Abdul Rahman Khan Paghmani, President of Tamiz (Chief Justice of Amanullah Khan) was an accomplice of Mojaddadi's and was arrested with them. Mohammad Sadiq Mojaddadi was the younger brother of Shamsul Mashaeq and Noorul Mashaeq, who played a major role in the independence of Afghanistan and Amanullah Khan's ascension to the throne.

Ghulam Masoom Mojaddadi was the son of Shamsul Mashaeq. Noorul Moshaeq and Shamsul Moshaeq's titles were bestowed upon these two in recognition of their services during the war of independence of Afghanistan.

Habibullah Attacks Kabul

The Chief Justice was executed on the order of Amanullah Khan, along with his two sons and a nephew. It was time for evening prayer, and I had gone home from office when I heard gunfire. The talk of the town was that Habibullah had attacked Kabul. Later, we learned Habibullah had a plan to enter the palace unannounced. He reached Kabul with lightning speed through a preemptive attack. Whomever they met on their way, they told they were going to the king to take arms and go to Shinwar to fight the rebellion.

Ironically enough, when they reached Shahrara they saw students of the military academy in combat uniform. Habibullah's friends fired, without even confirming what the matter was. The students were in fact training and had no ammunition in their guns. The gunfire alerted the palace, and Habibullah's plan was aborted.

With the battle raging in Kabul, Habibullah fought the government forces in Shahrara, and Baghebala and dug in to face the attack of the government forces. The Khogyanis also rebelled with the help of Shinwar. Amanullah Khan appointed Ali Ahmad Khan, his brother-in-law, as Administrator of Jalalabad. The hope of the government was tied to Ali Ahmad. The rebellious forces defeated the former Administrator, Sardar Sher Ahmad, earlier. Mutiny by the military helped defeat Sher Ahmad.

The soldiers considered themselves as conservative Muslims and part of the people. The young Generals of Amanullah Khan failed to understand the soldiers and could not win their confidence. Ali Ahmad Khan, instead of helping Amanullah, declared himself king on the way to Jalalabad. The people did not pledge allegiance to him, and the Khogyanis forced him to leave Afghanistan, escaping on foot to India.

The war minister of Amanullah Khan, Abdul Aziz Khan Barakzai, a heavily built man who boasted a long mustache, entered the war against Habibullah with full strength helped by artillery and air cover. He got badly beaten in every battle. Meanwhile the British planes flew over Kabul several times, dropping leaflets that no one should attack the British nationals.

Amanullah Khan watched the warfront every day through big binoculars mounted on a tripod stand. He ordered arms to be given to all government servants and students. Ironically, the government newspapers kept on reporting that Habibullah had been arrested, his friend Sayed Hussain had been killed, and Khogyani, Momand, and Shinwar rebels had been defeated and surrendered to the government forces. Every day, however, the wounded, the dead, and the defeated government soldiers were seen in Kabul.

Incidentally, the winter this year was severe. One electric power station was in operation in Jabal Seraj, which was built by Amir Habibullah (Amanullah Khan's father). This plant went out of commission when Habibullah's supporters sabotaged it. Commercial traffic was not flowing into Kabul so a food shortage hit the capital. While the government soldiers were short of food and supplies, the people of Kohdaman and Kohistan supplied the best possible food, fruits, and fuel to Habibullah's men free of charge, out of hatred for Amanullah Khan.

Every day Habibullah's Islamic resurrection kept expanding. The Kohdaman soldiers who were defeated in Jalalabad surrendered to Habibullah with their arms. Thus Habibullah's men received a continuous flow of arms from government depots except for heavy artillery and planes, which they did not have.

One day, during a battle, a piece of shrapnel from a bomb blast near the British Embassy hit Habibullah's shoulder and broke it. He lost a lot of blood. The Red Cross provided medical assistance to the wounded on both sides. Because the doctors wore white aprons and spoke a different language, some of the wounded took them to be angels from heaven. Habibullah was forced to retreat to Kohdaman. The government forces pushed their way up to Khair Khana Pass.

The insurrection took strength and unrest in Kabul increased. Amanullah Khan sent the queen and his sisters to

India via Kandahar. This further enhanced the unrest. Mahmud Beg Tarzi, politician and writer of Afghanistan and father of Queen Soraya predicted this and informed Amanullah Khan, who did not heed his advice. Mohammad Wali Khan Wakil had resigned a few months prior and was at his home. Brigadier Abdul Rahim Khan (Ghondmisher), along with 1,000 soldiers and 20 Afghanis and artillery, was summoned to Kabul from Mazar-i-Sharif.

Abdul Rahim Khan Safi

Abdul Rahim Khan, son of Abdul Qadir Khan of Safi tribe from Kohistan, was my maternal uncle. Abdur Rahim Khan was still on his way when some of Amanullah Khan's advisors thought against it, questioning that Abdur Rahim could be loyal when all his brothers and Khans of Kohistan are with Habibullah. It was too late, however. To tell the truth, I was also happy and wanted my uncle to join Habibullah. I realized with the passage of every day my enemies increased, yet the Minister of Finance continued to support me.

Habibullah's men and my relatives would come to me covertly, bringing news of the insurrection. They took back news from Kabul. Abdur Rahim Khan's advance continued and was reported in the Kabul papers. The news came to stop abruptly after Bamiyan. I was informed by the Kabul security police not to leave my residence and no one should come to my house.

It should be added that some time back, my uncle Mohammad Yosuf and I sent a sincere message to Amanullah Khan through Sardar Abdur Rahman, son of Sardar Abdul Wahab, a friend of my father, expressing our intention to serve for the upkeep of the security of the country. We also told Ghulam Mohammad Khan Wardhaki, the Minister of Interior. Abdul Rahman Khan carried our message to Amanullah Khan. Ghulam Mohammad Khan had resigned his post and told us Amanullah Khan does not listen to counsel. Some well-to-do people of Kabul, thinking that someday Habibullah might usurp the throne of Kabul, kept contact with us, although covertly.

One day, a director in the Ministry of Finance came out of the blue to my house and said the Minister wanted to see me. I was surprised and convinced something was cooking. I went to see him. As soon as he saw me, the Minister said, "Congratulations, Abdur Rahim Khan has reached Kabul safely." He hugged me and added, "The enemies left no stone unturned, but God is on our side. Abdur Rahim Khan is camping three kilometers from Kabul in Mahtab Qala."

In spite of my enthusiasm to see my uncle, I excused myself on the pretext of cold weather and not having winter clothes. The Minister understood. He knew I did not like the arrival of my uncle in Kabul.

The next morning Abdur Rahim Khan came to Chaman-e-Huzuri with his men, and Amanullah Khan went there to welcome him. He kissed his forehead and commended the soldiers. The leaders of the religion, elite and the majority of the people did not like his presence in Kabul. He was sent to the Ministry of Defense. Abdul Rahim Khan came to Kabul from Bamiyan, through Hajigak Pass during a heavy snowstorm.

I went to see him that night and asked him, "What would you answer to the question of the people of Kohistan and Kohdaman?"

He said, "I have not forgotten what Amanullah Khan did to you. Also, I deeply respect the insurrection of the people. It is about 20 years that I have been a soldier; however, and I have vowed on the Holy Koran to remain loyal to God, country and the king and not to be an embezzler. I had this money and arms, property of the government, and as a faithful Muslim and a loyal soldier I have brought this to Kabul, whatever be the will of God. To me, people and tribe come after God."

Amanullah Khan Tries to Amend His Proclamations, Addresses People

Amanullah Khan realized his shortcomings and wanted to compensate for them. He called a meeting of the people

in the public gardens near south of the Kabul River.

Addressing the people, he said, "I have never asked for the lifting of the veil. And I am not against polygamy. My enemies have fabricated all this."

Pointing toward the west (Qibla), he said, "There is the shrine of Shah Sahib of Qalai Qazi, and I am devoted to him." He repeated the Kalimah (There is no other God, but one God....).

I was present and heard him myself. Someone in the crowd stood up and said, "Thank God you have embraced Islam again."

Amanullah Khan said, "Habibullah, the robber, has been arrested. I am not afraid of these robbers. I am afraid of the people of Shinwar and Momand who have rebelled against me on the instigation of the British. I have issued orders that you should be armed to defend yourselves."

A youth shouted in a loud voice, "You have issued orders, but until your ministers do not take bribes, they will not issue guns."

The king was infuriated. He had the right, because in his entire life he had never faced the truth. Picking up his hat, he walked on foot to the palace. On the way he bought some nuts, handing out a gold coin. He was doing this to show the people everything was under control. Amanullah Khan had not yet reached the gate of the palace when a shell fell close to him. Amanullah Khan boasted, "The bullet that could kill me has not been manufactured yet."

Gunfire could be heard not very far away, and contrary to what Amanullah Khan said, Ahmad Ali Khan, the administrator of Kohdaman and Kohistan was forced to leave the Jabal Seraj citadel and escape to Kabul via Tagab.

The claims of the king that all is well, published in the Kabul papers, continued to be contradicted by the events and happenings on the other side of Khair Khana Pass, reducing the government's credibility. Abdur Rahim Khan requested the government's permission to go to Kohdaman and use his family influence to calm down the popular movement. The interest groups, however, painted a different picture of his intentions.

Instead of allowing Abdur Rahim Khan to go, the

government asked him to have his soldiers surrender their present arms and carry less modern weapons. The religious leaders sanctioned the announcement and pamphlets of Habibullah declared Amanullah Khan an infidel. The pamphlets were distributed every day in Kabul. Amanullah, sensing a popular uprising to his reforms, repealed some of the new laws. Friday was returned as weekend. The women again started wearing the veil. To win back the confidence of the people, he even married the daughter of his uncle (Naibul Saltana – Nasrullah Khan). He did this to show the people he was not against polygamy.

Amanullah Khan, through the Turkish ambassador, sought Mustafa Kamal Pasha's assistance. The Turks sent Kazim Pasha, a versatile general, to Kabul via air. Kazim Pasha went to the other side of the Khair Khana Pass to inspect the battlefront. He saw a well-equipped division of Amanullah Khan. Kazim Pasha was told Habibullah had besieged Hussain Kot. He was baffled to see an equipped division beset by an illiterate man and his few followers. He forgot the soldiers were children of the nation, and the nation had turned against Amanullah Khan.

Kazim Pasha ordered an attack on the besieging forces. Amanullah Khan's soldiers were defeated and fell back. Only the king's special guard from Kandahar loyal to Amanullah Khan fought while the rest of the soldiers either deserted or fought half-heartedly.

Amanullah Khan Abdicates, Handing Power to His Brother Inayatullah Khan

The next day, all government employees were summoned to the Dilkusha. I went along with other civil servants from the Ministries of Finance, Justice, and Home. Some of my acquaintances, who believed in Habibullah's victory, were very kind to me and some avoided me. Some assumed Amanullah Khan had been assassinated and we were being gathered to hear the news. Others said Habibullah had been arrested and would be paraded here. Still others expected government employees to be given arms and asked to go to war.

An elderly employee called out, "If I am given arms, I will start my battle right from here against Amanullah Khan." Some people opposed him.

We stood there hungry and thirsty. Luckily, it was a warm winter day, and the sun was shining. At about 2 p.m., a small battalion of soldiers (100 men) came out from the palace and lined up in the backdrop, not far away. Bullets fell even on the roof of the Dilkusha. Meanwhile, Sardar Inayatullah, elder brother of Amanullah Khan appeared from behind the man holding the Afghan flag and went to the southern side of the Dilkusha. The army unit commanded by Ahmad Ali Khan offered the salute, and we were surprised to see the development. After a few words from the Holy Koran, members of royalty and some distinguished elite in this gathering, Sardar Sher Ahmad, President of the Assembly who recently returned from Jalalabad, on behalf of the Assembly members (none of whom were present), recognized Inayatullah Khan as the new king. Mir Sayed Qasim Khan, Chief Secretary on behalf of Amanullah, read a note from him:

"I was the king for 10 years. Now that I have realized the people of Afghanistan are not happy with my rule, I have resigned. I pledge allegiance to Inayatullah, who also has the right to be King of Afghanistan."

Continuing to read Amanullah Khan's words, the Chief Secretary said, "Wherever I may go, I will pray for the prosperity of Afghanistan." The note was read twice in Persian and twice in Pashto.

After this, Inayatullah said, "I have the right to the throne and am the heir apparent to my father. From the very beginning, I did not want to be king. Even now, however, because I see the bloodshed among Afghans, I have accepted this heavy responsibility. You hear the gunfire. One brother is killing the other. I pray God help me to serve the country."

At the end, just as Amanullah Khan taught, the people applauded.

Suddenly, a loud and thunderous voice broke the routine.

"Still you are following Amanullah Khan's custom,"

the voice shouted. "Why don't you say, 'Allah-o-Akbar' (God is great)?"

I do not know who shouted those words, but the sound of 'God is great' filled the air after an absence of 10 years.

The people lunged forward to kiss the hands of Inayatullah as a sign of allegiance to his rule. I also wanted peace in the country, and Inayatullah was one for the sake of whose friendship my father was murdered. I also tried to reach him, but could not.

At sunset the new king with his followers started to return to the palace. I joined the crowd going inside, but Haji Madad Khan, one of my elderly relatives, asked me, "Where are you going?" He said, "Even before you reach the king, the enemies of the king will kill you on the pretext of your being Kohdamani."

Some other Kohdamani friends of mine accompanied me to the Ministry of Defense to see Abdur Rahim Khan.

I Meet My Uncle, Abdur Rahim Khan

Later, we came to know that at about 11 a.m. that day, Amanullah Khan headed to Kandahar by car, leaving behind many of his stepsisters and wives of his father and other women. On one hand, I was happy I was delivered from ten years of hunger, destitution, and hatred. On the other, I was distressed to see fratricide and bloodshed in my country. After offering evening prayers, I went to the Ministry of Defense. Abdur Rahim Khan was trying to reach Inayatullah on the telephone when I entered his office. He was happy to see me. He did not want to hear criticism of Amanullah Khan.

He cast a glance at me, and his eyes were filled with tears. Maybe because of the death of my father and ten years of my suffering, I also started crying. Even until this day I do not know what to call those tears. He consoled me and said, "My son, forget everything except God and country."

Finally, he was able to reach the new king on the telephone. He told him, "Khalilullah, son of Mustufi, and I congratulate you. What can I do for you?" The king thanked him and said he would let him know tomorrow. He

asked him to take care of the Ministry of Defense.

That night the only high ranking officer at the ministry was Abdur Rahim Khan. He sent me home escorted by four soldiers and asked them to take me down the back streets. The same night Habibullah launched a surprise attack on Khair Khana and Deh Kepak from Hussain Kot. The palace was besieged with Amir Inayatullah inside. All night long gun and cannon fire from Kohe-Sherdarwaza and Kohe-Asmai, the Arg and Bala Hissar shuddered the whole of Kabul. Amanullah's soldiers who had surrendered to Habibullah filled the streets.

The people of Kohistan, Kohdaman, Parwan, and suburbs of Kabul joined Habibullah in the thousands. Inayatullah's flag was still flying over the Arg. I went to the Ministry of Defense. The Mazar soldiers who had dispersed on the order of the government had returned to the ministry. There was still no high-ranking officer there except Abdul Rahim Khan. I went there to find out whether Abdur Rahim Khan contacted the new king and whether I was needed. I reached his office right at the time Abdur Rahim Khan was talking to Inayatullah on the telephone. He asked the king if he could try to arrange a mediation between Inayatullah and Habibullah to stop the bloodshed.

Inayatullah told him, "You do not need to go. I have sent a delegation consisting of Sardar Mohammad, Usman Khan, Mohammad Siddiq Khan, Mojaddadi, Sayed Mohammad Younus Khan, and Abdul Qayum Mirza, Chief Secretary and Mustufi-ul-Momalik."

Abdur Rahim Khan insisted he send him and Khalilullah too. The king did not accept. Abdur Rahim Khan distributed arms to his soldiers to get ready for an upcoming battle.

Inayatullah ordered Abdur Rahim Khan to go as close to Bahge-Bala as possible and not to allow the defeated soldiers to enter Kabul. He left for Baghe-Bala after dropping me off at home. He could not persuade the returning soldiers to go back to battle. At one point the returning soldiers were so angry they threatened to fire on Abdur Rahim Khan.

Habibullah Kalakani Proclaims Crown

Sardar Usman, at the head of the delegation, went to Habibullah and instead of reducing tension, further encouraged him to continue his movement against Amanullah. Usman Khan also proposed that Sardar Usman be made king. Sherjan Khan of Charekar, whose forefather fought the British, said, "When Inayatullah is not suitable, how can Sardar Usman be the king?" Sherjan had not yet finished his arguments when thousands of bullets were fired in the air by the people of Kohistan, Kohdaman, and suburbs of Kabul who accepted Habibullah as their king. Habibullah tried to excuse himself, telling them he was illiterate and had no training to be a ruler. The conquering brave young men paid no heed to him.

After a brief resistance the Kohistani and Kohdaman people entered Kabul from four sides. Amanullah Khan's soldiers guarding Sher Darwaza, Asmai, and Bala Hissar laid down their arms without a fight. Habibullah's victory was also the defeat of the ruling clans of Afghanistan. For the first time a man from among the people had come to power. Resentment led to a widespread campaign against Habibullah Kalakani by various ruling clans and nobility of Afghanistan. He was misnamed Bache Sagao (Son of the Water Carrier) and never got his proper place in history.

Habibullah's marksmen climbed the Kotwali tower and started battering the Arg. The next morning, a dialogue started and Inayatullah said he would open the palace doors if guaranteed safe passage to India with his family. Habibullah accepted the terms and let him leave for India.

The same night, some of my Kohistani and Kohdamani relatives came to guard my house. I sent a messenger for the whereabouts of Abdur Rahim Khan. I was informed he took arms and ammunition and moved to the Tape Maranjan citadel with his men, waiting to fight Habibullah.

First Day of Habibullah Khan's Rule

After spending one night in Baghe Bala, Habibullah Khan arrived in Kabul. Some of his close associates from

Kohdaman and Kohistan came to me and took me to the governorate of Kabul to see Habibullah. All the streets of Kabul were full of his victorious soldiers.

In the courtyard of the governorate the soldiers lit a campfire and sat around it, sipping tea. The main hall of the building, known as the guesthouse, which had been built by Amir Abdur Rahman, overflowed with people. I met Habibullah there. He was standing and members of the former royal family were standing with folded hands surrounded by the brave fighters.

His shoulder was bandaged. He hugged me with one side. He said, "Amanullah Khan turned away from God and God's wrath fell on him. Pray that God may not doom me."

The victorious warriors all around shouted, "Amir."

Malik Mohsin Kalakani, appointed governor of Kabul by Habibullah and later to become ruthless and bloodthirsty, stood beside him. Habibullah, turned toward Sherjan, asked, "Do you recall what we said about Khalilullah?"

Sherjan replied, "Yes, you wanted him to be Chief Secretary."

Habibullah said to me, "Congratulations, you are my Chief Secretary."

Hundreds of friends of my father, who would not even talk to me during Amanullah Khan's time, hugged me amid jubilation and tears. Habibullah told me to go to Abdur Rahim Khan and tell him to stop this insanity and come down from the mountains. I left directly from there for Tape Maranjan to meet Abdur Rahim Khan.

Abdur Rahim Khan was getting ready to defend the fort. Habibullah's men had taken position at Bala Hissar and Tape Behmaru, and also Chamane Huzoori to attack Tape Maranjan. Omra Khan Daoudzai commanded the forces. I told Omra Khan to hold off the attack so I could try to mediate to prevent bloodshed. Abdul Wakil Kharoti, the fourth commander of Habibullah, also reached there. Both men used to be guards of my father. They listened to me.

I reached Tape Maranjan. The gates opened for me. I asked Abdur Rahim Khan, "Whom are you going to fight?

Your brothers, Amanullah Khan and Inayatullah, have both left and Habibullah is in Kabul. Amanullah Khan's army has surrendered. What can these 1,000 Mazari do?"

After a prolonged dialogue, he agreed to surrender to Habibullah on the conditions his soldiers would be allowed to go to Mazar and he would be promised a safe conduct.

I ran back to Habibullah with the demands. He agreed. The next day I met Habibullah and Abdur Rahim Khan. Court was in progress in the Gulkhana's (palace) billiard room. Kabul nobility, former royal family members, and former ministers came to pledge allegiance to the new king. The religious leaders Hazrat Mojaddadi, Akhund Zadah Shahib of Tagab, and Mian Guljan surrounded Habibullah.

Habibullah Khan Meets Abdur Rahim Khan

Habibullah was wearing a Jaji tribal dress. Sardar Shah Mahmud Khan and Ahmad Shah Khan were also present. We made our way through the crowds of Kalakanis and Kohistanis. Abdur Rahim Khan's tall figure and manly appearance impressed Habibullah.

He asked one question: "Why?"

Abdur Rahim Khan answered, "Because I was a soldier and recognized Amanullah Khan and his father as king."

Brigadier Abdul Salam, elder brother of Abdur Rahim, was also sitting.

Habibullah asked Abdur Rahim, "Now, what will you do?"

He answered, "If the people of Afghanistan accept you as king, I accept you as king."

Generally, the audience was expecting Abdur Rahim to be reprimanded for his assistance to Amanullah Khan.

Habibullah said, instead, "I admire your bravery. Come forward and let me hug you."

Abdur Rahim Khan had a small box in his hand. People were guessing what he was up to, including myself. Abdul Rahim Khan said, "It is not proper to hold your hand while I am wearing this military cap."

He removed the military cap from his head, opened the small box and took out a headband, which he tied on his head instead.

Habibullah stood up and kissed Abdur Rahim's forehead and said, "No doubt you are a soldier."

Habibullah asked him what his military rank was. Upon being informed, he issued a decree for Abdur Rahim Khan's promotion up two ranks higher than he was.

Amir Habibullah Khan's Cabinet

After Habibullah said farewell to Abdur Rahim Khan, Sherjan, who did the court work, ordered a desk for me in the courtroom where Habibullah sat so I could perform my responsibilities efficiently.

I started my work. The courtroom was always filled with people. Sherjan was a versatile civil servant. He convened a meeting attended by Qazi Ghulam Hazrat of Qarabagh, Ataul Haq Khan, brother of Sherjan, former brigadier of Amanullah who was educated in the Soviet Union, Mohammad Azam Khan of Tutumdara, myself, and a few others. The following appointments were approved: Sayed Hussain Charekari as Naibul Saltana (regent); Hameedullah, Habibullah's brother, as Minister of Defense; Ataul Haq, Sherjan's brother, as Minister of Foreign Affairs; Khwaja Babu, as Minister of Interior; Qazi Ghulam Hazrat Khan, as Secretary of the Treasury; Mirza Ghulam Mujtaba, as Deputy Minister of Finance; myself as Chief Secretary, and Sayed Ahmad Khan was put in charge of the king's guards.

It was also decided a meeting of the eminent people be convened in Kabul under the name of Tanzimia Islamia, chaired by Mohammad Azam Khan. Most of these people and their fathers had taken part in Jihads. Sherjan was the grandson of Sahibzada Ghulam Jan, whose deeds of Jihad were published during King Zahir's rule. Khwaja Babu's father escaped to India with Amir Mohammad Yaqub Khan. Sayed Ahmad Khan was the grandson of Mir Bacha Khan Ghazi, after whom in King Zahir's time, Mir Bacha Kot was named. Mohammad Azam Khan was the son of

Jalandar Khan of Tutumdara, who fought along with Wazir Akbar Khan against the British.

It was also decided the only appointments made would be those approved by Habibullah Khan. The rest would have to wait until all of Afghanistan was brought under control and rule of the new regime.

The meeting also decided I should read all the firmans (decrees) to Habibullah Khan as he was not literate. Sherjan was supposed to sign them in red ink and I was to sign on the back. Habibullah Khan was to place his seal after he inspected the two signatures. I wrote more than 100 firmans a day. Many of them I wrote to safeguard the eminent families, members of the royal family, and relatives of the overthrown King Amanullah.

Ibrahim Khalil, a Kabul poet, was my assistant. I was happy and proud about my role in saving those families from the wrath of Habibullah's soldiers. All these firmans were recorded in the king's library.

We received news the Herat garrison had revolted and killed Mohammad Ibrahim Khan, the governor, and Abdur Rahman Khan, commander of Herat forces. He was also a cousin of Amanullah.

The garrison was upset at being summoned to Kandahar by Amanullah Khan to assist the forces there. Mohammad Ghaus Khan Barekzai (Firqa Mishr – Divisional Commander) became the commander of forces in Herat. Quickly, Amanullah Khan appointed Shujaudaula as Administrator of Herat (he was Afghanistan's Ambassador to London), but he could not calm the insurrection. Azimullah Popalzai, Administrator of Kataghan and Badakhshan, and Sardar Mohammad Rahim Khan, the military commander, had already sent their allegiance to Habibullah Kalakani.

On the third day of Habibullah's presence in Kabul he was recognized as king in an official ceremony. The eminent religious leader Hazrat Shamsul Haq Mojaddadi tied the traditional dastar (headband). The next day the newspaper, *Habibul Islam*, was established.

Burhanuddin Kushkaki, a prominent writer of Jalalabad, and a close ally of Amanullah, was named editor of the paper.

Habibullah took over the responsibility of the Ministry of Justice, and Mullah Mohammad Qasim was appointed Chief Justice. Unfortunately, rivalries reared their ugly heads. The regime divided into factions pursuing their interests. One group took sides with Sayed Hussain, a desperado. He was a glutton, womanizer, and coward, unlike Habibullah, who was brave, honest, simple, and kind-hearted. Habibullah was a gentleman.

All those who served in the Jihad against Amanullah Khan wanted a share of the power and influence. They all wanted to be part of the inner circle.

Amid all this, Malik Mohsin influenced Habibullah and had himself appointed governor of Kabul. No doubt he helped Habibullah through thick and thin of the Jihad. Malik Mohsin was also an illiterate man. Things between the three men spun out of hand. There were times when two to three firmans were issued on the same subject, one by Habibullah, another by Sayed Hussain, and a third by Malik Mohsin.

Habibullah tried his best to control this but failed. Foreign and local spies were at play. The yes-men were getting into Habibullah's inner circle and increasingly a gulf was created between Habibullah and Sayed Hussain. Habibullah, Sherjan, and some eminent people of Kohdaman and Kohistan tried to deliver the country from chaos and lawlessness, but alas, all was in vain.

Habibullah Khan Meets the King of Bokhara

At this time the king of Bokhara, known as Janabe Ali, who was disappointed by Amanullah Khan's close ties with the newly created Soviet Union, wanted an audience with the new Amir through Khwaja Babu. It should not be forgotten that when Habibullah first came to Kabul, Abdul Ghafoor Khan, a cousin of Inayatullah, became the Minister of Interior. Malik Mohsin assassinated him.

The king of Bokhara knew Khwaja Babu from

Kohdaman where he met many Khans. Habibullah received the former king of Bokhara at the Gulkhana. Sherjan, Khwaja Babu, and I were present during this meeting. Habibullah kissed his hand in consideration that the king of Bokhara was a Sayed (a descendent of Prophet Mohammad, PBUH). They talked as two friends. The king of Bokhara addressed Habibullah as "my son," saying he had met him somewhere.

With a smile, Habibullah said, "I am the one who brought your wild stallion under control at Hussain Kot when you were staying there. You ordered my name be added to the list of your servants. I did not accept the offer. I said whenever you wanted to go back to fight the Soviets, I would go with you."

With tears in his eyes, the King of Bokhara said, "Amanullah Khan deceived me." Habibullah assured him of his help. The two-day–old illiterate king and former vine seller (Take Angoor) from Kohdaman held out his hand to the king who had lost his throne and his country. Both stood up, faced the west (Qibla), and promised to work for the freedom of Bokhara.

With the increase in chaos and restlessness, I could not serve efficiently the interest of the people and Habibullah. I could not contemplate a clear path to progress and sought advice of Mohammad Azam Khan, uncle of my wife, and my paternal uncle Mohammad Yosuf Khan. I also sought counsel from Sherjan Khan on the fluid situation prevailing in Kabul. I discussed the matter with my maternal uncle Abdur Rahim Khan. He was in favor of leaving Kabul temporarily. He suggested I go to Mazar-i-Sharif for a brief period while he went to Herat and stayed there. He asked me to seek the approval of the Amir.

My Journey to Mazar-i-Sharif

I went to Habibullah and pleaded with him to let Abdur Rahim Khan go to Herat via Mazar and allow me to accompany him. I explained to Habibullah that Abdur Rahim Khan could calm both Mazar-i-Sharif and Herat, and deliver them for him without a fight. Sherjan was present during this meeting.

Sherjan, who considered Abdur Rahim Khan his rival, was happy to hear this. He also knew Abdur Rahim Khan had influence in Mazar and Herat and could deliver those garrisons without a fight.

The firman of Abdur Rahim Khan was issued, and I had Amir Habibullah sign it. In the meantime, a respected and well-known gentleman from Mazar-i-Sharif, Mirza Mohammad Qasim Khan, was under house arrest on the order of Amanullah. Mirza Mohammad Qasim was well known from Andaraab to Maimana. He was a respected and popular elderly man. Amanullah Khan envied his popularity and reputation as humble, generous, and truthful. He had his holdings confiscated, and Amanullah Khan placed him under house arrest in Kabul.

Abdur Rahim Khan said he would take care of the military, but we needed Mirza Mohammad Qasim Khan to bring the people on our side. Mohammad Azam Khan, who served as a civil servant in Mazar, agreed with this assessment. He immediately released Mohammad Qasim and appointed him administrator of Mazar. I was appointed his deputy and Abdur Rahim Khan as Naib-Salar (Commander) of Maimana and Herat.

A special meeting of close advisors was summoned, and the appointments were presented to Habibullah. Abdur Rahim Khan assured the Amir and the attendees he would solve the problem of Mazar without war. I said I would return after a brief stay and paying respect to the shrine of Hazrate Ali. Habibullah appointed my uncle Mirza Mohammad Yosuf in my place and also made him administrator of Logar. Amanullah Khan exiled Mirza Mohammad Yosuf in Logar. He earned respect of the population of Logar.

Abdur Rahim Khan sent the Mazar soldiers back to Mazar, ahead of his journey. He retained a handful of cavalrymen (16) for himself. In spite of a slight objection by Sherjan and some of Habibullah's advisors on my appointment, I left for Mazar-i-Sharif with Abdur Rahim Khan.

Also with us were Mirza Qasim Khan and Sayed

Ahmad Khan, who'd been placed in charge of customs. Khwaja Ainuddin Khan of Guldara, the brother of Khwaja Tajuddin, who had been appointed as Mayor of Kabul, was with us, too.

It was the month of Jaddi (December). We left amid heavy snow. To me this journey was adventurous. After years of deprivation and confinement I was travelling as a free man. It took us three nights to cross Ghorband. The people in Ghorband posed no threat because of tribal links.

Abdur Rahim Khan Meets Hazara Leaders

We received news on the way that Hazara of Sheikh Ali and Surkh Parsa were in a threatening posture in Shiber Pass. We conferred and decided if we returned, we would have to bear the wrath of Habibullah, and it would also be an act of cowardice. If we stood and fought, the odds were stacked against us. We were heavily outnumbered. Also, we would fail in our objective of reaching Mazar without a fight, in peace. It was decided to send a messenger to Hazara and inform them we had not come to fight but to pass in peace to Mazar. The mission was risky. We had to find a way to start a dialogue.

We could see through binoculars that the Hazara fighters continued to climb the Shiber Pass. I should mention here that before we left Kabul, Habibullah signed 100 blank firmans for us to use if needed. Things became rougher as an avalanche hit our location bringing tons of snow and stones all around. We could feel the earth moving from under us. Some people in our party suggested we return to Ghorband.

Abdur Rahim Khan emphasized that turning back would be a cowardly act. He volunteered to be the messenger, in spite of objections of some to the very dangerous rendezvous. He climbed the hill with one cavalryman who was holding and waving a white flag, a sign of peace. We followed them through binoculars as far as we could. Before his departure, Abdur Rahim Khan told me to wait for his coded letter after he reached the Hazara. The code was supposed to show the letter was not written under duress.

We waited around a campfire for three hours. Finally, we saw the cavalryman come back escorted by two Hazara fighters. They brought the letter from my uncle and after reading it we started our climb toward Abdur Rahim Khan. The elders of the Hazara tribe, led by Eissa Khan, met with Abdur Rahim Khan. My father was once posted in Surkh Parsa at the beginning of his career and was very friendly with the people of that area. As soon as they recognized me, they kissed my hand and agreed to no action until the fate of Mazar was decided. Undoubtedly, the presence of Mirza Mohammad Qasim Khan also helped.

I wrote the firmans in reference to the decisions taken and distributed them among elders of the tribe. We reached Bamiyan after three days. We saw the Ramadan crescent on the way. In spite of the hardship, Abdur Rahim Khan, Mohammad Qasim Khan, and Khwaja Ainuddin fasted.

After crossing Bamiyan, we were guests of the people. We came to Kamord via Aghrabat and Daudan Slikan passes. The sight of Bamiyan statues of Buddha left a deep impression on me. In Kamord we stayed at the qala of Wakil Khan Seghanchi. The glory of his house, his antics, and his priceless collections reminded us of the Kabul court. Wakil Khan was the first Afghan who attended a meeting of Islamic countries in Turkey during the reign of Amir Abdur Rahman. His writing reflects his proficiency in the language as is exemplified in his memoirs. During the time of Habibullah Khan Seraj, father of Amanullah Khan, he was magistrate (Hakim) of Laghman and was killed in Kalaghosh, where Habibullah Khan was assassinated.

From Kamord we went to Rooi and Doaab. We were informed Abdul Aziz Khan, Amanullah's governor, and Mohammad Akleel Khan, military commander, closed the Tashkurghan pass on us. We conferred again and decided Mohammad Qasim Khan would not say he has been appointed; instead, he would say Amanullah Khan left Kabul and is returning to his home and his family. Ainuddin Khan said he would go under the pretext of

business. However, Abdur Rahim Khan and I had no excuse, so we decided to go to Kamrod and wait for instructions from Kabul.

Later that evening, Abdur Rahim Khan suggested that after Mohammad Qasim and Khwaja Ainuddin left, we would decide. In the morning, both men left for Mazar while Sayed Ahmad Khan stayed with us. Abdur Rahim Khan decided to travel to Darrai Soof, which is overwhelmingly populated by the Hazara tribe. Abdur Rahim Khan had good relations with their leader Ghulam Nabi Beg, son of Ghulam Mim Bashi.

We talked to Ghulam Nabi Beg, and he appreciated our peaceful mission. We appointed him Governor and Hakim of Darrai Soof. Haji Shah Murad Beg and Abdul Samad Mir Bashi, the elders of Darrai Soof, who were from Mir Qasim's Uzbek tribe, surrendered after being informed Mir Qasim was with us.

The next day we came to Boi-Naqara. Here, Abdur Rahim Khan owned some land; some Safis (Pashtun tribe) lived here. Abdur Rahim Khan left for Qalai Jangi the same night. One man, Mohammad Hussain, accompanied him. I stayed back in Boi-Naqara with thirteen other men. Even though Abdur Rahim Khan went to Qalai Jangi with one cavalryman, he was well aware of the dissatisfaction among the troops about Amanullah Khan's rule. He was also sure the 1,000 Mazri soldiers who left Kabul earlier, must have reached Mazar. He reached Qalai Jangi in a few hours and called for a general meeting.

A day before his arrival, there was a popular unrest in the garrison. Sher Ali Khan Jabhadar of Kohdaman, Mandol Khan of Logar, and Pahalwan Hanif Tashkurghani mutinied and arrested all officers. The Mazari soldiers of Abdur Rahim Khan were already appointed to important positions. In the city of Mazar, Ata Mohammad Tokhi, the commander of the police, arrested the governor and other high-ranking civil servants of Amanullah and threw them in jail. They decided to execute all military officers in the presence of Abdur Rahim Khan. My uncle saved their lives and the next day took over the city. He sent me a message, and I followed him to Qalai Jangi. There, I was considered

a representative of Habibullah Kalakani and welcomed by 21 gun salute. Mohammad Qasim Khan also reached Mazar. Thus, Mazar was captured without a fight. Abdul Rahim Khan was a shrewd negotiator.

First Communist Invasion

The Soviets had consulates in Mazar and Herat where they were monitoring developments. Religious leaders contributed substantially toward consolidating Habibullah's nine-month rule, and allegiance of people from the countryside continued pouring in. Two religious leaders had great influence in northern Afghanistan: Abid Nazar Makhdoom, known as Khalifa Qizel Ayaq of Turkman tribe and Mullah Adina of Tashkurghan of the Arab tribe.

Khalifa Qizel Ayaq, after fighting against the Soviets in Bokhara, took refuge in Afghanistan with hundreds of thousands of families. They lived in deserts in Khirgah (tents). Their business was carpet weaving and horse breeding. About 10,000 mounted soldiers were always ready. Khalifa was an elderly scholar of the Naqshbandi school. The Turkmans specifically, and other people in general, had great respect for him. They knew him as a mujahid and enemy of the communists. He lived in Shiberghan among his people.

Mullah Adina was educated in Bokhara and witnessed persecutions in the Soviet Union. His influence in northern part helped him to be appointed later as a teacher at Darul Oloom in Kabul. I met him in Kabul. During the last year of Amanullah Khan he lived in Mazar.

Abdur Rahim Khan received an intelligence report that on behalf of Amanullah, Shujaudaula in Herat, Ghulam Gailani Khan in Maimana, and Ghulam Nabi Khan Charkhi in Mazar would be attacking with the help of the Soviets. Abdur Rahim Khan, who was opposed to Soviet intervention in Afghanistan, informed Kabul of the developments. He was instructed to leave immediately for Herat via Maimana and leave Mazar for Mohammad Qasim; Khalilullah should remain as auditor and deputy administrator.

Abdur Rahim Khan took 10,000 soldiers with him and

left the military affairs for Sher Ali Khan Kohdamani, promoting him to a general. Sher Ali served for many years in the army in Mazar. He was very sincere. Mohammad Qasim remained in Mazar with me, but had no military experience.

Abdur Rahim took control of Maimana before Ghulam Gailani could come in. No major confrontation occurred on his way to Maimana from Mazar except for a small incident in Andkhoi. Shujaudaula reached Herat before Abdur Rahim Khan. The military was in the hands of Ghaus Khan.

Ghulam Nabi Khan Charkhi

All was quiet in Mazar. Khwaja Ata Mohammad Kohistani was appointed as governor of Mazar. He was a drug addict. As soon as he took over, the administration broke down. He did not heed advice, but started taking bribes and confiscating people's property. I spent the month of Hamal 1348 AH (March 1929 AD) under a lot of pressure. Every day I had a dispute with the governor. The intelligence informed that Ghulam Nabi Khan Charkhi was coming to Afghanistan via Patak-Sir to attack Mazar with the help of the Soviets. It was the first time communist forces entered Afghan soil. The frontier in charge reported an army with Ghulam Nabi Charkhi as the commander, with officers and men speaking Russian heading toward Mazar.

Ghulam Nabi Charkhi distributed pamphlets in Mazar and throughout the countryside that said, "I have come to conquer the throne of Afghanistan for Ala Hazrat Amanullah and deliver the country from robbers. Whoever has cooperated with the robbers has been forgiven by Amanullah Khan." (Details are compiled in a booklet published by Khalili in Pakistan under the title of "First Soviet Invasion of Afghanistan." The original pamphlets were confiscated from Khalili's library by communists after the 1979 Soviet invasion of Afghanistan). The pamphlets asked people to kill all civil servants of Bache Saqao or arrest and bring them to him. It said, "Our friendly and brotherly state of the Soviet Union will give its unconditional support to us. The allegiance of the people of

Herat, Kandahar, and eastern provinces has been received by us." The pamphlets were signed by Ghulam Nabi Charkhi, Minister Plenipotentiary.

I sent the pamphlets, which caused a stir among the people, right as the new governor, Khwaja Ata Mohammad, was preparing for his marriage at 60 years of age, to Kabul. I was told to leave for Balkh at the head of detachment, and Sher Ali Khan would defend Qalai Jangi in Deh Dadi. Mohammad Qasim Khan and the governor would defend Mazar. In Qalai Jangi there were 4,000 soldiers. In Mazar there was only a police regiment and a small military unit. Ghulam Nabi spread the rumor he would attack Qalai Jangi via Balkh.

I took position at Bala Hissar of Balkh. Ghulam Nabi deceived everybody and came directly to undefended Mazar via Siah Gird Dasht. He took Mazar in two hours without much resistance. Mohammad Qasim Khan fled to Tashkurghan to campaign against Ghulam Nabi. Khwaja Ata Mohammad, leaving behind his day-old bride, took refuge in Qalai Jangi. Sher Ali sent me a message, and I came back to Qalai Jangi from Balkh.

Mazar Battle

Sher Ali Khan was conferring with his officers when I arrived. Ghulam Nabi Khan was military commander in Mazar some years back. The people knew him as a very sincere person, and also knew his father who was a Marshal in the military. Ghulam Nabi telephoned Sher Ali Khan to surrender and come in person to Mazar.

Ghulam Nabi promised amnesty to all, however, he claimed Amanullah had captured Kabul and killed Habibullah, when Habibullah's telegram reached Sher Ali Khan a day before, saying Amanullah escaped to Ghazni for Kandahar. Also, according to frontier intelligence received from Pata Kesar, Ghulam Nabi's army consisted of soldiers who spoke Russian.

Sher Ali Khan was happy to see me and started the meeting all over again. I reported that this was not a small incident, and until full details are received from Kabul or unless it is proved to us that Amanullah Khan has reached

Kabul, every measure taken by us would be detrimental to the cause of Afghanistan. The telephone rang, and I spoke to Ghulam Nabi Charkhi for the first time in my life. He greeted me warmly, addressing me as cousin, and said, "You are very lucky this case would be wrapped up in your name."

He added, "Have the military surrender and come in person to see me. I will inform Ala Hazrat (His Highness) and forget the past."

I expressed my regards and said, "I have forgotten the past, but what do you mean when you say Ala Hazrat?"

He said, "I mean Ala Hazrat Ghazi Amanullah."

"Where is Ala Hazrat?" I asked.

After a brief lull he answered, "In Kabul."

I told him to check the post office and governor's office that only yesterday Habibullah's telegram was received from Kabul. "We know Amanullah Khan was defeated in Ghazni and has escaped to Kandahar, and we have heard that foreign troops are helping you," I said.

He was angry and screamed, "You will be duly punished!" and slammed down the telephone.

Ghulam Nabi Khan took position in the city of Mazar and outskirts. We were positioned to fight in Deh Dadi and Qalai Jangi, where we had some Italian heavy guns and other modern weaponry, but unfortunately, no trained personnel. Everything was in boxes. We had a few six pounders and nine pounders made in Kabul and some other old guns.

The battle started.

Our men knew little about war maps and war techniques. Sometimes we moved up to Sher Abad square and sometimes our enemy moved there. We all took positions at different points and during the night rejoined at Deh Dadi. Intelligence reports continuously poured in from Mazar that Soviet officers and men were with Ghulam Nabi in Afghan uniform. Our artillery avoided direct hits on Mazar, respecting the Ziarat of Hazrate-Ali (Mausoleum). Ghulam Nabi distributed leaflets and so did we. We reported facts to the people.

Mullah Adina came to Qalai Jangi with some men and

after careful assessment of the situation declared Jihad. Khalifa Saheb Qizel Ayaq sent 500 armed cavalrymen to help us. Mirza Mohammad Qasim also came with a small force from Tashkurghan.

Ghulam Nabi Charkhi brought in five Soviet bombers and bombarded our positions. Our casualties were heavy with more than 1,000 men lost each day. Young men, in respect for Jihad, wore white shrouds in the presence of Mullah Adina and went to fight with rusted old swords against modern-equipped enemy.

Mullah Adina said, "Oh, my sons, the Prophet (PBUH) is waiting on you. It is the day of Jihad – life is immaterial." (May 1929).

We continuously sent messages to Kabul, but in vain. The telegraph office fell into the hands of the enemy. Cruelty and bloodshed were unprecedented. On the day of Eid Qurban, the Soviets, without Ghulam Nabi's knowledge, burned alive Colonel Yar Mohammad and eleven of his fighters. When informed of this incident, Ghulam Nabi was infuriated. He did not take part in the war for two days.

The Soviet officers who ordered the mass killing were sent back to the Soviet Union. The battle lasted for about a month. Deh Dadi and Qalai Jangi fell to Ghulam Nabi. We held an emergency meeting and decided I would go immediately to Kabul and take all documents with me while Mirza Mohammad Qasim Khan in Shiberghan and Sher Ali Khan in Balkh formed resistance groups to engage the enemy. We had completely run out of heavy ammunition.

I Meet Sayed Hussain

I left for Kabul via Dashte Bala Ali Sher to Tashkurghan with 30 men. Soviet planes bombarded Tashkurghan. I left Tashkurghan for Khanabad via Dashte Abdan Mir Alam. After I reached Khanabad, Ghulam Nabi bombarded the military garrison and the government house there. In Andarab, I met Sayed Hussain's army.

I realized my messages to Kabul had their effect. About 15,000 men were with Sayed Hussain. They brought arms in small quantities, expecting to take the rest from Tashkurghan and Khanabad. Sayed Hussain did not have a very organized army; however, about 1,000 men were trained soldiers. Habibullah's army was occupied in Paktia, Kandahar, and Jalalabad. Khans sent most of Sayed Hussain's men. These people were not trained, and they molested the population.

Ibrahim Beg of Bokhara also accompanied Sayed Hussain. Ibrahim Beg was a brave fighter who fought the Soviets several times. He was a scholar, too. About 500 men accompanied Ibrahim Beg from Bokhara. Sayed Hussain thought the news about Ghulam Nabi's army, airplanes and artillery was fabricated and was convinced he could beat him and even attack Bokhara. He accused us of cowardice. My friends and relatives with Sayed Hussain's army sent us a message to go directly to Kabul.

Because I was acting on behalf of the government, I considered it necessary to brief Sayed Hussain of the situation. I went to his campsite at 2 p.m., and he was sleeping. As soon as his men saw me, they woke him. Khans from the Shomali gathered. Sayed Hussain wanted to punish me then and there without asking any questions. I laid all the documents and letters in front of him and asked him to read them first before he took any action.

He gave the papers to Ghulam Qadir, his Chief Secretary. The Khans from Shomali insisted the papers be read then and there. The document signed by Mirza Qasim, Mullah Da Arab, and others had details of all the happenings. Mir Baba Saheb Khan Charekari, the Governor of Khanabad, also signed this document.

Sayed Hussain learned what was actually happening. He appointed me as his advisor, and I narrated the whole account. I wanted permission to go to Kabul, but realized Sayed Hussain would not like it because there appeared to be deep differences between Sayed Hussain and Habibullah.

I was given a tent. I met Ibrahim Beg and others that night. It seemed Sayed Hussain listened to no one. He wanted to go to Mazar disorganized and in disarray.

Sayed Hussain's military commander was Ghayas, an

illiterate and unknown young man from Mariki. Amiruddin Khan, who was Hakim of Paktia during Amanullah Khan, and who was later executed by Nadir, was also with Sayed Hussain.

I came to Nahreen with Sayed Hussain. Here, the men of Ibrahim Beg and Sayed Hussain nearly clashed. It was averted when Malik Ghulam Nabi Istalifi, Mirza Abdullah Ghani Khan Kohdamini, and I interfered. As a precaution after the incident, Ibrahim Beg traveled separately from Sayed Hussain's army. We learned 5,000 men were on their way from Kohdaman to Aibak to take arms and join Sayed Hussain. Some of his men were afraid I would be appointed Chief Secretary and interfere in their operation. They took a firman from Sayed Hussain and sent me to Aibak at the head of 100 men.

The 5,000 men who came from Kohdaman did not even have 100 guns. In the Aibak garrison except for a few rusted guns from Amir Abdul Rahman's time, there was nothing else to be found. My immediate concern was to find food to make sure the population was left alone. Then, I asked for arms from Kabul or Sayed Hussain. Kabul replied in one week, asking me to contact Sayed Hussain. Sayed Hussain's reply was that the people should fight with knives and swords. Sayed Hussain reached Tashkurghan and captured it after a surprise attack.

I was left at Tashkurghan with 5,000 unarmed and unorganized soldiers who were distributed among the local population to spend the night. A small force was left at government installations, at Jahan Numa gardens. At dawn, Ghulam Nabi attacked Tashkurghan by air and with heavy artillery. By the time Sayed Hussain's men could come together, Ghulam Nabi captured Tashkurghan.

The people of Tashkurghan, under the leadership of a man named Hanif Pahelwan and some Kohdamani, defended until the last moments. Thousands of people were killed. The survivors of Tashkurghan and Kohdaman made their fortifications in Tangi Tashkurghan, not allowing Ghulam Nabi to go to Aibak.

Sayed Hussain was bombarded in Dashte Abdan Mir Alam by Soviet planes helping Ghulam Nabi and was forced to flee to Kunduz. The Aibak men reached Tangi Tashkurghan to help their brothers. The Soviet army crossed at Bandar Kaldar and captured Tangi Tashkurghan, destroying property and killing people as far as Dashte Robatak.

According to statistics, out of 5,000 men from Aibak, only 1,800 survived. The rest were massacred. Sayed Hussain arrested a famous scholar of Khanabad, Maulavi Ghulam Sarwar Khan and a judge based on false reports of cooperating with the Soviets. He had them in a cage in downtown Khanabad. He executed the judge and cut the fingers of Maulavi Ghulam Sarwar. Maulavi Sarwar Khan was an adversary of Ghulam Nabi and a friend of Mullah Dah Arab. The people rescued Maulavi during the night. Sayed Hussain later repented his act and released all other prisoners.

I Return from Mazar to Kabul

Habibullah sent a messenger and asked me to come to Kabul via Pule Khumri. It was too late. I had left for Kabul via Salang.

I crossed Salang at night with great difficulty because there was no road and the snow was icy, increasing the chances of falling from a cliff. The Hakim of Jabal Seraj, who did not know the facts, arrested me for deserting Mazar. He did not believe Ghulam Nabi Charkhi would bring Soviet soldiers into Afghanistan or Amanullah Khan would be such a coward as to seek aid from the enemy of the religion and freedom of Afghanistan to recapture the throne. He could not believe the Soviets could defeat Sayed Hussain.

One of the qualities of Afghans is their pride, which sometimes goes against their best interest. The Hakim thought I was the only person escaping the war. Later, I was released and sent to Kabul.

After two days, Habibullah invited me in. Sherjan Khan, Mohammad Azam Khan, Minister of Foreign Affairs Ataul Haq, and Chief Secretary Mohammad Yosuf Khan (my uncle) were present. All the papers were read aloud for Habibullah. At the end, Ataul Haq was asked to summon

the Soviet envoy to the Foreign Ministry and demand an explanation. It was decided that I should be present during the meeting.

Soviet Envoy Summoned

The next day the Soviet envoy, a military attaché, was called to the Foreign Ministry. It was my first time meeting a foreign representative. The Soviet Ambassador, along with other ambassadors, left Kabul. Only the Turkish envoy remained, saying, "The blood of the Turks is not thicker than the blood of the Afghans. I will not leave Afghanistan."

Ataul Haq briefed me. He spoke Russian and learned to pilot airplanes while he served as the Afghan attaché in Moscow. The Deputy Minister of Foreign Affairs, Mirza Mohammad Khan Yaftali, also attended the meeting, which was held at the Foreign Minister's office. Ataul Haq Khan had a small beard and a very impressive personality. He did not rise from his chair when the Soviet envoy came in. He asked the envoy whether relations of the Soviet government were with Amanullah or the people of Afghanistan. He said, "Do you respect the mutual agreements on Afghanistan's territorial integrity?"

The Soviet attaché answered in the affirmative.

Ataul Haq said, "Then why do you interfere in our internal affairs? You have sent your soldiers and planes to Mazar, and have bombed our cities and killed our people. You are fighting without declaration of war."

The Soviet representative denied this and responded, "We would never interfere in the internal affairs of Afghanistan. Ghulam Nabi is not a Soviet, he is an Afghan."

Ataul Haq asked, "From where did these planes come?"

The Soviet replied, "I don't believe our planes have bombarded."

Ataul Haq took the pamphlets from me, gave them to the envoy, and asked the translator to read them, translating into Russian. At the end, the Soviet said, "I do not have full details. I will inform my government and ask for information."

Ataul Haq Khan asked the person in charge of the Eastern division to hand over the note to the Soviet on behalf of Habibullah. The attaché left the office. Ataul Haq went to Habibullah. As the envoy was leaving, a prearranged show of about 300 young men, fully armed, tall and well built, paraded outside to demonstrate the Afghans were ready to fight.

After ten years of deprivation and affliction I started thinking good days were finally coming back. Destiny took a different turn. While I was in Aibak I learned my wife, whom I loved very much, died, leaving behind our two children. Kabul was like a house of condolence for me. The disorganization in work and lack of administration disillusioned me.

Amanullah Khan Leaves Afghanistan

Although Amanullah Khan sought Soviet help to fight for his crown, when he realized the Soviets had their own designs on Afghanistan, he gave up the fight. I learned after his defeat in Ghazni and a few days in Kandahar, Amanullah Khan left Afghanistan for India. All his family followed suit. Ali Ahmad, his brother-in-law, who made the abortive attempt of declaring himself king at Jagdalak, had gone to Kandahar when Amanullah Khan was there and again proclaimed himself king. Habibullah's army captured Kandahar, and Ali Ahmad Khan was arrested.

In the victory of Kandahar, Buzurgjan Mojaddadi Kohdamani and Abdul Qadeer Khan of Kohdaman and the Taraki tribe played a pivotal role. Abdul Kadeer Khan was appointed governor of Kandahar, and the people of Kandahar remembered him for his sincere service.

Sherjan Khan, Mohammad Azam Khan, and Ghulam Mohammad Khan Wardhaki wanted me to remain in Kabul, but I wished to get out of this mess as soon as possible and by whatever means necessary. After a few days Ataul Haq called me to the Foreign Ministry.

He said, "Today I have a meeting with the Chargé d'Affaires of Britain (probably Sheikh Mehboob Ali). Because Mazar will be discussed the Amir wants you to be there and show these documents if needed."

The British Chargé d'Affaires came. He had a big potbelly and a small beard. Ataul Haq Khan knew Urdu, which he learned in India when he was young. Sheikh Mehboob Ali was probably asked by his government to find the truth about the Mazar episode. I narrated everything including dates and timings. This meeting lasted for three hours.

After two weeks we received news that Amanullah sent a telegram to Ghulam Nabi saying, "The Russians are deceiving us. They have their own interest. I do not want the throne at the cost of my beloved country. If you are working for yourself, do as you wish."

On the same day he received the telegram and realizing the danger, Ghulam Nabi left Mazar-i-Sharif. He went to the Soviet Union via Qarqeen and Khamyeb. The young Afghan soldiers who were with him split up; some went to Abdur Rahim Khan in Herat and some left for the Soviet Union (destroying as many arms as they could). Mirza Mohammad Qasim Khan and Sher Ali Khan went to Mazar-i-Sharif. Sayed Hussain waited three weeks, and after assuring himself of security, came to Mazar. On the pretext of cooperating with Ghulam Nabi, he created havoc for many families.

I tried to remain confined to my humble house in Kabul.

Victory in Herat and Maimana

According to a report from Herat, Abdur Rahim Khan reached Maimana with 1,000 men and after capturing Maimana had gone to Bala Murghab. From there he sent messages to Mohammad Ghaus Khan and Shujaudaula in Herat. He wrote to them: "I am sending this message for two reasons; first, for the sake of Afghanistan and second, because my wife and family are in Herat. I am coming to see them." Because Abdur Rahim Khan served in Herat for 16 years in the military, he also informed his friends.

Mohammad Ghaus Khan answered back, "It is better you go back from Bala Murghab otherwise I will come myself to arrest you."

We learned later Shujaudaula advised Mohammad

Ghaus Khan not to send this message, but Ghaus Khan replied, "Abdur Rahim Khan will flee back to Kabul," if he heard my name.

Abdur Rahim Khan, on the advice of Darveza Khan of Maimana and other leaders, raised an army. Mohammad Ghaus Khan left Herat for Bala Murghab with one division to fight Abdur Rahim. The division included 5,000 men, artillery, and cavalry. The battle started at Bala Murghab. Messages of help kept pouring in for Abdur Rahim Khan. Within four hours, Mohammad Ghaus Khan surrendered and fled to the Soviet Union.

Abdur Rahim Khan reached Herat. Shujaudaula left the city and went to Gazergah, taking refuge at the tomb of Khwaja Abdullah Ansari (as the tradition goes, those who took refuge at the tomb were not arrested and sometimes remained there for years). Ghulam Haider Khan Mir of Gazargah was the head of Waqaf (Trust), and people respected his scholarly skills. Amanullah Khan tried to do away with this custom but failed.

Abdur Rahim Khan conquered Herat without bloodshed. Two army divisions in Herat surrendered as soon as they learned that he arrived. The next day he addressed the scholars, leaders and Khans of Herat at the congregation mosque and declared, "I am not your ruler, but just a soldier who will defend your borders until the last drop of blood. After this day, the destiny of Herat is in the hands of its people."

The same day, a committee of 40 people was formed, and all former high-ranking government servants were suspended. The committee appointed new civil servants. It accepted Abdur Rahim Khan as Naib Salar (Deputy Commander in Chief) for military and civilian affairs, and pledged allegiance to Habibullah. At the congregational mosque, the Khutba was read in the name of Habibullah - Khademe Deene Rasullullah.

Kabul was informed by telegram of this development. The important issue was money because Amanullah Khan's men looted the treasury and three divisions of the army and government servants were without salary. Abdur Rahim Khan recommended minting new money out of old cannons and guns that were melted and cut in coins. One face of the coin read "Afghanistan-Herat," and the other face read "Majlise Ayan" (Senate). This helped for a few months, until taxes could be collected.

Abdur Rahim Khan sent a delegation of elders to Kabul to pledge allegiance. I sent Ustad Salahuddin Saljuqi back to Herat with the delegation. Mullahs in Kabul did not like him.

My Return to Mazar

In spite of my intention to remain aloof, one day Habibullah saw me in Darulaman. I was strolling on the sidewalk. Habibullah was driving and his wife, Bibi Benazir, granddaughter of Amir Dost Mohammad Khan, was beside him. As soon as he saw me, he stopped the car and asked me to come to the palace. I had no choice but to go.

The Queen went to Haram Sarai, and the Amir received me. As soon as he saw me he called out, "You have not yet gone to Mazar. You have not heard Sayed Hussain has lost control."

I told him, "I am sick, and my wife died recently."

He said, "It is time for the service of Islam, I should get your letter after ten days from Mazar."

Again, I pleaded.

He said, "You talk too much, I have to go to say evening prayers. Whatever I have said, you should do it."

He then left for the palace mosque, and I left for home.

The next day I went to Sherjan and Mohammad Azam Khan. Sherjan said, "There is no way out. You know Habibullah Kalakani, and now he is Amir Habibullah Khan."

In the evening of that day the Amir sent me a gift of a gun and pistol and 5,000 afghanis. After two days, he again summoned me to the court and asked me to write a firman that I be his appointee and envoy in Mazar.

I told him, "Sayed Hussain is your regent and assistant, it is better if you write the firman as advisor."

I took the firman nonchalantly and left for Mazar via Panjsher. About 60 men accompanied me. As a result of my father's friendship with people in Panjsher, I was their guest for ten days. I went to Mazar via Andarab, Nahreen, Khanabad, Kunduz, and Tashkurghan. Sayed Hussain was in Mazar.

My adversaries aggravated Sayed Hussain. They told him, "Habibullah doubts your integrity and therefore has sent Khalilullah."

The next morning Sayed Hussain summoned me in Baghehuzoor. I prayed at Hazrat Ali's tomb, first, anticipating death. When I arrived, Sayed Hussain was sitting in an open area surrounded by 300 armed men.

Upon seeing me, he screamed, "Why have you come?"

I answered, "The Amir has sent me to serve you."

He retorted, "I have heard you have been sent over me."

I replied, "You are the son of the Prophet (PBUH). I will never compete with you."

He softened a little. The Khans of Kohistan like Mir Baba Saheb Khan Charekari, Khwaja Mir Alam Khan, Abu Sattar Khan Bayani, Shah Ghazi, Mohammad Sayed, and many others came running. They pleaded on my behalf with Sayed Hussain and reminded him of my father. Sayed Hussain hugged me and said, "I know Khalilullah well." He gave me a separate tent and appointed a salary. I thanked God and left for my resting place.

Abdul Qayum Khan, Amanullah Khan's former general from Paghman, who fought against him, was appointed governor of Mazar. Mir Mohammad Azim Khan Charekari was appointed as military commander. I was very happy not to interfere in anything and if possible to help people and save their necks. I joined hands with some other friends and decided to search ways to stop Sayed Hussain from killing and punishing people.

Jashen Celebration (Independence Day)

It was time for Jashen Isteqlal (month of Assad). Charbagh was illuminated. In spite of all the killings by the Soviets, people happily participated in the celebration. Khalifa Qizel Ayaq and Dah Mullah Arab were present. A big camp was installed for Sayed Hussain. He ordered, besides the official flag, for a flag to be flown in his name

because he was Sayed. Mullah Mustafa Waiz of Charekar opened the Jashen celebration instead of Sayed Hussain.

The Mullah said, "Sayed Hussain has come to kill the infidels and redden the Amu River with their blood. Until we free Bokhara, we will not give up."

This declaration was greeted with "Allah-o-Akbar" ("God is great"). The Soviet consul, who spoke broken Bokhara language, stood up and without permission said, "I have come to congratulate on the Jashen, unfortunately I am hearing war cries."

Ghulam Nabi Istalifi asked me to answer the Soviet.

I congratulated the nation on the Jashen and said, "I have a duty from Sayed Hussain to be the official spokesman. I thank the consul for his greetings. In spite of the fact that one friendly and neighborly country interfered in our internal affairs and thousands of our young men have been killed, now the Soviet soldiers have left Afghanistan. This force that has come from Kabul is to protect the freedom and borders of Afghanistan. Bokhara belongs to the people of Bokhara, there is no doubt we share their sorrow. If the people of Bokhara and Samarqand want their freedom and need Afghanistan's help, the people of Afghanistan will then make their policy clear."

Maybe only a handful understood me. Sayed Hussain ordered the military band to play guard of honor for me. He left for recreation camp, and Abdul Ahad, the Director of Foreign Affairs in Mazar, told the consul that this gathering is exclusively for Afghans, and the Regent would meet him some other time. As the consul was on his way out, Ibrahim Beg came in and hugged me.

The next day Sayed Hussain appointed me his assistant and Mustufi of Mazar. The law and order situation was deteriorating. At this time, I fell ill.

Habibullah Khan Kalakani's Fall and Nadir Khan Reaches Kabul

We learned Sayed Hussain was abruptly leaving for Kabul. Mohammad Sayeed Khan (Kandahari), Director of Telephone and Telegraph, who was a friend of mine, told me, "The Arg has been besieged. Nadir has attacked from the south, and Habibullah is in the palace."

I was awakened early in the morning and told that Sayed Hussain left for Kabul with full force. He sent a firman from Tashkurghan that the Governor and the Military Commander should consult Khalilullah on all affairs. I summoned all Kohistani and Kohdamani government servants, and also Mirza Mohammad Qasim Khan and Da Mullah Arab and sought their opinions. At this time Abdul Qayum Khan, on his own, announced at the tomb of Hazrat Ali that Nadir Khan was king.

I told others, "Until the time we receive the correct news from Kabul we should wait and see what happens, and take no action." Abdul Qayum Khan went to Deh Dadi and was unaware of the developments. He condemned Habibullah in front of all the soldiers and announced Nadir's ascension to the throne.

The soldiers arrested Qayum Khan and imprisoned him. They said, "Until Kohistan, Kohdaman, and Logar announce their allegiance, we will support no one."

One military unit on its own moved toward Mazar to arrest the supporters of Nadir and Amanullah Khan. Mirza Mohammad Qasim Khan and I cooled them down. The army and the people named me as the governor of Mazar. We received Abdur Rahim Khan's telegram from Herat, and Nadir's pamphlets were sent to Mazar by plane saying that all supporters of Habibullah have changed sides to Nadir, have accepted Nadir as king, and Nadir declared public pardon.

I was able to send all Kohistani and Kohdamini officials to Kabul. I received a telegram from Nadir saying, "Mohammad Omar Khan Mohammad Zai has been appointed in Mazar. Go to Abdur Rahim Khan via Tashkent to Herat. The services of your late father have not been forgotten."

I also received a letter from the elders of Kohdaman and Kohistan that "we have pledged allegiance to Nadir," and "Do not resist. Go to Herat."

My Journey to Herat via Tashkent

I left for Tashkent via Qizel Ayaq on horseback. I wanted to go to Herat from inside Afghanistan if Khalifa of Qizel Ayaq could help me. The Khalifa did not see it as right. About 30 men crossed with me into the Soviet Union. The Soviets took us to Khatab Town and from Khatab to Karki City near Amu Daria.

They allowed us to travel during night only. After two days staying in the city and confiscating our guns and horses, they took us via boat across Amu to Tashkent on the train. We stayed in older part of the city of Tashkent and hardly had any money left. The Soviets would not give us permission to go to Herat. Abdur Rahim Khan, realizing our stay in Tashkent was prolonged, sent a message to me through a courier of the Foreign Ministry who was going to the Afghan consulate in Tashkent. I informed him that the Soviets were not allowing me to leave.

Abdur Rahim Khan informed Kabul and summoned the Soviet Consul General in Herat who told him to expedite my departure from Tashkent. Two of the men stayed back, marrying two beautiful girls of Tashkent.

Fortunately, at this time, Sayed Hashim Khan, a scholar and theologian, was appointed as General Consul of Afghanistan to Tashkent. Two or three days later he met me in my room. Sayed Hashim was the brother of Sayed Qasim, the Minister of Justice of Afghanistan. He was fluent in English, Arabic, and French, and whatever I say about his qualities is less. Sayed Hashim tried his best to send me to Herat, but was assassinated by the Soviets six months later, while on a journey from Tashkent to Iran.

Sayed Hashim became close to the Moslems of the area. He said everywhere, "If I am allowed, I will prove scientifically that communism is dangerous and disastrous for humanity, especially for the Moslems of the Middle East." Sayed Hashim's murderer was apprehended and later released. The Afghan government was told the murderer was sentenced to jail for ten years. I was in Herat when the news reached me that Sayed Hashim's body was being brought to Gazargah to be buried. The people took out a procession with black flags and marched to the Soviet consulate. They chanted anti-Soviet slogans and blamed the Soviet government for his death.

Abdur Rahim Khan sent armed guards to the consulate. As the news reached Kabul, Sayed Hashim's body was taken to Kabul and buried at Tape Maranjan. I think it was the first political murder of an Afghan by the communists.

I was able to reach Herat via Torghanli and Mahro by train.

I Am Among the Afghan Mujahideen

In December 1983 I received an official letter from my friend Qazi Mohammad Afzal Khan Chema, former Chief Justice of Pakistan. At the time he was Chairman of the Islamic Relations Committee of Pakistan. He was a learned man and scholar, and knew four languages: Arabic, English, Urdu, and Persian. In Pakistan he was considered an eminent personality. He had written to me that he "has been officially assigned to inform you on behalf of the President of Pakistan that you have been appointed as cultural advisor to the President of Pakistan in the cultural relations for the Afghan refugees."

I went to Pakistan and was warmly welcomed by the Mujahideen. I told the Qazi that if I am allowed to work as an advisor without an office schedule and just from my home, I would accept the job. The Qazi insisted that I should accept an office in the Presidential Palace and with an official car and driver and work on the basis of a schedule like others, but I could not do this. After a week I was appointed to work independently as advisor to the President.

I took up residence in Islamabad at Nazimuddin Road. My objective was two pronged: to provide accurate information to the Mujahideen and to get accurate reports from the Jehad front (struggle against Soviets) in the form of articles, poetry, and interviews to the outside world.

I might have written approximately 20 booklets on different topics and published them with the help of the leaders of the Afghan political parties. Safiullah Sabat, my student, took a leading part in publishing it.

In 1985, I was officially invited to the anniversary of Sheikh Saadi, which was sponsored by UNESCO and being held in Shiraz, Iran. I replied, "If you have invited someone from the puppet regime of Kabul (Communist regime sponsored by the Soviet Union April 1978-1992) and if the gathering is marred by any protest from our side, and if you are willing to accept that protest, I will definitely come."

Mr. Hussein Razamjo, Chairman of the 800-year commission of Saadi, replied to me, "We do not recognize the Kabul government, and we are not going to invite its henchmen."

Because the time was too short, I was unable to attend the meeting, but I was able to send my message, which was published by Sayed Attaullah Shirazi, Chargé d'Affaires of the Islamic Republic of Iran in Pakistan, in my third volume of poetry.

During my first journey to Pakistan in 1982, my booklets, books, and articles were published by the leaders of Afghan parties, Burhanuddin Rabbani, Sebghatullah Mojaddadi, and other Afghanis.

On both occasions when I travelled to Pakistan, the writers of Pakistan and Iranian writers living in Pakistan respected me. They held meetings and conferences to honor me. During the celebrations of Pakistan's national day, my poetry was read amid warm welcome and tears. I had said in that poetry:

Afghanistan and Pakistan are like two eyes.
One eye has been struck by an arrow and is bleeding;
the other eye should cry, shed tears and be awake.

The majority of Moslems of Pakistan have been deeply touched by the afflictions of Afghanistan. They want every kind of help to be provided to the refugees of Afghanistan. However, there are a few parties who are prey to Soviet deception and are against the presence of the Afghan refugees in Pakistan. It is a shame that I should name a few of the tribal leaders, who have been deceived by the Soviets and have forgotten their nationality, history, and Islam.

Zia ul-Haq is a person who thinks and relates to the

future of Pakistan and that of Islam in the region with the freedom of Afghanistan. In the 1,000-year history of the subcontinent there is nothing written or any action taken without the participation of Afghanistan. Since Mahmood of Ghazni to Ahmed Shah Baba to Zia ul-Haq this participation is seen in war, peace, in books, in thinking, in the school and in religious places.

The Persian language and Persian poetry has lost its position with the colonization of the subcontinent by the British. In spite of this the name of Maulana Rumi, Sanai, Hafez, Saadi, Amir Khusrau, and others are still illuminated like stars. The leaders of the mujahideen in Pakistan were divided into two parts.

The division was labeled as conservative and the other part as mild or western-oriented. But I do not think this was right. The fact is, one part was against the former regime and the other part was for the former regime.

Sayed Ahmad Gailani, Sebghatullah Mojaddadi, and Maulani Mohammad Nabi were thought to be supporters of the former regime. Ustad Burhanuddin Rabbani, Engineer Hekmatyar, Maulavi Younus Khan, and Abdul Rab Sayaf were against the former regime. I did not join any of them officially. I explained and clarified my position that we should divide Afghanistan on the basis of time: 1. Today, that the Soviet army is in Afghanistan, and 2. Tomorrow, that Soviet army leaves Afghanistan with the grace of God.

Today, all our activities should be directed to the Jihad of Afghanistan. That is, the Jihad should be organized: 1. The Commanders of various frontiers should "join" hands. 2. Needed and effective arms should reach the front line. 3. The petty differences lingering among the leaders of Jihad in Pakistan should be removed. 4. The future of Afghanistan should be left to the people of Afghanistan.

How long can we ignore the nation? How long can we forget the sacrifice of the nations? Why should we believe in the mirage that the people of Afghanistan, after all these sacrifices, cannot take care of their destiny? Whomever the people elect, they should have the power to question. Let's allow the people to get the power and elect their own leaders.

At this time an article appeared in *Wulus Mojahid*, written by Dr. Salim in Peshawar. This article was attributed to me. In this article the former King of Afghanistan was taken to task. But God be my witness, I did not write the article. If I had written it, there was no reason and no fear not to write my name. I gave no importance to this small circle of vagabonds, and I believe that the interest of the nation is higher than that.

The interest of the individual is the legacy of colonialism. It promotes a person or a family and bestows all power of the state and the nation on it and this is a major tool that always makes the spread of communism easier in such nations.

I was in touch with the commanders of the frontiers fighting the invaders. Twice my son Masood went to Panjsher and Herat. The letters of the commanders of Panjsher, Herat, Mozar, Parwan, etc., came to me regularly.

I was happy to see the commanders working closely and had realized that the threat of disunity is no less than the Soviet aggression. During the last month of my stay in Pakistan, May 1985, the leaders of the various parties were close to each other. After this I am sure the seed of disunity sown by the enemy will have no effect.

I had to return to the Unites States to see my wife and grandchildren, as well as for health reasons. I also needed to come to New Jersey for the possibility to talk to U.S. and international sources on behalf of Afghanistan.

I consider this as one of the most difficult moments of my life, to go to U.S. government offices as a refugee and to ask for assistance for myself and for my countrymen.

In the United States, materialism is at its highest level. From the land that has given birth to famous poets, ironically spiritualism and poetry no more exist. When I came to New Jersey I saw that my wife had moved from one apartment to the other with a few of my books and could not pay the rent. At the same time, I noticed at that time some of my books were still lying incomplete: 1) *Life in the Village*, 2) *From Kaaba to Kapisa [Mecca to Church]* and 3) *Naqshe Qadame Maulavii [Footprints of Maulavi]*. I also saw my memoirs written by my son- in-

law, Afzal Nasiri, in English, and now I start the part two of these memoirs.

Editor's Note: Part Two is pg. 145. This section was moved to better correlate with Khalili's 1985 thoughts about the Mujahideen.

News from the Moslems of Tashkent

Now that I am returning home, it would be regretful if I do not give the news of the Moslems of Tashkent (Uzbekistan) to the Moslems of Afghanistan.

No words, no pen, and no art can explain or draw the bloody and shameful acts of that time. My stay prolonged for three months in Tashkent. We were given rooms at the Pushkin Guest House, but when they realized we would not become communists, they confiscated our belongings. Fortunately, we were able to rent a small place in the old community of Orda, the center of the city's Moslem population. We could see around us graveyards with stones whose inscriptions had been broken and decaying mosques with their doors locked.

The landlord was still a Moslem and knew by heart verses from Holy Koran. It was winter and Tashkent was colder than Kabul; water had frozen into ice. My friends, wearing warm clothes, would stand in queue with the local people in front of stores to buy potatoes and coal or fuel for kerosene oil stoves, twice a day. Sometimes, they came back late at night empty-handed, and we went hungry. In our community of more than 20,000 households, there were not more than four or five stores from which to buy food and fuel supplies. Every few days we would hear the news that an old woman or child had died of the cold while standing in front of a store.

Our residence had two rooms; my three friends, Sayed Ahmad Khan, Director of Frontier and Customs; Mohammad Rafiq, Brigadier from Jabul Seraj; and my very noble friend, Mohammad Issa Totumdarai, stayed in the bigger room while I took the small room. Coal and wood heaters delivered us from the sheer death of the Tashkent winter. In contrast, in the building where the Soviets lived, all amenities were available. Most of the products of Tashkent were shipped out to Moscow and other states. Food and fuel were distributed through a coupon system. Uzbeks who had stood tall, with large heads and big stomachs, and who had for years shaken the whole of Asia, were now deprived of everything.

Except for an old tramcar as public transport, there was nothing else. Tashkent did not have more than 20 cars belonging to government officials. There were some carts without wheels pulled by horses. These were used for disabled and sick people.

Decades had passed but still the Russian, now Soviet, government occupied the Moslem nation. Killings and persecution continued. Most of these political murders occurred during the night. Even in the street where I lived, families were eliminated. During the night we heard gunfire and in the morning only bloodstained clothes were found. Uzbek neighbors made us understand through gestures that the women were taken to Siberia, and the men were killed.

What was very painful was the desecration of religious relics and monuments. A modern sewage system had not yet come to Uzbekistan. Pages from religious books and the Holy Koran were used as toilet paper.

In the whole of Tashkent, there was one old public library that was open two hours every day. All of the bookstores stocked only communist propaganda and nothing else. Children were forced to study communist ideology. Youth were taken to communes during the day and to bars at night. Old men and women were in pitiful condition, waiting to die, but still they had not given up their religion or culture.

Because Abdur Rahim Khan had threatened the Soviet Consul in Herat for holding us in Tashkent, the Directorate of Foreign Affairs accepted our demands. Sayed Hashim Khan, General Consul, also helped us in Tashkent. Ramadan would be the last month of our stay in Tashkent. Luckily, Abdur Rahim Khan sent some money through Sayed Mohammad, a political courier, to me so we could easily get sheep. We fasted, bought one sheep a day and ate it for Iftar and Sahar. Our Afghan cook prepared Afghan dishes. We invited our neighbors for dinner under the cover of darkness.

During the Ramadan nights, I would lead prayers with the congregation. The neighbors watched us from rooftops with sad eyes but did not join us because they were scared of the government. One Friday, we went to the congregation mosque of Sheikh Khan Tohoor. When Sayed Ahmed Khan sounded the first Takbeer (call to prayer), a few elderly people came running for prayers. They said, "We heard the sound of Takbeer after many years." The prayer was still in progress when armed soldiers entered the mosque. They recognized us as foreigners but arrested the elderly of the local community. They beat them with the butts of guns and took them to an unknown place. I told Sayed Ahmed Khan, "I don't know that you did a good or bad thing by this Takbeer."

When I came to Herat and told Abdur Rahim Khan about the Islamic books that were desecrated, the people of Herat were deeply touched. They contributed some money. Abdur Rahim Khan talked to the Soviet consul and after a lot of trouble, the consul agreed to buy three thousand volumes of religious books from Uzbekistan and brought them to Herat. The books were trusted to the library of the Masjid Jame of Herat. However, whatever I saw in Tashkent was the killing of this national spirit and annihilation of Islamic civilization and sabotaging of the foundation of the Islamic nation.

In Tashkent people would run away and avoid us because secret police had us under surveillance day and night. My pastime involved my three favorite things – friends, books, and chess. The books we would get covertly through our neighbors. I would write poetry reflecting my pain and suffering. Unfortunately, I lost everything in Herat.

Herat

One after another, I passed the Islamic cities on my way from Tashkent to the border of Afghanistan. The railroad was up to Sheikh Junaid, which is the last port in the Soviet

Union. Shah Joi and Merv Shah Jan, in greater Merv, were in a very old and poor state. Afghanistan had a consulate in Merv, but because the rail used to leave twice a week, we remained three days there.

The destroyed remains of Merv were located in a desert. The gunbud (dome) on the grave of the famous scholar of Islam, Sultan Sangar, was still standing. The sunset in Merv reminded me of this verse,

Evening prayer in Merv
Night prayer in Herat
Morning (Fajr) prayer in Chahpur
Afternoon prayer in Baghdad.

I have witnessed all four of these scenes.

A public bath (hamam) from the time of the King of Bokhara and his father was in its place. It was called Murghabi Hamam. The Murghab River rises from the mountains of Afghanistan and passes through Merv and ends in Shah Jan in the desert.

I had a great desire to see my country once again, and escape from the Tashkent detention, avoiding the tearful imprisoned eyes of the people of Uzbekistan, which bothered me. To see Herat was also one of my outstanding desires. The description of the historical writings and books and the desire of the people of Herat to learn, especially literature, had captured my heart. After full customs and a long search by the Soviet guards, still, they held us for one night in the town of Sheikh Junaid for interrogation.

Finally, we reached our own soil. It is regretful that Sheikh Junaid, about 50 years back from that date, was part of Panjdeh, an integral part of Afghanistan at the time of Amir Abdur Rahman, when the Russians occupied it. Civil and military officials on our side of the border warmly and respectfully welcomed us. They embraced each and every one of us. Our voices talking with the border security people were heard by the Soviets. We were calling loud, "Long live Afghanistan! Long live Islam!"

The land was covered with snow, and the sun was smiling at us. Because of the heavy snow there was no chance of an automobile coming from Herat. We came to the building that housed customs along with Afghan soldiers and under the high-flying Afghan flag. At that time, the area was called Qara Tepa; later, in the time of Zahir Shah, it was named Torghundi. We were guests of customs officers and the administration, Naib Salar (Deputy Commander in Chief). Abdur Rahim Khan ordered the frontier in charge that we should remain for one night in Torghundi and then go to Herat. We took horses for Herat via Chuqur Rabat and Yaka Darakht.

We reached Kamar Qala about the time of evening prayers. Naib Salar had come to welcome us along with high-ranking officials. All of them had white turbans over their civil and military uniform. I asked Naib Salar about the white turban: "Is it the same that you put on in Kabul in the Arg?"

He replied, "No, this is the tradition of 1,300 years of Islam."

We went to the Charbagh building via Khayaban in the old part of the city. Naib Salar would perform military duties in the Arg, (Fort) Qalai Ikhtiyaruddin, and civil duties in Charbagh.

From Kamar Qala to Herat, the first thing that attracted attention most was the tomb of Jami and the remains of Mosallah (Eid Gah), which was constructed in Timurid period (1405-1507) and was famous as "the bride of the east." Amir Abdur Rahman Khan destroyed Mosallah and history has recorded this black spot of his rule that is immortal. Still, the old wall of the city of Herat was standing.

I met my uncle, Abdur Rahim Khan, in Herat. We had a long discussion about the political developments. My uncle advised me to stay a few days with him and analyze the situation. I wanted to go to Kabul as soon as possible.

I remained in Herat for about two years. In these two years I took no part in the government. Abdur Rahim Khan was the military commander with the title of Naib Salar and governed Herat. The civil servants of Herat were all from Herat. These people were versatile in their duties. The government ran like a well-oiled machine.

I did not go to Kabul because Habibullah Khan

Kalakani, along with his friends, were executed and wherever they found someone having to do anything with his government, they were thrown in prison.

Nadir Shah had promised the people of Waziristan who had come from outside Afghanistan that if he conquered, he would let them have the bounty of Kohdaman and Kohistan. When he neared Kabul he announced through firmans the general pardon of the people of Kohdaman and Kohistan, who in turn, sincerely pledged their allegiance and returned to their homes. Thus, it was difficult to give the belongings of the people of Kohdaman and Kohistan as bounty to the Waziris. This problem was also solved by the Great Adversary who had sent the Wazaris to help Nadir Shah. The solution was to accuse the people of Kohdaman and Kohistan of a "sin" and on this pretext the state could break its promise of pardon. First, one renowned and innocent personality of Afghanistan would be murdered. Second, the Judge of Shariat court also would be killed.

Allah Nawaz Khan and Shahji went to Kohdaman secretly and executed the plot by bringing with them to Kohdaman people from outside. With their help, they murdered Abdul Wakil Khan Nouristani, and Abdur Rahman, the judge. Abdul Wakil Khan had to be sacrificed to fulfill the plot because in the war of freedom he had played a pivotal role – he was archenemy of the British. In the army, he had influence and was a friend of Amanullah Khan.

A few days before this incident some renowned people of Kohdaman, Charekar and Jabal Seraj were invited to attend a dinner in Kabul. Mirza Mohammad Yosuf Khan, my uncle, was appointed Hakim of Sarai - Khuja and knew nothing of the plot. He called Sardar Mohammad Hashim Khan on the phone and told him not to send Abdul Wakil Khan to Kohdaman because people would wonder why a military general is being sent to Kohdaman. However, Abdul Wakil Khan went to Kalakan (home of Habibullah Khan Kalakani) without his army guards and was murdered by unknown assailants. When the people wanted to gather in support to Abdul Wakil Khan, the army and the people of Waziristan attacked the Kohdaman people.

Mohammad Ghaus, Naib Salar, whose son was killed by Habibullah Khan Kalakani and was defeated by Abdur Rahim Khan in Herat, wanted to take revenge. He was the commander of the attacking force. He ordered that for one month Kohdaman, Jabal Seraj, and Charekar would be looted and those who resisted should be killed without being tried. From the Gulbahar River to the other side, people were not attacked and they were pardoned.

No doubt, in this one month of mass murder thousands of people were killed, houses were burned, belongings and cattle herds of the people were given to Waziri militia. Even girls and women were carried away by those people and sold. The old and rusted weapons the Waziri had bought were traded for new weapons and taken to Waziristan.

Whoever had a name and influence was killed, their property destroyed, and their remaining families escaped to neighboring countries to save massacre. For example, the sons of Mohammad Karim Khan from Murad Beg and Khwaja Jal of Qarabagh; like Qazi Ghulam Hazrat Khan and Khans of Farza; like Mohammad Zaman Khan and Khans of Laghman; like Khwaja Najmuddin Khan and Mir Baba Saheb Khan and Khans of Tutumdara; each of them was punished by murder and their property appropriated and given to people from Waziristan. The enmity between these two places remains.

Mohammad Yosuf Khan and all my family were thrown in jail. Even my cousins, Dr. Wassa and Dr. Essa, who at the time were not more than 14 or 15 years old, were imprisoned for three years.

Those were the reasons why I remained in Herat and why the Naib Salar also advised me against going to Kabul. I acquainted myself with Herat literature in those two years, and there is where I published my book *Assar-e-Herat* (History of Herat) in three volumes.

At that time Qazi Mullah Mohammad Siddiq Khan Kabuli was known as the leading scholar in Herat. The Saljoqi family was famous for scholarly and literary works.

Gazargah was there and Mir Ghulam Haider Khan was president of Gazargah Auqaf (Trust). He was a scholar, poet, and writer. He would invite me on Friday nights along with my friends at Namakdan. Allama Mohammad Siddiq, Maulavi Ziauddin, Mullah Jalal Tabil, and Abdul Hussein Munajim Bashi were among the literary figures who participated in these meetings.

According to the divisions from the time of Amir Abdul Rahman Khan, Herat included Ghorian, Badghis until Murghab River, Isfezar whose historical name was changed to Shindand, Ghorat and up to the border of Hazarajat. The land of Herat was a repository of historical remains. The Ghaznavid dynasty, the Saljoqui, Kurt and Temurids; each of these had worked in the development of Herat. In every place one could find a mosque, tomb, Khanqah (meeting place of Darvish), Fort, and Rabat City from ancient history. The tomb of Khwaja Abdullah Ansari in Gazargah, Khwaja Maudud Chisht, Khwaja Mohammad Kunje-Jahan, Masjid Jame of Herat, Qalai Arg Ikhtiaruddin, Rabats of the time of Sultan Hussein Mirza Pule-Malan (bridge) – all of these speak of the ancient grandeur of Herat. In Herat you can find every kind of game from deer to kulong (pheasant). The people loved hunting.

Herat boasts 63 varieties of grapes. Compared to all other countries, in Afghanistan the dak, pine, najo, and pistachio trees growing wild were in abundance. Every kind of agricultural farming was done in Herat. The land that could be cultivated in cases exceeded the needs of the people. Therefore they cultivated the land in turns: One year, one plot; and the next year, another plot.

All schools of Sufi thought and Tasawwuf (mystic) were found in Herat except for Shiites, who were a minority, but carried out their religious rites with all respects; the rest of the people followed Hanafi faith (Suni), followers of Imam Azam Abu Hanifa. The religious schools were run in the ancient patterns in countryside and the city. The people linked themselves to different nationalities, like Pashtun, Tajik, Char Aimaq, White Hazara, and Temuri.

The lands surrounding Herat were divided into 12 or 13 sections. Each section was called a block. Each block had a separate canal, which were dug from Harirud River. The division of water was done by Sultan Hussein Mirza Temuri through Maulavi Jami. There was a small booklet on this written by Jami, I had seen it myself. I do not know who has that book now. Takhte-Safar was one of the famous places of fall festival (maila). It is located in the footsteps of the northern hills of Herat. The Heratis say this place was first used in the time of Sultan Hussein Mirza. Whoever was found or caught drinking was sent to Takhte-Safar for building and cleaning. No one was exempt, including royalty.

The people of Herat would hold a number of mailas (jashens) or fairs during spring at Takhte-Safar, Bagh-e-Maulavi, Jami, Khazimullah-e-Kohi, and Imam Shashnoor were the famous places for melas (fairs). Men and women participated separately. The ancient names were still there on canals and villages, like Jibreel (Gabriel), Engeel, Saq Salman, Ghor Darwaza, Mai Farosh, Ziaratgah, Alimjan, Guzara, Dadshan, etc. Among the local dishes of Herat, kabab qao (full lamb roast) was on top of the list. To cook it, first an open pit oven was prepared big enough to hold a sheep, and sufficient quantities of pista and baloot wood were lit. The sheep was skinned, the intestine and other parts were taken out, and the sheep was put on seekh (spit) and hung in tandoor a foot above the fire after the flames had died down. A big sheep took six hours to cook; a small lamb, two hours. It was then placed on a big platter and served. The farmers would prepare two kinds of dry foods for winter, one with water and the other with milk, ghulor sheer (milk) and ghulor tursh (sour). Pigeon remains fertilized the cultivated lands and vineyards. In every village four or five tall towers were built. Thousands of desert pigeons would find shelter in them. Their remains (stool) were used as fertilizer, and the places were named as kaftarkhana (pigeon homes). The windmill was still used to produce flour. In Herat, people complained of wind for six months. Eye infections spread with these winds. The winds of Herat, when they were harsh, were called siahbad (dark wind), and when gentle, they were called farahbad (happy wind).

The people of Herat were well built, tall, and had

literary and artistic tastes. Literacy was highest in Herat. They were sincere and had a deep belief in their religion, country, and the preservation of their historical relics.

A bitter experience of the Heratis was the treacherous occupation of Panjdeh (Afghan territory south of the Oxus River) by the Russians during the time of Amir Abdur Rahman Khan (1885). It was still a topic of discussion in private gatherings.

Despite the lack of literary value to his poetry, every year people pay respect to the grave of Herati poet Sayedah, whose grave is near Kharmadozan Bridge, because in one of the battles against the attack of Iran he was martyred. In the wintery nights the topic of discussion among the elderly was the Sufis and men of letters. The gatherings of the youth discussed their national heroes.

Music in Herat was based on the same old notes. Sitar, tambor, robab, daf, and nai (flute) were prevalent. For every occasion they had a different composer. Indian music had also found a way through Kabul into Herat.

Persecution

During my stay in Herat, two or three important incidents happened. The first was the assassination of Sayed Hashim Khan by the Soviets, while he was on a journey from Tashkent to Iran. The second incident was the influx of refugees from the Soviet Union to Herat. Not a day passed when an incident did not occur on the border. The communists pressured the Moslems. They did not back away from killing, destroying, and annihilating the people.

Among these refugees were Karim Khan Baluch and Junaid Khan from Turkmanistan. They were very famous. Karim Khan brought with him more than 2,000 families. Hundreds of women and children were killed by Soviets on their way to freedom. Turkmans were also undergoing the same fate. Naib Salar Abdul Rahim Khan gave to all of them land and a place to live. The people of Herat also warmly welcomed these refugees. The Soviet Consul in Herat and their embassy in Kabul protested this.

The refugees were so afflicted and poor that no one could resist helping them. At the same time a tourist

caravan called the Yellow Caravan came to Herat via Iran
from France. Their objective was to travel to China. In the
Karta Gardens near Herat City they found a place to live.
The leader of the caravan was a well-known personality of
France. This caravan left for Kabul via Kandahar. The
leader of the Yellow Caravan met Naib Salar, and Naib
Salar showed him the refugee camps.

Return to Kabul

At this time, the last firman of Nadir Shah, forgiving
me, reached Herat. According to the news that had reached
from Kabul earlier, the Kohdaman plot that was hatched
outside Afghanistan had ended.

My uncle, Mirza Mohammad Yosuf Khan, his four sons
and my two brothers were in jail. Mohammad Islam
Maihan, who was sincere to education development, was
also one of my cousins to have been jailed. I thought to
myself, unless I go to Kabul, these people will not be
released. It was very bitter and difficult for me to see the
beautiful Kohdaman under blood and destruction. Its
leaders were either killed or in prison; its beautiful
vineyards and gardens looted and trampled; its pride
shattered and even some of its women taken away from it
to unknown lands. Anyway, I bade goodbye to my friends
in Herat.

My Journey Toward Kabul

Shireen Sukhan, the poet of Herat, accompanied me. I
tried to discourage him from going, but he did not listen.
We left for Kabul on a lorry with two or three soldiers via
Isfazar, Farah and Girishk, and reached Kandahar. The
historic name Isfazar had not been changed to Shindand.
There was no security, and we were compelled to take our
own measures to protect ourselves. In the lorry, we crossed
the Farah, Hermand, and Arghardab Rivers on a boat. The
Hermand River was torrential, roaring, and full of waves.
Two strong men rowed the wooden boat.

Mohammad Gul Khan Momand was the Administrator

in Kandahar. It was rumored he was against the supporters of Habibullah Khan Kalakani. I sent Shireen Sukhan ahead from Arghardab so he could arrange my stay in Kandahar in one of the Caravan Sarais. However, Mohammad Gul Khan had gotten the news of my arrival and had summoned Shireen Sukhan to his office. He was kind to him and told him I would be his guest and should stay at the Arg of Kandahar. Because the weather was hot, the respected poet, as soon as he saw the government guesthouse, fell asleep. He was young and had a long beard. I sat waiting for him near Arghardab River. I thought Shireen Sukhan has been imprisoned and I, too, should go to Kandahar and sit beside my friend. Near the Herat entrance of Kandahar city Mohammad Gul Khan with all his glory was waiting to welcome me. He accompanied me to the Arg. I was his guest for one week, and he was kind to me. He gave me a personal letter to Mohammad Hashim Khan and vouched for me.

Mohammad Gul Khan had graduated from military school at the time of Amir Habibullah Khan Seraj, and had gone to Turkey during the time of Amir Amanullah Khan on an Afghanistan publicity mission. He spoke the Turkish language well. During the Amani period he reached the rank of Firqa Mishr (company commander). He was considered as one of the revolutionary leaders.

During Habibullah Khan Kalakani's time, he assisted Nadir Shah. During Nadir Shah's time, he was appointed Minister of Interior and Administrator of Kandahar. During Zahir Shah's time, he was appointed Administrator of Northern Provinces (Mazar-i-Sharif, Kataghan, Maimana), and ultimately, he opposed the government of Mohammad Hashim Khan. He resigned from his post and later died. Undoubtedly, he was a sincere servant of Afghanistan.

Leaving Kandahar for Kabul

From Kandahar we left for Ghazni. Near Qalat we came across the supporters of Abdul Rahman Taraki. He was the leader of the Ghilzai tribe; he opposed Nadir Shah but later gave up. (It should be mentioned here that Noor Mohammad Taraki was not related to him and forged his identity; it was never true.) Near Kande Pusht village his supporters stopped our lorry and Abdul Rahman Taraki sent me a message saying, "It is dangerous for you to go to Kabul. It is better you stay with us. If you want to go, you are free to do so." I thanked him and left for Ghazni in the morning.

The governor of Ghazni was Nasrullah Khan Logari. Mohammad Gul Khan had informed Nasrullah Khan of my arrival. My delay in Kande Pusht worried him. It was the first time I was visiting the land of Hakim Sanai. Shireen Sukhan and I decided to go directly to the tomb of Hakim Sanai and send the others to the hotel. The light of the tomb of Hakim Sanai attracted us from far away. The gumbad (dome) of the Ziarat and the mosque still had the ancient structure. The colored paintings of Ghazni on the wood and the boundaries were beautiful. The grave was covered with fresh roses. The Mujavir (caretaker) was sitting at the door. Two elderly men were busy reading verses from the Holy Koran.

The flickering light emanating from the oil lamps, the capitulating reading of Holy Koran, the smell of roses and the faces of the mystic Noorani (Holy-luminous) brought a glory and greatness to the place. Shireen Sukhan and I were lost in our thoughts. He put his fingers in his ears and recited a verse from Hafez in his Herati accent.

We read a few verses from the Holy Koran and soon it was dawn.

After two days in Ghazni, we left for Kabul. Our worries increased as we neared the city. Because Sardar Hashim Khan was acquainted with Naib Salar, and Naib Salar had saved his life in the uprising of Herat at the time of the assassination of Amir Habibullah Khan Seraj, we decided to go directly to him. I thought he would support me. The biggest challenge was reaching him.

Every good act has a good result, sometimes instantly and sometimes later in time. By chance near Maidan, an officer stopped our vehicle so we could give him a lift. My heart melted when we picked him up. During the discourse with him we learned he was Jan Mohammad, a captain of Royal Guard. The name of my father was still well known in the countryside. Jan Mohammad, as soon as he recognized me, paid respects to me.

I asked, "Is it possible for you to take me to the Gulkhana in the Arg and to Hashim Khan?"

He happily consented. But I said, "I will only accept this offer if I am sure you will not be harmed."

As a proof of Afghan bravery he said proudly, "Do not worry, I'll take you to the Gulkhana."

We reached Kabul in the evening. I prayed at the Shah-e-do-shamshera mosque and prayed to the soul of my mother on her grave, which is at Shah-e-do-shamshera. Still, the Soviet flag was flying at my father's house (now the Russian Embassy).

From the gates of the Arg no one was allowed without a pass that had a photograph and the name of the person. Jan Mohammad accompanied us in his uniform.

Shireen Sukhan and I went to the Gulkhana, and Jan Mohammad took our leave. My other companions remained outside the gates. This was a huge gamble I took, entering the Arg secretly without permission. The Gulkhana was on the northern side of the Arg and was built by Amir Habibullah Khan. Nadir Shah lived in Haram Sarai, attached to the Gulkhana on the western side of the Arg. Sometimes he worked in the Dilkusha, sometimes, the Gulkhana. Hashim Khan, although he was of good age, slept in lower section of the Gulkhana and during the day, worked in the Zainul Imarat (the Apple of the Eye), which was on the northwestern side of Kabul and later named Qassare-Sidarat (Prime Ministry). Nasrullah Khan, Moinus Saltana (Caretaker of the Crown), bought the blueprint himself after he returned from London during the time of Amir Habibullah and had Zainul Imarat built.

Indirectly, I reached Kabul the night Sardar Hashim Khan invited the head of the Yellow Caravan at the Stor Palace. The caravan leader mentioned the warm welcome he received in Herat and about the Naib Salar. Hashim Khan had a very faithful servant, Nazir Mohammad Hakim, who acted as personal secretary and butler. At the time Hashim Khan was Naib Salar in Herat, this man introduced him to Abdul Rahim Khan. Naib Salar Abdul Rahim Khan had also sent some gifts to him. He paid respects to myself and Shireen Sukhan and took us to his room and gave us tea. We sat there until Hashim Khan came.

Hashim Khan was tall, good looking, fair complexioned, with a French cut beard, and wearing an Afghan Soor (black) cap and a smoking jacket. As soon as he saw Shireen Sukhan and me, he reacted sharply, worry creasing his forehead. He was surprised at how we came into the Arg without permission and that we had also, in the night, entered his personal servant's quarters. Before replying to our greetings he asked, "Who are these people?"

Nazir answered, "Khalilullah, nephew of Naib Salar."

He said, "Why don't you say the son of late Mustufi-ul-Momalik (Finance Minister)?"

After a couple of minutes of asking our welfare while standing, Hashim Khan went to his bedroom.

It was the first time I had seen a smoking jacket. I told Shireen Sukhan, "That man in this dress looks like a penguin."

I asked Nazir Hakim to ask Hashim Khan where I should stay in the night, because my brothers were in prison and I didn't have a house in Kabul. Nazir Hakim brought the message, "Wala Hazrat (His Highness) says, 'Go wherever you want to. If you stay in the Arg, the enemies of the government will say you have been imprisoned.'"

I was satisfied I was free and left for my house, which I had inherited from my mother, and was in Khayaban near the Arg. It was deserted. Kohdaman and Kohistan were filled with blood. My brothers were in prison. Two of my children were with friends of mine, hiding them from one place to the other. I remained in the house for two months and no one came to visit, afraid of the government's wrath. My friends were waiting for my destiny. After two months the Prime Minister summoned me to his office and appointed me the Director of the First Secretariat. No one ever dared question his decisions. I, too, accepted the appointment with gratitude.

Prime Minister's Office

The Prime Minister himself exclusively ran the Office of the Prime Minister. The office included the Criminal Investigation department and three Directorates of Secretariat, including the Directorate of Archives, the Directorate of Applications, and the Directorate of Payroll and Expenses. All of these directorates were answerable to the Prime Minister. Criminal Investigation had large and prominent role. This department had undercover detectives for overt and covert activities. The downfall or bad omen was that even the judges and government employees had to have their backgrounds checked by the Director of Criminal Investigation. For example, in spite of the independence of the judiciary system, only the judges who were cleared by Criminal Investigation were to be trusted.

It was therefore that nationalism, competency, sincerity, and honesty were not factors for appointment. Someone who was incompetent and had not those thorough qualities could have been appointed in high offices through Criminal Investigation. For informers, treachery was not sin and law had no meaning. They would do whatever he wanted. I had composed some poems and my enemies took them to the Prime Minister; however, it had no effect. Those poems were at my library in Kabul and were destroyed during the communists' takeover. This is part of one of those poems:

The informant,
because of you the country was destroyed
O infidel, this should stop.
The state and the people have been separated.
This has to stop.
O infidel, this should stop.

The Prime Minister's secretariat was responsible for different ministries. The ministers would bring their reports that included applications for which they needed instructions. The Defense Ministry, Justice, and Commerce were under my office.

The Ministry of Defense, which was run by Shah Mahmoud Khan (1885-1953), did not bring reports. Shah

Mahmoud Khan, the brother of Hashim Khan, would make his own decisions and was free to do so. Still, the Ministry of Public Works, Health, and Communications did not exist. The Public Works and other works were the Commerce Ministry's responsibility. Every minister would write whatever he wanted on a piece of paper and bring to the Prime Minister and read it before him. The rest was in the hands of the Prime Minister. After listening to the application, the Prime Minister would give instructions, and the secretary would write the instructions on the paper. Even the appointments of the postmen, cooks, etc., were done after instruction from the Prime Minister. At the end, the Prime Minister signed the papers. The Minister had the right to read the papers, and the secretary only wrote them down. The Prime Minister decided everything. Many of the matters were sent to the Criminal Investigation department.

Every day the ministers saw themselves not being trusted, but did not speak up. Only one servant, who was deaf and dumb, had the right to be present during the meetings of the ministers with the Prime Minister. Even two years after the death of Nadir Shah, Hashim Khan still came to work every day at 11 a.m. and stayed until 5 p.m. The Prime Minister interfered in technical affairs, too. For example, the Prime Minister changed the blueprints of the buildings, bridges, and factories that were designed by foreign (expatriate) architects, and the architects had no right to say anything. During the third and fourth years of Hashim Khan's administration as Prime Minister Mondays were the ministers' meetings. The ministers came to the Prime Minister's office, and the secretary of the meeting presented the resolutions and everybody signed. After the creation of the Parliament and Senate, the Speaker of the House of Representatives and Senate also signed. In spite of freedom of the three branches as allowed by the constitution – legislative, judiciary, and executive – separation of powers was not there. The Speaker of the House of Representatives and Senate signed in the ministers' meeting and in the meetings of the council.

The ministers meeting worked in three phases: First, regular works. Second, comparatively important decisions were first discussed and made in a meeting of the Prime Minister, Defense, Commerce and Foreign Ministers and then brought to the meeting of the ministers. Third, confidential and national security importance affairs were only discussed by elders of the Royal Family in the Arg. Sundays were assigned for general meetings of the Prime Minister. About 200 people would come from around the country to attend the meetings and have lunch with him. At that time the Prime Minister wore a traditional turban and had a beard. We would eat on the floor on dastarkhwan (special sheets) spread for the lunch.

Sundays after 2 p.m. was the time for the special meeting for applications and grievances. People wrote their grievances on official applications beforehand and presented the applications and grievances to the department at the Prime Ministry.

One advisor in the beginning, Khair Mohammad Khan Kandahari, and later Ghulam Qadir, famous as colonel of road communications, and one director named Mir Abdullah and a clerk by the name of Niaz Mohammad, would read these applications to the Prime Minister in the presence of the people at the palace gardens. Every application was read aloud, and the Prime Minister gave instructions.

Every application cost ten afghanis. Here, too, the clerk was trusted because he was connected to Criminal Investigation. The instructions were like a lottery, and depended on the luck of the applicant. Some decisions were justifiable; others had no justification. Most grievances were turned back to the source.

Wednesdays after 3 p.m., the Prime Minister would go to Dehmazang Prison, which housed about 2,000 detainees. All of them were shackled, some, in chains. Apparently, the Prime Minister would go to see the welfare of the prisoners and teach them vocations like kleem weaving and stone cutting and carpentry, but there was no program for educating them or raising their morals.

The adversaries of the Prime Minister had rumored that the Prime Minister got a kick out of hearing the noise of the shackles and chains. At Dehmazang, political and nonpolitical prisoners were housed together. Most were from Kohdaman and Kohistan and progressive people of Kabul. The prison was built from a blueprint prepared by the Prime Minister. While Mohammad Nadir Shah was alive, the Prime Ministry was under the jurisdiction of the king.

Improvements

Some important steps and measures were taken during the rule of Nadir Shah. The government created the House of Representatives and wrote a constitution that was an improved version of Amanullah's constitution. The government improved the Shikari Valley (Darrai-Shikari) Road from Mazar to Kabul, and named the Darul Aman palace Darul-Funoon (House of Arts – Liberal Art). The medical school and later, the medical college, were established with the help of Turks. The Amani and Amania schools were named Isteqal and Nejat. In the renovation of Shikari road, for the first time my family and tribal influence was used. I was against this and hated the feudalism of Khans. I was asked to go to Kohdaman and Kohistan and bring 1,000 young men who could help the Shikari road crew. In the past this was done from the time of Amir Abdur Rahman to Amanullah by the Mazare tribe, and they were called sappermen. This was forced labor. The government thought that maybe the people of Kohdaman and Kohistan, too, would think it a punishment. I went to Kohistan and invited the people at Qalai Sidqabad, Sayed Khel, and Gulbahar mosque and spoke to them about the benefits of the road and its usefulness. I gave them the greetings of Nadir Shah and told the people that for the sake of the mosque of my father, they should improve the road. Still some of the elderly who had escaped death and imprisonment knew me and understood that if they did not agree they would be forced to do this. They accepted my pleas. Instead of 1,000 people, they agreed to give 500 men. Mohammad Rafiq Khan of Kohistan (my mother's uncle) was selected as a colonel and was given 500 men against a good salary and food. People started working, and Shikari road was built.

The reason the government remembered me for this job

was that Sardar Mohammad Aziz Khan, the elder brother of Mohammad Nadir Khan and father of Mohammad Daoud, was Ambassador of Afghanistan in Moscow. In 1351 AH (1932 AD) Abdul Majid Zabuli was to return to Kabul. The road from Kabul was only good to Bamiyan and from Mazar it was up to Aibak. I went to Bamiyan with Mohammad Hashim Khan, and on our return, he was the guest of the people one night in Charekar and one night in Istalef. In both these feasts, when the people saw me near Mohammad Hashim Khan, they thanked the government, prayed for my welfare and remembered my father. This was the reason the government selected me to go to the people when they needed men to build the road.

In 1352 AH (1933 AD), the government decided to build a regular army and draft the young men from Kohdaman, too. Nadir Shah ordered me to be responsible for the Kohdaman and Kohistan conscription. This was a great responsibility put on my shoulders. The plan was that the hakims (district magistrates) would record the names of people in logs and send them to me, and I would select up to 5,000 men varying in age from 22 to 30 years. In spite of the feeling of revenge that the people of Kohistan had for what they had seen during the attacks on Kohdaman, the people agreed to give up their young men for draft.

Conscription

Until the end of Amani period young men were drafted on a voluntary basis. After that, a law was promulgated that one out of every seven young men would be needed for military. Before the soldiers were selected, the government would inform the villages and cities of its need. For example, if the government needed 60,000 men, one out of every eight 27-year-olds was selected, based on their age. If the number needed was not met, then the rest were taken from a higher age group. This was called the "Group of Eight." Sometimes a group of soldiers was selected as career soldiers.

Toward the end of the Amani period, the practice became to select people on the basis of a raffle. I was appointed to select people on the basis of a raffle from

Tagab to Bamiyan, including Kohdaman and Kohistan. The raffle worked in this fashion: The hakim of each place would log in the names of the eligible men and send them to me. I was supposed to select the draftees. To avoid nepotism, the column of names was hidden under a piece of paper, and I would select people according to their age.

I would advise the soldiers selected to be true to their motherland. Because the budget did not provide sufficient funds for photographing each draftee, the clerks were asked to describe the features of each soldier, such as height, eye color, nose, and any marks on the skin of the body.

After the completion of this assignment the Prime Minister thanked me.

First Meeting with Nadir Shah

I had seen Nadir Shah a few times during my father's time, but that was in my childhood. At the time of his rule the enemies used to scare me from him. At the beginning, when I was appointed to the Prime Ministry (1931), Nadir Shah invited me to the Dilkusha. At that time Ahmed Shah Khan, his cousin, was Minister of Court; however, his deputy did the work. Nawroz Logari was Chief Secretary. At about 11 a.m. at the Dilkusha, Haider Khan, the deputy of the Ministry of Court, took me to the king. Nadir Shah was on the second floor in the small room on the west side of the Arg. He intimidated me because the orders for execution, exile, and imprisonment of hundreds of people came out from this small room.

As I have said earlier, at the opening of the Dilkusha Palace, when I was four years old, I had seen Amir Habibullah Khan in this same room. Now, Nadir Shah sat behind a big desk in the darker side of the room. Sayed Sharif Khan, his aide-de-camp, took me by the hand. He was a highly educated person from the Sayeds of Kunar; he was well built, handsome, and impressive. The military uniform looked beautiful on him. I offered my regards to him. Nadir Shah waved the aide to go out, and I kissed the king's hand. All my opposition to him in Mazar came before my eyes; his smile gave me relief.

He asked me to sit. He inquired about Herat and Naib

Salar and said, "Amanullah made a big mistake to forget the services of your father and execute him without any reason. I have read your writing and poetry in the publications from Herat. I wanted you to be in my court, but the Prime Minister, my brother, took you, him being a friend of your uncle." He smiled and said, "May you be in God's protection."

He called in Nawroz Khan and ordered him to proclaim the firman for the forgiveness of my brothers. He did not give me time to say anything about my uncle and cousins. He said, "The case of Mirza Mohammad Khan and his sons is being investigated."

To change the subject, he showed me the first volume of the history of Herat. He admonished me not to forget the literary works. That was the end of the meeting. I was still at the stairs of the Dilkusha when the sound of the feet of Sar Yavar, his head of security, stopped me. He said, "The king has ordered that you dine with him at lunch."

I was escorted to the waiting room. The employees of the court who paid no attention when I first came in, now gathered around me. They congratulated me that the king had pardoned me.

Lunch was announced in the dining room on the same floor where Nadir Shah's office was located. I was standing in line with Sardar Assadullah Khan, nephew of the king and Chief of the Guard and two deputies of the Ministry of Court: Saleh Mohammad Khan, former Commander-in-chief who was now advisor, and Haji Nawab Khan Logari, and another advisor, and Mohammad Sarwar Khan from Argandeh. The king entered, sat down on his chair, and waved us to sit. The Imam of the Masjid of the Arg and eight soldiers from the king's guard also sat at the table. Every day soldiers were brought in turn to eat with the king. During lunch, the king talked mostly about Herat, its relics and the feasts my father had given to Amir Habibullah Khan Seraj in Hussein Kot, Kohistan, and Kabul. He talked graciously and politely.

After lunch, Sardar Assadullah Khan sent with me one of the army officers to go to the prison and bring back my brothers. The new prison had yet to be built. This old prison was located near the western wall of the Arg where not even a ray of sunlight could penetrate.

The prison commandant in charge had been informed of my arrival. The prisoners that were from Kohdaman and Kohistan were expecting a new guest. They thought I would be imprisoned. Most of them were my relatives and friends. Some of them were in shackles and some in chains. Hunger, exhaustion, misfortune, and pain all could be seen on their faces. The elderly prisoners, when they saw me, started crying. It was very difficult for me to take my brother from among these people and leave, especially my aging uncle and his sons.

The jailer announced no one was allowed to talk, and all prisoners were directed to go to their rooms. I could not even pay my regards to my uncle.

My brother was in chains. We had to wait until the blacksmith came from the bazaar. It took about two hours for him to arrive and breaking the shackles was as difficult as putting them on. The feet of the prisoner were stretched across a big stone and a heavy hammer or claw was used to break the shackles off. When the blacksmith raised the axe to cut the iron, it was scary, because a little mistake could cut the leg. Finally, the shackles were off, and I brought my brother home to his wife and sister. The bitterness of seeing my relatives and friends in prison and leaving them, and seeing how my uncle's wife was waiting for her husband still, had taken away the happiness of bringing my brother home.

Independence Celebration

During the Amani times Independence Day was celebrated on 27 Assad (July) every year for eight days in Paghman. During Nadiri time, the date of Jashen (fair) was changed to end of Sumbula (September) and moved from Paghman to Chaman-Huzuri (downtown Kabul). The city was decorated with lights and different exhibitions and sports like wrestling, horseracing, and pegging were held. Nadir Shah would open Jashen with an address near the Minar of Isteqlal (Minaret of Freedom) on the eastern side of the Arg.

The foreign ambassadors, the cabinet, representatives, senators, members of the Jamiatul Ulema (council of scholars), and other civil servants gathered around the Minar of Isteqlal and heard the address. A military parade was held on the first day in Chaman. Nadir Shah would ride on horseback and accept the guard of honor. Whoever entered Chaman after the parade purchased a ticket for one afghani.

Hundreds of people who loved independence and freedom, came from the countryside to participate. Exhibitions were brought in from as far as India through Rustam Ji, a Parsi (sponsor) from Bombay. In all the provinces and governorates, the governors celebrated Jashen.

During the second year of my work at the Prime Ministry I was asked to coordinate Jashen affairs. Because I loved to take part in the work for the freedom of the country, I accepted the job. A brigadier from the Ministry of Defense and a director from every ministry were assigned to me. Every year for 10 years I would be in Chaman looking after the affairs of Jashen. During the first year I stayed in a camp and later in an apartment on top of the shops. Some of the best days of my life were spent here. The people's fervor for independence and their satisfaction at being free was evident from the colorful lights under the lapis blue skies.

Jashen was a playground and a place of competition for wrestlers, lancers, horsemen, and craftsmen. It was also a showplace for musicians, who were hired to play music for the people every night. Ustad Qasim (1878-1957) was the leader of all the musicians at that time. He would recite poems for two hours nightly in praise of the freedom and bravery of the nation of Afghanistan.

With the sound of the call of prayer from Eid Gah (Congregation Mosque), the lights were turned off and the music stopped. The call of prayer engulfed the whole city. The dawn and the sunrise appeared from the eastern mountains of Kabul. The people thought that the land and the sky were saying congratulations to the free people of Afghanistan. On the last day of Jashen, the king would honor the most senior general of the military of Afghanistan and give presents to him in public. The presents included a replica of the Minar of Isteqlal, a cannon and a metal mehrab and member (Islamic arch and pulpit). On the day of the military parade, what excited the people most were two cannons made in Kabul that had taken part in the War of Freedom.

After work, I would sit with my literary friends all night: Abdul Haq Betab, Shaiq Kabuli, Ustad Hashim Shaiqi-Afandi, and Herati Shereen Sukhan were usually part of it. Ustad Qasim and Ustad Ghulam Hussain, father of Ustad Sarahang (famous classical singer), sometimes came and joined us.

In 1932, a rumor reached the government that Herat considered itself independent of Kabul. Nadir Shah said, "If we invite Abdul Rahim Khan for Jashen, he will definitely come because he is a true soldier." I was asked to send a ciphered telegram to Abdul Rahim Khan, inviting him to attend Jashen on behalf of Nadir Shah. I was afraid that if he came and was subjected to an unfortunate fate, the family would accuse me. After two days of telegrams, Naib Salar telephoned that he was leaving for Kabul the next day. Unfortunately, there were only two days left in Jashen. The roads were unpaved, and there was no air transport. As soon as I informed Hashim Khan, he informed Nadir Shah and assigned the Ministry of the Interior to house Abdul Rahim Khan providing all comfort. On the second day of Jashen, Abdul Rahim Khan reached Qalai Qazi where his friend, the Minister of Court, Ahmed Shah Khan, received him. Abdul Rahim Khan arrived at the Prime Ministry by evening prayers. A military unit welcomed him and the Prime Minister himself came to the ministry gates. Abdul Rahim Khan took part in Jashen and was permitted to visit Kohdaman and Kohistan and talk to the people. On the last day of Jashen, Nadir Shah ordered the Present of Freedom be given on his behalf by Abdul Rahim Khan to the most senior general of the military. The ceremony was to take place in the stadium at the eastern side of Chaman. Ironically, this year the present was to be given to Mohammad Ghauz Khan, Naib Salar. As thousands of people watched, Abdul Rahim Khan presented Mohammad Ghauz Khan with the honor. They were remembering how Mohammad Ghauz Khan had once experienced defeat at the hands of Abdul Rahim Khan (insurrection). Abdul Rahim Khan left for Herat after a month against the wishes of his enemies.

Next year, in 1933, an incident took place involving Ghulam Nabi Khan Charkhi, the son of Ghulam Haider Khan Charkhi, who at the time of Amir Abdul Rahman Khan (who ruled 1880-1901) conquered Nooristan and was given the title of Naib Salar. Charkh is 50 kilometers from Kabul in the province of Logar. In Ghulam Haider Khan Charkhi's family, Ghulam Nabi was the eldest son; Ghulam Jailani was the second son; Abdul Aziz, the third son and Ghulam Siddique was the fourth son. Ghulam Nabi Khan Charkhi was brigadier at the time of Amir Habibullah Khan Seraj and at the time of Amani was a General in Mazar and later Afghan ambassador in Moscow and Paris. Ghulam Jailani was Amanullah's ambassador in Turkey, Abdul Aziz was governor of Mazar and Ghulam Siddique was the last foreign minister of Amanullah. Ghulam Nabi Khan Charkhi was famous for bravery and chivalry. He was considered to be an intellectual and a writer. He was of short build, with a large stomach, small eyes, and the wheat-colored complexion that resembled the Uzbek people of Afghanistan. People liked him. The youth always praised him for his chivalry and generosity. During the early days of Nadir Shah, Ghulam Jailani came to Kabul, while Ghulam Nabi Khan Charkhi and Ghulam Siddique stayed in Europe. Nadir Shah wanted Ghulam Nabi's daughter for his nephew Mohammad Daoud Khan; however, Ghulam Jailani did not accept it.

In 1933, Shah Wali Khan, brother of Nadir Shah, who was the Afghan ambassador in Paris, came to Kabul. Surprisingly enough, Ghulam Nabi Khan Charkhi was with him. Government employees and military officers who lined up as far as the eastern gates of the Arg welcomed Shah Wali Khan. While Shah Wali Khan passed through the lines of the people and youth, they paid their respects most earnestly to Ghulam Nabi Khan Charkhi. It was the first time I had seen him there. I was standing in the line of departmental heads. As soon as he recognized me, he took me in his arms and smilingly said, "Wouldn't you stop me coming here?"

I respectfully answered, "You are the national leader of your country. The past is past."

Shah Wali Khan and Ghulam Nabi Khan Charkhi went to see Nadir Shah the same day. During lunch, Nadir Shah said, "Ghulam Nabi, what is the matter? Your hairs have not turned gray. Do you dye them?"

Ghulam Nabi Khan Charkhi replied, "I don't play with colors like others."

Ghulam Nabi Khan Charkhi went to stay at his home. He lived near Masjid Shah-e-do-shamshera (King of Two Swords). Every day hundreds of young men and tribal leaders came to see him. He gave them gifts and invited them to join him in dinner. However, people of Kohdaman and Kohistan had not forgotten the bloodshed of their kin during the attack of Mazar by Soviets accompanied by Ghulam Nabi Khan Charkhi.

In the family of Ghulam Nabi Khan Charkhi were two generals who had helped Nadir Shah a great deal in his battles against Amir Habibullah Khan Kalakani. One of them was Jan Baz, and the other was Sher Mohammad Khan. Two or three months passed. People observed that in the evening, Nadir Shah, accompanied by the two generals and Ghulam Nabi Khan Charkhi, always went for leisure driving. His enemies exploited the information and reported every move of Ghulam Nabi Khan Charkhi to the government.

I had gone to Kohistan for a long hunting weekend on Aqrab (October) 14, 1933, and I stayed at the Sidqabad Fort. Unexpectedly, I received a message from Lieutenant Governor Abdul Razaq Khan that I should proceed immediately to Charekar. I reached Charekar at night on horseback. There, Lieutenant Governor (Hakim Alaa) said, "Today, Aqrab 16 at 4 p.m., Ghulam Nabi Khan Charkhi was executed on the orders of the King Nadir Shah in the gardens of Dilkusha Palace. The Prime Minister has ordered that you return to Kabul immediately."

I hurried back to Kabul. Along the way, I saw security forces on the main roads. Martial law had been proclaimed.

The next day I went to the Arg, and Mohammad Hashim Khan told me to inform Herat of the execution of Ghulam Nabi Khan Charkhi.

Murder of Ghulam Nabi Khan Charkhi

On Wednesday, Ghulam Nabi Khan Charkhi was sitting in the sun waiting for a court vehicle to arrive to take him to the palace, when a military lorry with Sayed Sharif, Chief Aide, showed up instead. Ghulam Nabi Khan Charkhi went inside on the pretext of changing his dress. He told his brother Ghulam Jailani, "I should kill Sayed Sharif here and leave for Logar on this military lorry. If I reach Logar alive, I can save myself from the government. If I die on my way, it is better for me. I know Nadir Shah, he is bringing me there to murder me." However, his brother prevailed upon him to change his mind.

So instead, Ghulam Nabi Khan Charkhi put on his French dress and left for the Dilkusha Palace with his brother and Sayed Sharif. Near the southern stairs of the Dilkusha, Ghulam Nabi Khan Charkhi and his brother got off the lorry and were held there. General Jan Baz and Sher Mohammad Khan came out, and then, after about half an hour, Nadir Shah came out of the palace. He was accompanied by Ameenullah Khan Jabbar Khel, deputy to Ministry of Justice and a powerful tribal leader, Zulfiqar Khan, advisor to the Prime Ministry, and Mohammad Nauroz, Chief Secretary. Nadir Shah stood on the stairs and told Ghulam Nabi Khan Charkhi, "What has the government done to you, that you incite people every day?"

Ghulam Nabi Khan Charkhi answered, "May God forbid! It's not true!"

He wanted to continue to speak in his defense, but Nadir Shah ordered the soldiers to beat him. The soldiers beat him so severely with the butts of their guns that he died on the spot. Nadir Shah then ordered Ghulam Jailani, the two generals, and all of his family to be thrown in jail and his property confiscated. He gave orders for Ghulum Nabi Khan Charkhi to be buried in his garden. Incidently, a very big thunderstorm hit that same evening, and Nadir Shah could not go for his leisure driving. The people said this was a sign of the innocence of Ghulam Nabi Khan Charkhi.

One week had not passed before Mohammad Hashim Khan ordered me to go to see Nadir Shan with the Khans of Kohdaman and Kohistan, Panjsher, Tagab, and Najrab. Only a few Khans were left from Kohdaman and Kohistan. The rest were either in jail or executed. From among these few people left were Sayed Ahmed, grandson of Mir Bacha Khan; Malik Ghulam Nabi Khan from Istalif; Malik Mohammad Tahsildar and Mohammad Ibrahim Khan from Qarabagh; and my cousins from Kohistan: the sons of Abdul Wahab Khan from Kohistan and Abdul Satar Khan, son of Abdul Ghiaz Khan Bajar, my maternal uncle. I did not want to be called Khan or to be known as Safi. One reason was because my father was killed, and the other reason was that whenever someone was famous by tribe or Khan they were always subdued. The Kings of Afghanistan never liked anybody to be popular except themselves or their families.

So I went to the second floor of the Gulkhana with these people as Mohammad Hashim Khan ordered. It was evening and all of us stood in line on the order of Haider Khan, the Deputy of the Court. I was trying to stay behind, but the people pushed me in front. Nadir Shah, wearing a grey dress and displaying his full regal power, entered from the western door. He shook hands with me and smiled as he asked the others how they were.

In spite of the fact he knew most of the people present, he ordered me to introduce each one of them. I followed the orders. He expressed warmth to some. He asked me to seat each one of them where I felt they should sit. He was standing until all were seated. Then Nadir Shah addressed us for about 20 minutes. He spoke some sentences softly and others harshly. He mentioned the vital role of the people from the north in fighting the foreign enemy and praised them for their bravery, faith, and piety. For reasons best known to him, he wanted to convince people that the revolution of Habibullah Khan Kalakani was the fault of

Amanullah and his government. He did not insult Habibullah by calling him "Bache Saqqa" (the son of a watercarrier). Instead, he recalled my father and his friendship and closeness to Amir Habibullah Khan Seraj and said Amanullah made a mistake in killing Mustufi-ul-Momalik.

Then, he justified the murder. He said, "Ghulam Nabi Khan Charkhi wanted to create dissension among people. He thought I would remain uninformed like Amanullah. He did not know I am Mohammad Nadir Shah." He also reminded us Ghulam Nabi Khan Charkhi had, on the pretext of friendship with Amanullah, brought Soviet soldiers to Mazar, where they killed thousands of Moslems.

"If your people and the people of Mazar had not risen to the occasion, the Soviet soldiers would have come to Kabul and Afghanistan would have become another Bokhara," Nadir Shah said. "I punished Ghulam Nabi Khan Charkhi in the national interest of Afghanistan. To me, a person or class of people who work against the government is not pardonable."

The people who had seen the killings and disaster in Kohdaman and Kohistan prayed for the well being of the present king.

Nadir Shah responded, "I want you to have the same respect and honor in my court as you had during the time of Amir Habibullah Seraj."

Malik Ghulam Nabi Khan innocently said, "Whatever favors the king does to the son of Mustofi Malik, is done to us."

Everybody said, "Our representative is Khalilullah."

I spoke a few words, weighing them carefully before uttering. I was afraid Nadir Shah would think I had asked the people to select me as their representative. I did not want him to think I am interested in Khanism. I did not want to say anything that would offend him or Mohammad Hashim Khan.

Nadir Shah told me to select two people for the senate and four young men for the army. These four men would start as army colonels. The poor people who did not expect this treatment prayed for the health and long life of the

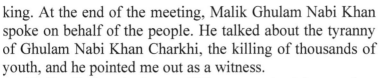

king. At the end of the meeting, Malik Ghulam Nabi Khan spoke on behalf of the people. He talked about the tyranny of Ghulam Nabi Khan Charkhi, the killing of thousands of youth, and he pointed me out as a witness.

Nadir Shah asked me, "Were you in Mazar when Ghulam Nabi Khan Charkhi came?"

I replied, "Yes, from the beginning until the end."

He responded, "Now I remember. You should compile all this in the form of a booklet. Bring it to me, and I will order it be published."

We left the court without being invited for tea or refreshments. I went to the Prime Ministry and reported everything to Mohammad Hashim Khan. He did not give me a chance to select anyone as requested by the king. He said, "I would advise that Malik Ghulam Nabi Khan from Istalif and Abdul Sattar, son of Abdul Wahab, be appointed to the senate. Who could say no to it?"

I thanked God I was saved from selecting the men.

Sardar Mohammad Aziz Khan

Sardar Mohammad Aziz Khan was the elder brother of Nadir Shah. He was very weak and timid, and was the real brother of Hashim Khan and Mohammad Ali. Their mother was from the family of Nawab Mohammad Aziz Khan, brother of Amir Dost Mohammad Khan (1793-1863). He was appointed the governor of Kashmir in place of Sardar Atta Mohammad Khan during the time of Amir Dost Mohammad. Because he had mental problems the people of Kashmir had written to the Amir this poem:

You have taken Atta Mohammad Khan from us
And have forced upon us a great monster.

The people said Mohammad Hashim Khan and Mohammad Daoud Khan inherited this mental flaw.

Mohammad Nadir Shah, Shah Wali Khan, and Shah Mahmud Khan were from one mother. Their mother's ancestor was Ahmad Shah Durrani (1722-1772) first of the Saddozai rulers of Afghanistan and founder of the Durrani Empire).

Mohammad Aziz Khan during the time of Amir Habibullah Khan Seraj worked as Chief of Protocol for the Ministry of Foreign Affairs. During the Amani period, he was Guardian of the Afghan students in Paris.

As soon as Nadir Shah became king, Mohammad Aziz Khan was summoned to Kabul to begin work as Naibul Sultana (representative of the crown) for Mazar, Takharistan, Badakstan, and Maimana. Mohammad Aziz did not see himself capable and turned down the offer. He was then appointed to the Afghan Embassy in Moscow. He was very mild mannered, sensitive, and anxious. He never shook hands with anybody for fear of catching someone else's germs. Even when he kissed his own children, he would put his palm on their cheek and kiss the back of his own hand. He was ridiculously superstitious. On Tuesdays, he never left his house and on Wednesdays, he never spent money. His best side was that he enjoyed both dressing well and eating fine food. His contact with foreigners was documented in detail 80 years ago by A.C. Jewett (an American and Chief Engineer during the time of Amir Habibullah Seraj). Jewett, a former hydroelectric engineer for General Electric, remained in Afghanistan for eight years, 1911-1919).

Sardar Aziz Khan went to the court of the representatives of the proletariat in Moscow with these qualities. Mohammad Hashim Khan appointed Ghulam Jailani Khan, one of his acquaintances as counsellor to Abdul Aziz Khan in Moscow. Ghulam Jailani Khan was a graduate of Habibiya High School. He was a fellow classmate of Sardar Ali Mohammad Khan and Faiz Mohammad Khan (foreign ministers) and was from Kabul. Ghulam Jailani Khan was a patriot and nationalist, but unfortunately he could not stay in Moscow because of the delicate sensitivities of the ambassador. The servants of the embassy planted the seed of hatred between the ambassador and the counsellor. Ghulam Jailani Khan, seeing that every day the ambassador's behavior was getting worst, left the job and went to Hitler's Germany. At that time Ghulam Siddique Khan, brother of Ghulam Nabi Khan Charkhi was also in Germany. Mohammad Aziz Khan wanted to live a

European life and had himself transferred to Berlin.

In Berlin, there were a lot of Afghan students who came to the embassy for their business. A young man by the name of Sayed Kamal from Kabul went to the embassy several times; he had no money, and hoped to get some from the embassy, but was disappointed because the ambassador did not meet with him. Ghulam Siddique Khan, who was well-to-do, helped Sayed Kamal and may have incited him. I have been told Kamal acquired a gun through Ghulam Jailani Khan and Ghulam Siddique Khan. One day, he came to the embassy and insisted on an appointment with the ambassador. Sayed Kamal had seen that the ambassador met with people who were from well-to-do families, but not people like him. He refused to leave the embassy. The ambassador cursed him and asked the guards to throw him out. This son of a shopkeeper who was considered to be related to Prophet Mohammad (PBUH) pulled out the gun and fired three shots at point blank range, killing Sardar Mohammad Aziz Khan, the ambassador of Afghanistan, brother of the king. Mohammad Aziz Khan was rushed to the hospital but died before reaching there. One of the bullets hit Sardar Mohammad Attiq in his arm by mistake, slightly injuring him.

Fate played three roles. One, Mohammad Aziz Khan became famous in the family as Agha Jan Shaheed (martyr). Two, Sayed Kamal turned himself in and Hitler's government, against all laws, executed him. Third, the sister of Malika (Queen) Humairah, daughter of Ahmad Shah Khan, was married to Sardar Mohammad Attiq Khan because he was injured in the attack on Mohammad Aziz Khan.

Funeral of Mohammad Aziz Khan

The body of Mohammad Aziz Khan came to Kabul via Iran and Herat. In Kandahar, Ghazni and Kabul it was welcomed by people and government officials. Abdul Rahim Khan sent a few ulamas of Herat, along with his son, Abdul Aleem, to accompany them to Kabul. The Prime Minister, the cabinet and members of the family were standing near Baghe Bala Palace (south of Kabul on a hill) which now leads to the intercontinental hotel. Hazrat Nourul Mashaeq was leading the mourners. The people of the city had lined the two sides of the road up to Tape Maranjan (hill where dignitaries are buried). The body was transferred from a black lorry to a four-horse driven carriage. Sardar Faiz Mohammad Khan, the foreign minister sat near the carriage driver. The Prime Minister went forward and bowed in respect. Daoud, who was a young military student at the time, cried out loudly, "Oh father, I will revenge your blood."

Nourul Mashaeq held the Prime Minister by the shoulder and did not let him fall down. The prayers for the dead were said at the Eid Gah (traditionally, every city in Muslim countries have a place for annual Eid prayers). Nadir Shah and members of the family did not see the casket. For three days, Nadir Shah held mourning out of the eastern gates of the Arg called Salamkana (greeting room). People came all around the suburbs. The king repeated this sentence, "May God bless the Afghan nation. If Mohammad Aziz has died, it was fate." All over Afghanistan condolence meetings were held. This was the first funeral during the Nadir rule from his family. Sardar Mohammad Khan Telai (1795-1861), the great grandfather of this family, had been buried there earlier.

The blood of Mohammad Aziz Khan renewed the enmity between the families of Amanullah Khan and Ghulam Nabi Charkhi and Nadir Shah. People used to say that Ghulam Siddique, Minister of Foreign Affairs of Amanullah and Shujadullah, Minister of Security had a hand in the killing, at the instigation of Amanullah. Hundreds of people were thrown in jail in Kabul on the crime of being related or being close to the family of Ghulam Nabi Charkhi.

Forgiveness of the King

In the spring of 1933 the hunting season arrived and I, as usual, went to Kohistan and Qalai Buland for bird hunting (kulong - pheasant).

One day while returning through the market of Qalai

Murad Beg, Nadir Shah's car broke down on the way back to Kabul. The people had formed a circle around him. It was an interesting sight. An old woman had put a clay pot on her head full of fire and was standing in the middle of the road and crying. I gave my birds to a friend and got down from the bus and went to the car of Nadir Shah. He was riding in a black Buick. The red crown's flag with the mehrab and member (arch and pulpit) was flying on the front side of the car.

After inquiring I found the king had come for a leisure drive to Hussain Kot and the car gotten stuck here in mud. It was afternoon prayer time. The king accepted my regards. Two aides of the king were trying to move the woman from near the car, but she was pleading in a loud voice, "On your order they killed my two sons! Whatever I had they confiscated! No one gives me a place to live because they are afraid of you!"

The aides were trying to stop her, but the woman kept wailing. Nadir Shah asked me to take the woman away from the car. I asked the woman, who was she? She said, "I am the wife of Mohammad Karim Khan Qalai Murad Begi, my husband is in jail." I recognized her, that he was the administrator of the area at the time of Habibullah Khan Kalakani and had defeated Amanullah. Her two sons, who were military school graduates, were killed. The woman kept on ranting, "For God's sake, help me!"

As soon as she recognized me, she calmed down. I took the pot of fire from her head and put it down.

In Afghanistan it is part of the culture that if you have no way to get justice then they take a pot of fire in their hands or hold it above their heads. I held her by the hand and brought her to the king and introduced her. Nadir Shah gave me a few gold coins to give to her, but that brave woman did not accept it. She said, "Give me my house where I could live or kill me." She spread her spotted veil and said, "When they tied my sons to the cannon and fired I collected the bits of flesh which flew around in this veil and these are spots of their blood."

Nadir Shah said, "Give your application to this man, and I will ask the Prime Minister to give back your house."

The woman said, "For God's sake, do not leave it to the Prime Minister. He is not even afraid of God, and he does not care." The king promised he would, himself, take care of this.

I put the gold coins in the veil of that woman. Nadir Shah ordered I should accompany the king in his car. The car was a limousine and had two seats behind and one in front. Saleh Mohammad Khan Sepah Salar, Commander-in-chief of Amanullah, Haji Nawab Khan Logari, Mohammad Nauroz Khan, Sar Munshi, Chief Secretary, were with the king. The king told me, "If your father would have been alive, he would have been my Prime Minister."

He asked me, "Is the revenue from your land sufficient for you?" I kept quiet. He asked again.

I said, "We have nothing which belonged to my father."

He said, "They don't give you the rent from the Russian Embassy?"

I said, "They give me nothing."

He ordered his Chief Secretary to write a firman as soon as we reached Kabul. Because my financial condition was very weak, I prayed earnestly. I thought to myself, "Maybe I can have some good times with the return of the land."

Saleh Mohammad Khan and Nawab Khan, and Nauroz Khan, who were friends of my father, prayed and thanked him. Saleh Mohammad Khan said, "Your Highness, do you remember the day at Sarajol Imarat Gardens in Jalalabad and Mustufi-ul-Momalik? It's good you kept your promise."

The king did not want to talk on this topic, but Haji Nawab Khan asked Haji Mohammad Khan about the story. I, too, who had not heard the story, became interested.

Sepah Salar, the Commander-in-chief, said, "One day in Jalalabad in the Sarajol Imarat Gardens we were sitting and waiting for Amir Habibullah Khan, Sardar Mohammad Yousuf Khan, father of Nadir Shah and Mohammad Asif, uncle of Nadir Shah. Nadir Shah, Sardar Wali Khan, and Sardar Mahmud all were together. At this time Mustufi came, father of the king gave him a seat next to him. During the discourse the story of carelessness of the Amir and firing of a pistol shot in Sher Bazar came up. Mustufi said, 'If, God forbidding, Amir is not there, I would not be there, too. My sons are young. They will grow in bad company.' Sardar Mohammad Yousuf Khan said, 'May God not bring that day. If this happens, my sons will not forget your friendship. And Nadir Shah put his hand on the sword and said, "The will of my father will always remain in my ears."

At the same time, I reminded the king of Mohammad Islam Khan Mahan and his brothers, my cousins, who were in jail. Nadir Shah said they should be released today. We reached the Arg after evening prayers and rushed home so my birds that I had hunted could be shared with my friends.

My friends who heard about this came home. I promised to some of them land, house, and work even before the firman was written. Rumors prevailed in Kabul and Kohistan, and the people thanked God. I was waiting every day for the king's firman. One day after noon prayers I received a firman. My heart throbbed with happiness. I was thrilled. I opened the packet and read. I was so upset and angered. Instead of my land, gardens, and houses, I was given 13 jeribs of land (six and one-half acres) with a house.

I thought it was a misunderstanding. I called the Chief Secretary who said the king instructed this. I was young and had a short temper. I picked up the pen and wrote to the Chief Secretary that I have not rendered any service that would have called for 13 jeribs of land. Nadir Shah, in spite of being a king, has not kept his promise. I will, too, not keep this land. I returned the firman along with my letter right away. I paid no attention to the fact that this was a grave crime to return the king's firman.

The next day I went to my friend Faiz Mohammad Khan, the Minister of Foreign Affairs. I would go to him on every occasion, good or bad. He smiled at me and said, "You made a mistake, why didn't you seek my advice before you did this?" I realized he knew about the episode. He said, "It is not the fault of the king. He talked to his brother, Mohammad Hashim Khan." I asked what would happen to me now. He said, "God is with you and the king does not consider you guilty."

Mohammad Hashim Khan did not ask me to come to his office for anything. After a week he called me in. He was angry. Whenever he got mad, his nostrils flared, his face turned red, and his eyes looked scary. He would speak Persian in an Indian accent and often recited an Indian proverb.

Surprisingly, he said, "If I had not intervened on your behalf with the king, he would have severely punished you." Then, out of great anger, he added, "If you have served a long time you will get 100 jeribs; if less, 50 jeribs. Instead, since you served a long time you will get 50 jeribs; if you had served less, you would have gotten 100 jeribs."

I replied, "May God keep you under his blessing. I will try to serve less and get 100 jeribs." He did not understand my sarcasm.

Assassination of Nadir Shah

Days passed and I could not go to Kohdaman, ashamed to face the people. I was young and did not realize the shame was not on me, it was, ironically, on him who broke his promise. Fall approached, and the work on the road to Darre Shikare (the hunting valley) came to an end. For the first time Kabul was being connected to the northern provinces via machinery. Nadir Shah considered this a feather in his cap. The government decided the Prime Minister should open the road and should also see closely the affairs of the northern provinces. These people accompanied the Prime Minister on his journey: Faiz Mohammad Khan Yaftali, Minister of Commerce (finance, roads, canals, agriculture, and minerals were also part of his job); Abdul Ahmed Khan Wardhak, speaker of the first Direct Council, a Director at the Prime Ministry and Secretary General of the delegation; Abdullah Malik Yakr, in charge of third Directorate of the Prime Ministry; and some detectives and members of the police force and also some clerks. Also, a unit of the court for hotels and other boarding facilities came along. It was probably the first week of October 1933 when we left for Mazar. On the way there was no hotel or a place to stay overnight. The Prime

Minister opened the Shikare road. We thanked the workers and engineers.

[NOTE: The record of the assassination of Mohammad Nadir Shah (April 9, 1883-November 8, 1933) by a student, Abdul Khaliq Hazara, during Nadir Shah's presentation at a high school graduation ceremony was lost during our moves from place to place in the United States. Khalili had described the experience and its effects in detail.]

Events after Nadir Shah's Assassination

The year 1352 AH (1933 AD) was a bloody and eventful. Every week, people were thrown in prison for their political leanings and activity. The opportunists and anti-nationals were having a heyday. Not only men were thrown in jails, but the custom of arresting women and putting them in prison had also started. The family of Ghulam Nabi Charkhi, who was under house arrest by the order of Nadir Shah, was also thrown in jail. Even children were not spared. Every month some prisoners were executed without a trial or defense. All this was vengeance against those thought to be involved in Nadir Shah's assassination.

Revival of Daily Newspapers

The press and media in Afghanistan were almost non-existent. There were two newspapers in Kabul at that time: *Islah* and *Anis*. *Islah* was established during the time of Nadir Shah, and its editor was Burhanuddin Kushkaki. Burhanuddin was from the village of Kishk in Nangarhar province and was educated in India. He had long standing connection with Nadir Shah. At the time when Nadir Shah was the head of Kataghan and Badakhshan Administration (Tanzimiyah) during the time of King Amanullah, Burhanuddin traveled with him on a journey to Pamir. He wrote and printed a book about that time, *Guide to Kataghan and Badakhshan*. It is a good book.

Burhanuddin published *Haqiqat*, a newspaper during the time of King Amanullah and Habibul Islam during the brief period of Habibullah Kalakani's rule. When Nadir

Khan became king, it was thought Burhanuddin Kushkaki would fall from grace; however, because of his past relationship with the king, he appointed him editor of *Islah*. Burhanuddin lived a respectful life until his death.

The other newspaper was called *Anis*. The editor had been Ghulam Mohiuddin Khan, whose father, Ghulan Naqsh, was exiled during the time of Amir Abdur Rahman Khan for reasons unknown. Mohiuddin Khan was born in Egypt to an Egyptian mother and his Afghan father. He was educated in Egypt and was progressive in his thought. Toward the end of Amanullah Khan's rule, he returned to Kabul and established *Anis* as the first national newspaper. He was a handsome man, soft spoken, who conversed in elegant Persian with a slight Arabic accent. He wrote objectively, sometimes critical of the government. Amanullah Khan did not say anything to him. *Anis* was taken away from Ghulam Mohiuddin Khan, and he was thrown in jail for being pro-Amanullah. Despite that, he authored a book about Nadir Khan, called *Deliverance of Kabul from Habibullah Khan of Kalakan.*

Anis was given to Mohammad Amin Khan of Khogyan. He was also from Nangarhar and was famously known as Khogyani. His father's name was Maulana Mohammad Israel. He had many followers and students. He was killed in a robbery attempt between Jalalabad and Khogyan.

Mohammad Amin Khan knew Arabic, Pashto, and Persian. There was a standing rivalry between *Anis* and *Islah*. Both papers published my articles, especially *Anis* because of Mohammad Amin Khan. His father was a friend of my father.

The press and media remained frozen after the death of Nadir Shah. Freedom of the press was nonexistent. The Literary Academy was left alone to function; however, some of its members were behind bars. One of the academy members jailed was poet Mohammad Anwar Bismil, son of Nazir Mohammad Safar Khan. He and his brother Mohammad Ibrahim Safa were being punished for being supporters of Amanullah Khan. *Anis* and *Islah* were revived during the time of Zahir Shah.

By this time I was becoming famous as a writer. I was

being asked to evaluate articles of other writers. I remember a poem by Mohammad Ibrahim Alamshahi was published in a newspaper. Mohammad Sarwar Goya was asked to critique the poem and published his critique in the paper. Alamshahi wrote a very sharp reply to Goya's criticism. It was a dialogue between friends. I was asked by Mohammad Naim Khan (brother of Mohammad Daoud Khan), advisor to the king, to evaluate the poem and the criticism on it. I wrote the truth in a literary magazine. For a while I lost both of my friends. Eventually, we made up and rekindled our friendship.

Sayed Ibrahim Alamshahi

The grandfather of Alamshahi took refuge in Mashhad, Iran during the time of Amir Abdur Rahman Khan's campaign against Hazaras. Alamshahi and his father were both born in Iran. He studied law and political science there and had a beautiful handwriting. He was also a poet, though his Persian prose was much better than his poetry. He was an intellectual writer and researcher who deeply believed in religion and patriotism. Alamshahi was a good friend of mine.

During the beginning of King Zahir Shah's reign, he contacted Abdur Rahim Khan, Deputy Commander-in-chief, expressing his desire to return to Afghanistan. He knew that the time had arrived when Hazaras were not considered slaves anymore, as they were perceived during the time of Amir Abdur Rahman Khan. Thanks to Amanullah Khan, they were free to pursue their lives. He could even get back his ancestral land, previously confiscated. With these desires and thoughts he came to Herat covertly. From there Abdur Rahim Khan sent him to me in Kabul. I took him to meet Sardar Hashim Khan. Eventually, he was appointed as a clerk at the Presidential Secretariat. He had his own law practice, opened law courses at his work, and had quite a few students. He also wrote books and stayed at the Secretariat for a long time.

After the communist coup in Kabul (1978), Alamshahi was taken from his home and thrown in jail like thousands of others. He may have died while incarcerated like other

innocent people whose only crime was that they were patriots.

His daughter, Danish, who is in the United States, had no information of his whereabouts. In the good old days, I spent many days and nights with my friend Alamshahi. He would travel with me to Istalef, Qarahbagh, Kohistan, Jalalabad, etc. I have always cherished memories of him.

Demarcation of Afghanistan's Western Border at Herat (1934)

In 1934, I was given an opportunity to go to Herat and serve my country. The situation was the demarcation of the borders of Afghanistan and Iran, which had been dormant since the time of Amir Abdul Rahman Khan. Amir Abdul Rahman Khan decided, based on agreements he had with the British, to demarcate Afghanistan's borders among his neighbors, those being: the Soviet Union and Afghanistan's closest Muslim neighbor, Iran. The British appointed a special delegation for this purpose. History is witness that this delegation went up to Panjdeh under the leadership of Captain Rejavi.

The delegation included a number of Indian soldiers, whose objective was to indicate our border to the Soviet Union; however, the Soviets did not agree, and British soldiers were forced to retreat.

The people of Afghanistan fought (March 1885) against the Soviets in a bloody battle in which Colonel Shah Murad Khan of Kabul fought to the death. To this day, the people of Herat remember his bravery. On the day the battle started, it was snowing heavily. The guns used by the Afghans were old, front-loading muskets requiring gunpowder. When gunpowder gets wet, the guns are useless. The young Colonel Shah Murad Khan led a Kandak (battalion) across the Murghab Bridge to face the Soviets. Fierce fighting ensued leaving hundreds of young Afghan men and boys dead. Even the women of Panjdeh took part in the fighting while the Soviets ruthlessly barraged the Afghan army with guns and heavy cannon.

The fighting lasted two to three days. Colonel Shah Murad chained the legs of his horse and threw the key into the Murghab River. People asked, "Why did you do that?"

He responded, "I do not want to flee the battle on horseback. I will stay here and fight to the death."

He commanded his soldiers from the Murghab Bridge. The Soviet soldiers were pursuing the Afghan soldiers. The Colonel pulled a revolver out of his belt, aimed at the officer leading the Soviet soldiers and shot him dead. The Soviets directed their fire at the Colonel, killing him. His body was laid down on the other side of Panjdeh with bodies of Soviet officers. The Soviets erected a minar with a chain wrapped around it to mark the spot where their soldiers fell. Colonel Shah Murad is also buried there.

The people of Herat have a saying associated with this legendary soldier: Dowr-i Shah Murad-i Divana... meaning, "around crazy Shah Murad they've put a chain to ensure he doesn't rise to avenge Afghanistan's loss of Panjdeh to the Soviets."

The situation at Panjdeh ended in disgrace. During this time, Amir Abdul Rahman was in Rawalpindi as the guest of Great Britain. The British delayed him there, but once the battle in Panjdeh was lost, the British allowed the Amir to return to Kabul. Unable to rouse an opposition, he quietly acquiesced to Panjdeh's fate.

It is said Sardar Mohammad Ayoub Khan Ghazi, "the Conqueror of Maiwand," (July 1880) who was under house arrest in Lahore, requested the British allow him to go to Afghanistan to fight the Soviets. "If I die in the war, that's okay, and if I come out alive, I will surrender myself to Amir Abdul Rahman so he can put me in chains and send me back to you," he implored. The British, however, did not agree to this.

Coming back to the case of Herat, the British had a General Counsel by the name of Col. Henry McMahon (1903-1905). The Demarcation of the border between Afghanistan and Iran was assigned to him. What a shame that, between two Muslim nations, the task of defining borders was assigned to a man from the English Isles. Amir Abdul Rahman Khan accepted this. McMahon started the demarcation by putting up pillars indicating the division. General Ghausuddin Khan-i-Logari, the military commander of Herat at that time, was appointed as the head of the Afghan delegation. The General went to the border to meet the Iranian delegation. McMahon came with the Iranians, and they met at Pillar 39.

To aggravate the situation between Afghanistan and Iran, McMahon altered the demarcation into Afghan territory and attempted to cede that territory to Iran. At this time, the General Logati was unsure what to do. On one hand, the Amir already conceded to McMahon's assertions, but on the other, should he stay silent, Afghanistan would lose sovereignty over the region. Logari devised a plan. Upon reaching Pillar 39, he dropped himself from his horse, breaking his ankle. He yelled in pain that he broke his leg. He was brought to Herat for treatment and thus the work stopped at Pillar 39. McMahon had no other choice but to return to Iran and wait until the head of the Afghan delegation recuperated. The work was suspended.

The work remained suspended until the time of Amir Habibullah Khan Seraj. There was tension between Afghanistan and Iran at that time. Iran claimed the demarcation proposed by McMahon was correct and Pillar 39 should be placed inside the borders of Afghanistan, thus ceding part of Afghan territory to Iran. According to the Afghans, this was an integral part of Afghanistan, and they would not accept this demarcation under any condition.

This stalemate continued until the time of King Nader Khan. During his reign, this tension again boiled to the top of the pot of Afghan-Iranian relations. Since both Amir Amanullah Khan and Amir Habibullah Khan endorsed all of the agreements of Amir Abdul Rahman Khan, Nadir Khan decided his only option was to seek the arbitration of Turkey.

Entry of Abdul Rahim Khan in the Demarcation of Herat's Borders

Abdul Rahim Khan was consulted (1934) regarding the negotiations about Herat's border and was asked to review the situation. He was referred to as Naib Salar, a highly decorated title in Afghanistan and was well versed in the border situation of Afghanistan. He knew every nook and cranny and understood well the psychology of the people of Herat. He was convinced the people of Herat would not accept Henry McMahon's proposal. He wrote, in his opinion, that it was impossible to impose McMahon's will on the Muslim people of Herat. If Turkish arbitration was sought; however, the people of Afghanistan may be more willing to accept that. His observation was based on the fact that the people of Afghanistan considered the Turkish people as their own Muslim brothers and would accept such arbitration in the name of Islam. I, too, had the same opinion.

While this news was communicated to Kabul two events happened. First, Nadir Khan was martyred. Second, Turkey appointed General Fakhruddin Altai, a prominent general in the Turkish army, to mediate and arbitrate between Afghanistan and Iran to settle the border dispute. Kamal Ataturk was still alive and in power in Turkey at the time. The Afghan government decided a delegation should travel to Herat to welcome the Iranian delegation, as well as review the border situation. Abdul Rahim Khan sent a letter to Kabul explaining that demarcation and arbitration could not take place unless and until the Afghan delegation made a proper assessment of the border region.

Sardar Muhammad Hashim Khan, the Prime Minister at the time and the late Nadir Shah's brother, was concerned regarding Abdul Rahim Khan's letter. He summoned me to his next cabinet meeting and shared his frustration because he felt Abdul Rahim Khan was delaying the resolution of the dispute between Afghanistan and Iran.

I said, "In my opinion, he's not wrong. He wants the situation to be transparent to everyone prior to the arbitration and to ensure it is based on sound facts. Our assigned delegation should have all the facts going into the negotiations."

The cabinet agreed with my point of view and issued a decree appointing the Afghan delegation and naming me as its General Secretary.

Section Two

Afghan Delegation for the Demarcation of Herat Border

The Afghan delegation included the late Mohammad Usman Khan Amir, Deputy Minister of Foreign Affairs; Sayed Abdullah Khan, Director of Political Affairs; Abdullah Rahman Khan Popal and Abdullah Kareem Khan, members of the ruling council from Mazar-i-Sharif, and Engineer Mir Hamad Khan, who earned his Engineering degree from Germany. The delegation also included Colonel Mahmud Abu Ahmad Khan Kheli, son of General Shoaib Hamad Khan Kheli, and me.

The Iranian delegation was headed by Mehdi Farrukh, one time Iranian ambassador to Afghanistan, and was comprised of a few other members, whose names I do not remember.

On the Turkish side, General Fakhruddin Altai headed the delegation. Kazim Baig, who at one time was a teacher in Afghanistan, was also a member. There was a military representative and two handsome assistants who were also part of the Turkish delegation.

I was ordered to take an automobile and get to Herat as soon as possible. I was to carry with me the firmans of Prime Minister Mohammad Hashim Khan. In these firmans, which I wrote, the Prime Minister advised the delegation to strive its utmost to stick to the words and spirit of the firmans. He emphasized there should not be even the slightest deviation from the firmans. The delegation was to be careful that any issues between Afghanistan and Iran should be decided in an amicable atmosphere, without any tension.

The Ministry of Court sent tents, chefs, and materials to ensure the guests would have comfortable lodging and board. I asked the Prime Minister, "Who will head the Afghan delegation?"

He replied, "The Deputy Minister of Foreign Affairs."

I asked, "What position should Abdul Rahim Khan hold?"

The Prime Minister responded, "He's the Governor of Herat, and an army general. He should be the deputy head and first member of the delegation."

Since I knew the psyche of Abdul Rahim Khan and was familiar with the people of Herat, I advised the Prime Minister, "That is not possible." I warned him, "The people of Herat will not accept that the Deputy Commander, whom they selected themselves for their state, will be answerable to Usman Khan Amir while deciding their national interest." Initially, the Prime Minister did not pay attention to my words. Later, he consulted with his advisors and decided that Abdul Rahim Khan should be the head of the delegation and Usman Khan Amir, his first deputy.

I took this firman and was very excited. The same day, in the afternoon, I got a new car whose driver was a Sikh gentleman (Afghanistan has a small minority population of Sikhs). I took along with me Naik Mohammad, who at one time was employed by my father. He was from the Hazara tribe. Naik was an experienced hand and very sincere to my father, God bless his soul.

I started my journey from Kabul to Ghazni on the evening of the 25th of Sumbulah 1313 (September 1934). The roads were not paved yet. We traveled through fields and desert, reaching Ghazni the first night. The chief magistrate of Ghazni welcomed us with lighted torches. He told us, "I want you to stay at the Ghazni Hotel; however, please accept my apologies. The Prime Minister wants you to continue your journey and not stay in Ghazni." Even though we were tired, we continued our journey after a little respite and having a cup of tea.

The second day, around noon, we reached Kandahar. Ghulam Farooq (Naib-ul-Hokooma) was the deputy governor of Kandahar. He was my childhood friend. He had a sweet tongue, was fair spoken, and had a sense of humor, but he could be abusive at the same time. Whatever came to his mind he would blurt out – he was very blunt. Ghulam Farooq belonged to the Mohammad Zai clan and had prominent roots. His father was a very renowned man.

We accompanied the Naib-ul-Hokooma for dinner and enjoyed his sense of humor. We slept for a few hours and again resumed on our journey. A man named Munshi Mullah Amir Khan, may God bless his soul, was a secretary to Deputy Commander Naib Salar and had traveled from Herat with some blueprints. He also accompanied us in the car. The Munshi belonged to the Qainat people. In Herat the Munshis (secretaries) were considered to be very experienced, intelligent, learned, and politically savvy people. One Munshi named Munshi Ahmad was from the Jamshaidi people. He had worked with Shoja-ud-daulah, the Minister of Security (Amnia) or Gendarmerie. Another Munshi was Mullah Amir, the student of Munshi Mullah Ahmad. Mullah Amir had a beautiful handwriting. He was a very patriotic, experienced, and wise man. We had a long conversation during our journey so our time would pass easily. Sometimes he would sleep while I was awake, and at other times it would be the other way around. We could not let the Sikh driver sleep. We would give him coffee or tea to keep him awake.

By the time we reached Farah, we were exhausted. We thought we would be killed in a crash if we continued to push the driver, who was also extremely tired. So we picked up a new driver from Farah and allowed the Sikh gentleman to nap next to him. In Farah, we ate dinner with Mohammad Anwar Khan (Naib Salar). Then, we started again for Herat. A few hours later we reached Sabz Var or Isfazar. It was renamed Shindand. Renaming Sabz Var was not a good move. It was inappropriate because they tried to change history.

Reaching Herat

When we reached Herat we were unpleasantly surprised. No one was there to greet us. I asked, "Where is Naib Salar?" They answered, "He has gone on a hunting trip." That was strange to me. I had come from Kabul as fast as I could with these firmans and instructions from the Prime Minister, who had contacted Naib Salar on the phone, repeatedly and now he was on a hunting trip?

I went to see my sister, Haleema, who was married to Abdul Aleem, the son of Abdul Raheem Khan. I kissed her forehead, and then I went to sleep, very upset. It was in the afternoon that Naib Salar returned. He embraced me right away in front of everyone. He loved me more than his son and was always very kind to me. I thought he would take me aside privately to ask, "What is going on?" or "What's happening?" However, he just sat in the living room with the others and ordered tea. When he'd had his tea and gradually the company left, finally I said to him, "You went on a hunting trip today? I have been sent from Kabul with urgency to see you."

He responded, "You know the people of Herat are very emotional, and these are emotional times. They think the government has sold part of Herat to the Iranians. If I had stayed back, waiting for you, giving importance to your arrival and pulling you aside for a private conversation in front of these people, they would have been convinced something was going on."

He continued, "My son, not even a miniscule part of Afghanistan, as small as my thumbnail, will be given to anyone. This is my conviction, and it is the faith of the people of Herat. No power can subjugate or control these people for that purpose. Now, tell me, what do you have?"

I pulled out all the firmans and showed them to him. He was pleased. "If they had not appointed me head of the delegation, I would have sent my resignation to Kabul," he responded. "And like any other soldier, as I vowed during the time of Habibullah Khan Kalakani when I came to Herat, I would have done the same and defended the rights of the soldiers. I would have stayed here and done that, and then gone back to Kabul."

In the end, we stayed in Herat, and the delegation followed us there, including Dr. Fawad Turk. Dr. Turk was a friend of mine, a friend of Afghanistan, and an optometrist in Kabul. He was fair spoken and had a sense of humor. We spent a great deal of time together until news came that the Iranian delegation, which was traveling from Tehran to Herat via Islam Qala, was near.

Before the Iranians arrived, Naib Salar, Usman Jan Amir, and Sayed Abdullah Khan got together and traveled toward the border, some of us on horseback and some by motorcar. We went to see the demarcation points contested by both sides. We talked to the Afghan people who were living alongside the disputed border. They told us, "Our fathers and forefathers have lived here. We have deeds to this land and other documents proving our ownership." We observed that the headstones on graves proclaimed that their fathers and forefathers had lived in this area. On one grave after another we saw the names of Alkozai, Ghilji, Aimaq, Taimuri, and Tajik of Herat. These names were found in other graveyards in Herat, also. The deeds and documents pointed out these same people as owners of the land. We returned to Herat amid news of the arrival date of the Iranian delegation.

The delegation included a high-ranking military officer, Mohammad Qasim Sharifee of the Mohammad Zai (ruling clan). Sharifee later became a military general in Kabul. He was a governor of Herat, a governor of Kataghan and Badakhshan, and an ambassador to Iraq. Unfortunately, he is now serving in Kabul under Babrak Karmal. What a pity.

Let me talk a little about Osman Khan Amir and Sayed Abdullah.

Osman Khan Amir was the son of Sardar Amir Mohammad Khan and grandson of Sardar Shah Mohammad Khan. Their genealogy can be traced to Sardar Paindah Mohammad Khan. Osman Khan was educated in Kabul and Ghazni. His father was Administrator of Ghazni at one time. Osman Khan knew many scholars from Ghazni and was familiar with every corner of that place. He was an accomplished writer. He started at the Ministry of Foreign Affairs as a clerk and rose to be the Deputy Foreign Minister and the Minister of Foreign Affairs. Later, he became the Ambassador of Afghanistan to Iran and Italy. He was taken to Russia for medical treatment, and there the poor man died. Before he died, he left instructions in his will that his body be taken to Ghazni and buried in the Ali Lala graveyard, even though his ancestral cemetery was in Kabul. Osman Khan loved Ghazni. He would talk to me constantly about it. I remember him saying, "Whenever I go to the mausoleum of Ali Lala, it seems the land pulls me toward it. I think, one day, my grave will be somewhere here." Eventually his prophecy was true, and his body was

buried there. Osman Khan was a very learned gentleman
and scholar. He was a patriot and a good man.

Sayed Abdullah belonged to the Sayed family of Kabul.
He was the son of Ahmad Agha. I remember, there were
three or four brothers; namely Sayed Khudadad, Sayed
Masoom, and Sayed Ahmad. They were veterans of the
British War and friends of Sardar Mohammad Ayub Khan.
Sayed Abdullah was a graduate of Habibiya School. He
became a clerk at the Habibiya School of Amir Habibullah
Khan. Later, he went to the Ministry of Foreign Affairs and
rose through the ranks to become Director of Political
Affairs. He was a gem of a man, wise and intelligent. He
was also very kind and brave. He was on a mission for
demarcation of the northern border of Afghanistan near
Darqad, riding on horseback along the bank of the Amu
(Oxus) River, when one of the embankments gave way, and
he fell into the river and drowned. The people who
accompanied him and witnessed the incident said that the
embankment was intentionally sabotaged by the Soviets to
cause the death of this great Afghan man. His body was
recovered downriver 40 to 50 days after he fell in, and was
buried with honor. His son, Sayed Wahid Abdullah, who
during the time of Mohammad Daoud Khan became the
Deputy Foreign Minister of Afghanistan, was killed by the
Communists during the Soviet invasion. May God bless
him.

Fakhruddin Altai (Turkish) Reaches Herat

We went to Ghoryan in Islam Qala and waited for the
arbitration delegation to arrive. Islam Qala had a well-
established population. Before the time of Amania, Islam
Qala was known as Kafir (Infidel) Qala. I imagine
Shujaudaula Khan renamed this place Islam Qala. There
was a very beautiful hotel (sarai) built in the Moghul style
architecture. The hotel consisted of eight to ten rooms
constructed around a circular courtyard underneath a brick
and mortar dome. Hassan Khan Shamilo built the hotel
during the time of the Safavid dynasty when Herat was

temporarily under the Iranian influence. Shamilo was the Governor of Herat and a very famous man in the history of Safavid. We arrived at Islam Qala amid news that Fakhruddin Altai would be there the next day.

Among the Heratis assigned to our delegation was Qazi Mohammad Siddiq Khan, a judge (qazi) of Herat who had a good grasp of the borders of Afghanistan. He and several others had set the stage for a meeting place and provided us an abundance of fresh and dried fruits. It was toward the end of Sumbula (September), and Herat's orchards were filled with fruits ready for harvest: melons, grapes, and many other fruits. There were at least 63 kinds of grapes, some of them called Shaikh Bahai. If all 63 varieties were not on the table, at least 40 of them were present. Moosa Abad was a place famous for watermelons. The desert oases in that area produce high quality watermelons. There were some on the table that day.

There is a kind of reptile about four to five lengths of a finger or ten inches long. It has two hands and lives in the desert sands, where it hides. Every two to three hours it comes out of the sand and jumps up in the air two or three meters as if it is flying. Then, it goes back into the sand. People call this Saqanqor fish (flying fish). They say it is very useful and effective for virility to eat it. If you catch one and run a knife through it, take its flesh and mix it with some zedoary (perennial herbs) and eat it, it will turn an 80-year-old man into a 14-year-old boy! (Editor's note: Not unlike the generative power of our modern day Viagra). There were other insects and reptiles also.

Hazrat Pasha came in a motorcar up to the border of Moosa Abad. We had with us very well bred horses. One of them was brought from Iran and came from the family of Raza Khan. This horse was very spirited, a strong and lively horse. Naib Salar wanted to mount this horse that was very spirited, so he gave his horse to Pasha. The rest of us had well-trained, calm horses to ourselves.

Fakhruddin Altai was a little upset that Naib Salar chose to ride the best horse instead of presenting the horse to him. He assumed Naib Salar thought the Turkish officer would not be able to control the horse, so he decided to handle the spirited horse himself. Without permission, the Turkish officer mounted the horse. He took off riding toward Moosa Abad as fast as he could. There was a hue and cry to stop him, and for him to slow down. Naib Salar mounted another horse, and we all mounted our calm and trained horses and followed him and reached the Afghanistan camp.

At the camp a small squadron gave them a respectful military salute and officially welcomed the delegation. The Turkish officer reached there with his delegation, and then the Iranian delegation reached the camp. It was time for evening prayers. The Turkish officer came toward the table where the fruits were laid out and stood there. He was very tall and well built, with broad shoulders, and a dignified and majestic presence. His face radiated the bravery and monumental confidence of the Turks. There were others from the delegation and also from Herat who stood up in respect and sat in the corners of the gathering.

Pasha took a knife and wanted to cut a melon. Before cutting the melon he told Naib Salar, "Pillar 39 is here."

Naib Salar responded, "Yes."

Pasha said, "What right do you have to Pillar 39? You have held it while Henry McMahon, the British arbitrator, had given Pillar 39 to the Iranians."

Naib Salar said, "McMahon was an Englishman. He wanted to create a rift between two nations, two brothers, and two friends who have a common language. Just as you want to cut this watermelon into two, he wanted to knife through two brothers and to separate them. This Pillar 39 has never been a divisional point that the people of Afghanistan are ever going to accept. This undoubtedly and categorically is the right and ownership of Afghanistan. You should investigate. Then only will you find that what I am saying is correct. Now please, go ahead and eat watermelon."

The translator translated Naib Salar's discourse into Turkish for Pasha. Gradually Pasha started paying attention to Naib Salar's words. Naib Salar took the knife and cut through watermelon and said, "These are two parts of a heart. You, as a Muslim, either want to bring the two parts together or, like the Englishman McMahon, you want to keep the two brothers separate from each other."

He responded, "No. I am a Turk. I have come here to cultivate brotherly relations between Afghanistan and Iran and remove this bone of contention between you."

Naib Salar concluded, "May God give you the strength and victory. I will cooperate with you as much as I can."

We all dispersed toward our camp to have dinner. When Fakhruddin Altai saw his majestic camp, with the beautiful tent from Abdul Rahim Khan in Moosa Abad and the comforts available in the tent in the heart of the desert he abruptly exclaimed to Naib Salar, "They told me there was nothing available in this area. But everything is available here and better than anywhere else." He did not say in Iran, but he said here, everything is available.

Naib Salar responded, "I have prepared a soldier's bedroll for you. You are a soldier, and a soldier is comfortable under a tent."

Relations between Afghanistan and Turkey

The Iranian delegation left after dinner. Fakhruddin Altai sat there and while the sun was setting in Moosa Abad amid the beautiful scenery he asked for blueprints of the border. He studied each and every one very carefully and asked detailed questions.

Here, I would like to talk a little about Afghan and Turkish relations. Historically Afghans have always had friendly and brotherly relations with the Turks. At the time of Amir Habibullah Khan Seraj, even though Afghanistan did not have the right to exchange envoys with other countries yet, it hired some Turkish people to serve in Afghanistan.

When the Ottoman Turks were busy in the war with the Allied Forces the Persian newspaper at the time, *Seraj-ul-Akhbar,* reported that the people asked the King of Afghanistan to send Afghan youth as volunteers to fight on the side of the Turks against the Allies.

Amir Habibullah Khan himself collected money from his family, from the treasury of Afghanistan, and from the people of Afghanistan and sent it to Turkey. I do not remember how he sent it or what the amount was. I do remember when he was doing this at the Salam Khana (palace) he read one verse of a poetic couplet that said:

Nigah gar nashuud qabile roi dost
Feghan raa rassanem bah jai keh ou hast

If I cannot see my friend face to face,
At least I can send forth my sorrowful cries to where he is
living.

In other words, if he cannot join this Islamic Jehad in person, we should send people representing us, so that Afghanistan is standing shoulder to shoulder with its brothers.

At the time of Habibullah Khan, a military hospital was established in Afghanistan by the name of Harbia Serajia (Seraj military hospital). This hospital was near Kabul River, close to bridge of Qalai Mahmood Khan (Fort). It was a well-organized hospital. Some Turkish technical people had come to work in the military and produce white gunpowder and other army materiels. A physician at this hospital, named Muneer Beg, came from Turkey. I vividly remember he was a short fellow with black eyes and broad shoulders. The twirled sides of his yellow mustache were very prominent on his face and could be spotted from far away. He was in Afghanistan a very long time and married an Afghan woman. When his contract ended, he left for Turkey during the time of Amir Amanullah Khan, when Afghanistan had warm and close relations with Turkey.

One of the reasons for these close relations was that Mahmood Beg Tarzi, the Foreign Minister of Afghanistan, was the father of Queen Soraya (wife of Amir Amanullah Khan). Tarzi was educated in Syria at the time of Ottoman. His father had a title and a stipend from the Ottoman Empire. Tarzi was fluent in the Turkish language. He printed books in Kabul that were translated from Turkish into Persian. He always tried to improve the relations between Afghanistan and Turkey and was very successful in his efforts. At the time of Amir Amanullah Khan some students, both girls and boys, were sent to Turkey for higher education in the military and civilian fields.

A doctor named Rufqi Beg came to Afghanistan from Turkey. He was an influential man and a friend of Mustafa Kamal, the leader of Turkey. There was also a law scholar and two or three teachers who also came from Turkey. Let's not forget that Amanullah Khan wanted to recruit Indians who were against the British Empire to serve in Afghanistan. During his time, a gentleman named Allah Nawaz, who belonged to a prominent family of Chitral (current Pakistan), worked in the Department of Education. Some Indian refugees also worked in the education system of Afghanistan. The Turks were well respected during the time of Nadir Shah.

This doctor, Rufqi Beg, was a close advisor to King Nadir Shah. He helped establish the medical school in Kabul. During the time of Nadir Shah about 30 students graduated from that school and were practicing medicine. Rufqi Beg also built the sanatorium building in Aliabad, a neighborhood of Kabul, and helped built the Aliabad Hospital. There were two or three other medical doctors from Turkey in Kabul who were influential and trustworthy. A doctor named Rabie Beg practiced internal medicine in Kabul, and Dr. Fawad Beg practiced optometry. There were Turkish political advisors at the Ministry of Foreign Affairs; similarly, there were a few other advisors from Turkey whose names I have forgotten. It was for this reason that Dr. Fawad Beg was included in the Afghan delegation during the demarcation talks of Afghanistan's western border.

Relations with Turkey were so close that when the people of Afghanistan rose against Amanullah Khan and Amir Habibullah Khan Kalakani attacked Kabul, Mustafa Kamal sent Fauzi Chaqmaq (Chief of Army Staff of Turkey) to Kabul. His mission was to help Amanullah Khan and review the military situation and battlefield operations, but he arrived a little too late. Habibullah Khan Kalakani had already conquered Kabul (1929).

Another example of the close friendship between Afghanistan and Turkey was during the revolution of Habibullah Khan Kalakani, when most of the foreign ambassadors had left Kabul, and the Turkish ambassador remained. He said, "My blood is not redder (or thicker) than the blood of the people of Afghanistan." After the revolution, Turkey continued to have relations with Habibullah Khan Kalakani and worked toward calming the situation in Afghanistan.

Another Turkish visitor, during the time of Amir Habibullah Khan Seraj, was Mahmoud Sami Pasha. Mahmoud Sami was famous in Afghanistan as General Afandi. His forefathers had migrated from Afghanistan to Baghdad (Iraq) and from there to Turkey. Mahmoud Sami Pasha studied at a military school in Turkey and came to Afghanistan to serve in the Afghan Armed Forces at the time of Amir Habibullah Khan Seraj. At the time, Habibullah Khan established the Serajia Military School and Mahmoud Sami was a teacher there. Even though the Regent Inayatullah Khan did not like him (we don't know the reason), Amanullah Khan had a great deal of respect for him. Once, Amir Habibullah Khan, on the recommendation of Sardar Inayatullah, Regent, exiled Mahmoud Sami Pasha from Afghanistan, but then, he forgave him and let him return.

As soon as Amanullah Khan took over the throne, Mahmoud Sami Pasha was awarded the title of Naib Salar (Vice Commander). He became a trusted advisor to Amanullah Khan. Mahmoud Sami was the author of the mixed Arabic and Persian anthem of Amanullah Khan. I do remember a couplet from it:

Our Sardar became the king,
The flag of the religion was raised.

The lyrics further pleaded:

O God, give us victory here and give victory to our king,
the Afghan Amir Amanullah Khan Ghazi.

154

This anthem was sung in every school, and Mahmoud Sami Pasha composed its music. He held a great deal of respect before King Amanullah Khan until the time of Nadir Shah became king. Nadir Shah threw him in jail on the pretext of the crime of treason with Habibullah Khan Kalakani. Mahmoud Sami Pasha was charged with the crime and ultimately executed.

During the time of Amir Amanullah Khan, another person came to Afghanistan by the name of Hussain Afandi. He belonged to Alcozai tribe. His forefathers lived in Baghdad, where they had taken refuge at the time of Amir Abdur Rahman Khan. Afandi was educated in Customs Law. He improved and rewrote the customs laws of Afghanistan that were originally compiled by the Turks. During the time of Habibullah Khan Seraj, the Turks also helped establish the Afghanistan taxation ledgers and books. Mirza Ghulam Mustafa Khan was one of the pioneers of the tax law changes, and his teacher was a Turk. Hussain Afandi remained in Afghanistan to the end and lived in the Baghe Alam Ganj neighborhood in Kabal, which was across from the Nejat, or formerly, Amani School. He had a building there, and Amanullah Khan had deeded him the land. Hussain Afandi was a very virtuous and pious man. He built a small mosque near the Kabul River. He died in Kabul and was buried in Shohadai Saleheen cemetery. He was a very likable man.

The relationship between the Turks and the Afghans lasted through Nadir Shah's rule (1929-1933) and for two to three years during the time of Zahir Shah (1933-1973). As soon as Sardar Mohammad Daoud Khan (1973-1978, overthrown by communists) and Sardar Mohammad Naim (his brother) came to power, the Turkish influence waned. The Turks were removed from the Ministry of Health, the Ministry of Defense, and other places, and asked to leave. They were replaced by the Soviets, who brought us to the present misfortune. Similarly, they did the same to the French. The Afghan nation had a great affinity for the Turks and always looked at the Ottoman Empire (Khilafat) with a great deal of respect. They used to say Sultan Saheb

(which means Mister) with a lot of love.

Indo-Afghan Relations

I should add here that the Indian (Muslim) doctors who came to Afghanistan were highly respected by the Afghan people. Dr. Ghulam Mohammad Khan came during the time of Amir Habibullah Khan Seraj. I remember that Dr. Allah Joya was the Amir's personal physician. Dr. Abdul Aziz Khan, Dr. Rashiduddin Khan, and Dr. Sayed Abdul Ghani Khan all came during the time of Amir Habibullah Khan, Amanullah Khan, and Nadir Shah. They served Afghanistan sincerely.

At the time of Amir Habibullah Khan Seraj, my father built a small hospital in our compound. This hospital was mentioned in the newspapers. A physician from Punjab was hired by the name of Dr. Mohammad Hayat. Surprisingly, he practiced both optometry and internal medicine. He had a gray beard and wore a Turkish or Ottoman cap called a fez or rumi that was maroon in color with a tassel at the top. The Indian Muslims wore these caps, even in Afghanistan, with a great deal of pride and considered them good luck. The hospital remained in our compound at Baghban Koocha as a free clinic. Dr. Hayat installed 11 beds and treated his patients there. He wanted to teach me English first; however, my mullah (religious teacher), may God bless him, was critical of this and said, "I will not allow my student to learn English and become infidel." Dr. Hayat later started teaching me Urdu. I still remember his teachings and his Urdu lessons.

After three years at the completion of his contract, Dr. Hayat left Kabul on horseback, heading for Peshawar. From Peshawar he went to Punjab. I cannot remember where he lived in Punjab. I know that he has died. I wish I could meet his descendants and try to retrieve the letters my father sent to him. Dr. Hayat also had pictures of my childhood. I would have loved to look at the pictures and see if I can remember more. I am still a child at heart.

General Altai Resumes Work on Demarcation

Every day we would present our proof of land ownership, and on the other side, the Iranians did the same. These daily meetings sometimes took place on the Afghan side of the border. Other times we had to cross the Iranian border into Tayabad. When the meeting was held on the Afghan side, the Iranian delegation came with Mehdi Farrukh. When we went to Iran, we would travel to the border with Naib Salar by car. We sat there from morning to evening and presented documents of proof to the Pasha. Pasha would read and review them and write notes for himself. He would not say anything to us. Both the Iranians and our delegation were held in suspense of his decision. The Iranian delegation was afraid of their Emperor. They knew if they failed, they would be subject to reprisal for themselves, their families, and their descendants. I was afraid of two things. First, that if we failed, we may give part of Afghanistan to the Iranians. Second, I was convinced Naib Salar would not accept any loss of land, and this would lead us to a war. I was afraid of harm to both sides and that our enemies would laugh at us.

The daily meetings lasted for almost six months. One day, Munshi Mullah Amir of Herat was with us along with two or three other Heratis who were part of the delegation. They were supposed to give details of certain things. Pasha was in a place near Herat. There was an older Afghan gentleman with flowing gray beard passing by. Pasha asked him, "What are you doing here? This is not your land."

The elder answered in a Herati accent, "This is my father's land. This is the land of my gardens and my orchards. This is the land of my forefathers, and the land we have owned for hundreds of years."

I don't know what came over Pasha, but he abruptly slapped the old man in the face for his candidness, which was very shocking.

The Heratis who were with us and witnessed this incident were also shocked. Pasha saw that he was alone in this. He walked away from us. Meanwhile an Iranian

157

officer who was passing by asked him the same question, "What are you doing here? This is not your land." The Iranian officer exclaimed, "This land categorically belongs to the Iranian Empire." He pointed out toward our land and said, "This also belongs to the Iranian Empire. What are these Afghans doing here? They have forced their way in and are sitting here."

Pasha confronted him, "Did you see them coming here by force?" An altercation took place between Pasha and this soldier. Finally, both sides calmed down. The next day a meeting took place again. The head of the Iranian delegation was a very rude man who stuttered and was always upset. During this meeting he blurted out, "The Afghan army has the fighting techniques of 400 years ago!" Naib Salar, who was a military man and a General of Afghanistan, heard this. The Heratis also heard this and translated it for the Pasha. Naib Salar did not react. The meeting ended this way.

Pasha asked Naib Salar, "You heard the man?"

He answered, "Yes."

Pasha tried to apologize to Naib Salar. Naib Salar shrugged it off, saying, "It doesn't matter."

I don't know where this fight started. Either the two Heratis who witnessed it reported it to others, or others spread the rumor. The rumor of Naib Salar and the Afghans being insulted spread like wildfire. Tensions spread as well. Fighting broke out among the people of Zindabad, Khawaf, and Wakhir. Eight security personnel from the Iranian side were killed. People from Khawaf and Wakhir took refuge in Afghanistan.

The news traveled fast to Tehran. King Reza Shah of Iran sent a telegram to the King of Afghanistan, Zahir Shah, urging him to stop the arbitration. In his message he reproached the Afghans for coming not to negotiate, but to fight.

The news was not taken lightly in Kabul either. Sultan Fazal Ahmad Khan Herati Mojaddadi, the Minister of Justice, rushed to Herat with Mohammad Younus Khan to investigate the matter. Sardar Sher Ahmad Khan, the Afghan Ambassador to Iran, was part of this delegation and

I was asked to join, also. On the Iranian side, Mahmoud Jam and Hassan Pakravan, the Governor of Mashhad, were named to investigate the incident. We were all asked to go to the place where the security personnel were killed.

It was wintertime, and snow was on the ground. We traveled by automobile as far as the road could take us, and then we rode on horseback up to the Zulfiqar police station. We met our Iranian brothers from the other delegation there and discussed the issue. Those summoned from Afghanistan for the investigation stated they came by their own free will. No one forced them. When questioned, they stated the Iranian border guards were very abusive and disrespectful. "They intimidated us and told us we should not read the Koran. They suggested we should read *Shahnama* (the epic "Book of Kings" of Iranian poet Abu'l-Qasim Hasan Firdausi). They tried to force us to change our religion."

The delegations were taken to the place where the security personnel were killed. When we arrived, we could see some military uniforms lying on top of the snow. The Iranian who spoke on behalf of his delegation pointed out, "Do you see the uniforms soaked in blood? See the casings of the bullets that belong to the Afghans?"

I asked him, "How many days have passed since this incident?"

He answered, "Ten days."

I asked, "When did it last snow here?"

He answered, "Two days ago."

I shook my head. "Then how can it be possible that the uniforms and bullet casings are lying on top of the snow?"

Our argument prevailed, and they accepted that the Afghans did not do this. Mr. Jam was very upset that whoever staged this scene of transgression was responsible and not the Afghans. The Iranian government was responsible. For no reason, this incident was staged, and we had to come here. Finally, a protocol was written, and both sides signed documents. The Afghans were vindicated. Mr. Jam and Mr. Pakravan left for Mashhad. Our ambassador also left with them.

My First Journey to Iran

After the documents were completed and protocols signed, we left on horseback, following the Iranian delegation toward Mashhad. No one asked us where we were going. However, we were anxious because we knew we had no passports or visas. This was my first time treading onto Iranian soil. With me was Mr. Fazal Ahmad Khan, Minister of Justice. He was a very patriotic and scholarly man, a writer and a literary person. Mr. Mohammad Younus Khan, who later became the governor of Kandahar, also accompanied us. He was my former student and a very close friend. Mr. Abdul Rahman Popalzai and Munshi Mullah Amir from Herat also rode with us.

The weather was very cold. It seemed we would freeze to death on the journey, which took us seven to eight hours. Finally, from far away, we could see the lights of the city of Mashhad, and the dome of the holy Imam's mausoleum. For years, I had longed to cast my eyes on this sacred dome. My eyes widened in awe at the manifestation of the dome and to think of all the sacred, cultural and historic Islamic architecture in the beautiful city of Toos (an Iranian city in Khorasan). Soon, I would be able to visit the grave of poet Firdausi and the library of Mashhad. God gave me this opportunity. Even though the winds and rain came around, God fulfilled my dream. We reached the city by nightfall, and we were taken to Mr. Assadi's house. He was the curator of the mausoleum and a friend of King Reza Shah. He was considered to be a personality of national stature, renowned throughout Iran. We came to a beautiful building that looked like a palace, a part of the mausoleum complex.

We were greeted warmly as respected guests, but our own Ambassador to Iran was a little upset to find out we traveled without passports or visas. We explained we thought it was in the national interest of Afghanistan to come right away, and we didn't think it was necessary to ask permission. Mr. Assadi assured us we had no need for papers here. They prepared a place for us to stay in one of the buildings. We were soon warm and dry, and spent a very pleasant and comfortable night.

In the morning, we rose early for prayers. The Minister of Justice was familiar with Mashhad. He belonged to the Mojaddidi family of Herat and was the son of Abdul Wahab Khan. His forefathers had holdings in Khawaf and Wakhir in Iran. After making ablutions, we eagerly hurried toward the mausoleum. What an affect it had on us! I cannot translate my feelings into words. I was astonished. I did not believe I was awake. I thought I was dreaming. The dome was made of gold, as were the flowers. It was breathtaking. We heard a lot about the Imam. He was called Imam Zamin in Kabul and Imam Samin (the Guarantor). He was the apple of the eye of Prophet Mohammad's family (PBUH).

A young man, dressed very chic with no head covering, came forward out of the blue and greeted us. "Gentlemen," he said. "I have been appointed by the Governor, on behalf of the province of Khorasan, to be your host." We replied we were very fortunate to have him as a host. "I am Mahmoud Farrukh," he introduced himself.

I recognized his name and was happy to see him. "Sir, you are a poet and a writer," I said. I had read his poetry and articles in Iranian magazines several times.

"No, sir," he replied, humbly. "I'm neither a poet nor a writer. I am a Sayed (related to Prophet Mohammad, PBUH)."

I was glad to see he had a good personality, and I told him, "You are a very respectful person."

He asked me who I was. I said, "I am Khalili, and this is the Mr. Mojaddidi." I could tell he had also read my poetry and knew my taste because he took us into the library and showed us many books. He brought us to the Gauharshad School, where he showed us documents about calculating the equator, which had been prepared at the Bahauddin Amili School.

At Gauharshad, we watched while one of the clergy (I don't remember his name) was lecturing a group of students. They were sitting around him, and there were books placed next to every student. He was very respectful and spoke very eloquently, from memory, about a different subject.

When he finished his lecture, we were introduced to him. He said, "Yes, yes! I have been to Herat. I have a fondness for Heratis, and I am also fond of Afghans. We are brothers." He turned toward Mr. Farrukh and said, "The governments have created these differences. Here, among our schools and our books, we don't have these differences."

We stayed there for three days and signed a protocol, with the grace of God. I must have bought 10 to 15 books. Some were given to us as gifts. I remember I bought *Rahbar-e-khirad (A Guide to Wisdom or Intellect in Logic)*. The best thing that happened was my friendship with Mr. Farrukh. He took us to the resting place of the poet Firdausi, which recently had been renovated and looked very grand and impressive. I thought to myself, "There was a day when the body of Firdausi was not even allowed in their cemetery. Today, the same people have built him a very beautiful and ornate grave."

While in Mashhad, we toured an official school for regular students. We entered a classroom where the students were being taught the Persian language. The teacher was repeating the word "Naji" and asking the students, "What does it mean?" He saw us, but ignored us. We felt a little disrespected, especially since the Minister of Justice – one of the prominent people of Afghanistan – was with us. He continued his lesson. In a flattering way, he told the students the emperor is the Naji of Iran, implying that Naji means savior (but Naji means saved, Munji means savior).

When the lesson was over, we moved forward to pay our respects. I knew he had mixed up "saved" with "savior," and I felt I should say something about his error. When you are young, you do things like that. I asked the teacher if Naji was Persian or Arabic.

He said, in a very rude tone, "It's Arabic. Why are you asking?"

I said, "If it's Arabic, what does it mean in Persian?"

He replied, "One who saves or is the savior."

I told him, "I don't think so. The meaning of 'Naji' is 'the saved.' It's a transitive word."

The teacher suddenly became aware and attentive. "This word is famous for being mistaken by many people," he said.

I responded, "I don't know where it has become famous." In my heart I knew that the same mistake is made in Afghanistan. There, they say the King (Nadir Shah) is the Naji of Afghanistan. That is the wrong word. Naji is the one who is saved, and Munji is the person who is the savior.

I saw the students looking at each other. I realized I should not have put down the teacher in front of his students. However, he did not leave me an alternative.

We left the school and got into our automobiles with the many gifts given to us by Mr. Assadi. Mr. Assadi was from the Alizais of Farah or Kandahar. His forefathers migrated to sacred Mushhad, and he was born there. Later, we heard that Mr. Assadi was arrested in the incident of Shapo (an uprising). Even though he was a close friend of the King, Reza Shah, without any further investigation Reza Shah had him executed. I read in one of the Iranian newspapers that if Mr. Assadi had not had foreign blood in him, he would not have been treated like this. We also heard later the young King of Iran said his father misjudged these people. Assadi had done nothing wrong. I did not hear it myself, but I have been told it was written in one of their books. This also happened to Sheikh Bahlool when he came to Afghanistan.

After this, an argument about a small stream of water, called Ghash Loshi, gained attention. Ghash Loshi was located on the border of Afghanistan. It was not worth fighting over, but tensions mounted from both sides. Finally, the matter was referred to the Iranian capital of Tehran, and the Iranian King sent Mirza Mohammad Ali Khan Farroghi, the Prime Minister of Iran, to investigate the issue. Farroghi was dispatched to Yosufabad and Tayababad. We were in Islam Qala when the telephone call came that the Prime Minister had arrived on behalf of the King, and our delegation was summoned right away. The telephone call came from Fakhruddin Altai. We left immediately. It was important to me to meet Mr. Farrukh because I had read his book, *Rahbar-e-khirad (A Guide to Wisdom or Intellect in Logic).*

My Acquaintance with Mahjooba Heravi

I came to know Mahjooba Heravi in Herat. She was a poet who belonged to the Aimaqs, a tribe of Afghanistan. I've forgotten her father's name. Her handwriting was very beautiful, and her poetic expression was excellent. She used to write poetry in the Iraqi style, which was popular with many Herati poets. Of her contemporaries, only Hazrat Allama Mohammad Siddiq Khan Qazi followed the Indian style.

Mahjooba's husband was a very conservative man. He did not want anybody to see the beauty of his wife or her poetry. He did not permit her to publish her poetry beyond the four walls of his house. It was only through Khalifa Mohammad Hassan, who was famous as a smooth talker, that I received one of her poems. I still remember one of the couplets:

> *The Heavens have made truthful Yousef a slave*
> *Destiny rendered Mahjooba also a slave girl.*

I was shocked to read this couplet and realized how poor her financial condition was. I summoned her husband. Fortunately, like me, he belonged to the Safi tribe. His name was Mirza Ghulam Jan. I did whatever I could do to help them. I also convinced him to allow Mahjooba to have her poetry published in the newspapers and magazines of Herat, and if possible, send it to Kabul for publication also. Mahjooba and I exchanged poems. Both of our poems were published in Kabul and Herat.

We Travel Back to Kabul

On this journey, besides seeing many friends, we explored all the historical sites within the borders of Herat and became familiar with the landscape, including the abundant birds and animals of the desert. Finally, we said goodbye to our friends, relatives, and the beautiful Herat and left for Kabul.

We traveled by car with the same lorries (trucks) from the Ministry of the Court and the Royal Guard following us that had gone with us to welcome the Fakhruddin Pasha in Herat. By this time, harsh winter had set in. We passed the town of *Qalat* with fair weather, but by the time we arrived in Moqor, tons of snow had fallen, and the sheer volume of it made it impossible for us to move any further.

We were together with Fazal Ahmad Khan, the Minister of Justice, and head of the delegation, Osman Khan Amir, Abdul Rahman Khan Popal, Qasim Sharifi, myself, and a couple of others. We were stuck in the Moqor Hotel for seven days because of bad weather. The nights were very unpleasant. Our clothes were in the cars that were following us and were left behind because of the snow. Unfortunately, I was used to smoking, and my cartons of cigarettes were in the cars behind us. We could not find cigarettes in Moqor. That left us with our only alternative, smoking tobacco the social way, through a hookah or water pipe that is shared by several smokers. Every day the hookah was prepared. Loose tobacco was placed in the chalam (a small funnel-looking clay pot) and lit. Osman Khan, Younus Khan, and I would share it. (As the smoker draws on the hose or pipe, the smoke passes through bubbling water to cool and humidify it). We found a book of poetry by Mirza Abdul Qadir Bedil (Persian poet of New Delhi, 1642-1720) in one of the local stores and bought it. It was very complex. We sat around until late in the night, reading his poetry, discussing it, and smoking the hookah.

Some Sweet and Sour Memories of the Moqor Hotel

Because there were a limited number of rooms in the hotel, five of us shared one room: the Minister of Justice, Dr. Fawad Turk, Mohammad Younus Khan, Osman Khan Amir, and I. As a matter of habit the Minister of Justice and

Mr. Younus Khan were facing each other. Our *chapar khots* (cots or beds) were placed a little further down. I wonder if *chapar khot*, an iron bed with four legs, is derived from the Persian phrase *chapra ghat*, meaning "a very powerful and strong man."

In our crowded room, there was a small table between the *chapar khots* of the Minister of Justice and Mr. Younus Khan. On this table were two water glasses. These were much desired because the hotel had no water glasses, and all the cutlery and utensils of the Ministry of the Court were also lagging behind us in the snowbound cars. These were the only available glasses in the room, and at night the Minister of Justice and Mr. Younus Khan took possession of one each.

One night a funny thing happened. The Minister of Justice wore a bridge of two artificial front teeth. At night, he would take the bridge out before going to bed and put it in the glass filled with water and place the glass on the little table. Younus Khan also had a habit of leaving a full glass of water for himself on the little table. He would place a saucer on top and put his cigarette in the saucer. We were not allowed to touch these glasses until the morning. If we wanted to drink water we had to go out at night and drink from the mouth of the water pitcher. That was difficult to do, so we thought about playing a joke on them so they wouldn't control the glasses any more.

That night, after the kerosene lamp was extinguished, we quietly took the glass with the teeth of the Minister of Justice in it and switched it with the glass under the saucer on the other side. Around midnight, there was sudden hue and cry, with screams from Sardar Mohammad Younus Khan. Because there was no electricity at that time in Hotel Moqor, we lit a match and turned the wick of the lamp. I was lying on my cot, watching underneath my covers and guessed what may have happened. Younus Khan said, "Something was in the water, and it's stuck in my throat!" The Minister of Justice exclaimed, "It must be my teeth!" It was a funny situation. Dr. Fawad sized up the situation, found his medical tongs, and carefully extracted the teeth from the bloody throat of Younus Khan. We laughed until morning.

Another Story of Hotel Moqor

A few years after this incident, I traveled through Moqor again on our way from Kandahar to Kabul with the King of Afghanistan. I was in a car with Sardar Khalilullah Khan, son of Inayatullah Khan (brother of Amanullah Khan), and Mir Haidar Khan Hussaini, Minister of Justice, who was the son of the famous Herati academician, and scholar, Mr. Ata Mohammad Khan Hussaini, President of the House of Ayan (House of Lords or Elders). The King was in one car with Ali Mohammad Khan, Minister of Foreign Affairs and a couple of other friends.

It was wintertime, and the weather was very cold. We slowed down and let the royal caravan pull ahead of us. After they passed, we stopped several times along the way at scenic places. We would rest by the side of a stream or river, eat our food, talk, and exchange poetry. We slowly continued on our travel route and reached Moqor around evening prayers.

As we headed into the hotel, we were told the King was very angry and upset that we lingered behind and took so much time getting to Moqor. He had just ordered a search party to go and look for us, concerned that something may have happened to us on the way here. I knew we were in serious disfavor, because the King of Afghanistan never gets angry. We entered the small banquet hall and saw the Governor and the people from Kandahar, the army officers and also the well-wishers from Kabul and Ghazni all gathered there. They were sitting around a stove that was burning wood and coal, and the room was thick with smoke. There was no room to sit in the back, so for the three of us, they brought chairs right up front. We sat down and found ourselves facing the King and Ali Mohammad Khan, the Minister of Foreign Affairs. It was very awkward. No one paid attention to us; we were being ignored.

My discomfort was physical as well. Unfortunately, I used to have boils or skin abscesses that would break out on the lower part of my body. I was using a sulfur medication, but I was having an allergic reaction to it, which made things worse. The rash was very painful, especially while traveling on unpaved roads. Every bump in the road aggravated my condition.

No one greeted us. The people were quiet because they were afraid of the King, who was very angry. Ali Mohammad Khan waited for the right moment to break the silence. He was very fond of me and wanted to change the atmosphere into a more amicable one. In his typical beautiful style of conversation he called me Khalil *Jan* (like "Mister," a form of respect or courtesy). He said, "Khalil Jan, you must have had a very uncomfortable journey. Any time our car hit a bump, I would be reminded of your wounds and felt very bad for you. I was worried about you." As he spoke, he pointed toward my lower body. I was already quite tired, and this joke was not very welcome to me. I wasn't very happy that he made this remark in front of everyone, especially the King. Suddenly, I remembered this couplet of Hazrat Sheikh Bedil. I pointed out toward his lower body and replied,

Because time has brought pain to one part of the body
It does not leave the other parts of the body without pain.

My reciting this couplet and pointing to his lower body changed the atmosphere in that place immediately. Some people started laughing. Even the King broke out in a smile. He did not want to lose his dignity in front of the people. The joke cleared the air.

Ali Mohammad Khan burst into laughter, and then cut his laughter short when he realized the King was not laughing. Things changed after that. When I left to go to my room, other people followed me.

I have another bittersweet memory from Moqor. I came to the Hotel Moqor with my wife and children on the eve of my exile to Kandahar. We stayed in the hotel our last night together, and in the morning I said goodbye to them amid my tears. They went home to Kabul, to the pleasant weather and instead, I was sent to Kandahar, with its hot weather, and the loneliness of exile.

The next morning we left Moqor for Ghazni, where we stayed overnight. The King went to the Mausoleum of Sultan Mahmoud Ghaznavi and prayed there. We were all together, and since I was versatile in the history of the Ghaznavid dynasty, I was peppered with numerous questions, which I answered for everybody. We spent the night at the Hotel Ghazni and left for Kabul the next day.

As soon as we had returned from our journey to Herat, we were supposed to present a full report to Sardar Mohammad Hashim Khan and provide him specifics of the activities of the Turkish and Afghan delegations in the matter of the demarcation of the borders. I had compiled the report, and my files contained detailed information, blueprints, etc. There were a couple of engineers with us who helped in this compilation.

We went before Prime Minister Hashim Khan. As soon as the Minister of Justice and other members were seated, I opened the file to begin my presentation. Sardar Hashim Khan (brother of King Nadir Shah), who belonged to the royal family, interrupted me and said, "There's no need to read the report. I'm aware of all your activities and all the work of Abdul Rahim Khan." In other words, Abdul Rahim Khan wanted to muddy the water and catch fish. Luckily, it didn't happen.

All of our efforts, research, and diplomacy for the sake of the country were in vain. Instead of thanking us and showing gratitude, Sardar Hashim Khan was dismissive of all of our sincere work. What can one do in such a situation? All I could do was mutter under my breath, "May God keep His Highness alive," and sit down.

Kabul and My Friends

We passed mornings and evenings idly. One more year went by. Our family was under surveillance. Abdul Rahim Khan was recalled from Herat on the excuse of consultation. Back in Kabul, he was appointed Minister of Public Works.

Fortunately, in Kabul I had many literary friends. Sardar Najibullah Khan was working at the Ministry of Foreign Affairs as head of the Eastern Division. He had recently graduated from Isteqala (Independence) School and was fluent in French. He wrote beautiful Persian and had an inclination toward poetry. He was a pious, handsome young man. Similarly, Osman Khan Amir, with whom I became acquainted during my journey to Herat, had an affinity for literature. As was the custom in the royal family, he had studied many books while growing up.

Mohammad Ibrahim Khan worked as the Prime Minister's secretary and was the grandson of Sardar Mohammad Younus Khan, who at one time was General Counsel of Afghanistan in Tashkent and later worked as Director of Documents at the Secretariat. The Director of Documents kept track of all the documents in many different offices of the Secretariat, so he knew quite a few things. Bedil's poetry was his favorite, as was literature and music. He liked to eat well and dress well. He was a gentleman. His duties also included carrying documents to the Prime Minister. Whenever someone came to see the Prime Minister, the meeting was recorded, and clerks collected the documents. That gave us little to do, other than to sit back, talk, and enjoy our conversations. Abdullah Khan Malikyar (later Afghan Ambassador to the U.S. during the rule of Mohammad Daoud Khan) was also appointed to our department at this time. I was closer to Ibrahim Khan. We did everything together.

My Reclamation of Some of My Father's Land in Qarabagh and Kohdaman

Sardar Mohammad Hashim Khan approved part of my father's holdings, north of Kabul, to be returned to me. This was based on the recommendation of His Highness Mohammad Nadir Shah. He returned 37 jeribs or acres of land to my possession, as well as one orchard and one qala (country home). I was very happy to receive all of this back. I was not getting a return from this land or the orchard; however, we had plenty of grapes to eat and had a place to get together for our friends to visit. His qala had a big dome from the time of my father. You could see the whole of Kohdaman from this dome. The qala also had three to four rooms. I vividly remember that before the qala was built in Hussain Kot, my father and my mother used to spend summers there. The people of Qarabagh were master vintners – experts in the cultivation and growing of grapes. They grew various kinds of grapes there.

On Thursday nights when offices were closed for the weekend (the Afghan weekend is Thursday evening through Saturday morning) I used to take Ibrahim Khan and sometimes Sardar Najibullah Khan and Osman Khan with me, and we would take a car or public transportation and stay in Qarabagh overnight. Sometimes our other friends Younus Khan and Sayed Abdullah would go there, too. We would talk, recite poetry, play chess, debate issues, and criticize the government. Our main topic of discussion was Sardar Hashim Khan. We would complain about the prevailing conditions of the country.

If they couldn't go with me, I took another friend named Qari Abdul Sattar Khan (Qari is one who could recite Koran by memory). He taught me during my childhood. He was a very pleasant man and had a resonant voice, which made listening to him recite poetry and the Koran a beautiful experience. He was a gentleman.

I had a couple of other friends in Kabul, Mirza Mohammad Khan Murshid, and Sheikh Abdul Hussain, who was from Kohdaman. We used to call him Qazi because his father and his grandfather were qazis (judges). He, however, was himself, illiterate. He had a large orchard and land, and a prosperous life that he had inherited from his father. The government confiscated all his holdings after they accused him of cooperation with Habibullah Khan Kalakani (who overthrew Amanullah Khan in the popular religious uprising). He requisitioned his father's land and was able to successfully reclaim part of it when Sardar Mohammad Hashim Khan finally gave it back to him. I played a positive role in getting this land back to him.

Abdul Hussain Khan was also a very impressive personality. While he was soft spoken, he was a good talker and had a pleasant way of speaking. He was not very handsome. He had allowed his beard to grow so long that it reached his navel. He was a generous and brave man. We would go to Qarabagh once in a while and spend nights at his place and go hunting for crane and pheasants. Sometimes we would go with Abdul Rahim Khan (Naib Salar) in his car from Kabul to his qala in Sidqabad. We used to go crane hunting and passed pleasant times there. As much as Sardar Mohammad Hashim Khan was a harsh and short-tempered leader, we considered ourselves more liberated during these outings.

I should also add here that my friend Alim Shahi used to go with us to Qarabagh and Kohdaman. He was a generous friend. We used to play chess and discuss poetry together. He had many good qualities. He was a humanist and was later martyred. May God bless his soul.

My Journey to Ghazni

I began to read and write books. I wanted to write a book about Hazrat Hakim Sanai of Ghazni (1044-1150). Rumi said this about Sanai:

Attar is the soul and Sanai its two eyes; I came after Sanai and Attar.

Until this time, No one had written a stand-alone book about Sanai. I decided to write about him.

We left for Ghazni, and it was a beautiful sojourn. With me were Osman Khan, Najibullah Khan, and Saheb Dadd Khan, who was a photographer and at that time, Sardar Najibullah Khan's employee.

Let me introduce Najibullah Khan. He was the son of General Mohammad Younus Khan, a Commandant of the Royal Guard of Amir Habibullah Khan Seraj. He was the grandson of Sardar Mohammad Yousef Khan and the great-grandson of Amir Dost Mohammad Khan. His father, Mohammad Younus Khan, was married to the sister of Amir Habibullah Khan Seraj. She had a title of Ukhtul Seraj (sister of Seraj). In other words, Najibullah Khan and his brother Annus Khan were the sons of the sister of Habibullah Khan. However, Amanullah Khan did not like them.

172

Najibullah Khan, Osman Khan Amir, and Saheb Dadd Khan went to Ghazni. The reason Osman Khan went with us was first, because he was my friend, and second, because he loved Ghazni. His father, Amir Mohammad Khan, was the Governor of Ghazni for many years. During the time of Amir Habibullah Khan Seraj, Osman Khan spent most of his youth in Ghazni. He was educated there, and he had friends in Ghazni. People always recalled his father with respect. They also respected Osman Khan very much. He used to say, "Whenever I die, bury me in Ghazni next to Ali La Lai Ghaznavi," even though his ancestral cemetery was in Kabul.

We traveled to Ghazni. It was springtime, and the roses had bloomed. I had just read the *History by Baihaqi* (the Afghan historian) and *Riazul-Al-Waah,* a book written by Sheikh Mohammad Reza Sohail during the time of Amir Habibullah Khan Seraj. I had read other books in Arabic and Persian about Ghazni like *A Full History of Ibne Aseer*, *History of Abul Feda*, *History of Farishta*, *History of Habibul-Sair*, *History of Rowza,* and others. I had almost become "Ghazni" myself.

Naijbullah Khan and Osman Jan Amir

On our way to Ghazni we passed all the places I had read about, and I was eager to share that rich history with my companions. I wanted to proclaim to everyone that the Rowza Shrine was here, or the Seemgran Street (garment district) was there, or the Khayaban-e-Zareen Kumran, which Baihaqi mentions, was within our sight. We could see the Nau Bagh (new garden), which Baihaqi also mentions and the Kakh-e-Mahmood (palace).

Najibullah Khan and I were both very proficient in history. He had read French materials extensively regarding Ghazni. I was bursting to discuss these things. Unfortunately Osman Jan, who was older than us, continuously talked about minutia, without allowing us to speak. We would pass one significant place and he would say, "Remember Saheb Dadd Khan, right there is where my father pitched our tent when we came together on this day or that day in Ghazni." As soon as we passed that place, he would interrupt again. "Oh, and remember when my father came to this place? You were with me. The people of the area sacrificed a sheep for him." His interruptions about little things like tents or sheep were becoming unbearable to me. Finally, he pointed to another place and said, "Look! Do you remember my father came here, riding an orange-colored horse? There were other riders, 30 to 40 of them with him. They pitched a tent over there."

I abruptly said, "Stop the car!" When the driver pulled over, I threatened to get out. "We are not talking about the great Sultan Mahmood Ghaznavi and his three thousand elephants and the empire of Mahmood Ghaznavi and his conquests and victories! We are talking about the little orange horse your father was riding! I have not come to Ghazni for this. We want to talk about the grand things of history. I will walk to Ghazni. You, my friends, may continue your travel."

Every one burst into laughter. Osman Jan went silent and did not bring up his stories about his travels with his father again.

We went to the hotel in Ghazni and spent a few days there. What a remarkable few nights those were. I cherish their memory. Every morning after prayers we would read couplets and odes of Farrukhi (the renowned Persian poet). We read the poetry of Ansuri too. We would visit every nook and cranny of Ghazni, every garden, every historical heritage, and every house. Then, we would read the history of Baihaqi and discuss it until bedtime.

One day we stopped to eat while visiting the Shrine of Khwaja Balghar. We ordered the famous kabobs of Ghazni. They brought the kabobs for us, and out of nowhere an uninvited man, an indigent beggar or Dervish appeared among us. He had a small beard and beautiful eyes. His appearance had a mesmerizing effect. Some people whispered, "He's a very famous and frenzied Dervish of Ghazni. If he slaps anyone on the face, it will bring good fortune for that person. That person will have both spiritual and financial success."

I, being simple hearted and deprived of both these things –spiritual and financial success – I put my face forward and said in a flattering way to the Dervish, "Your eyes rival the eyes of Hakim Sanai; your beard reflects Bemlooh-e-Dana (knowledge)...your face mirrors that of Ali Lala! Why don't you slap my face for the sake of God?"

He slapped me softly. I turned my other cheek and said, "Slap me on this side, as well."

He slapped me softly again and suddenly started laughing. He spoke beautifully. "Brother," he said, "Who am I that I should slap you for good fortune? May God himself strike you! May all the forces of Ghazni strike you! I am nothing to slap you. My slapping you is not sufficient!" Hearing his humble words, we all laughed, went back to the hotel and reluctantly ended our journey.

Sardar Faiz Mohammad Khan Zikriya

One of my very dear friends with whom we always got together, Sardar Faiz Mohammad Khan Zikriya, was the Minister of Foreign Affairs at that time. He enjoyed the number three spot in the hierarchy of power in Kabul. Zikriya Khan had superior qualities. He was a graduate of Habibiya Serajia School. His writing was polished and immaculate. He was an eloquent speaker. Your appetite was never satisfied with hearing him talk. He was very sincere and true to his faith. He was as devout and pious as a Dervish. He was handsome, with beautiful, captivating eyes. He was very dignified and carried himself well as a Minister of Foreign Affairs.

Sardar Ibrahim Khan relied on Zikriya Khan for his intelligence and his grasp of foreign affairs. Every three or four weeks, he would either come to my humble abode or call me on the phone and say, "Khalil Khan, come over, and let's go somewhere." My father was a friend of his father. Zikriya Khan was one of the Sardars of Kabul (royal family). He was related to Mohammad Nadir Khan. We would get in a car and ride away from Kabul. In winter, we would go to Jalalabad. In spring, we would go to Kohistan or Gulbahar or to Yaka Toot, where he had his own house and garden and orchards. Yaka Toot is about 90 miles

175

northeast of Kabul on the banks of the Rud Khana River. This is where Zikriya Khan had inherited land from his father.

He was a good marksman and liked to go hunting and fishing. I enjoyed his company. It was very fruitful, and his discourse was very informative. He had a very sweet tongue. He used to address the personnel of the Ministry of Foreign Affairs every day and also taught them. As God's witness, I would vouch that when Sardar Mohammad Daoud and Sardar Mohammad Naim Khan (two brothers, sons of Abdul Aziz Khan) came to power, he used to say, "They have a tendency toward being pro-Soviet. I know that Afghanistan will be lost." When he said this, he would touch his beard (an Afghan way of vouching). I remember his words: "Wait and see, very soon the Red fire will engulf Afghanistan. Wait, either today or tomorrow. It is fast approaching." This was long before the pro-Communists and pro-Soviet coup in Afghanistan.

Finally, he was removed from Kabul and appointed Ambassador to Turkey and Saudi Arabia.

But at that time, when we were in Kabul and were subjected to intimidation, he used to come to our side to help. He was well versed in Bedil (the Persian poet) and had written and published a small booklet in Iran, titled *What Does Bedil Say?*

We had good relations with the literary circles of Iran. Sayed Nafisi came to Afghanistan at that time. We went up to Ghazni to welcome him and brought him to Kabul as a very dignified and respected guest. He was welcomed very warmly. Prime Minister Sardar Mohammad Hashim Khan frowned upon all of these activities. We knew that he did not like it, and if Najibullah Khan had not been part of these activities, we would have been thrown into jail.

Hazrat (Messers) Shamsul Mashaiq and Noorul Mashaiq

At this time a young man returned to Afghanistan from Egypt. His name was Hazrat Mohammad Masoom Mojaddidi. He was the son of Hazrat Shamsul Mashaiq, the older brother of Hazrat Noorul Mashaiq.

Shamsul Mashaiq and Noorul Mashaiq were famous as Hazrats (spiritual leaders) of Shor Bazar. Hazrat is a title of respect that means Excellency or is sometimes used for prophets. Shor Bazar is a very populated and congested neighborhood in downtown Kabul. They were descendants of Hazrat Mojaddidul-Alif Saani and part of the freedom fighters during the War of Independence against the British (May 6-August 8, 1919). Amir Amanullah Khan had given them land, other recognitions and bestowed on them the titles of Shamsul Mashaiq and Noorul Mashaiq. They were among the leading spiritual and scholarly families of Afghanistan.

Upon his return from Egypt to Kabul, Mohammad Masoom Khan, one day came looking for me at my house. Actually, it was not my house, but a very humble room where I lived. I was informed that Hazrat Saheb (which both mean Excellency) had arrived. I had a great deal of respect for Shamsul Mashaiq and Noorul Mashaiq because they had opposed Amanullah Khan in the killing of my father. I ran as fast as I could to the outside door. There, I saw a young man with a cap on his head, just like any Arab youth. He had a very small beard. He was wearing chic clothing and was handsome and good looking. He smiled. I thought he was the forbearer of the news that Hazrat Saheb is himself coming.

I shook his hand and asked, "Where is Hazrat Saheb?"

He inquired, "Which Hazrat are you talking about?"

I replied, "Masoom Jan Agha."

He replied, "Even though I am Masoom (which means innocent), I'm not that innocent. These days, you cannot find an innocent man."

I greeted him warmly. "Come, let's go upstairs to my room," I invited.

He was a very gracious man, very respectful, and had scholarly qualities. Everything that I can think about his personality was good. That day, we became friends. He honored us by joining our circle of friends.

Sayed Shamsuddin Majrooh

Another young man came from Kunar in Nangarhar, an Afghan province with the major city of Jalalabad. His name was Sayed Shamsuddin Majrooh. He was the brother of Shaal Pacha, whom I liked very much. His father's name was Sayed Pacha Saheb of Tagari (Sayed means related to Prophet Mohammad, PBUH). I had the utmost respect for him. The Prime Minister appointed him as a member of the House of Elders. When I was informed that Sayed Shamsuddin Pacha was outside, I went out, and we saw each other for the first time. I liked him very much. He had a very good way of communication, and he was very personable. He talked about poetry and prose, and philosophy and history. He was very witty and pleasant, and he liked to banter and jest. It seemed that we had known each other for years. Thus Hazrat Sayed Masoom Jan (famous as Mian Jan Agha), Sayed Shamsuddin Majrooh, Sardar Najibullah Khan, Osman Jan, and I became friends. We used to gather always on Friday nights, either in my room or at Sarwar Goya's. (In his memoirs, Majrooh remembers Khalili very fondly).

Mohammad Sarwar Goya

Mohammad Sarwar Goya was the grandson of Prime Minister Abdul Quddos Khan. He was a good friend of mine. I wrote an ode about him upon his death. We would spend days and nights together at his place. All our friends gathered there. He had no wife or children. Our friends included Ghulam Masoom Mojaddadi, Sayed Shamsuddin Khan Majrooh, Mohammad Anus Khan, and Najibullah Khan. He served traditional Afghan dishes, and we read books together until dawn, talking about literature and poetry and sometimes criticizing the government. Sarwar Goya was well known in Iran. The Afghan government did not like his popularity with the Iranians.

He was very fluent in poetry and was a good literary critic. He was a tall, handsome man, very eloquent, humble, Dervishi, and a confirmed bachelor all his life.

At times, he stayed in a room at the power station in Deh Mazang, an old Kabul neighborhood, or lived in a room above a shop. The room above the shop in Deh Mazang was especially for us. Four or five of us would get together on Friday nights at the house of Goya Saheb. We would go to his room, close the door, and feel safe that we would not be disturbed. We would sit together, and he would cook for us himself and prepare some tasty dishes. Where ever he could find the best of fruits, he would bring them for us. We would sit around and read and talk about Bedil, and we always had a tussle among us who would read Bedil first. I would do that, or Goya Saheb, or on occasion, Sayed Shamsuddin Khan. Sardar Najibullah Khan would also get his share. In that room, we would forget the trail of time. The night passed, and the day dawned on us, with a beautiful sunrise. Most of the time, we talked about poetry, on occasion we talked about the incompetence of the government and criticized Sardar Mohammad Hashim Khan.

Abdul Rahman Pazwak

Abdul Rahman Pazwak came to Kabul. He was the son of Abdullah Khan. His father headed the Justice Committee in the House of Elders. He was a respected personality from Baghbani in Jalalabad. His father was a friend of my father. Pazwak was a good-looking young man. He went to Habibiya School, and from there he went to the medical school, where he studied for two years. There he had to deal with urine and pus, and discovered he did not like dealing with bodily fluids, so he quit medical school. He had a good literary understanding and wrote well. He became friends with Sarwar Goya. He started writing poetry and became a poet. He used to send the first drafts of his poems to me to look at and improve them. However, I do not remember that I improved any of his poems.

He had a great vitality in poetry. He also joined our circle of friends. He was very sensitive and got upset easily. I remember he would get a little hot under the collar and lose his temper quickly. Sometimes our friends would try to avoid Pazwak Sahib to keep away from any tension.

However, I loved him very much and respected him.

During the day we would go to the Prime Ministry for our official jobs, and we knew that while we were there, we had no rights. Every day we would walk to work, passing the house of Sardar Mohammad Daoud and Sardar Mohammad Naim Khan. Pacha Saheb or I, or sometimes Miam Jan Agha, would recite this line from poetry:

O, God, destroy this house of injustice and oppression....

We did not realize that the day would come when this house would be destroyed, and we would be destroyed with it.

Dr. Mohammad Annus Khan

Sardar Mohammad Annus Khan returned from Turkey. He was the younger brother of Najibullah Khan. When we first met him, he seemed like a very dry, rigid, and inflexible man – rough and rude. He had a face that was white and round like the moon. You could not see any warmth in his face. We met at the house of Najibullah Khan and eventually became friends. I found out he had a world of information. He was well versed in the German, Turkish, and Arabic languages. His Persian was very good, and he was familiar with English. He held a PhD in Mathematics. He was a kind man. The only negative about him was that he was very frugal. He was not generous toward others. As the saying goes, a bird could never find anything to eat, if he ate first.

He was very witty and a man of letters. He had a mastery of words, and his eloquence was unquestionable. If I were to write about his mastery, it would take a book. Unfortunately, he died and did not leave any journals or memoirs. He was Deputy Minister of Education, then Minister of Education and later, Minister of Information and Culture. He was also the President of the Kabul University at one time. During the ugly times of the Communists in Kabul, he died in vain.

Fall of Bokhara

I finished writing the book on Hakim Sanai Ghaznavi and titled it, *The Biography and Works of Hakim Sanai*. It was well received by those who read it. My friends wrote introductions and forewords to it. Hashim Shaiq Afandi, who was a respected and revered professor, wrote a foreword. Karim Nazihi, a very famous literary figure, also wrote an introduction.

Hashim Shaiq Afandi was from Bokhara. Going back in history, when the Communists deceived the youth of Bokhara, they staged a revolt against the government and established a new system in Bokhara. They forced the King of Bokhara to seek refuge in Afghanistan. This was at the advent of the rule of Amanullah Khan, approximately 1920.

Hashim Shaiq Afandi was appointed as the Ambassador to Kabul for the young state of Bokhara. The Bokhara Embassy was near the banks of the Kabul River. It had a flag fluttering above it and a staff of two or three personnel who worked there. There is no doubt that the people of Kabul looked toward the embassy of Bokhara with respect; however, the refugees who had crossed into Afghanistan from Bokhara did not like the Embassy. They were not happy with the new government in Bokhara, either. They called the government a puppet of the Soviets, and the result of a deceitful conspiracy of the Communists to take over Bokhara. They predicted that this puppet government would fall soon, that the Communists would totally annihilate the name of Bokhara, and that it would never be free.

Hashim Shaiq Afandi, Last Ambassador to Afghanistan from Bokhara

Hashim Shaiq Afandi was at the Embassy in Kabul. I think he lasted a couple of years before the new government of Bokhara finally fell. The Foreign Ministry of Afghanistan wanted to inform Afandi about the fall of the government. I am paraphrasing Osman Jan Amir here, as I was in Kohistan at the time. Osman Jan was a head clerk at that time at the Ministry of Foreign Affairs in Kabul. He was a very trustworthy and straight talker. He said that Mahmoud Baig Tarzi, the Minister of Foreign Affairs was very upset at the fall of Bokhara. He even had tears in his eyes at this incident. He directed Sardar Abdul Rahman Khan (brother of Sardar Abdul Wahab Khan), who was the Second Deputy Minister of Foreign Affairs, to summon the Ambassador of Bokhara and inform him about the fall of the government so he could remove the flag from his embassy (1917, establishment of Soviet rule). Abdul Rahman Khan accepted this assignment reluctantly. The Foreign Minister had tears in his eyes when he told him to relay the bad news to the Ambassador of a friendly and brotherly Islamic country. Osman Jan said, "I was young, and I wanted to see how an Ambassador declares the fall of his government and how will it come to an end."

Hashim Shaiq came to the Ministry of Foreign Affairs in a horse-drawn buggy, and as usual, he was received with respect and a guard of honor. This was done at the behest of Mahmoud Baig Tarzi. Hashim Shaiq was brought into the reception room of the Ministry. The Ministry of Foreign Affairs was where it is located now. It was called Stor Palace at that time, and it was one of the cornerstones of Amir Habibullah Khan Seraj.

The Ambassador made his entrance. He was a scholarly man and spoke in Persian with his Bokhara accent. He exchanged greetings with Sardar Abdul Rahman Khan, who was also a very learned man. He welcomed the Ambassador very warmly; however, he did not serve tea.

He said, "I regret to give you bad news."

The Ambassador asked, "Is it about my young son, who was sick in Bokhara? Has he passed away?"

"No," said Sardar Abdul Rahman Khan. "I wish your son had died, and this was the news about his death."

"Did my wife die?" asked the Ambassador, growing more alarmed.

"I wish it had been your wife," he answered.

"So what has happened?" asked Hashim Shaiq. "Please hurry up!"

"I cannot bring myself to tell you what has happened,"

he replied.

The ambassador was insistent. Sardar Abdul Rahman Khan said, "The sacred Bokhara has fallen, and the government has been dissolved. Some people have been killed, and the Communists have captured Bokhara totally."

This man, who was always very dignified, suddenly started shaking and turned his face toward the sky. His eyes rolled up, and he fell down, passing out on the floor. Sardar Abdul Rahman Khan ordered the staff to bring rosewater, which is a mixture of sweet water with rose extract. They helped the Ambassador drink the rosewater, and he returned to full consciousness.

Abdul Rahman Khan said, "This is what I wanted to tell you." However, he did not mention anything about the removal of the flag. The Ambassador saw to that himself. He went back to the Embassy and told others what had happened. They refused to take down their flag. So he asked one of the Afghan guards to do this, and the Bokhara flag was taken down.

The Flag after the Defeat of Hitler

I remember when Nazi Germany fell in 1943 during World War II, Sardar Najibullah Khan, then Political Director General, was asked to inform the German Ambassador to lower their flag. Najibullah Khan said it was a strange experience. He went to the German Embassy, which was near the Shrine of Shah-e-do Shamshera (King of Two Swords), and he was pretty upset about how to break this news. However, he discovered that when he went there, the Ambassador already knew what had happened.

"After an exchange of greetings, I passed on the news, and I told him that my government has said that you are a guest of the government of Afghanistan during the time you are here," said Najibullah Khan. "However, it is better that you lower your flag."

The German Ambassador answered, "Yes, this is customary, and I will do that. I cannot do it myself, but I will ask my Chargé d'Affaires."

The Chargé d'Affaires refused. If I remember well, there was a gray-bearded German man named Fisher, who was a medical doctor. I do not want him to be mixed up with the other Dr. Fisher who was hired by the municipality of Kabul to practice medicine in Kabul and was in the employ of Afghanistan. But this German doctor, who was the exclusive physician for the Embassy said, "I will take care of it." He said that when bad times come human beings turn to three things: If they are God-fearing, they turn to God and trust that whatever happens is at the behest of God, because God is beautiful, wise, and all knowing. God will not do anything that will hurt the interest of his creation.

If they do not recognize God and are more inclined toward philosophy and metaphysics, then they will look in bad times toward what their beliefs say about the rise and fall of worldly social states, and find satisfaction through this.

And if they do not believe in God or philosophy, then in bad times it's very simple: they will turn toward history. They look at history and see that it is full of such occurrences, especially the history of the people of Germany, which is full of ups and downs, peaks and valleys.

He said, "The fall of the Third Reich (Nazi Germany 1945) is also an example. Germany has come out of a lot of valleys and will come out of this as well. I believe in all these things, and my faith convinces me that it is happening at the behest of God. Based on my beliefs, I will go and lower this flag."

With shaking hands and unsteady steps he went up on the ladder and brought down the flag. When he came down he looked very much affected by the whole experience.

The Story of Bokhara Continues

Thus Hashim Shaiq Afandi remained in Kabul, and the government of Amanullah Khan welcomed and respected him. Hashim Shaiq said, "I will not return to Bokhara, even though I know that I have a wife, a son, and a daughter there. I will have to leave all of them. They may be killed, but I'm not going to return. It is not my country any more. It has been expropriated by the Soviets, taken over by the

Communists, and it is the country of atheists. If you accept me, I will remain in Afghanistan; if Afghanistan will not accept me, I will move on."

Amanullah Khan accepted him, and he was given political asylum in Kabul. Because Afghan-Soviet relations were on a good footing, these small things did not bother the Soviets.

Hashim Shaiq Afandi was a man of letters. He had completed his higher education in Turkey. He had memorized 18 chapters of the Holy Koran. He was a very good writer and a poet. He was also an accomplished researcher. He was fluent in three languages: Turkish, Persian, and Arabic. He was appointed at the Ministry of Education as the head of the Compilation Department. He was also assigned to edit the literary and cultural magazine called *Aiinai-e-Urfan* (Mirror of Knowledge). On the masthead of the magazine he would always carry this verse:

Faulad me fisharam
va aiina me kunam.

I press the steel
And turn it into mirror.

Gradually, Hashim Shaiq established himself. Sardar Azizullah Khan, the son of Sardar Nasrullah Khan, was the Regent and the son of Amanullah Khan's uncle (cousin of Amanullah Khan). He gave his daughter in marriage to Hashim Shaiq Afandi, of course, with the blessing of Amanullah Khan. Thus, Hashim Shaiq was patched into the royal family of the time.

Azizullah Khan was a scholar and a poet. He was the Ambassador of Afghanistan to Iran during the time of Nadir Shah. His pen name was Qateel, and his collection of poetry was published in Tehran under the title, *Divan-e-Qateel*. His father, Sardar Nasrullah Khan the Regent was also a learned and well-read man. On his direction, the collection of Mirza Abdul Qadir (Bedil) was published up to the Persian letter of Daal. He was the Regent who knew the Holy Koran by heart. He was the first Mohammad Zai (ruling class) prince who, during the time of Amir Abdul Rahman Khan (reigned May 31, 1880 to October 1, 1901) represented Afghanistan and went to London to attend the Court of Queen Victoria (reigned June 20, 1837 to January 22, 1901). His sojourn was very much talked about at that time. Unfortunately, those writings have been lost.

Sardar Mohammad Hassan Khan, Famous as Hassan Siyah (Black)

One of the companions of Sardar Nasrullah Khan was Sardar Mohammad Hassan Khan Siyah. He was the grandson of Wazir Fateh Khan. Sardar Hassan Khan was an educated man and a good poet, with beautiful handwriting. He was very dark in complexion, tall, and well built – a heavy man, as is obvious from his photographs. He had also accompanied the Regent. He had written a pamphlet or treatise entitled, *The Journey of the Regent*. Sardar Hassan Khan composed it in his own handwriting. At one time, this pamphlet was in possession of Sardar Mohammad Siddique Khan Waziri, the grandson of Sardar Hassan Khan Siyah. We tried our best to have this pamphlet published in Kabul, but the government would not allow it for some unspoken or hidden reason. I do not know who has that pamphlet now. It was a beautifully written literary work with very lively stories.

As the saying goes, "Talk gives rise to talk," or stories follow stories. Even though the pamphlet is gone, I still remember some of the stories included in it.

For example, he had written a story about the time, when the Regent was in London, that he was invited to a target-shooting exhibition. One of Sayeds of Kunar was with him. I do not remember his name, but I recall seeing him. He was one of those revolutionary Sayeds of Kunar who had taken part in the Afghan War of Independence against Britain (1880). He appeared to be a spiritual man and was dressed in traditional robes with roped braids and a turban. When the Sayed of Kunar picked up the gun and aimed for the target, some of the Englishmen who were around and accompanying him, laughed. One of them said, "This man with a beard and strange clothes has no chance of hitting the target."

The Sayed did not like the reaction of the people around. He proved them wrong by hitting the target with three bullets in such rapid succession that it tore the target away from where it was secured.

Through an interpreter, they asked him, "Where did you learn such marksmanship?"

He replied, "I was part of the Battle of Maiwand (1880). I learned it there, fighting the British."

This was a slap in the face of the Englishmen because Britain had lost the battle of Maiwand.

Another interesting story from Sardar Hassan Khan, which he wrote, is this: One night, the British held a reception for Sardar Nasrullah Khan at either Buckingham Palace or another palace in London. It was a very majestic affair. After a couple of nights, as a matter of protocol, the Regent was obligated to reciprocate and throw a reception in honor of the Queen. This was also a very elegant party that featured Afghan cuisine. Chefs and servers had accompanied the Regent from Kabul and dressed in traditional Afghan garb. The Sardar said, "I was standing with two or three other people at the entrance, welcoming the guests. Groups of men and women were entering the hall. We paid our respects to them according to the protocol."

"At this time we saw across the room an older gentleman, bald, wearing a military uniform with lots of insignia on his chest. I was told that he was Lt. General Frederick Roberts (he marched on Kandahar and took part in the Battle of Baba Wali, Second Anglo-Afghan War, September 1880, in southern Afghanistan). This was the general who had come to Afghanistan and had fought against the Afghans, killing many of them. (To the British Army regiments he was 'Our Bob.' To the Indian Army regiments he was 'Bob Bahadur' (Bob the Lion). Afghans called him 'Roberts the Bald.'

The Sardar continued. "I had a flashback to this memory, and I felt resentment in my heart like a hard knot.

He came close to me and tried to shake hands with me. Because he was old and I was young and very strong, I pressed his hand hard several times, so that he was forced to bow in front of me. His face showed that he realized I had done this intentionally.

He stopped and through an interpreter asked, "Who are you?"

I said, "My name is Hassan Siyah. I am the grandson of Wazir Fateh Khan."

He said, "You don't recognize me?"

I said, "No, I don't remember who you are." I did it on purpose.

He said, "I am General Frederick Roberts."

I answered, "Very well. I do not recognize you by your face or front. Why don't you turn around? If I see you from the back, I might recollect who you are because I may have seen you running away from the battle. Let me assure myself whether you are the same person who I had seen running away or not."

The translator did his job, and the General was very offended. He went ahead and attended the party, which must have been difficult for him.

He continued the story. "Either the next day, or the following day, an official letter arrived from the British Ministry of Foreign Affairs. It was addressed to Nasrullah Khan. The letter stated that 'it is unfortunate that one of the well-known personalities of Great Britain, a very versatile general came to your house and one of your staff, Mohammad Hassan Siyah insulted him. Mohammad Hassan should apologize to him.'

This letter was read to Sardar Nasrullah Khan. It was customary to send the English letter with the translation in Persian (Dari). I realized what the matter was and why the letter had arrived. During our stay in England the Sardar was being very careful not to deviate from the policy and program, which was assigned to him by Amir Abdul Rahman Khan. The protocol and directions on the Afghan delegation's behavior in London was detailed in almost 200 pages.

However, my reaction to General Robert was not part

of the script. The Regent called me in and laid it on me. "You see what you have done! Who is going to answer my father? He will punish me and you both!"

I said, "Your Highness, Sardar Saheb, I'm the one who did this. And I'm the one who should answer this. Please allow me to answer the letter. Please send him my reply. If the British government accepts my letter with my argument, fine. Otherwise, I am going with you to Afghanistan. Your father will not punish you. I will tell him that in spite of your opinion and warning, I did this. Please, let me accept my responsibility. If you have to kill me, I'm here. If you want to put me on the gallows, I accept. If you want to tie me to a tree and hang me there, I accept."

He said, "Well, you should not have done this, but go ahead, write a reply."

Hassan Khan wrote the letter on behalf of the Ministry of Foreign Affairs. The letter said: We summoned Hassan Siyah, and he said, "Never has the Afghan government looked toward the government of Great Britain with enmity. We have never attacked the land of Great Britain. However, three times the British government attacked Afghanistan without any obvious reason. When you established a friendship between the British government and Afghanistan and you hosted a reception for us, we thought we should forget what happened in the past, and we accepted your invitation. We assumed that this friendship will flourish, and the roots of enmity will have been dissolved.

Unfortunately, Hassan Khan says, when we came here the same general who had killed thousands of innocent Afghans was also invited to this gala. We took it for granted that the British government still feels proud of the generals who kill the people of Afghanistan and the people of other countries it colonizes.

Hassan Khan says that while we are the guests of your government, we have not given our right to look at someone as our enemy. We believe that someone like that is not only our enemy, but your enemy, also. We consider someone like that the common enemy of Afghanistan and Great Britain.

Hassan Khan admits to what you are charging. Now, Hassan Khan is going back with us to Afghanistan and will narrate the incident to my father. Whatever is his fate, he will be dealt with in Afghanistan according to Afghan laws. We will keep you posted upon the decision of my father regarding Hassan Khan."

There were a few other stories in that pamphlet or treatise. He also wrote about the ladies of Paris. He said that while in Paris we went to Champs Elysees (Shanza Lysee). "Every morning we would sit in the sidewalk cafés and people thought that I was either a wrestler or a giant because I was big, black, and heavy. I would sit in a big chair and fold my sleeves back, exposing my black forearms, heavy with hair. I could be seen from far away. There were girls who came around me, and I would pick up a book to act nonchalant, but I would catch glimpses at the girls from the corner of my eye. These girls were so beautiful, that my heart would come to my throat. However, I had no power to act on my feelings. So I would get up and leave, missing all those ladies with their long hair and short skirts. I used to enjoy those moments." There were other stories, which I'm not going to narrate at this time.

Hashim Shaiq Afandi married the daughter of Azizullah Khan and made Kabul his home. We became good friends. He had a very rich library in his house. Since Sardar Nasrullah Khan's possessions were confiscated, some of his manuscripts were passed on to Sardar Azizullah Khan. Sardar Azizullah Khan also died and his daughters received these priceless manuscripts as their inheritance. Some of those rare books ended up at Hashim Afandi's house as inheritance.

His house was located near the Kabul River in a neighborhood of downtown Kabul called Pul-e-khishte (brick bridge). He was very generous. On one side of his house he had built a room as a library, and he opened it to students. I also used to go there to sit and read. Sometimes Kareem Nazihi would join me. Najibullah Khan also came. We would read books, recite poetry, and have a full literary discourse. We would have dinner at Afandi's house.

Sometimes we would lose track of time and would be there until morning. Gradually each of us would leave and go to our own houses.

He also owned a small orchard in Paghman, a resort area about 10 kilometers from Kabul. He was very proud of it and would invite us there during the springtime. He was a good elder friend and a great scholar. The only regret was that whenever we used to go walking together in winter and see the surrounding snow, Hazrat Afandi would begin reciting poetry under his breath in his Bokhara accent. He knew the meaning of the poetry, and he would go into a trance, with tears rolling down his cheeks and through his glasses. We knew what was happening and asked him if he was all right. He would say, "I remember Bokhara." A line from his poetry, about "the same wind blowing from Bokhara brushes against my face here," was very touching and was always about his country and his feelings toward it. He was expressing his feelings of pride.

During his lifetime, when the city was being expanded, the government mapped out his property. He was very upset about this. He moved to Jade Maiwand, a famous street in downtown Kabul and lived in an apartment there toward the end of his life. After a long illness, he died in that apartment. I was there with him during his last hours. I was afflicted by sorrow.

He told me, "Khalili, you should write the epitaph on my grave."

I told him, "God willing, you'll be alive, and you will write an ode for me."

He said, "I have willed that after my death I should be buried south of Kohe Sherdarwaza (a neighborhood in Kabul). Even though the Shuhadai Saleheen (Martyrs Cemetery) is a great place, bury me north of Kohe-Asmai (mountain) close to the grave of Sardar Nasullah Khan at Qole Chakan. (All of these are historic names that are part of the honored heritage of Kabul.)

I asked him why, and he said, "Because the wind from Bokhara reaches there faster." He said this and closed his eyes. I remembered these things when I dictated these memoirs in New Jersey (1985-86). May God bless my recounting of these stories and my Ustad (teacher).

May God bless him and keep him under his covenant, may God bless him and keep him under his covenant, may God bless him and keep him under his covenant.

May God engulf him in his benevolence and confer on him his benevolence.

Kareem Nazihi

Kareem Nazihi was the son of Qazi Baba Murad. He was from Maimana and Andkhoi (provinces in northern Afghanistan). He belonged to the Uzbek tribe. His father was a famous Qazi (judge). He died in Mazar-i-Sharif. When he was a young and wealthy man, of the middle class, I came to know him. He was well educated and fluent in English. I admit I have lost affection for him because of his action in later years. It is said that toward the end of his life he had connections with the Communists in Kabul. I earnestly hope that this was not true. He was a poet too, but unfortunately, he has not left a book or a magazine with his writing, though I believe some of his writing may have appeared in *Ariana* and *Kabul* magazines. There is no doubt he was a learned man and a good researcher.

During this time I was a simple clerk at the Secretariat without an office. I used to help out by working with appointments and in provincial affairs. Gradually, I realized I was under surveillance and was turning into a political prisoner.

Hashim Khan Departs to Europe for Treatment; Shah Wali Khan Takes Over as Prime Minister

One year, during the autumn on a Wednesday, when Sardar Mohammad Hashim Khan was seated in the Secretariat living room along with Mirza Mohammad Khan, the Minister of State, he said, "Regretfully, something ominous has occurred." (Sardar Mohammad Hashim Khan ruled Afghanistan as Royal Prime Minister from November 14, 1929 to May 1946. He was born in

1885 and died in 1953. During his tenure he turned to Germany for economic assistance.)

Mirza Khan said, "Your Highness, what has happened? Please tell us."

Pointing to his lower body, Hashim Khan said, "I am not feeling well, and I have excruciating pain." (He described a pain in his testicles, symptoms of the same cancer that took his father's life, Sardar Yousef Khan). Hashim Khan reminisced lovingly about his father and described his courageous battle with the illness.

Mirza Mohammad Khan said, "Your Highness is very busy with the work of the state and does not have time to care for himself and his well-being."

Hashim Khan disclosed he had already called in a doctor. "I have been advised to travel to Europe as soon as possible for a procedure."

Mirza Mohammad Khan, and almost all of us, wanted him to have the operation. We told him in unison, "Your Highness should go for treatment as soon as possible. Your health is extremely important. Without you in sound health, this country will face disaster."

With pleading from all around, he concurred and admitted he had already sent a telegram to His Highness, Wakil Saheb. Sardar Shah Wali Khan Ghazi was also known as Field Marshal (if you are killed in Jehad you're called *shaheed* or martyr; if you survive Jehad, you are called *ghazi*). He was Afghanistan's Ambassador to France or London. I do not remember very well. The Prime Minister said, "As soon as he gets here, he will take over the Prime Ministry, and I will leave." (Shah Wali Khan was acting Prime Minister from 1936 to 1937. He was also called *Fateh Kabul*, or Conqueror of Kabul. His career extended from 1906 to 1949.)

Mirza Mohammad Khan answered, "Until he arrives, you should stop working and rest. The work will continue. Your health is paramount to all of us."

Sardar Hashim Khan had no choice except to rest. Sardar Shah Wali Khan would come back to Afghanistan and set up his office at the Prime Ministry. Meanwhile, I worked with Sardar Hashim Khan to compose a speech, which would announce the news he would be leaving due to illness. "I have served Afghanistan and have no other desire," it began. "Now that I am afflicted with a life-threatening illness, I would respectfully request my brothers of the Afghan nation to pray for my recovery. No matter where I am in the world, I will be serving Afghanistan. It is my duty. I have great love for Afghanistan. And I cannot forget it." He liked what I had written and read it aloud several times.

Sardar Hashim Khan had a habit of giving a speech as a decree and whenever he did that he would ask me to write it. He would pour out his thoughts, and I would take them and go to the subject. When he would reread them, he often remarked, "This is exactly what I wanted to say, and you wrote it!" I was careful to have him review any transcript before it was released. I did not want to be accused of committing treachery or perjury. I also did not want to be part of any action that might hurt Afghanistan's interests.

We were intimidated by the news of Marshal Shah Wali's arrival. We feared unknown changes and assumed because he was a military man, he must be very rigid and rude. We were also aware of the competition and rivalry among the five sons of Sardar Yousef Khan. (Nadir Khan, Shah Wali Khan, and Shah Mahmoud Khan had one mother. Hashim Khan and Abdul Aziz Khan had another. All five had Sardar Yousef Khan as their father.)

I had never met Shah Wali Khan, though I may have seen him a few times in public. When he arrived, I saw that he was a slim man, built very lean, and polite. He came to the Prime Ministry, and we lined up to receive him. He embraced all of us and kissed us on the forehead. He looked at me and said, "Khalilullah Jan," which was surprising to me. "Your father was a good friend of mine. He had an affection for me and a friendship with me."

Shah Wali Khan talked frankly about my father and even shared a few jokes that my father had told him. I was flabbergasted at his friendly behavior in the same place, and in the same office where we had endured anger, rudeness, and heavy handedness for nearly four years. Now, we were being addressed with respect, politeness, and personal talk.

Sardar Mohammad Hashim Khan left for Europe with Germany as his destination. He was supposed to drive up to Peshawar by car and take a plane from there. Many people came to say goodbye to him, but it was staged to show the foreigners that Sardar Mohammad Hashim Khan is a popular figure in Kabul. We had a tradition when someone was leaving for a journey, someone else would give *Aazan*, the Islamic call for prayers (God is great, *Allah-o-akbar*, repeated three times).

A military general stepped forward for the *Aazan*; however, he made a mistake. Instead of facing *Qiblah* (Mecca) he faced the east because Sardar Hashim Khan's car was facing east. The Prime Minister called out from the car, "Turn your face toward *Qiblah*." He turned his face toward *Qiblah*, but he was embarrassed to come forward and give *Aazan*. We also had a cultural tradition of throwing water behind the person who was leaving on the journey. As the custom goes, water was thrown behind Hashim Khan's car.

Sardar Mohammad Ali Khan ran after the car and said, "Sir, you should recite on your way!" The driver hit the brakes, almost hitting Sardar Mohammad Ali Khan. He ran to the car window and repeated to Sardar Hashim Khan, "Please recite on your way *ya (oh) salaam, ya salaam, ya salaam.*"

Finally, the automobile pulled away, taking Hashim Khan toward Europe. We went back to the Prime Ministry and brought our files to Shah Wali Khan. He was kind and compassionate. If someone pretitioned against the prison for someone who was in jail and was innocent, or being oppressed or tortured, he appointed an investigative committee right away. I was part of many committees. He would tell us, "Investigate and get to the truth." If the issues were simple, he decided them himself. More complicated issues were reviewed by the King and, at times, deferred for future review by Hashim Khan on his return.

We received a report that a few prisoners had escaped from jail and had taken refuge at Hazrat Nurul Mashaeq

Saheb's house (the home of one of the Sayeds, related to Prophet Mohammad, PBUH). There were people who wanted to make a big deal about this incident in order to muddy the water and create a wedge between Sardar Shah Wali Khan and his growing popularity.

The Hazrats or religious elders were very respected at this time. An officer named Commander Asif Khan was sent to the residence of Hazrat Saheb. The two escaped prisoners were brought to the mosque, and Hazrat Saheb said, "Take them to Shariah court and let them be dealt with according to what is required by Shariah law. If their crime is proved, they should be punished. If not, they should be released."

The two escapees pled that they were innocent. It was said that their biggest crime was that they escaped against the order of His Highness, the Prime Minister, and they were imprisoned upon his orders. Hazrat Nurul Mashaeq mentioned in passing, "Let them go to the court" and "the order of Sardar Hashim Khan is not an order coming from the Prophet (PBUH) or from God." It is possible he may have erred.

Commander Asif, who had come to collect these prisoners, was an audacious person. He said impudently, "Sir, it is better that you keep quiet."

The Hazrat became very upset and told him, "I am not going to hold back my tongue. My tongue is the tongue of Justice. When your women sought refuge in my house when Habibullah Khan Kalakani came to my house, I gave them refuge and kept them here. My house is the house of Dervishons and a house of refuge and poor people. It is like the house of Hazrat Omar." (Prophet Omar is the original Caliph of Islam in the 7th Century).

He continued, "Anybody can take refuge in my house. These prisoners have sought refuge in my house and if you take them away from here, may God devastate and destroy your home also. I have not done anything wrong except to keep them here. If you treat them justifiably, according to the Shariah law, all is well. If not, I will be their defense lawyer, and I will defend them. Take them away."

They took the prisoners away and the words Hazrat

196

Saheb had uttered about the royal women coming to his house and being protected were repeated, magnified, and vilified. By the time they were reported in front of Wakil Saheb they had totally changed the story. The kindness that had existed between the two was affected, and their relationship was damaged.

It should be remembered here that Hazrat Saheb played a pivotal role during the coronation and ascension to the throne of King Zahir Shah. Born October 14, 1914 in Kabul, Zahir Shah was the son of Mohammad Nadir Shah of the Barakzai family, who was Commander in Chief of the Army under Amanullah Khan. Zahir Shah became King on November 8, 1933 at the age of 19 after the assassination of his father. He ruled Afghanistan until July 17, 1973 when he was overthrown by his cousin and brother-in-law Mohammad Daoud Khan in a palace coup.

Hazrat Saheb was the first person to give allegiance to Zahir Shah and had placed the crown over his head and bestowed upon him the title of Al Motawakkil Allallah (Trustee of God). Hazrat Saheb was offended, and his followers were also upset. Those who had an ax to grind against the government were happy at this incident. (Hazrat Saheb died July 23, 2007 at age 92 and is buried at Maranjan Hill.)

Return of Hashim Khan from Europe

Sardar Mohammad Hashim Khan returned from Germany after nearly five months. Thousands of poor people were staged at the entrance of the post at Dakka near Abbottabad in Pakistan to welcome him into Afghanistan. They were forced to go there to line his route. He spent one night in Jalalabad, the next night a ways farther, and finally he reached Kabul. We all went out to welcome him. There was no work for two days. Finally, the offices were open for business.

Hakim Sanai's Book and Hashim Khan's Wrath

Being an "Honest Abe," I took along with me the book

about Hakim Sanai that I had published earlier. I had mentioned in the foreword of the book that I was very grateful to his Highness, the Prime Minister, who paid special attention to this book and enabled it to be published during his time. I thought it would make him feel proud. As the poet says, *"On the day of judgment everyone will have a letter about their life in their hand."* I would also be present with the picture of my beloved under my arm.

I went to welcome Hashim Khan with the book of Sanai under my arm. When I went before him, and I presented him the book, it seemed that he had already read it. He took it with show of anger and tossed it on the table next to him. "Khalilullah Jan, whatever you have done behind my back, I have been informed," he said.

I was taken aback. I replied, "May God keep his Highness alive, I have no knowledge or idea of what I have done."

He announced, "You will be informed about it soon."

I was very insulted. He had rebuked me in front of everybody. This was against my dignity. The meeting ended.

The next day, Hashim Khan summoned me to meet alone with him.

"You have committed two wrongs," he said. "First, as soon as you saw Shah Jan (his personal name for Shah Wali Khan), you forgot all about us. You were doing everything, and you were doing all his work."

I protested, "Saheb, he was your substitute, and he was not familiar with the operation. I went with him to help him."

He said, "Okay, okay, fine," in a nonchalant way, meaning he did not approve.

Then, he gestured to the table. "What is this?" he asked.

I answered, "Saheb, this is the book of Sanai that I wrote. Please read it."

He said, "No. In the back of the book, you have written the name of Mohammad Yousef, and you sent him a copy. What right did you have to send a book to a prisoner?"

I said, "Saheb, he is my elderly uncle who mentored me. I wanted him to read the book I wrote about Hakim

Sanai. It elucidates about Sufism."

He did not accept my answer. "How did the prisoner get this book?" he asked again.

I said, "I sent it through an official of the prison."

"Okay, you sent a book to a prisoner, but why, on top of it did you write this couplet on the side of the book?" He picked up the book and told me to read it.

There was a custom in our culture that whenever you give a book to somebody you write a poem or couplet in it. I don't remember the name of the poet whose bad fortune it was to compose this couplet, but I read it aloud.

We gave you the treasure of purpose
... though I have not reached there, maybe you will.

I found out later, the prison official, instead of giving this book to my uncle, took it to Sardar Assadullah Khan, the Commander of the Royal Guard at the Palace. Sardar Assadullah Khan interpreted it quite differently. He took the couplet to mean, "if I have not been able to assassinate his Highness, maybe you, my uncle, can do that for me."

This book, which I had written about Hakim Sanai Ghaznavi, the Pride of Afghanistan, and had praised the Prime Minister in it, should have worked in my favor, not against me. I sent the book to my uncle as a token of remembrance. It became my undoing, an albatross.

The couplet refers to the treasure of Sufism, which is wisdom, literature, knowledge, and divinity that we have given to you, the reader. If I cannot reach these goals and my actions fall short, maybe you will read the book and you may achieve those goals. "Reaching" means "understanding or perception." It doesn't mean reaching someone to attack or kill them.

The Prime Minister was always paranoid about assassination. He thought every word of "reaching" meant "assassination." He thought I said, "If I have not been able to reach the objective of hatching a plot against the Royal Nadir Shah Family myself, then you, Mohammad Yousef, a prisoner for seven years, should get together with other prisoners and devise a plan to take action from there to bring down this family and reach our goal."

But I can vouch by the Great God that there was not a grain of truth in this, and we had never thought about it.

Because I became the subject of wrath and indignation, Sardar Mohammad Hashim Khan did not look at me with trust and affection any more. At that time I was one of the unfortunate directors of the Prime Minister's Secretariat. Sometimes, I would do things inadvertently, thinking that it was the prudent thing to do. Whatever I said in my defense did not work. They had formed their opinion, and my reasons did not make any dent.

General Mohammad Siddiq Khan

Saheb Zada Attaul Haq was the Minister of Foreign Affairs of Habibullah Khan Kalakani. He was being held in the palace prison along with his two nephews (the sons of General Mohammad Siddiq Khan). The general was an honest, patriotic army man, and was a friend of Nardir Shahi family. He was a true servant of Afghanistan.

During the War of Independence of Afghanistan in Jalalabad, Sepah Salar (the Commander in Chief) left the field of battle and continued fighting a guerilla war against the English along with Soor (Supreme) General Mohammad Omar Khan and Akleel Khan of Badakhshan (a province in the north of Afghanistan near the Chinese border).

When the body of Sardar Mohammad Yousef Khan (father of Mohammad Hashim Khan) was brought to Afghanistan from India during Amani time to bury him at the Ziyarat (shrine) of Mehtarlam in Laghman, Amanullah Khan ordered that no one should accompany the funeral or show any respect. Mohammad Siddiq Khan, a general in the Afghan Army at Jalalabad, not only welcomed the funeral and attended it, in spite of this restriction, but he also served as one of the pallbearers, helping to carry Yousef Khan's body to his grave and lowering him into it. Siddiq Khan also hosted a condolence meeting, or wake, in Jalalabad afterward. When Amanullah Khan questioned him, Siddiq Khan responded, "Your Highness, you have the right to do what you want, however Nardir Khan was a

friend of mine, and I knew his father."

In spite of all this, Mohammad Siddiq Khan, who had a broken leg, was killed along with others who were close to Habibullah Khan Kalakani. His two young sons were also imprisoned. One of his brothers, Mohammad Karim Jan Saheb Zada, escaped Kabul and took refuge in India, where he lived for a while.

Attaullah Khan had a son by the name of Abdul Haq Wallah (he had not used his pen name Wallah yet). Sher Jan, the brother of Mohammad Siddiq Khan and Attaullah Khan, was the Minister of Court of Habibullah Khan Kalakani. Sher Jan's son's name was Nemat. Both of these young boys, Nemat and Abdul Haq, were not allowed to go to school. The mother of Sher Jan Khan was a very intellectual and brave lady from Kohistan. She was an outstanding woman of her era. She was one of my distant cousins, and she asked me to become a mentor to the two boys and educate them so they would not grow up illiterate.

Let's not forget that the mother of Attaullah Khan was the same lady whom Amir Sher Ali Khan had accepted as his daughter-in-law for the Regent and his beloved son, Abdullah Jan. (Sher Ali Khan, born in 1825, was the son of Dost Mohammad Khan, father of the Barakzai dynasty in Afghanistan. Sher Ali Khan became Amir of Afghanistan in 1863 until 1866, when his older brother ousted him. He regained power again and ruled from 1868 until his death in 1879. Because Abdullah Jan had preceded him in death, when Sher Ali Khan died in Mazar-i-Sharif, he left the throne to his son, Mohammad Yakub Khan).

This young lady was the widow of Abdullah Jan. She was also the daughter of the Khan of Kohistan, Abdul Karim. He was considered to be a mujahidor freedom fighter of Afghanistan (against the British).

Because Amir Mohammad Yakub Khan was not on good terms with his father, when Amir Sher Ali Khan died, he ascended to the throne and as revenge, summoned Abdul Karim Khan to Bala Hissar, a famous and historic citadel of Kabul, and had him killed. His body was torn into 17 parts, and his entire family was eliminated. Amir Yakub Khan did this because he thought Abdul Karim Khan had his daughter engaged to Abdullah Jan because he wanted Abdullah Jan to be king after Amir Sher Khan.

When Abdul Raman Khan came to power, he also was against Abdul Karim Khan. He had the seven sons of Abdul Karim Khan, who had escaped death earlier, arrested. They, along with all their family, were killed, and their land and their 14 grain mills were confiscated.

Only this girl was spared, and she escaped to India with one of her nephews, a child named Abdul Wahab, the grandson of Abdul Karim Khan. In India, they got in touch with Sardar Mohammad Ayub Khan (the Conqueror of Maiwand). He was kind to them. The father of Sher Jan Khan married this girl. Sher Jan Khan, Attaullah Khan, Mohammad Siddiq Khan, and Karim Jan are her sons.

This lady had my highest respect and also the respect of the people of Kohdaman and Kohistan, both fertile valleys north of Kabul. I respected her request and gladly started teaching these two young boys, Nemat and Abdul Haq, her grandsons. I would invite them every day to my house. Abdullah Jan at that time was 13 years old. Nemat Jan was about nine years old. I would teach them *alif ba* (Persian A-B-C's). For almost two years I taught them until they were well versed in Persian and Arabic. I was unaware of the fact that these two young boys were under surveillance, and detectives reported to the Intelligence Department that these two were coming to my house every day. The information became part of my file with Intelligence. However, the Chief of Intelligence, Mirza Mohammad Shah Khan, who was a friend of Mohammad Siddiq Khan, showed some restraint and did not report to Mohammad Hashim Khan the everyday activities of these boys unless questioned by him. Being unaware of the circumstances, I continued teaching them.

The Request of a Dying Mother to See Her Son

According to information received, this lady, Asheera Safi, the mother of Attaullah Khan, became very ill and was near death. She did not have permission to go to

Kohistan or Kohdaman. All her family's land and holdings were confiscated. They were living in Kabul in an old rented place. She had done some favors for Mohammad Hashim Khan, and he was obliged to her. The favor was extended when Mohammad Hashim Khan was Amanullah Khan's Ambassador to Moscow. Her son, Attaullah Khan, was president of the Army Military Students Union in Moscow. When relations between Amanullah Khan and Nadir Khan fell to low ebb, Amanullah Khan did not allow his sister Nurul Seraj to be married to Mohammad Hashim Khan even though they were engaged; instead, he married her to his cousin Hassan Jan (thus Mohammad Hashim Khan remained a chronic bachelor all his life). Mohammad Nadir Khan resigned his post as Ambassador to Paris, and the relationship between Amanullah Khan and the Nadir family fell even further. Hashim Khan also was relieved of his duties in Moscow and was replaced by Mirza Mohammad Yaftali. The new Ambassador wanted to take charge from Hashim Khan and go over the embassy accounts. Hashim Khan did not want to prolong his stay in Moscow. I have heard this in person from Attaullah Khan and Ghulam Jilani Khan, who was the Charge d'Affaires.

Attaullah Khan went to Mirza Mohammad Khan and told him, "Whatever money Mohammad Hashim Khan owes to the embassy, I stand responsible for and will reimburse. Allow him to go to Paris because his brother, Mohammad Nadir Khan is sick."

Mirza Mohammad Khan reluctantly accepted it, and Attaullah Khan offered his personal guarantee and wrote it down officially on paper. Thus, Sardar Mohammad Hashim Khan was allowed to proceed to Paris.

Even though he was praiseworthy for what he did, Attaul Haq Khan was thrown in the palace jail along with my uncle and other elders from the north valley of Kabul. When I came to know of Asheera Safi's illness, it was a wintery afternoon, and I hurried on my way to Deh Afghanan (an ancient Kabul neighborhood) to see this lady, the mother of Attaullah Haq and Sher Jan.

The house was old and piled high with snow. Inside, the room was cold. This tall, very beautiful lady was lying on the floor in very dire condition. She was like a strong cypress tree that had fallen with the force of the fall winds.

One of her grandsons, Buzurg Jan, was there. He later married the sister of my dear friend Masoom Jan Mujaddadi, and became part of the Mujaddadi family of Charekar (a town north of Kabul) through marriage. I don't have any news about him. Maybe the Soviets kidnapped him or killed him.

Her other grandsons Nemat and Abdul Haq, my students, were also there. Her young daughters-in-law were also sitting around her. (Women wore the hejab, the Islamic head covering, in public, but when they were at home, among family who were close relatives, they did not cover their heads).

When I entered the room, Asheera Safi recognized me and spoke. "I have one request from you," she said in a frail voice that was weak and shaky. She was nearing death.

I answered, "Please, tell me."

She said, "Ask Mohammad Hashim to allow Agha Jan five minutes respite to come and see me. In my last moments, I would like to look into the beautiful eyes of my son, after which, I can say goodbye to this world."

I became tearful and kissed her feet. Here was this intelligent and very literate lady, who had been a scholar and had completed her education in Kohistan and India. She had vast knowledge and had interpreted the Holy Koran. And now, she lay dying in a shabby room as cold as a prison. I didn't even have money in my pocket or at home to help them out.

I left them and hurried toward the Prime Minister's Secretariat. In my heart, I was talking to God, hoping that Mohammad Hashim Khan would be there and praying that I may do something for these people. I found the courage deep down, maybe because of my faith and my respect for this honorable lady. I thought, instead of just pleading verbally to Mohammad Hashim Khan, let me quickly write a quote from a poem by Bedil that will soften his heart. I wrote, "Your Highness,

How much I have suffered in your absence

'Til you come to my grave and I am dead!"

I reached his office close to sunset and saw Mohammad Hashim Khan exiting. His limousine was waiting to take him to the Arg (palace). I handed him the piece of paper. He said, "I don't understand the meaning."

I replied, "Sir, it is a Bedil poem. The mother of Attaullah Khan uttered something similar to me. She asked me to come into your presence, your Highness, and plead with you."

"Where is Attaullah's mother?" he asked rudely.

"Sir, she and her family have a place in Deh Afghanan," I replied. "They are living in extreme poverty, and she is on her deathbed. She may die at any time."

"I cannot cure her," he said, dismissively. "She's an old woman. If she dies, she dies."

"Sir," I said, "She wants only to see her son Attaullah Haq for five minutes. Please allow this, for her sake. Let him leave the prison for five minutes so that his dying mother can see him and say goodbye to her son."

"I cannot let every prisoner who has a dying mother out of prison so that they can visit," he snapped.

He walked away a couple of steps and then stopped. I don't know what God put in his heart, but he turned around, reconsidering, and asked, "Will you guarantee he comes back to the Arg prison?"

"Yes, sir," I replied. "I will be responsible, and I guarantee. Please allow him to come for five minutes accompanied by the prison guard, and I will return him after that."

"Write this down," he said. "The Qala Begi (Commander of the Palace) is to allow Attaullah Haq to go for half an hour to see his mother. The guard should be with him. He should go with handcuffs and shackles and come back directly to the Arg prison afterwards."

I took my cap off my head (an Afghan custom of paying respects to God when your prayer is granted). I prayed, thanking God, and then wrote what Hashim Khan asked for on the paper. I was already running back to Asheera Safi's house in my thoughts.

But first I had to submit the paper to Abdul Ghani Gardezi, the Qala Begi. He did not give me possession of the prisoner, but instead, said he would send him directly. I hurried back to the house to give the good news to the lady. It was Maghreb (sunset), the time of evening prayers.

Soon, we heard the clanking noise made by a prisoner's shackles. I went outside and was shocked. The Attaullah Haq I remembered had mesmerizing eyes, a clean shaven face, wore good quality, and attractive clothes and was considered one of the handsome young men of Afghanistan. My uncle used to talk about how well dressed and good-looking he was.

This Attaullah Haq who stood before me had a beard that reached his navel. He was wearing an old, dirty, and ripped waistcoat, and he had a Charekari Kaish (the customary Afghan shawl) wrapped around his hunched shoulders. Shackles on his hands and feet debilitated him as he stood there. While one guard was prepared to bring him inside, two other guards would stand outside.

"There are women and girls inside the room, and his mother is very sick," I told them. "You also have mothers and sisters. Please respect that and don't come inside."

The guards agreed. "We will not come in the room, even though we have been strictly ordered to do so," said one guard. "How can we do that? We also have family, and we do not want to come inside and see the bare faces of Saheb Zada Saheb's wife and mother."

It seemed they knew these were Khwajas (Sahebs) and understood they belonged to a family of freedom fighters of Afghanistan. The guards remained outside. A small fire stove was set out for them to sit around and keep themselves warm.

While his mother was still unconscious, Attaullah Khan stood up to offer evening prayers. I followed him because Attaullah Khan could recite the Koran by heart. He started reciting in a very slow, arresting, and grief-stricken voice. He first recited Surai Fateha (the chapter of the Koran that is traditionally recited at the beginning of prayers). After the optional rakaats (prayer), and as we prepared to pray further, his mother returned to consciousness and asked,

"Who is this tall person? He looks like Agha Jan!"

The others replied, "Yes, it is Agha Jan. He has come here to see you. God is great!"

She bid them, "Go ahead and complete your prayers."

Attaullah Khan finished his prayers and threw himself on his mother's feet, but neither the mother nor the son cried. Finally, the mother spoke. "Son," she said, "I am leaving. My life is no more valuable than Sher Khan or Mohammad Siddiq Khan. Do not worry. It is good to see you. I will pray for you. You pray for me. Both of us should pray, 'May God keep the Muslims under His care. Deliver them from these difficult times.' May God bring success to your children, that they may reach their goals. May God be happy with you, my son, as I am happy with you. Go, with the grace of God. They will not allow you to stay tonight with me?"

He answered, "Yes, mother I am not allowed to stay the night. I will sit with you for a few more minutes."

His mother turned toward the others and said, "Bring the green tea, the one that I drink, and I have kept some for Agha Jan. Please, prepare it for him. He likes it."

The green tea was brought, and Agha Jan drank it.

We could not control our tears, no matter how we tried to hide them. Time passed, more than what the time period allowed. The guards said, "Please, let us go before we are punished for delay." Attaullah Khan's mother said goodbye to him and amid the sound of shackles and chains he left the house and joined the guards. You could hear the sound of the shackles gradually disappearing until the sound and his shadow were lost in the snow.

Awhile later his mother started reciting the Kalima of Shahada (the oneness of God, the declaration of belief that is required for a person to become a Muslim). She died as she was reciting Kalima. I also started reciting the Koran. God is great! What a scene. The world passes, and mankind cannot forget these moments. God is great.

Advent of World War II, 1939-1945

In this same year, 1939, World War II began. Oil disappeared first, and an illegal business or black market for oil started. Sardar Mohammad Hashim Khan would sometimes take a horse and carriage to go to visit his lands in Shakardarah (a fertile valley north of Kabul). He purchased a lot of land at bargain prices. He acquired a place called Gogamanda from Gabbar Khel in Shakardarah. He bought up the lands of Ali Khan Pasni, and in Jalalabad, he had also obtained land in Butkhak. He came to own vast tracts of land, as the poet says,

From Halab to Kashghar is the Maidan of Sultan Sanjar
(Fields)

(Maidan means "fields." The lyrical phrase is similar to Woody Guthrie's "this land is your land" or Irving Berlin's "from the mountains to the prairies").

There was a time when Amanullah Khan was criticized for holding land and ignoring its return (to the original owners). Time has passed now, and I don't want to talk behind their backs. They have gone, and we are going to go also.

Once again Sardar Hashim Khan became further incensed or upset with me. Those days my friends Sardar Najibullah Khan, Sardar Mohammad Osman Khan Amir, and Annus Khan would visit me very often or I would visit them. They knew Sardar Hashim Khan did not like me. In spite of that, they would come to inquire of my well-being. People from Kohdaman and Kohistan used to visit me too. I had a few students living in my house. During the time of fresh fruit I would receive fruit from all over, and during the time of dry fruits, they would bring dry fruits for us. I was busy reading books, studying, and writing. I would write articles also. Occasionally, I would go to visit Hashim Shaiq Afandi and would stay late at night at his house.

Ustad Betab and Qari Abdullah

Once in a while I would go to visit my esteemed Ustad Betab (the Professor). (Note: Three of the most prominent poets of Afghanistan were Qari Abdullah, Abdul Haq Betab, and Khalilullah Khalili. Qari and Betab followed the Hendi style of poetry; the youngest, Khalili, was drawn to the Khorasan style.) Abdul Haq Betab was like an uncle to me. His sister, Bibi Ko, was my father's first wife. She bore no children. After my mother's death, and especially after the assassination of my father, she was as kind to me as a mother. As long as she lived, she did everything in her power to help me and to be kind and affectionate to me. Every year, before the anniversary of my father's death, she would stitch three or four head caps with real threads of gold sewn inside. She did this even though her eyesight was weakening. She would take the caps and sell them in the market. With the proceeds, she would bring in mullahs to recite the Koran (Fateha), in commemoration of my father's death, and she would participate in the commemoration. She was a widow living in a humble abode, as Amanullah Khan had confiscated her house and her holdings, too. She took what little jewelry she had left from her time with my father and dug a hole in the earth to hide her few valuables, as was the custom among Afghans when they saw the British airplanes. However, someone informed the authorities, and her meager treasures were dug up and confiscated. Even though she was rendered poor and desolate, she maintained her high morals and hope.

Betab Saheb was the brother of this lady. Betab's mother was from Laghman (a province in Afghanistan). He belonged to an intellectual family of Laghman. There is no doubt that Laghman had some very esteemed intellectuals. Betab himself was a Sufi. He followed the Chishti doctrine. He was a follower of the Chishti Darveshs in Ghor, a province in the north of Afghanistan. Like Darvesh Shah Amanullah, he followed the Shahans of Chisht who lived in Ghor. He was their disciple. He was not married yet. He had a passion for music and had written a beautiful booklet about music. At times, when he was alone in his house, he would pick up the tambour (a long necked lute) and play it and sing so beautifully, it would put him into a trance. When he did this he lost himself, like becoming high and going under the influence of the music, expressing his love of God.

In literature and writing, he was very precise and

meticulous. He wrote poetry in the Hendi style. I always told him his research and his prose were much better than his poetry. I thought his poetic vision was limited by his factual views, when it should be independent, free, and passionate. He was a very esteemed and a great teacher. He was very popular at Habibiya School among all the other teachers. He considered himself to be a student of Malik-ush-shora Qari Abdullah (poet laureate of Afghanistan).

There is no doubt Qari Abdullah Khan was a very intellectual and scholarly man. He memorized the Koran and had beautiful handwriting. He was from the city of Kabul. He was a very careful, humble, and modest man. However, he was a very nervous public speaker who avoided addressing an audience. He pursued the Hendi style of poetry, like Betab.

I did not like Qari Abdullah's poetry, and this always drew his wrath. He would advise me not to write poetry. He would say, "Why don't you go and learn bookkeeping or accounting or research the heritage of your father's land? Poetry will get you nothing." He would criticize my poetry in public meetings. Sometimes, I would get upset and criticize his poetry behind his back.

Betab Saheb would also get angry at me since he was my teacher, and since I had studied many subjects under him, including astrology and the foretelling of signs. I would not say anything. Betab's power and strength in research was higher than Qari Abdullah's; however, both of them were not very familiar with the history of literature. Both of them followed the Hendi style of poetry, and the poets for whom they had the most faith, were Mirza Abdul Qadir Badil, Waqef, and Mirza Mazhar.

The Rise of Music and Ustad Qasim

Let me talk about music. Music took root during the time of Amir Habibullah Khan Seraj. Respect for music gradually grew in Kabul – a little during the Amani time and more during Nadir Khan and Zahir Shah's time.

There was one shortcoming. People used to cast demeaning looks at musicians. It was to the extent that in gatherings and at dinners they would provide a separate eating facility for the musicians. Musicians were not invited to eat with the host and guests.

During both the Amani time and the time of Nadir Shah and Zahir Shah, Ustad Qasim Jo was very famous. Ustad Qasim Jo was the son of Ustad Sitarjo, whom I did not meet, and his mother's name was Allahdeti. They had, most probably, come from India. People with names like Jo and Ji migrated to Afghanistan during both the Amani time and the time of Nadir Shah and Zahir Shah. (Qasim Jo was born in 1878 and died in 1957 in the Gozar Barana area of Kabul. His father was Sitarjo, a renowned musician himself. Amir Habibullah Khan Seraj invited Sitarjo to Kabul from Kashmir. Sitarjo married in Kabul and remained there).

Even though there were other musicians in Kabul like Khalifa Ghulam Hussain Nataki, the real Ustad was Ustad Qasim. He was an indisputable Ustad (versatile individuals in their professions were bestowed the title of Ustad). Not only did he understand music, he had another rare quality. In the words of Ghulam Ali Azad, who wrote *Tazkirai Khazanai Amirah*, Ustad Qasim always recognized the moment and recited the couplet that captured the feelings of the moment. He knew a tremendous amount of poetry by heart and would pluck the right poem for the right occasion. He knew how to resonate with his audience and make them his fans. He did not have a very strong memory, but was still able to produce the right words for the right moment. His poetry matched the audience.

Let me tell you a story. During the time of Amanullah Khan one of the sons of the Sardar (royal family) of Afghanistan was arrested for an attempt on the life of Amanullah Khan. The King imprisoned him. Ustad Qasim was giving a concert in the audience of Amanullah Khan and had selected poems in honor of the Independence of Afghanistan. Amanullah Khan loved the music and the poetry and approached Qasim Khan and said, "Ask me whatever you want and I'll give it to you."

Qasim Khan said, "Your Highness, promise me you will do it."

Amanullah Khan was kind of taken aback and said, "Yes, I will do it."

Ustad Qasim asked, "Please release the Sardar whom you have imprisoned."

Amanullah Khan said, "Since I have promised you, even though he was imprisoned for an attempt on my life, I have pardoned him."

Ustad Qasim was very thankful and indebted to Amanullah Khan. During the time of Nadir Shah and Zahir Shah he was considered to be a supporter of Amanullah Khan. He was not much liked by Sardar Mohammad Hashim Khan.

One year, Ustad Qasim traveled to Delhi at the advent of Zahir Shah's rule and was given time on national India Radio to present his music. He sent a telegram to Amanullah Khan in Italy (when he was dethroned in 1929, Amanulluh Khan took political asylum in Italy and lived there until he died and was buried in Afghanistan). He telegraphed him, "Tonight, I will recite poetry on the radio in your memory. Please listen to it."

One of the poems Ustad Qasim recited translates as:

I sacrificed my life to you, orange in hand (meaning the essence of orange).
I am keeping myself alive by smelling your essence, wherever you are.
You do not come and you do not send any messages.
Maybe you have become a kafir (infidel) *and you are worshipping a statue.*

Another couplet of his poetry translates like this:

Without you, O Yousef (Joseph in Bible)
Not only the house of Yaqoob (Jacob) *is gloomy.*
The entire homeland is suffering.
Without you, Canaan is deserted (Joseph's homeland).

Ustad Qasim's son was named Yaqoob. Everyone who heard this poetry said what he meant was, "Amanullah Khan, without you not only the house of Qasim is gloomy,

but the whole of Afghanistan is affected and missing you."
The radio broadcast reached the ears of Mohammad
Hashim Khan. He was provoked to consider jailing Qasim,
but Mohammad Zahir Khan did not let this happen. He told
himself, "It's not good during my reign that I arrest and jail
a musician of that caliber (star) for this small crime."

I do remember one anecdote. One day, at the Prime
Ministry, the ministers were all congregated, along with the
Iranian and Turkish ambassadors. Hashim Khan entered
with his stately gait and arrogance while Qasim was
singing Bedil's poetry. The Turkish ambassador, Mamdouh
Shaukat, knew Persian very well and was a very learned
man. Mr. Bahman, the Iranian ambassador, was also a
scholar and a man of letters and Persian was his mother
tongue.

At this time, Sardar Mohammad Naim Khan came in.
Everyone stood up as a sign of respect to him except for
Mohammad Hashim Khan. Ustad Mohammad Qasim
stopped singing and stood up. Sardar Naim Khan
acknowledged everyone else and ignored Mohammad
Qasim. He paid Qasim no attention. As soon as everyone
sat, Ustad Qasim started this poem of Bedil:

From the young you cannot expect the appreciation of
an older man.
You cannot expect the arrow to show you the target
the way you can see it from the side of the bow.

He also sang a few other poems, especially in
appreciation of the young in condemnation of the arrogance
of the moment. The whole assembly was overshadowed
with this.

Unfortunately, the article I wrote about Ustad Qasim's
clever ways of reciting the right poem at the right time,
which was published a few years back in *Zuandoon*
magazine in Kabul, is gone. I can't recall his timely
recitation of poems on other occasions. I have forgotten
about all of them except what I just related. Ustad Qasim
drew the anger and wrath of Sardar Mohammad Hashim
Khan just as I had.

Hitler's Status in Afghanistan

During World War II, the people of Afghanistan were eagerly tuned to the current events. Hitler's initial victories drew their interest and attention. The Afghan people thought if Hitler was victorious, then the conditions of the Eastern countries would improve, and these tough controls over Afghanistan and Iran would give way to a softer attitude.

German radio stations broadcasted in Persian and spoke about the victories of Germany and Italy. Wherever there was a radio in Kabul, people congregated around it to listen. I would go, along with Sayed Mia Jan Agha and Sayed Shamsuddin Khan Majrooh, to the house of Mr. Sarwar Goya and would sit around the radio behind closed doors. The government did not allow civil servants to listen to the Persian programming of Deutchland. However, we listened, discussed and criticized the events.

One of my cousins, Mohammad Anwar, had gone toward Darulaman on his bicycle. He was riding his bike when it went down with mechanical trouble. As he was standing on the side of the road, the Secretary of the German Embassy drove by in his car and blew a tire. Seeing Anwar close by, he called on him to help him fix the tire. He said he would pay him for his labor.

Anwar laid down his bike and went toward the car to help him fix the tire. He approached the Secretary not because he was attracted by the offer of payment, but because that was his nature to help a stranger in his country, including a German.

One of the policemen from the Prime Ministry witnessed this whole episode. As soon as the Secretary of the German Embassy left, the policeman slapped Anwar across the face and arrested him. Poor Anwar was only a student at that time.

The policeman brought him to the Prime Ministry. Unfortunately, Mirza Mohammad Shah, the head of Intelligence, was not in his office. He knew Anwar's father from the time of Amir Habibullah Khan. Anwar was thrown into prison and tortured. We came to know about this incident two or three days later. The husband of Anwar's sister, Paindah Mohammad Khan, who later became the Director of the Department of Investigation for the Prime Ministry also heard about this. At the time, he was Deputy Governor of Takharistan, and Anwar's sister lived with him there. Paindah Khan had influence at the Prime Ministry and was able to persuade Sardar Mohammad Hashim Khan to bail Anwar out of prison.

Anwar left Kabul for Takharistan. As bad luck would have it, one night he was visiting downtown Takharistan and the same policeman from Kabul happened to be there. When the policeman saw Anwar, he said, "You are a traitor and a German spy. Have you come here to report to Germans what you have seen?"

Anwar tried to defend himself. "As God is my witness, this is not true! I'm here because my sister lives here," he told the policeman.

The policeman tormented him further, saying, "Well, let me go back to Kabul and report what I've seen here. Count on it, I will get back to you."

This simple and humble young man came home distraught and wrote a detailed letter to his sister and his brother, Mohammad Islam Maihan, saying, "My life is in vain. I am accused of being a spy and a traitor. Wherever I go, the police will follow me. This will bring down the good name of my family. I would rather kill myself."

Anwar had some chemicals at home that were used for developing photographs. He swallowed them. In the morning, when his mother and his only sister opened his room, they found his body. He had left a bouquet of flowers next to himself and wrote in the letter, "Every year, on the anniversary of my death, please place a bouquet of flowers on my grave."

Anwar's mother wailed and repeated his name. "Anwar! Anwar! Anwar!" He did not reply. There was no sound underneath the comforter. The doctor was summoned and declared Anwar dead.

Wrath of Hashim Khan toward Me

When this story was told to Hashim Khan, it further

added to my downfall. Hashim Khan asked me, "Why did you let him go to Pul-e-khumri?"

I replied, "Sir, I had nothing to do with it. They are free people. His sister lives there. He killed himself and sir, you should be asking that policeman. Your anger is misplaced." This further downgraded my stock with Hashim Khan.

As destiny might have it, Hashim Khan encountered me one night as he was riding a horse.

Abdul Razzaq Khan, the son of Abdul Aziz Khan Qateel, was the brother of Abdul Hakim Khan, who later became Chief Justice of Afghanistan. He was a very good friend of mine. As a young man, he would come to my house so I could teach him how to correctly read Aurad (the blessings – *dua* – Hizbul Bahar and Hizbul Nasr) in Shazly, the Book of Prayers (*duas*).

Whenever he came to my house, both of us would go out for a walk. At that time in Karteh Parwan, these buildings had not been built yet, and there were wheat fields all over. We would walk toward the main road after the evening prayers and talk. I would be wearing a jalalabadi dress, with a thin, soft shawl around my shoulders and a lunghi (head covering) or turban. Abdul Razzaq Khan wore a similar dress, and we each had sandals on our feet. This form of dress was not the approved uniform of a civil servant, and Mohammad Hashim Khan did not like this.

The Prime Minister was returning from his land holdings in Shakardarah when his entourage pulled close to us on the road. He was riding a horse, leading 10 to 12 other horsemen, escorted by armed men on bicycles at the front and rear. The bicycle riders in the front showed a light in our faces. We walked away from the main road toward the fields; however, they recognized us.

The next day, when I went to the Prime Ministry, I had no idea what was waiting for me. I would have never guessed that this was a crime to walk on the main road. As usual I had some files from the Ministry of Commerce to be presented to the Prime Minister. When I presented the files to him in his office, he snatched them from my hand and dumped them on the table on one side and placed his hat on top of it. In his typical Indian accent (Hashim Khan and his other brothers grew up in Dehradun, India), he said, "Khalilullah Khan."

I answered, "Yes, sir?"

"Go and improve yourself," he reprimanded. "Then come and bring these files back to me."

I was flabbergasted. With all the courage I could collect, I said, "Sir, what have I done that I should go and improve myself? I don't see anything wrong with me, or what I may have done against you or the state."

He said, "I have put you on notice to go improve yourself. This is a warning. Otherwise..."

Others in the room pulled me away from the office of the Prime Minister, before I could say anything to put myself in further jeopardy.

Two or three weeks passed. Hashim Khan again summoned me. He was pacing in the garden of the Prime Ministry. When he saw me, he said, "Did you realize your mistakes?"

I replied, "Sir, I did not."

He said, "That night you were walking on the side of the road. Did you know who that man was? That dress you were wearing was not a civilized dress (what he actually said was that it 'was not a dress for a human being to wear')."

I replied, "Sir, the shawl on my shoulders, the jalalabadi dress, the lunghi turban and the sandals on my feet are the dress of the people of Afghanistan. Even the shirts and trousers I was wearing were all made in Afghanistan. The lunghi is an Islamic turban."

He did not respond to that. Instead he asked, "Who was that man with whom you were walking?"

I answered, "Abdul Razzaq Khan, son of Abdul Aziz Khan."

"Yes, yes!" he said. "You are still in contact with the family of Amanullah Khan!"

Ironically after a few months he himself adopted Abdul Razzaq Khan as his son, and he became a very respected person, close to him.

I defended myself. "I have no connection with this.

217

Abdul Razzaq Khan is not connected anymore to Amanullah Khan. Amanullah Khan killed his grandfather Nasrullah Khan. He comes to me and studies the Koran with me. We go over the prayers and blessings."

Hashim Khan continued, "This Maulavi Fazal Rabbi who also comes to you, I know about him, too."

I said, "Yes, sir. He does come to my place, and I have contacts with him."

Maulavi Fazal Rabbi was from the Frontier and was living in Afghanistan.

Maulavi Fazal Rabbi

Earlier we talked about Maulavi Fazal Rabbi. Even though it is very trivial, the point here is that the people of Afghanistan and the mullahs and spiritual leaders were against the government. They always taught that the government helps support the survival of the great British Empire, and if Hitler wins, maybe these governments will ease up on them. Maulavi Fazal Rabbi was a part of the Indian rebellion against the British. He was living in Afghanistan for many years, from the time of Amanullah Khan. He was gray haired and was a delightful person.

One day Maulavi predicted that Hitler would definitely be victorious. He based his conviction on Arabic (abjad) calculations. Alphabets are assigned numerical codes, and Hitler is 635, which coincides with the time of the famous Islamic Commander Khaled. Commander Khaled was one of the renowned companions of Prophet Mohammad (PBUH). Since Khaled had always been victorious in his campaigns; therefore, Hitler would also be victorious, according to Maulavi.

The spies of the government intelligence picked up his words and communicated them to Sardar Mohammad Hashim Khan. Hashim Khan sat on this information and as soon as the war was over, he summoned Maulavi Fazal Rabbi and gave him a piece of his mind. He told him, "You are a Muslim, yet you compare a frangi (foreigner) to a companion of the Prophet (PBUH)!"

Maulavi Fazal Rabbi retorted, "I was not aware of the

latter actions of Hitler. However, in the beginning when he started his campaign, I thought it was in the interest of Islam."

Mohammad Hashim Khan demanded, "What were his actions in the interest of Islam?"

Maulavi replied that one of Hitler's actions in the interest of Islam was to promise freedom of expression in Afghanistan. "Freedom of expression and the pen are one of the pillars of Islam," he said. "I would have been able to write and talk freely about the freedom of India and would have actively continued my campaign. Now that Hitler has done what he has done, the worst, which is against human dignity, I have nothing to say about it any further."

Hashim Khan wanted to throw Maulavi in the prison; however, his brother Sardar Shah Mahmoud Khan, who knew Maulavi very well, saved him from prison.

Our Nation's Hatred, vis-à-vis, the Government

With every passing day the gap between the nation and the government continued to widen. The Mohammad Nadir family considered themselves to have served the Afghan nation and delivered it from the clutches of, according to them, a robber, Habibullah Khan Kalakani (who was born in the village Kalakan north of Kabul in the 1890s and ruled from January to October 1929 before being killed by Nadir Shah).

The Nadir family laid the foundation that would have put Afghanistan on the path to prosperity. All this was derailed. A deep hatred ensued between the nation and the government. The king sat in the palace and had little control over anything. Sardar Mohammad Hashim Khan did things that the people hated. On a personal front he appropriated as much land as he could in every part of Afghanistan at cheap prices. Places as I mentioned before, like in Gogamanda, Shakardarah, and places like Chihilsetoon. He collected produce of the land. He also bought hundreds of acres of land in Ahangran between Maidan and Logar. He spent quite some time in maintaining and reaping the benefit from this land.

I remember one day I accompanied Mohammad Osman Khan Amir, who was Mayor of Kabul, when he came to the Prime Minister to file a complaint. He said, "Your Highness, the price of flour has shot up extremely. We are expecting a tough winter ahead, and people are raising their voice against it. They are standing in protest on the roads leading to Jalalabad near the Yak Lingah Kotal (single leg-pass) in the north, Kotal-e-Khair Khana, and on the road toward Kandahar. They are blocking the thoroughfares in protest. They're not allowing any grain to reach Kabul, and they are boycotting the export of wheat."

Mohammad Hashim Khan got angry and said, "Who is doing this? Go and bring Mirza Mohammad Shah!"

The head of Intelligence, Mirza Mohammad Shah was summoned. He did not know about the development and said he had no idea who was doing this.

The Prime Minister said, "Alright, I will investigate."

Later, it was revealed that Mirza Mohammad Shah himself had ordered the blockade. This would raise the price of Hashim Khan's produce coming from Shakardarah, Butkhak, Ahangran, and Gogamanda Sorobi. Maybe Hashim Khan did not know about this. His assistants or lackeys may have done that to appease the Prime Minister so he would reap the benefit and get the best price.

Building a Prison in Dehmazang

These things happened every day, and no one listened to the people's complaints. Hashim Khan started building a prison in Dehmazang. Before Dehmazang there was a prison in Kabul near Gonbad-e-Kotwali. Amir Abdul Raman Khan built the Gonbad-e-Kotwali prison, which was later named as Maidane Pashtoonistan or Pashtoonistan Square. This Gombad (dome) was very impressive and well built. It was considered one of the magnificent treasures of Eastern architecture. There was one prison there and another prison inside the city called Sehta prison. Sardar Hashim Khan decided to build the prison in Dehmazang on the west side of Kabul, close to the Minaret of Intelligence and Ignorance, which had been built by Amanullah Khan.

Hashim Khan appropriated land there. He appointed architects who followed his instructions and came up with elaborate blueprints that divided this prison into four parts or divisions. There would be a division for civilian or regular prisoners, a division for political prisoners, one for women prisoners (with a section for deranged/disabled women), and a division for children. No one knew why he was assigning one part of the prison for children.

Hashim Khan had a great interest in this and wanted to see it completed. Wherever he went, he would tell people he was doing this to provide a comfortable abode for prisoners.

In reality, after his prison was completed, his political prisoner section was very scary and horrifying. Although brand new, it was dingy, dreary, and dark. In summer, the prisoners would encounter snakes and scorpions. In the winter, they were subjected to damp and cold.

The Prime Minister himself had an interest in seeing the prisoners face to face. On Wednesdays, he would go to the prison after one o'clock and be there until four or five o'clock in the afternoon. He would observe the prisoners and assign duties to them. He would allocate hard work to certain prisoners like breaking down stone from Chihilsetoon to produce the cut pieces necessary for building or even finer pieces to produce bricks. He would appoint other prisoners to weave kilems (Afghan gilum) or carpets. He would assign other prisoners to do the iron smithing work. He would do whatever he wanted with the prisoners.

Some of the prisoners had shackles and others had chains on their bodies. It was a very pathetic scene. Others had shackles, chains, and even wood bars to restrict their hands – all three things attached to their bodies. His Highness would review all this and make sure each prisoner had shackles and chains on their bodies. If a prisoner dared complain to him, he would be further subjected to torture.

Khwaja Babu, a prisoner, was one of the nobles of Kohdaman who had taken care of the security of Nardir

Shah's family during the time of Habibullah Khan Kalakani (his father had taken refuge in India with Sardar Mohammad Ayub Khan). Khwaja Babu was the Minister of Interior of Habibullah Khan Kalakani. Now, he was old and weak, and subjected to chains and shackles in the prison.

Khwaja Babu knew the Urdu language and realized anyone speaking in Urdu would be understood better by Hashim Khan (who grew up in India). One day, when Hashim Khan was in the prison, Khwaja Babu cried out in Urdu and said, "Oh, Your Highness, I have a request! I have a request!"

The Prime Minister was taken aback at this person who was speaking to him in the Urdu language. He ordered the guards to go and bring him. He said, "What are you trying to say?"

Khwaja Babu said, "I was a Minister for nine months, and I am in this prison for nine years now. I am an old man with a gray beard. I took care of your family. My land, my property, my house have all been confiscated. My family is living in poverty with different people."

Hashim Khan turned toward the guards and said, "Quickly, take him and place him in solitary confinement." He didn't want Khwaja Babu to see or talk to anybody. Incidents like this continued to happen every Wednesday. No one could stand against Hashim Khan or dare talk to him.

The Pul-e-Charkhi Prison

As if this prison was not enough, it was decided a prison be built away from Kabul. The land appropriated for Pul-e-Charkhi was totally flat and open to extreme weather, so prisoners would be vulnerable to the relentless sun of summer and chilling strong winds of winter. With this land, the prison would be situated to the East of Kabul close to the Kabul River but farther away from people, on the way to Nangarhar. This was done to make sure that relatives of the prisoners could not reach the prison easily. I remember this prison was being designed to hold 13,000 prisoners. Even Mohammad Hashim Khan called it a big prison.

Italian and German architects were sought out to design it so that the prison could accommodate the 13,000 prisoners and have space to share for 400 families. Hashim Khan thought that maybe, some day, families with their children would be lodged in the prison.

When Sardar Shah Mahmoud Khan became Prime Minister he recommended to the king to shelve the plan, and the first decree of the king under Prime Minister Mohammad Hashim Khan was regarding the prison. Later, Sardar Mohammad Daoud Khan revised those plans and saw to its completion. Now, the same prison works as an internment place for Afghans by the Communists. The Afghan people are tortured there.

Selecting Uniforms for Civil Servants

Another symptom of the government's dysfunction was the cult of showing off. The ambassadors of other friendly countries who were stationed in Kabul would hold diplomatic parties and the government of Afghanistan wanted to put the best foot forward. The government thought the way to impress these people was by changing the style of dress of high-ranking Afghan civil servants. Specifically, high-ranking civil servants were supposed to wear formal dress, from dinner jackets and black trousers to tuxedos, tailcoats and smoking jackets, which followed the trend of Western diplomats. The government thought that by doing this, Afghanistan and Mohammad Hashim Khan's government would earn a good name and the foreign community in Kabul would consider them progressive.

On this shaky foundation, Rustamji, a big businessman who owned his own tailoring company in Bombay, was summoned to Kabul. Under his guidance, a team of professional tailors were brought from India to Kabul to measure and custom sew three sets of stylish tailcoats, dinner jackets, smoking jackets, and trousers for each civil servant up to the status of Director General. They were also fitted for imported shirts, shoes, and accessories like bow ties. These were the people who would be invited by foreign missions to diplomatic parties and social events. We were forced to wear these clothes, selecting a dinner jacket or a tailcoat from our wardrobe based on the degree of formality of the invitation.

It was laughable, as many of these high-ranking officials had no transportation. Even horse-drawn carriages were not available. So many of them would arrive at social events on foot, having walked a great distance with their formal wear tucked in a bag under their arm to protect it from the mud and dirt.

We did the same, and when we got near the Prime Minister's office, we would go to the security room and change there. This became a cottage industry for the doormen and security people because they charged one Afghani every time someone used their office to change.

We were not forced to pay up front for these clothes; however, the government charged us, whatever they wanted, and took it out of our monthly paychecks. At times it was difficult to give up the money because we needed it to feed our families.

The irony is, they failed to realize the foreign envoys, journalists, and other workers saw Afghanistan in the poor condition it actually was in. Our clothes in an official reception setting would not help them change their mind. They saw in the whole city of Kabul there were no public bathrooms. In winter, they watched as the soldiers on duty went in the early morning hours to break the ice on the frozen Kabul River and used the icy water to clean themselves. Even if a soldier was sick and coughing or had a fever, he still went to the frozen river to break the ice and clean himself and change his clothes. The policemen were doing the same thing. The foreign legions and delegations could easily see people in tattered clothes and no shoes on their feet, on the streets. They could see that men and women did not have proper clothing. Yet the government thought the dinner jackets and tuxedos would cover all these disparities. They were wrong. The shortcomings could not be denied, and the foreigners could not ignore the poverty that prevailed outside these social events.

The government was shortsighted on other fronts as well. They failed to realize that all the foreign teachers working at Kabul high schools would relay the information to their governments about the students being hungry and wearing poor clothing, in fact, the same clothes, summer, or winter. It was clear to the teachers these people couldn't buy a bar of soap, wash their faces, or take a shower and then come to school. The teachers knew the students had very little to eat at lunchtime as well. They saw the hawkers selling chickpeas and vinegar (shor-nakhud) outside the schools and noticed the students were unable to buy any, even though their mouths watered. They watched as the students tried to find a penny or two from someplace to quench their hunger. However, amid this, the government was busy providing three sets of dress clothes to the civil servants to appear as a progressive nation.

Well, this may have been the trend in some other eastern countries also. I have called it "showing off," and I have incorporated this in my poem, which I titled after the one who picks thorns from a field, *Naalai Kharkan* (Cries of a Thorn Picker).

If readers hear my poem, they will see why, in the middle of all this government pomp and glamour, I wrote an ode at that time. Even though I was a Director of a Department in the Prime Ministry, a high-ranking official, and I owned a few acres of land in the north, I was still affected by this disparity.

One day a friend of mine invited us for dinner. One of my sons, Nejatullah, was with me. It was a winter evening, and I cannot forget it. Nejat wore a coat. The host offered to hang it up, but my son resisted. The house was warm. The more the host insisted, the more my son clung to his clothes, signaling he did not want to take the coat off. Finally, his mother told the host to leave him with the coat. After the dinner, on our way back home, I asked him, "Why didn't you take off your coat?"

He answered, "Dad, every day you are either at the Court or in your office. You never see this. Under this coat, my shirt and my clothes are ripped in several places. I did not want to reveal this for my friends to see in their house, so I did not want to take off my coat."

I was embarrassed to hear this from my son. That's when I wrote the poem (ghazal). It has been published in my poetry collection.

I'm not going to complain on behalf of my family or myself because there were thousands and thousands of people who deserved more than I did and were caught in this whirlpool. The poem I wrote on this occasion caught the essence of the prevailing conditions.

This state of affairs in Afghanistan lasted for a long time. When the Spinzar Hotel was built in downtown Kabul, we were invited to the night of the grand opening, as was his Highness, the King of Afghanistan. I remember the bathrooms of the hotel were inlaid with lapis lazuli (blue stone found in Afghanistan and Chile) to impress the foreigners who were supposed to stay in this hotel. But right in front of the hotel, you could see from the windows of the rooms and balconies the mud and dirt of the Kabul River and smell the defecation around it. They could see people trying to clean themselves with icy water from the river in the winter. In the summer, they saw people walk in the street with torn clothes and shoeless feet. I saw this same showing off for civil servants in my travels to Iran, but not to the extent as in Afghanistan.

Sayed Mobashir Tarazi

Toward the end of World War II a notable incident happened in Kabul. Scholars from Bokhara, Samarqand, and Farghana lived in the city. Some were busy in trade; some had taken up teaching. The government absorbed others as civil servants, and of course, some were unemployed. They were poor refugees who had left their land. I understand how they must have felt leaving their land. (Khalili himself lived as a refugee in Maywood, New Jersey, 1979-1986).

Among them was a gentleman named Mobashir Tarazi from Farghana (Bokhara). Tarazi was also a Sayed, with linkage to the Prophet (PBUH). Sayed Tarazi was an intellectual and a scholar. He had written several books and also had some poetry to his credit. His writings were well researched. He knew Arabic very well and had fought Jehad against the Soviets. King Nadir Shah had hired him as his educational advisor (science). This act (of hiring a

226

veteran of war against the Soviets) shows how bold a step was taken by Nadir Shah.

During the first year of his rule, Nadir Shah sent a delegation to represent him at Holy Mecca (Kaaba). He authorized them to purchase a room-and-board place called *caravanserai* for the Afghan pilgrims (*hajis*). Sayed Mobashir Tarazi was part of this delegation, which was led by Ahmad Shah Khan, the Minister of Court, and included Haji Nawab Khan Logari, among others.

King Abdul Aziz of Saudi Arabia received the delegation. Sayed Mobashir Tarazi was one of those who addressed King Abdul Aziz. He brought up the subject of Bokhara and Samarqand, loud enough for everybody to hear.

After Nadir Shah was assassinated, Sayed Tarazi was appointed a teacher at Isteqlal High School (Independence High School) in Afghanistan. He was an esteemed person and taught the religious curriculum well. I think he taught the religious curriculum at other schools too. He was a very respected person. I was not his student, but I had a high opinion of him.

The King of Bokhara (Janabe Ali) and the German Invasion of Russia

At the time the former king of Bokhara, Amir Mohammad Alim Khan, was living in exile in Kabul. (A direct descendent of Ghenghis Khan, Mohammad Alim Khan, 1880-1944, was the last king of Bokhara. He ruled between 1911 and 1920.) He announced, "I will bestow a very handsome reward on the first person who brings me the good news that the Germans have invaded Russia and declared war on them."

One of my friends was Abdul Rahim Khan. He belonged to the Mirza families of Kabul (accountants) and was a Director at the Ministry of Court. He was also a writer and an eloquent speaker.

On the night that it was announced on the radio the Germans had invaded Russia, Abdul Rahim Khan ran immediately to the house of Janabe Ali (His Highness) in the historic Kabul neighborhood of Murad Khani. The King of Bokhara was known in Kabul as Janabe Ali. It was a title extended by the state of Afghanistan.

Janabe Ali was inside the main house or Haram; however, Abdul Rahim knew his aide-de-camp and told him he had good news for the King. The King left his bedroom and came out to see Abdul Rahim. He asked, "What news have you brought me?" Before Abdul Rahim could say anything the King predicted, "Oh, the Germans have attacked the Russians!"

Abdul Rahim said, "Yes, I have this good news for you that I just learned from the radio."

The King asked his aide to go and bring his pocket watch. Abdul Rahim thought the King asked for the watch so he could see the time of the night in this late hour. When the pocket watch was brought, the King of Bokhara rewarded Abdul Rahim with it, and said, "Congratulations to you!"

Abdul Rahim Khan did not believe his eyes when he saw it. This pocket watch was studded with real diamonds in the case and other jewels in the chain. His father, the former King of Bokhara, left the watch to Janabe Ali.

"If Bokhara is freed or not, this news is great for me that the Germans have attacked the Russians," said Janabe Ali. "Even if only one Russian is killed, it is worth a thousand of these watches."

Abdul Rahim Khan accepted the watch, kissed the hands of the King and left.

There was a tradition from the time of Amanullah Khan and especially at the time of Habibullah Khan Kalakani, and the time of Nadir Shah and Zahir Shah that the King of Bokhara was invited to attend the prayers and break the fast on Eid with a holiday feast. Janabe Ali was also invited at the Court on the day of Eid by the King. He put on his boots and his Bokharai dress and Bokharai headgear and arrived in an automobile. His financial situation seemed all right. Amanullah Khan had promised him a political pension; it was reduced, but it was sufficient for him. He also had brought some wealth from Bokhara, which he would sell to live on. He still had an aide-de-camp, a doorman, and a secretary around him. The Bokhara people had a tremendous respect for him.

One day a strange thing happened. I don't recall if it was Eid of Ramadan (fasting) or maybe Eid of Qurban (sacrifice), but it was during the time of World War II. Stories give rise to stories as the saying goes, but this is what I witnessed. We were offering prayers at the Arg (palace). Janabe Ali was sitting in the first row along with the King of Afghanistan. We were sitting in the second row wearing our Western dress of tuxedo jackets and trousers, which are not made to kneel and offer prayers in. If I had realized this beforehand, I would have recommended that for Eid prayers, we Afghans be given respite from Western dress and allowed to wear traditional Afghan dress. This Western formal wear had a shirtfront that was starched and stiff with a high collar. When we bent forward with prayers (rukoo) the collar material would pierce our necks and leave bloody marks around the collar.

At this time the prayer leader (Khateeb) was reciting the sermon or the speech (khutba) before the prayers. The tradition was the Khateeb would pray for the King, for his longevity and that of state and the nation, and how he and his son who would be appointed after him as guardians of Islam.

Suddenly, as the Khateeb was reciting these words, a wailing cry arose from the crowd. Someone shouted, "Hold him! He may fall and die!"

According to tradition, the imams would not allow the security guards with guns to attend the prayers. They stood inside the Arg mosque, which was small and could not hold more than 300 or 400 people. The Eid Gah Mosque (the Eid congregation mosque) was closed by Mohammad Hashim Khan and turned into a warehouse for wheat and barley. He was afraid the Eid Gah Mosque could hold many more people and if it were open, the King would be obligated to go and be part of the prayers. This posed security threats for attempts on his life (he was paranoid of assassination) and thus the reason he turned the beautiful mosque into a storage warehouse with high walls surrounding it. When Sardar Shah Mahmoud Khan came into power, he redressed this.

When the commotion happened, I looked up. The Khateeb did not stop his sermon. It was said later that when Janabe Ali heard the Khateeb talk about the King, the state and the guardianship of Islam, he was overcome with grief and emotion. These were the days when the German army was being defeated. The King of Bokhara was attended to and injected with medication. Slowly, his condition improved. He was sent along with the doctors to his home.

Imprisoning of People of Bokhara in Kabul and the Degradation of Their King

Those days, when the World War II was at its peak and the Germans and the Soviets were fighting, Janabe Ali, in consultation with Sayed Mobashir Tarazi, agreed to send Bokharais and Samarqandis across the Amu River (Oxus River) to start a rebellious insurrection. Probably, they had received some information from the Republics of Tajekistan and Uzbekistan that a couple of Germans were also seen very discreetly visiting Kabul and may have brought messages of intelligence from the respective governments. Later, we all read there were letters and documents attesting to the fact that the people in those parts were ready for an insurrection.

They brought together all these unarmed people and promised as soon as they crossed the Amu River they would receive arms and ammunition. This showed these Republics were involved in providing weapons, and they will all join in a war against the Soviets. These poor oppressed people were small business and shop owners or held petty jobs. Some sold their belongings and homes and left on foot or by automobile and in secret toward Mazar-i-Sharif and Takharistan. They wanted to cross the river and join the other insurgents in their quest for freedom.

The Soviet government came to know of this movement, and the British government also played a role in aborting this mission by threatening the Afghanistan government with repercussions. This was sufficient for Sardar Mohammad Hashim Khan to intercede. Mohammad

Hashim Khan decreed that all these people, who were on the move toward Bokhara and Samarqand, be arrested. Some of them were arrested while on their way; others were picked up from their homes. Chaos erupted. Their possessions were confiscated and destroyed. They were thrown in jail. Sayed Mobashir Tarazi was also jailed and was not offered any respect for his contributions or for being a Sayed or scholar or advisor to Nadir Shah.

Sardar Mohammad Hashim Khan's men went to the house of the Amir of Bokhara, Janabe Ali, and forced him out of the haram. He had never experienced this degradation before. He protested, "Why am I being taken outside? Why have I been asked to come out?"

The men told him they were under orders. He came out and was subjected to an inquisition as an accused. They showed him a document that questioned why he had incited the people to insurrection.

Janabe Ali asked, "Are you questioning me?"

The men replied, "Yes."

The King of Bokhara answered, "Why don't you leave it to my secretary to answer it in writing? I have never written down answers to questions like these."

The men insisted they needed his response on the document in his own handwriting.

I am paraphrasing here, but the gist of what he wrote down is this: "If you were in my place in Bokhara, and Afghanistan was occupied by an infidel foreign power, I would have rewarded you for your courage if you had taken an action like this. Do whatever you want. I did this, and I know this is right. Don't harass me anymore. If you want to kill me, or whatever punishment you decide, go ahead with it. I did what I had to do."

Janabe Ali signed his statement and gave it to them. "This is what I've written, and I'm not denying anything," he said. "My country has been occupied by the Soviets. I am a Muslim and also a Sayed."

I should add here that leaving aside anything he did in Bokhara, unfortunately Janabe Ali was caught off guard and deceived, just as we were all deceived, despite being an educated person and a scholar who had studied in

Leningrad (Petrograd at the time) and having gone to the military school. (He studied government and modern military techniques in St. Petersburg for three years.) He spoke Russian fluently, as well as Persian and Uzbeki.

While others were thrown in jail, Janabe Ali was not imprisoned. To satisfy the Soviets, he was placed under house arrest and banned from leaving his haram. When the Muslim people of Kabul got wind of this, they were very upset and gathered at the Pul-e-Khishti mosque. All the mullahs and imams stood in the pulpit and prayed for the interest and victory of the Muslims of Bokhara and rejected the actions of the government of Afghanistan. A few of these mullahs were jailed. We also lost our patience and may God bless them, Mia Jan Agha and Hazrat Nurul Mashaiq further condemned these actions. They said this brings a bad name to Afghanistan and does not bode well for the entire Islamic world. All this stopped any further actions against people. No one was executed or exiled. These people were living in hard times. The governors of the provinces were notified to keep an eye on these activities.

End of World War II and the Fate of Germans in Afghanistan

Finally, the World War II came to an end and here an act of Afghan bravery was displayed. The Allies demanded the surrender of the Germans in Afghanistan, both those who worked at the German Embassy and others. They wanted them interned and sent to contact points to be turned over to the Allied Forces. This created a wave of resistance in Afghanistan.

Sardar Mohammad Hashim Khan was caught in the middle, between a rock and a hard place, on how to deal with this and what to tell the Afghan nation. He knew that the Afghan people had an affinity toward Germany. If he refused to turn them over, what would he tell the Allies? The demand created turmoil in the country, and I am not exaggerating. The Afghan people were upset at both Germany's defeat and the victory of the Soviet atheists.

Their sacrifices and prayers created an even greater atmosphere of tension.

The call came for a jirga (a tribal assembly of elders that makes decisions by consensus). During World War I Amir Habibullah Khan had called for a jirga when the country needed to make a decision about whether or not to assist the Germans. Thus, a jirga was needed again. This request was sent out to all the provinces in Afghanistan, and a delegation was sought from them. The delegates who were appointed were not very independent and were pre-approved by the government.

Whether they were pre-approved by the government or independent, they were all united in their opinion. I was appointed as a secretary to oversee and support logistics for the loya jirga (greater assembly). Whatever we could, we did, and we did not hold back. The salaam khana (main court) was held in a big auditorium. Sardar Mohammad Hashim Khan, using the speech I had written for him, opened the jirga. After that Ali Mohammad Khan, an eloquent speaker, provided the details to the loya jirga. After him came Janab Hazrat Saheb Nurul Mashaiq. The whole auditorium was reverberating with his voice and his words. He talked about Islam, and the bravery of Islam and about Afghanistan and the bravery of the Afghans. He recalled the history of war in Afghanistan and said, "Until we have one drop of blood left in the throats of the Afghans, this will not happen." He pointed out that surrendering the Germans to the Allies was against the Shariat of Islam (Islamic jurisprudence) and against the traditions of Afghanistan. He said, "We will fight it!" and gave a cry of "Allah-o-Akbar (God is great)!"

The reaction to this tremendous slogan was a reverberating cry in unison by the delegates of "Allah-o-Akbar!" The jirga decided that until they received a guarantee the Germans in Afghanistan would not be harmed by the Allies, Afghanistan would not turn them over. The Germans should be allowed to leave Afghanistan in peace and be safeguarded from molestation. This was an historic moment for the people of Afghanistan. This action by the government is still a subject of pride. All the neutrality Afghanistan had demonstrated during the war worked in its favor. The Allies did not interfere and quietly accepted the outcome.

End of World War II and its Effects on Afghan Politics

After World War II a few incidents happened causing fear in those who had favored one side or the other during the war, or had been at crossroads with official policy, and would face the wrath of the government. The people worried the Prime Minister would implement new ideas and force whatever punishments he deemed necessary on those who had dissented.

One incident involved a young man named Mohammad Azim, a graduate of Habibiya High School and the son of Munshi Nazir. Munshi Nazir was among those people who came to Afghanistan during the time of Amir Abdul Rahman Khan. He was assigned to the city cleaning services, and people jokingly called him Munshi *Parro* (head of manure). I knew Munshi Parro's son Mohammad Azim. He was a swarthy young man. I don't recall if he was a supporter of Amanullah Khan, but he was very antagonistic toward the Nadir Shah dynasty. One day, Mohammad Azim attempted to assassinate Sardar Faiz Mohammad Khan. He was not successful, so he moved on to the British Embassy with the intent to kill the Ambassador. He was thwarted from doing so, but in the process, he killed two or three guards, putting the British Embassy in an uproar. How and why Azim did this, no one knew. The government decided this was a conspiracy hatched by Mohammad Wali Khan Wakil and six others: Mohammad Medhi Jan Qizilbash; Fakir Ahmed Khan the president of Forest Division; Khwaja Hayatullah; Sher Mohammad Khan; General Mohammad Khan; and Ghulam Jilani Khan, brother of Ghulam Nabi Khan Charkhi (former Ambassador). These people had no outside contact because they had been lingering in jail for a long time as political prisoners. No one was allowed to come even close to them. Yet, strangely, the government held to the conspiracy theory.

Some people say that the British Embassy demanded these people be executed because they conspired to kill the Embassy guards, and therefore, they were the enemy of the British government. Others theorize the Afghan government saw these political prisoners as a thorn in their side and was looking for an excuse to eliminate them. Mohammad Wali Khan, along with others, was taken out of the Arg prison in shackles. After spending five to eight years in solitary confinement, they were taken to Dehmazang prison and hung on the gallows.

It is said that before Mohammad Wali Khan was hanged, he said, "I wish I had never become a Minister or Wakil (representative of the King). I should have stayed in remote Badakhshan and served my mother like any peasant and died, breathing my last, in the lap of my mother." The guards were ordered to hit him in the face and the mouth for saying these things. They bloodied his mouth.

I may have already mentioned this; Nadir Shah himself imprisoned Mohammad Wali Khan. When he was in prison many governments sent telegrams and voiced their support for his freedom. He had played a role in the Independence of Afghanistan, and foreign governments asked for a pardon so he would not be executed. However, he was jailed for eight years. As far as I know, he was a very noble and honest man, and one of the princes of Darwaz, Badakhshan.

He was accused of having contact with Habibullah Khan Kalakani; in fact, they said he sent his gun to Habibullah Khan Kalakani. This is a total farce. There is no doubt Habibullah Khan Kalakani had the gun of Mohammad Wali Khan.

This is the truth: Amanullah Khan gave my father's property in Hussan Kot to Mohammad Wali Khan. Wali Khan had a manager named Khalifa Zahman, who worked in Istalif. Zahman had a gun belonging to Mohammad Wali Khan. Habibullah Khan Kalakani went at night to his place and took the gun by force from Zahman. It wasn't like Mohammad Wali Khan had given his gun to Habibullah Khan Kalakani.

When Amanullah Khan returned from Europe and began working toward the speedy progress of Afghanistan, like removing the hejab, changing the weekend from Friday to Thursday, and replacing the Islamic calendar with a Western calendar, Mohammad Wali Khan staunchly opposed his actions at the time. He tendered his resignation and was confined to his home. Mohammad Wali Khan was not the type of person who would take up arms to join Habibullah Khan Kalakani. In fact, Mohammad Wali Khan would have been the first one killed by Habibullah Khan Kalakani because of the tradition of not trusting the imposter who was not loyal to the previous employer (Amanullah Khan).

This was the story of Mohammad Wali Khan. He and his fellow prisoners were all executed. This contributed to the hatred of the people against the government.

There were other anecdotes I should mention here, that made people hate the ruling class. One example: It was a norm to promote hiring from within the ruling class tribes. People did not like that. The younger generation of Afghanistan was totally against this policy. Also, a rumor circulated in Kabul that the government of Afghanistan did not want to hire from the Shia sect, or people of Hazarahjat, to work in political affairs or at the Ministry of Foreign Affairs. I should add here, Abdul Khaliq, who was from the people of Hazarahjat, assassinated Nadir Shah. (Nadir Shah was born April 1883 in Dehradun, India and was a Mohammadzai of Barakzai Pashtun. Abdul Khaliq was a teenager when he assassinated Nadir Shah in 1933 during the graduation ceremony at a school. Khaliq was executed by cutting his body into pieces and his immediate family, father, and uncle, were hung in deference. (See *Fire in Afghanistan 1914-1929* by Rhea Talley Stewart.)

Sardar Mohammad Aziz Khan, the father of Sardar Mohammad Daoud Khan and Sardar Mohammad Naim Khan, was also killed by a student (in Berlin in 1933, while serving as the Afghan Ambassador to Germany). Mohammad Hashim Khan, being paranoid of assassination, did not visit any schools fearing an attempt on his life. He never met with any students, and he never discussed education with anyone. He would always try to infiltrate his spies into the education system, another reason why the youth of Afghanistan hated Mohammad Hashim Khan. The construction of Dehmazang Prison added to the people's despair.

Sardar Mohammad Daoud Khan and Sardar Mohammad Naim Khan

After Nadir Shah's assassination and during Sardar Mohammad's prime ministry, what attracted the people's attention most to the royal family was the appointment of two princes who newly emerged on the political scene, Mohammad Daoud Khan and Mohammad Naim Khan.

Both were sons of Sardar Mohammad Aziz Khan, the brother of Sardar Mohammad Hashim Khan. They were from the same mother and father. This was the reason Mohammad Hashim Khan loved his nephews more than any other. He did his best to recreate the same circumstances for them as he experienced while growing up. He trained them to be egotistical and arrogant; skeptical and suspicious; mistrusting and dependent on a spy network.

Once these two young men were brought onto the scene, they were moved into positions of power with electric speed. When Sardar Mohammad Daoud Khan was unable to complete his schooling in France, he was brought to Kabul and put under the tutelage of a German instructor, who led him through a condensed military course. As soon as he completed the course he was appointed as Military Commander in Jalalabad, and soon after that, Governor of Jalalabad. Daoud Khan was an inexperienced young man who had not seen the ups and downs of the world and was unfamiliar with the Afghan nation. Summarily, he became the leader, and he did whatever his heart desired. I'm not saying he was corrupt or had any personal motives, but he was unsuccessful in his endeavors on account of his spitefulness, arrogance, and his dependence on information gained only from intelligence and spying.

Daoud Khan was summoned to Kabul from Jalalabad

and promoted to Chief of the General Staff of Afghanistan's Army. He hadn't finished his tour of duty when he was appointed the Governor of Kandahar and assigned to the military affairs of the province. Sardar Mohammad Hashim Khan maneuvered his nephew into strategic places so he could create a center of power, gain influence, and learn about Afghanistan and its people. He was unable to win people's hearts; the people could see through him to his real attributes. The people of Kandahar, who had seen his rebellious, stubborn ways, used to call him the Crazy Sardar or the Insane Sardar or Lunatic Sardar. Daoud Khan's friends would defend him, saying proudly because the Sardar was a blunt and hot-tempered man, people called him crazy.

Daoud Khan was recalled from Kandahar to Kabul and appointed Minister of the Interior. From there he became Prime Minister and eventually the President of the Republic of Afghanistan after the coup d'etat of July 18, 1973 against his brother-in-law and first cousin Mohammad Zahir Shah. (Mohammad Daoud Khan lived from 1909-1978, and was Prime Minister, 1953-1963, and President, July 1973-April 1978 when he was assassinated by the Communists.)

Sardar Mohammad Naim Khan

The other brother was Sardar Mohammad Naim Khan. He was tall and well-built, and he loved hunting. He was a scholar and an intellectual, but while he studied a few years in the Isteqlal High School, he didn't graduate. Mohammad Hashim Khan was anxious to train this young man as his protégé as quickly as possible. He moved him into the Ministry of Foreign Affairs to start working there. When Abdul Majid Khan was promoted from President of the Bank of Afghanistan to Minister of Finance, Naim Khan took his place at the bank, even though he had never studied or worked in economics or finance. Naim Khan made a meteoric rise to the Minister of Education. Besides being head of the Bank and Minister of Education, he was also the first Deputy Prime Minister.

There's no doubt that Mohammad Naim Khan was

intelligent and had an interest in culture and education. Regretfully his teacher, Sardar Mohammad Hashim Khan, would not let him digress from his agenda.

In the prime of his youth and in spite of his pride and condescension, Sardar Mohammad Naim Khan took the reins of three important posts. He controlled the Ministry of Culture of Afghanistan, the financial centers of Afghanistan, and the Deputy Prime Minister of Afghanistan. Every two or three months at the Prime Ministry we would see evidence of and hear the sounds of floggings, whip lashings, and slapping. We would hear the voices saying the Sardar is very angry, and he had slapped around so-and-so, the head of this department or had flogged so-and-so, the head of that department. There was a gentleman named Mr. Ghulam Sakhi who became the deputy head of the bank and director general of the accounting department for the Ministry of Education. He was dragged into a whiplashing. There was another gentleman named Farhadi who was a commercial attaché in Peshwar, who was flogged one day without any court of justice or due process of law. Many other incidents like this occurred.

Sardar Mohammad Hashim Khan tried his best to ensure people were afraid of the brothers by propagating the fear-mongering. He didn't allow them to associate with anybody, and he kept them out of the midst of public. During World War II, when petroleum was scarce and not available in Kabul, they came to the Prime Ministry by horse-driven carriage. Sardar Mohammad Naim Khan would ride in the buggy reading a newspaper so he would not and could not return people's greetings. Sometimes he trotted by on horseback, and people had to run to get away from him as the horses hooves could have hurt them.

The Establishment of Radio Kabul

Radio Kabul was established at this time (Amanullah Khan and Mohammad Nadir Shah both had small 200-watt transmitters, but the upgrade in 1940 to a new 20 kilowatt transmitter, operating at 600 kHz is considered the official start of Radio Kabul – see Wikipedia). Mohammad Naim Khan, because he was the Minister of Education, had the Department of Radio under his jurisdiction. He acted as if he was the very experienced head of Communications, even though official radio had been newly established in Afghanistan. Ustad Salahuddin Khan Saljoqi was a seasoned and learned scholar among Afghan intellectuals and President of the Information and Media Department of the political media of Afghanistan. Even poor Saljoqi was forced to fold his hands and take instructions from his Highness Naim Khan every day, generating reports of minute details for him, which had no practical use.

Naim Khan ordered the construction of a building opposite the Eid Gah Mosque in Kabul by the name of Radio Clubhouse. The ruins of this abandoned building may still exist in Kabul. The building was totally different from the principles of Eastern architecture of Afghanistan. It looked like a European hat and could be seen from far away. In winter, it was impossible to warm it, and in summer, it was so hot the insufferable heat could cause heat stroke and take people's lives. All writers and journalists of Afghanistan were required to be there at least two to three evenings a week to write material for the radio. I was also part of it. We were divided into small teams or committees. At the instruction of his Highness, I was a member of the history and literary committee. My other friends were also part of this committee, and we used to go there together.

We were required to write hundreds of articles and filled many, many files. We used to go there every Saturday and on the days when his Highness would not show up, we would be thrilled. It was freedom then. We would shoot the breeze. As soon as his Highness arrived, there would be such silence, you could hear a pin drop. Our heads would be bowed, and no one had courage to talk.

Whatever articles we had researched and written about literature, history, philosophy, Shariat or mathematics, we had to present to his Highness and recite them in front of him. His Highness would critique each article, and we were supposed to welcome his criticism and accept it. On occasions, when one of us would press hard to retain our own writing, his Highness would not like it, and gradually, that person was eased out of the club.

Sardar Mohammad Naim Khan came to the conclusion that Afghanistan, which had political freedom, should also have cultural and linguistic freedom. Attention was paid to the Pashtu language. The Sardar himself did not know Pashtu, so he established a Pashtu Institute in Kabul. We became members of the Pashtu Institute and would work there every day. If I remember correctly Mr. Gul Pacha Ulfat, who was a renowned poet, a revolutionary and a brave man of Afghanistan, became the head of Pashtu Institute. Abdul Hai Habbibi and Abdul Rauf Benawa would also be there, and there were many other young men running around. Unfortunately, this act, which was realized later, intentional or unintentional, created a divide between Pashtu-and Dari-speaking people.

Publication of Historical Works

Another major step taken was to embark on writing down the country's history and publishing it so the Afghan nation would have its own independent version of history. This history would encompass culture, literature, and the political development of Afghanistan. It would cover the span of time from the pre-Islamic period up to the rule of his Highness Nadir Shah.

The government decided the work on writing the history should take place in the evenings in Kabul. Ustad Salahuddin Saljoqi was our designated leader, even though history was not his favorite subject. He was more inclined toward literature, philosophy, sociology, and ethics.

We were divided into committees again and each committee assigned various periods of history to work on. The pre-Islamic period was given to Ali Ahmad Khan Kohzad, as he was well versed in this part. I think the Saljoqi period was assigned to Qadeer Khan Taraki. I presume the Mohammad Zai period went to Mir Ghulam Mohammad Ghobar. One part was given to Mohammad Karim Nazihi. While each committee was given three to four people to help with the research, I accepted to tackle my project by myself. I was given the Ghaznavid period (975-1187). Others attested to my capacity for writing the history of Ghaznavid. (Ustad Khalilullah Khalili wrote and published the *History of the Ghaznavid Period* in four volumes).

We launched our project. For three to four months we worked from our houses and visited libraries, of which there were quite a few in Kabul. The public library of Kabul housed the remains of the library of Amir Abdul Rahman Khan. As much as I know, Abdul Rahman Khan had almost 120,000 printed books and manuscripts in his library. However, when his Highness Nadir Shah came to Kabul, the libraries were looted and plundered by the people of the Wazir and Masood tribes. A major part of the books did survive. There's no doubt the credit for safeguarding the books goes to Sardar Shah Wali Khan (April 16, 1888 – April 1977. He was one of the uncles of King Mohammad Zahir Shah and held many important posts.). According to him, the looters carried away big bags of books and sometimes a dozen at a time, wrapped in their shawls. He went after them, brought back as many as he could, and then put the books under lock and key and appointed a guard to watch over them.

There were books from the time of Amir Habibullah Khan Seraj, and some books from the library of Sardar Nasrullah Khan. Nasrullah Khan had preserved some very rare manuscripts in his library. If my father's libraries had not been pillaged, his books would have ended up in the public library. His library had almost 30,000 books, as well as a collection of almost 11,000 books in Hussain Kot fort. (Mohammad Hussain, Minister of Finance, father of Khalili, was a very powerful man under Amir Habibullah Khan Seraj. Amanullah Khan killed him for accusing him of conspiring in the assassination of his father.) Part of this collection was destroyed. I have seen some of the stolen manuscripts in London with my own eyes. I know who brought them there, but I do not want to name the person here. When the property of my father was confiscated during the time of Amanullah Khan, all his manuscripts were stolen from his library. I was an eyewitness to some of the rare manuscripts that were displayed in the libraries of London, Paris, and Turkey. I saw my father's stamp on them.

The royal library in Kabul was enriched during the time of the rule of Mohammad Zahir Shah. This royal repository of books included 400 to 500 very rare manuscripts. One of them that I remember was a catalogue of poetry by Mirza Abdul Qadir Bedil. I apologize, it was a different book, a catalog of poetry by Hazrat Shekh Saadi, which was written and compiled about 20 years after Saadi's death. This book, written by Mohammad Bin Mohammad Maroof, was very rare. There is no other manuscript older than this one. At this time, the poetry was not in alphabetical order. The *Bostan* of Saadi had been written as Saadi *Naamah*. There were a myriad of differences between this volume and the ones printed and published. For example, I compared the *Gulistan* of Saadi in the original manuscript to the printed volume of *Gulistan* – what a vast difference! I compiled a correct list of all these books. The list was lost when the Communists pillaged my library in Kabul. My books ended up at different places, and I have heard they were stolen again from those places. I don't know where they are now. This had become the *modus operandi* of destroying books of history in Afghanistan. Many actions like these happened all over the country.

Coming back to our project, we all worked and wrote our assignments. Sardar Mohammad Naim Khan again presided over the meetings in the evening at the Prime Ministry. Hazrat Saljoqi, with his powerful eloquence and sense of humor would try to cheer up Naim Khan and remove the frown lines from his forehead so he would pay more attention to the recitation of the books.

Sardar Najibullah Khan, who was working at the Ministry of Foreign Affairs at the time, had also taken an assignment. I don't remember which part he worked on, but he did a superb job. We took our turns and recited our writings aloud. I did the same, and my writing was accepted with few changes; a new word or interpretation here or there, was added, with which I agreed. These corrections were very minor. All accepted my book, and it was sent for publication. All other books were also sent for publication.

This was a remarkable thing happening. I was tired of the life we were leading, which mounted to working on files and taking them to the Prime Ministry. It had become a one-track life. I was watching my youth slip away. I was depressed and sorrowful. I had no power or right to speak my mind freely and protest openly. I would only discuss my complaints in private, among friends, venting against the government with them.

I did not feel this was morally correct. Sayed Shamsuddin Pacha, may his place be in the Heavens, Hazrat Saheb Mia Jan Agha, and I were always venting together. Sometimes Sardar Najibullah Khan and other friends joined us. Somehow reports of our sessions were magnified and transmitted to the government.

I observed the changing attitudes. I was willing to go to provinces, such as Kandahar or Herat, as a civil servant or governor. I would have been happy because this would deliver me from the current situation. It was difficult to get transferred. Sardar Faiz Mohammad Khan tried his level best to take me with him when he was appointed Ambassador to Turkey; however, Mohammad Hashim Khan vetoed his request. I could feel in my bones that I was under surveillance.

Teaching at Schools and the University

I was given another responsibility, to teach at the faculty of literature at the University of Kabul. I was assigned to teach history and literature. I also found assignments to teach at the various high schools in Kabul: Habibiya, Ghazi, Isteqlal, and Nejat. I taught at girls' high schools, Mala-Lai and Zarghona. In this way, I was able to make extra money to buy books and keep myself busy because my financial situation was very dire. At night, I would prepare lessons for the morning and during the day go to the university on foot and to the schools later and teach. I would also go back to my main work at the Prime Ministry.

One day Sardar Mohammad Hashim Khan inquired

about me. I was at the university teaching. I went to see him and he asked me, "What were you doing at the university?"

In my heart I wanted to say, "I go to university to ride horses. What would one do at the university? Either teach or be taught."

Instead, I answered, "Yes, I went there." I didn't say I went to teach. I thought if I said that, he would suspend me right away. I answered him, "At the order of Sardar Mohammad Naim Khan, I'm working there. I go there and do some research."

He said, "Okay, Naim Jan had appointed you."

I confirmed, "Yes, His Highness Naim Jan appointed me, and I went there."

He abruptly picked up the phone in front of me and called his nephew to confirm. When Naim Khan answered, he inquired about me on the phone. I assumed that on the other end of the line, Naim Khan said, "Yes, I have asked him to go to teach there and a couple of other places." Hashim Khan said something to him and hung up.

Two or three weeks later I was suspended from teaching at the high schools. I was only allowed to teach at the university. Whenever I went to the university, the students would gather around me when my period was over, and they would request I hang around for a few minutes and teach them further. I tried to avoid social subjects; however, it was impossible to do.

For example, one day I remember I had been teaching about Nasir Khusrow (Persian poet, 1004-1088). Much of his poetry was against the establishment of his time. When I would read these poems to the students, it was taken out of context, and I was accused of reading revolutionary poetry to the students. I was teaching about one of Hazrat Sherkh Saadi's poems, PBUH (peace be upon him), and there were repercussions. A line from his poetry was:

The external appearance is not helpful (hypocrisy);
one should work on inwardly conscience.

The lines of this poem were sent to his Highness with

the comments that, "See, when he teaches about the external appearance of Zahir, he's pointing at the King." God forbid, I was accused of saying this about Mohammad Zahir Shah. I was talked to and disciplined and told not to read this poem. I said, "For God's sake, this is the poetry of Saadi. He said this 700 years ago, "That hypocrisy is not helpful. One should always look inward to his own conscience, which helps you."

Later, I found out these discussions were always being held in the Arg (palace) at personal gatherings of the royal family. There, sometimes, even His Highness Zahir Shah and Mohammad Naim Khan supported me. They would explain this was a lesson, a lecture about a poem by Saadi, and that it's not wrong or the fault of this teacher what the meaning of poetry is. With these things hanging over my head, my life was bitter. During this time Radio Kabul was established, and I was a member. I was also a member of the historical society and was teaching at Kabul University as part of the Faculty of Literature. I still kept my job at the Prime Ministry. In spite of all this, I could feel in my heart that I was in a prison.

Section Three

Sayed Jamaluddin Afghani's Remains Come Home

In 1944, we received the news the remains of the late Sayed Jamaluddin Afghani would be brought to Kabul. (He was born in Afghanistan in 1838, but died overseas in 1897. He was a political activist, an Islamic ideologist in the Muslim world, and an advocate of pan-Islamic unity, according to *Arab Awakening and Islamic Revival* by Martin S. Kramer).

The government decided to bring the remains from Turkey to Afghanistan after learning the Turkish cemetery, which housed his tomb, stood in the way of mapping for a major highway. Some of our Iranian brothers raised a hue and cry that he belonged to Iran claiming he came from Assadabad, Hamadan. They had used this method before, but it did not make any headway. The Turks had a very close relationship with Afghanistan and knew the Sayed was born in Assadabad, Kunduz, Afghanistan. They also knew the Sayed had always said, "I am Afghan."

Abdur Rahman Khan Popal, brother of Ali Ahmad Khan Popal, was the Minister Plenipotentiary in Iraq for Afghanistan (a plenipotentiary is a diplomatic agent higher in rank than the ambassador). He was appointed to go to Turkey and accompany the remains of Sayed Jamaluddin Afghani back to Afghanistan via India to avoid any untoward happening in Iran. In transit, the Sayed's remains were warmly welcomed by Indian Muslims and reached Kabul via Dakka. A mausoleum was to be erected for him on a piece of land in Aliabad, across from the University of Kabul, in anticipation of a dedication ceremony.

I, along with many other poets in Afghanistan, was asked to write a poem or ode for the occasion of welcoming Sayed Jamaluddin Afghani's remains home. The poem would be read at the tomb. As God is my witness, if I had known that my teacher and mentor Hazrat, Poet Laureate, Betab was also participating, or if I had any inkling people would compare my poetry to his, or consider my poetry better than his, I would not have written the ode. Or, if I had written it, I would have given it a different style. I should have asked for his blessing before writing it. Unfortunately, this didn't happen, and I wrote my poem.

I Am Named Ustad

The poetry compiled by all other poets of Afghanistan was gathered and taken to Ustad of Ustads (professor of professors), Hazrat Ustad Saljoqi, PBUH. He was to select one poem that would be read at the dedication ceremony of the tomb of Sayed Jamaluddin Afghani. The occasion was anticipated to be attended by a large gathering.

As soon as Hazrat Ustad Saljoqi saw my poem, which I had written in the stanza style (in poetry, a stanza is a unit within a large poem), he took my poem to his Highness Sardar Mohammad Naim Khan and said, "Wah Wah" (an Afghan expression of praise, similar to "Bravo!").

After reading it, Naim Khan responded, "Poetry cannot be better than this! This is beautiful! Khalili's poem should definitely be read, and the title of Ustad should also be bestowed on him." The Sardar continued, "I wish this had occurred a few days before this, so that the Poet Laureate title could have been bestowed on him, too." When I learned what was said, I abhorred the idea. I did not want to be Poet Laureate. I, to this day, do not like that.

Ustad Saljoqi wrote to me instantly. "I, on behalf of the Ministry of Publication of Afghanistan, and on behalf of the Writers' Society of Afghanistan, have the responsibility to recognize you and address you as Ustad of Literature." I kept his original letter, which was also stolen from my library. Ustad Saljoqi kindly repeated these words again when he wrote them as an introduction to my published collection of poems.

I have published in the third volume of my writings on Herat that Ustad Saljoqi was himself a powerful poet. I remember he wrote an ode for Amir Habibullah Khan Seraj in the Khaqani style (Khaqani was a famous Persian poet). Ustad Saljoqi wanted to bring his expression and idiomatic (characteristic of a particular dialect) understanding into his poetry.

One of his poems, a part of which was published in a Persian textbook, consisted of over 200 quatrains or stanzas.

I remember one day Ustad Saljoqi came to our literary meeting. He was General Consul of Afghanistan in Bombay, India. One of the members of the literary society was Ghulam Jailani Khan Azami. He was a young man who belonged to a noble family of Kabul. Azami had written a few couplets satirizing Ustad Saljoqi with vulgar and bawdy words and pushed the paper in front of him. Ustad Saljoqi read the paper. He waited to see if he would spar with Azami in a jesting and witty way, as he was known to do with everybody. Ustad Saljoqi picked up a pencil, tapped it a couple of times on the paper, and then wrote a couple of stanzas in response. It went something like this:

Azami has satirized me with vulgar and bawdy words.
The nightingale, instead of landing from one branch to the other,
Has landed in garbage.
Like the dog, who makes no deference when excreting
Between the thorns or the nastarang (name of flower)*,*
Satirizing literary people is like
Farting in the midst of cultured society.

Coming back to my original story, Ustad Saljoqi took my ode, and the ceremony started. The coffin of Sayed Jamaluddin Afghani was brought to rest at the designated place for burial across from the University of Kabul. Scores of people came to pay their respects. As it was my habit not to read my own poetry in public, due to my bashfulness and stuttering (I had grown up fearing everything around me), the late Sarwar Goya read my ode with great enthusiasm. He read in a loud and attractive voice. My ode was long; however, here is one of the couplets:

Sayed! Bring forth your hand from out of the coffin
So that all the people may kiss your hand and receive
you

The sons of your soil are waiting for you
Stand up so that everybody can see you!

This ode consisted of 50 to 60 couplets. I was showered with congratulations from every corner. I noticed that my dear Ustad Betab Saheb, may PBUH, who loved me very much and was very proud of me as his student, left the viewing stand before the reading of the poem had ended and the dedication was complete. He left the commemoration and went to his home.

Everyone saw Betab Saheb was a little offended. Some people whispered comments behind him, and he could not take any more. I was very upset and still feel bad about it.

I was also given two to three thousand Afghanis that night by Sardar Mohammad Naim Khan as a gift on behalf of the Ministry of Education and the Ministry of Publication. I took the money and, along with my friends, we left for my hideout in Qarabagh, rejoicing with the spirit of Sayed Jamaluddin Afghani.

Life continued to pass with bittersweet memories. A mausoleum was constructed over the Sayed's grave, but this building, in my opinion, fell short of his status. It should have been more ornate. The minaret they built did not look like Eastern or Western architecture. Still, Sayed Jamaluddin was given a lot of respect as this dedication was followed every year afterwards by a ceremony on his burial day.

Insurrection in Kunar Province

World War II was gradually coming to an end, but a dour and sad incident happened during this time. Due to the rise of taxes, the people of Kunar became involved in an insurrection against the government. These people were poor with hardly any income. Some of them wore clothing made of animal pelts. They were in distress and even ate the grain mostly assigned for animals.

Most of them were from the Safi tribe. We, too, are from the Safi tribe. My uncle, Abdur Rahim Khan, was under a lot of stress. He was a military man, and he felt the heat of indignities every day. His first wife had passed away, and he had married a lady from among Sayeds of Kunar, the granddaughter of Sheikh Pacha. The government of Sardar Mohammad Hashim Khan held this family in contempt. Hashim Khan was not happy in this marriage.

Long story short, the people of Kunar joined in the insurrection, and soldiers were sent from Kabul to suppress it. As the proverb goes ("a rich man will rule over the poor and the borrower is subject to the man who lends") we were aware of our debt, but had no idea who started the insurrection. There's no doubt Abdur Rahim Khan had a connection with the people of Kunar through his marriage and on occasion the elders of Kunar would visit him in his house and stay overnight. He would always admonish them toward unity, friendship, and submission to the government. He would never encourage them to revolt. He knew these insurrections are the result of ignorance. What can poor people do when faced with guns, bombs, and planes of the government?

At this time, while Sardar Shah Mahmud Khan was the Minister of Defense, Mohammad Daoud Khan held the real power as the Commander of the Central Forces. The insurrection fed on its own influence, and the relations between Afghanistan and Pakistan went sour. Under the order of Sardar Mohammad Daoud Khan more soldiers, young army officers, armored vehicles, and cannons were sent from Kabul to the affected area.

The government usually hid insurrections from the general public to avoid any outbreaks in Kabul directly. Local media was mum while foreign media reported the news.

I told my uncle while may God take care of our future, the government's attitude towards us was very different. Anywhere I went, I found myself followed by Intelligence. "You're also being followed," I told him. "The government thinks we instigated the insurrection. What should we do? Should we preempt this before we are arrested?"

He said, "No, my son. I have pledged allegiance to the government. It's not right for me to do anything. I am a soldier. How can I go against my Islamic government?"

I said, "All right, whatever you say."

The year was 1944 still, and there was an invitation for a celebration in the city of Tashkent (Uzbek) for Amir Ali Sher Nawai. A hotel named for Nawai had been built there. An Afghan delegation was invited, headed by Annus Khan. Goya Saheb was also invited. Upon their return, they brought with them a lot of candies. It was very heavy winter, and my older daughter from my first wife, whose name was Rabia, fell sick.

Moving to the Karteh Char House

Yes, my daughter Marie, you have again insisted I continue to write the story of my life. This is not an easy thing to do. A new life is needed to repeat all these stories, incidents, happenings, and anecdotes.

Very well, this was toward the end of the rule of the Prime Ministry of Sardar Mohammad Hashim Khan. All those indignations, despairs, intelligence surveillance, and life being on one track and financial limitations and constraints, all became meaningless when my young daughter Rabia fell sick. She was very learned, educated, and intelligent. She used to compile poetry; one of her poems was published in the daily Persian newspaper, *Anees*. If you look deeper into the archives you may find the issue of the newspaper with her poetry in it. My esteemed Ustad Saljoqi has written about her in his foreward to my first volume of poetry. She had a heart ailment and rheumatism. One reason for her suffering was we did not have a house, and I moved from one place to the other.

When she fell ill and was confined to bed, I did my best to find a place of my own, which led me to Sardar Najibullah Khan. He was kind enough to help me purchase one of the newly constructed houses in Karteh Char on installments. He had to go through Sardar Naim Khan. This house gave me a new life. I was so happy to finally have a place in Kabul and call it my own.

My Good Neighbors

The house was in a good neighborhood with very caring people living there. Dr. Mir Najmuddin Khan Ansari was my neighbor. I had a longstanding relationship with his family. His father had a lineage from Hazrat Haji Saheb Ansari Saaduddin Majzoob, who was considered to be a source of knowledge of Afghanistan. He had written books entitled *Shor-e-Ishq* (Passion of Love), *Shorish-e-Ishq* (Insurrection of Love) and *Josh-e-Ishq* (Enthusiasm of Love). He also wrote an interpretation of *Maadanul-Asrar* (Interpretation of Secrets) and a book about the letters of Hazrat Imam Rabbani. Ansari's grave and tomb is still standing near the border of Kohdaman in Kabul. One of his devotees, Sardar Ali Ahmad Khan Popalzai Kandahari, designed and built the mausoleum and the dome. Through his connections, he brought stone cutters from Isfahan (Iran) and painters from Kashmir. He was the father of Mir Najmuddin Khan Ansari. He was a Unani (Greek) medical practitioner and a good friend of my father. He was our family physician (Hakim).

My father had purchased a house for him in the Baghban-Koocha neighborhood. He used to come to our house and was part of my father's social circle. He was a scholarly man with three or four sons. One of these sons was Dr. Mir Najmuddin Khan Ansari. Dr. Ansari was educated in the United States as a dentist. When he returned to Kabul, he gave up dentistry. The reason was that one day Sardar Mohammad Hashim Khan had a toothache, and he went to him to pull his tooth out. He had a very short stature. Because of his lack of height, he was not able to pull the tooth out smoothly. He said, "Your tooth looks like a pillar!"

This was considered an insult. The Prime Minister chastised him and ordered him never to return to treat him again, because of his lack of respect and impoliteness. When the doctor heard this, he quit his practice. He joined the Ministry of Education, and since he was a very competent and learned person, he was appointed as a member of the Book Publication Department, and finally, he was appointed as Director of the Teachers Association (teachers' training school).

I had another connection with Dr. Mir Najmuddin Khan Ansari. As a child, my mother had nursed him along with me, and his mother had nursed me along with him. In our culture, that makes us foster brothers.

Having him live in the house next to mine was good for me. We would socialize together. If sometimes we were short of anything in our house, his mother, while she was alive, would help us. We called her Koh Koh (a respectful nickname for an older lady).

Goya Saheb

Goya Saheb's place was located in Karteh Char. He did not own a house, but rented one in our neighborhood. Alamshahi also lived there. He was right across from our house. Thus, Karteh Char was good for me from every angle.

Coming back to my daughter, Rabia, she was ailing. I had written a poem about our nomadic life and presented it to his Highness, the King of Afghanistan. It was published in my first volume of poetry. Sadly, I don't remember it at this time. Maybe I will remember it later, and tell you about it at our next sitting. That way you may remember it when you are thinking about your sister.

The mother of your sister had already died at that time, and I had married your mother, who was my cousin, the daughter of my uncle, Abdul Rahim Khan Naib Salar, the Minister of Public Works. I was very happy to have a place to live and to have your mother as my wife. I was living a happy life. This is what I wanted.

Similarly, a young man from Jurm, Badakhshan named Abdullah Khan Badakhshi became famous as Shah Abdullah Badakhshi. He was a trustworthy person and had a deep influence in Badakhshan. The authorities decided not to let him stay in Badakhshan; instead, he was appointed to a position at the Prime Ministry. He used to sit next to me. Shah Abdullah Khan was a lean and delicate man of fair complexion. He was soft spoken and very eloquent. He would talk point by point and was witty.

Sometimes he used to write poetry. He had written a book, published in Kabul that is still considered to be a resource for both East and West. This book is about the different dialects of the Pamir language (Pamir, Shighnan, and Badakhshani).

Shah Abdullah Badakhshi was stricken with tuberculosis. He tried his best to get the government's permission to go to India for treatment but was denied exit. I do not remember the exact time or day, but during the time of Shah Mahmud Khan, he died. His body was sent back to Badakhshan and buried there. He left behind a daughter and a library with some manuscripts in it. He was a real gentleman and a humanist.

Translating the Holy Koran in Persian and Pashtu

God was kind to me, and Sardar Mohammad Hashim Khan decided the Holy Koran should be translated and interpreted in Persian and Pashtu in Kabul. The first thing his Highness Nadir Shah Shaheed (martyr) had done when he became king was to order the printing of the Holy Koran in Kabul's printing press. Sardar Hashim Khan, in order to show he was a very devoted Muslim, decided to have the Holy Koran translated again and reprinted in Kabul. He gave the assignment of supervising this interpretation and translation project to Sardar Naim Khan.

Naim Khan and Ali Mohammad Khan got together and invited this humble servant to join them. They also wrote a decree on behalf of the Prime Minister appointing me in charge of the Persian translation of the Holy Koran. Abdul Haq Khan Betab and Maulavi Mohammad Qasim Badakhshi, brother of Shah Abdullah, were appointed to assist me.

I recommended that, because of this augural (sacred) moment, it would be appropriate to use the rich sources of the scholars and academia of Afghanistan to compile the new interpretation and translation in multiple languages: Arabic, Persian, Urdu, and Turkish. This would bring about a modern publication, printed in Kabul, that people throughout the world could use. It would create a good defense and fortification, as strong as any army, against unbelievers and Communists. Sardar Mohammad Hashim Khan overruled this and ordered the Persian and Pashtu be translated and printed, using one source, the interpretation of Maulana Shabbir Ahmad Nomani. We accepted him as an authoritative source. We had no other avenue of choice. There is no doubt that Nomani's interpretation is an excellent source. In my view, however, a better approach would have been to bring together all the scholars and academia in Afghanistan to tackle the delicate subject of the interpretation and translation of the Holy Koran. It may have resulted in a more comprehensive and authoritative resource. However, since his Highness knew only the Urdu language and used to read that translation occasionally, he decided Shabbir Ahmad's translation should be used as a source.

To avoid negative consequences, I decided to go along and give up any resistance. We accepted that translation. It reminds me of an Arabic poem:

The pull of the sword
makes the dark and untrue words acceptable.
They asked us, "Is that right?"
And our answer was, "Yes, you are right."

When we got together, I realized we needed the help of more than just Hazrat Ustad Betab and Maulavi Mohammad Qasim Khan. Afghanistan had a repository of extraordinary scholars and in the matter of the Holy Koran we were very, very careful. If even one word deviated from the translation, they could declare us infidels. If that happened, Mohammad Hashim Khan would not take responsibility and would not hesitate in naming the person to be sacrificed. I recommended and got permission to include Maulavi Ghulam Nabi Khan of Kama, Nangarhar. He was educated in Deoband School of Islamic Studies (in India) and was an authority on the Contemplative Sciences. He was a great scholar, no less than anybody I know, and very deep in his thinking. He could easily write about philosophy and logic. Unfortunately, he was very sensitive and would lose his temper easily.

Maulana Abdul Hai Panjsheri

I also recommended Hazrat Maulana Abdul Hai Panjsheri, a renowned scholar of Afghanistan, be assigned to this committee. Sardar Hashim Khan held Maulana Abdul Hai in high esteem as well. I did not know the reason. Maulana Abdul Hai was one of the leading scholars of his time, educated in Deoband, India. His real name was Maulavi Paendah Mohammad. After earning his degree and graduating in India, they gave him the title of Abdul Hai the Second, in memory of Maulana Abdul Hai of Lucknow, India, who had also graduated from Deoband and was considered to be a leading scholar of Islamic studies in India. Abdul Hai was our Maulavi and was a terrific scholar in Afghanistan. This title was a great honor. He had a profound knowledge of Islamic studies. He memorized the Holy Koran in 30 days, and I should tell this story here.

When Anwar Pasha declared Jehad, without approval of Amanullah Khan, against the Russians in Bokhara from Kabul, his father, Habibullah Khan Kalakani, and some people from Panjsher proceeded to join him. I've seen the letter with my own eyes, which Maulana Abdul Hai received from Anwar Beg. In the letter, Anwar Beg addresses him as Sheikh-ul-Islam. He was with Anwar Beg to the last. His father was martyred in this war and after Anwar Beg was killed they returned to Afghanistan. Maulana Abdul Hai, on the orders of Amanullah Khan, was arrested in Khanabad and imprisoned. The governor of Khanabad beat Maulavi Saheb publicly. People opposed it, but still Maulavi Saheb was put in prison.

The Maulavi knew 10 chapters of the Holy Koran by heart. He told us he was in prison during the month of Ramadan. The prisoners wanted to complete the recitation of Holy Koran for that period. I would learn some passages from the Holy Koran during the day and read them as I led the prayers at night. Since I had memorized 10 chapters earlier, I memorized the rest of the 20 chapters in 30 days. According to him, until the end of the month of Ramadan he continued to read one chapter every night during the Taraveh prayers (special prayers offered during the 30 days of Ramadan), and the Holy Koran was completed that month. Whatever the esteemed Maulana had said about memorizing the Holy Koran in one month, it was witnessed by several (political) prisoners who were in jail with him.

Strangely enough the Maulana also knew the *Shahnamah (The Book of Kings)* by Persian poet Firdausi (977-1010 AD), an epic poem (60,000 verses that describes the history of Iran from creation through the Islamic conquest of Persia in the 7th century). He knew the *Shahnamah* by heart and memorized the story of *Sikandernamah (Alexander the Great)*, by (12th century Persian poet) Nizami.

He would recite these epic stories from memory in a very dramatic voice, which left the audience flabbergasted. He would hide the books from others and read them when he was alone. "It is against my academic dignity to read these (secular) books in the presence of my student scholars of knowledge and Arabic," he used to say.

He was also a poet, and his alias was Parwanah (Moth). Unfortunately, toward the end of his life, he washed away the ink with which he had written all of his poems and said, "The Prophet, PBUH, did not write poetry. I, also, do not want to leave any of my poetry behind. The knowledge of the Holy Koran in my heart is enough."

He was very articulate and expressed himself clearly. He was proficient in Urdu, Arabic, Persian, and Pashtu. He also knew a little Uzbeki from when he lived in Bokhara. He was a very handsome and impressive man, with the type of personality that attracted women. In fact, two girls from Panjsher married Maulana Panjsheri. He was witty, and at the same time, very sensitive and would lose his temper at any moment. The same is said of Sayed Jamaluddin. Most probably Sheikh Mohammad Abdou (Jamaluddin's most famous pupil and one of the pioneers of the modernist movement in the Arab world) said this about him: whatever he would construct while he was calm, he would destroy when he was upset. Maulana did the same thing. He would be very nice and do constructive things, and then all of a

sudden, lose all to his whims.

Starting Translation of Holy Koran

Finally, the committee translating the Holy Koran met. Sardar Mohammad Hashim Khan gave a copy of the Urdu translation of the Holy Koran to Yaqoob Hassan. We were not content and said that Maulana Mansur Ansari, who was from India and was one of the leading scholars of that country, should be brought in to translate from Urdu to Persian. We achieved our wish, and the Maulana came and wrote with us. He had a beautiful handwriting. He translated in the Indian style.

The Prime Ministry was like heaven to us. In the office where we wrote the official lingo, compiling different things about different subjects, filling up files, day in and day out, writing the decrees Hashim Khan would sign, now all that drudgery was taken over by the new work of translating the Holy Koran.

We assigned only one day a week for administrative duties. The rest of the week we would gather in an upstairs room, surrounded by scholars reading the Holy Koran very carefully, and then translate it, passage by passage.

When the Persian translation was read, I would correct it myself, in my own handwriting, the same way I wrote prose. After any corrections, I would make all the other scholars sign it, thank God. I'm glad I did that. If I didn't have those signatures, later on there was the possibility they could create a conspiracy about me and throw me in jail.

Some nights when we worked late, I would invite two or three scholars to my house afterwards and, in spite of my financial constraints, I would ask my wife to prepare a meal for all of us. Hazrat Maulavi Rabbi was a frequent visitor, and we would discuss the work on the Holy Koran. I had reached to the chapter of Surah Nahal when I was thrown in jail. I will talk about this later.

Those who sell medicine for the ailing heart;
When my turn came, sold torments and persecution.

During the translation sometimes I would write poetry.

Hazrat Ustad Poet Laureate Betab was neither a fan of my prose nor my poetry. He would lecture me, "You have a new style and you speak new words. This is not poetry. In poetry, bringing up social justice and other controversial topics is not appropriate. Poetry should speak of love, of the beloved, and of the beauty of women and their tresses of hair. You should be writing about the moon and the pain of yearning that comes when you are parted from your beloved."

In short, I would be insolent and write my own style and read it in the presence of Ustad Betab with the objective of enticing him to write along these lines. But he would not. There is no doubt Ustad Betab was one of the most prolific and erudite writers of Persian literature. He was very meticulous. I have yet to meet anyone else who was that precise. In spite of his gray hairs, I have not seen anyone compare with his courage either.

During the period when we were translating the Holy Koran, there was an insurrection among the people of Suleiman Khel tribe. Sardar Mohammad Hashim Khan instructed us to hastily translate the last chapter of the Holy Koran in Pashtu first so it could be printed as soon as possible and sent to the people of Suleimon Khel. He wanted them to realize the government of Afghanistan is an Islamic government.

To rush this translation in Pashtu, Burhanuddin Khan Kushkaki and two or three other scholars were assigned to the immediate task. Burhanuddin did his best and was able to finish the Pashtu translation earlier than Persian. The last chapter of the Holy Koran was the one delaying the Persian translation. Somehow, Hashim Khan was informed that it was I, Khalili, who caused the delay. Since people talked a lot against me behind my back, His Highness accepted the story as truth. Stories like this created even more of a rift between him and me. He was not very happy with Maulana Hai or Maulana Mansur Ansari either.

When the hasty translation in Pashtu was brought to our committee, the Maulana Hai and Ghulam Nabi Saheb pointed out some minor objections in two or three places in the last chapter of the Holy Koran.

For example, Burhanuddin Khan used the word *Cheikhtan,* which means God in Pashtu instead of *Allah* or *Khuda* (the name of God). Instead of S*oore Israfel* (trumpet of the archangel), he had used instead the Pashtu word of *shipeilai,* which means whistle (*ishpelaq* in Persian). These are small words, but large in meaning. (The archangel who will sound the Day of Judgment, heralding the end of the world, will do so on a trumpet, not a whistle).

These objections were taken to Burhanuddin Khan, which made him very upset. Instead of talking to me, he went straight to Sardar Mohammad Hashim Khan.

Hashim Khan had yet to summon us about these objections when Burhanuddin Khan came to a meeting and challenged us, saying, "What right do you have to correct my translation?"

As I had mentioned earlier, Maulana Abdul Hai lost his temper easily. He replied, "Be quiet you *Firaun* (Pharoah - a derogatory term)." He went a step further and slapped Burhanuddin Khan, who was a famous figure in Afghanistan.

Burhanuddin Khan went directly back to Sardar Hashim Khan. Maulana Abdul Hai and others, as well as I were called in. Hashim Khan stood with his cane in his hand fuming. He said, "Abdul Hai, what right do you have to call someone *Firaun* and slap that person?"

Abdul Hai replied, "Who did I call *Firaun*?"

The Prime Minister answered, "Didn't you call Burhanuddin Khan that?" He turned toward us and added, "Weren't you all there when he said Burhanuddin was *Firaun*?" We kept quiet and waited for this to play out.

The Maulana said, "Yes, I'm not going to deny this, but I did not say that he was *Firaun*. I said he looks like *Firaun,* not that, God forbid, he is *Firaun.* Burhanuddin is short stature and wears a tall head covering or hat. You know very well that *Firaun* was short in stature and always wore a tall hat. I told him he resembled *Firaun* because of that. If you don't believe me, read about it (he gave the name of a book and the place to find it)."

The Prime Minister softened his attitude with a slight smirk on his face. He asked, "Why did you slap him?"

Maulana said, "Just because we are always fooling around. *Mousa* (Moses) drowned *Firaun*. I only slapped him on the face."

Sardar Hashim Khan softened up further, and his smirk broadened. He turned to Burhanuddin Khan. As soon as Burhanuddin Khan's eyes met the Prime Minister's, he said, "Your Highness, he also called me a *jola*."

Maulana said, "Sir, he is lying. I did not call him a *jola* (spider). I called him a *jolaha* (weaver). Saheb, you know in Islam, *jolaha* is not a bad word. The Prophet, PBUH, has said, 'al-kasib is loved by Allah's people in vocations are loved by God). I wish I was a *jolaha* or my father had been a *jolaha*, because we would have weaved our beautiful local silk cloth and worn it." He pointed at the dress of his fellow ministers. "This is the dress of foreigners, which we wear because we cannot weave our own clothes."

The Prime Minister ignored all these complaints and pronounced, "Henceforth, I do not want to hear any more of these petty differences, and if I do, I'll be coming down hard on you. Go away now, and tomorrow we will meet here with everybody and continue this discussion."

We came out of this office in one piece and thanked our lucky stars. The next day the meeting was held at Gulkhana (the Flower House) in the Prime Ministry. Ali Mohammad Khan, Sardar Naim Khan and Ghulam Moulavi Nabi Saheb were there. Abdul Rahman Pazhwak, who had recently started literary writing, was also invited to join the meeting. Mohammad Annus Khan and Sardar Najibullah Khan were there as well. Everyone was sitting when I entered the room. I had the translation of the Holy Koran in my hands. Sardar Hashim Khan, in a sign of respect for the Holy Koran, stood up. I placed the Holy Koran on the table.

Burhanuddin Khan acted as though Sardar Hashim Khan had stood up from his place as a sign of respect to me. He stood up to passionately defend his grievance. "These people are slandering my translation in Pashtu. Maulana Abdul Hai has made very light of my complaint and tried to diminish and diffuse it into simple stories."

Maulana Hai said, "Yes, sir, he had written *Cheikhtan* for God. The word *Cheikhtan* is neither understood well in

Pashtu nor in Persian. I have no qualms with Pashtu. As a matter of fact, I'm more proficient in Pashtu than him. I know by heart the odes of Khushal Khan Khattak (1613-1689) and Rahman Baba (1650-1715, both were prominent Pashtu poets). In my opinion, the word *Khuda* is better, and if we had used *Allah*, it is better than both."

Burhanuddin Khan Kushkaki defended, "I'm trying to popularize the Holy Koran in the Pashtu language as commanded. You, Maulana, are obstructing."

Maulana Abdul Hai rose to speak calmly. "Your Highness, it is very easy to decide this matter. Why don't you call in a couple of your soldiers who are used to slapping and beating people? Bring them in here and let them slap Burhanuddin Khan Kushkaki and let's observe if, under the excruciating pain, he calls out 'for the sake of *Cheikhtan!*', or if he cries 'for the sake of *Allah*, leave me alone!' If he cries out for the sake of *Allah*, we are right, and if he calls out for the sake of *Cheikhtan*, then he is right."

The Prime Minister interrupted, "God forbid, we are not going to slap Burhanuddin Khan!"

Maulana Abdul Hai continued, pointing at the translation, "Saheb, this is the Holy Koran, and you are printing it for the use of the people. It is a very honorable gesture. Why don't we use the words which our elders and sages have used for ages; elders like Hazrat Shah Wali Saheb. Why don't we use the word *Allah* or *Khuda,* which we have always used, you have always used and your forefathers have always used? When you pray to God, how do you address him? Do you say *Allah* or *Khuda* or *Cheikhtan?"*

The Prime Minister responded, "I always pronounce *Allah* or *Khuda*."

Moving forward, we discussed the Pashtu word of *shipeilai,* which means whistle, or *ishpelaq* in Persian, which was replacing *Soore Israfel.* The Maulana explained, "The whistle is used by children when calling someone. This is not a whistle. It is a trumpet blown on the day of resurrection (judgment) by the archangel Raphel. *Soore Israfel* should not be translated. The word *Soore* (trumpet) is famous. It will not hurt if we use the original word and not translate it."

Ali Mohammad Khan and Najibullah Khan also sided with us. A decision was made, and orders passed that from this time forward, any Pashtu translation by Burhanuddin Khan would be copied and given to Ghulam Moulavi Nabi and Maulana Abdul Hai. Thus we all broke off, kissed each other, and left the room. Days and nights passed in translation. We had reached the chapter of Surah Nahal. It was a wintery Friday, and as I said earlier, we were sent to jail on this day.

I Am in Prison along with Abdul Rahim Khan, Naib Salar

My imprisonment may have been caused by the Insurrection in Kunar province. I received daily reports from Kohistan and from my village of Qarabagh that security police and undercover detectives were looming at our property. We were told that they were coming to the house and asking questions. We don't know why. The Administrator of Kohistan came himself several times. It was suspenseful, creating anxiety. They were even counting the horses and the cars at the house of Abdul Rahim Khan, Naib Salar. I informed Naib Salar, who was my uncle, about these developments. He said, "Let God be our guide and our security. We have not done anything, so there is no need to be afraid."

It was the month of Jadi (10th month of the Afghan year, December-January) in 1945, on a Friday. Sardar Mohammad Annus Khan and Goya Saheb had just returned from Tashkent. Snow blanketed Kabul. My older daughter was still very sick. And as God is my witness, we had not a single penny in our house. It was to the extent I did not have coal to burn in my Sandali. (A Sandali is a low table, placed in the middle of a room with a manqal or container of charcoal fire underneath and covered by a large quilt. The family would gather around and put their legs under the quilt to stay warm.)

That Friday, I was informed that Goya Saheb wanted to

invite me for lunch at his house. I was happy to go and even thought of borrowing some money from him so I could send it back home to purchase some coal fuel.

He came and presented me with a bottle of Russian cologne and some candy. He said, "I'm going to Shah Abdullah Khan's house to get him too." I said, "Fine," and he left. I went back inside my house to pick up my aba (cloak) so I could start walking toward the house of Goya Saheb.

I heard a knock on the outside door and someone informed me the police were outside. I said, "May God help me."

I went outside, and there stood a police officer from Kohistan. I recognized him. I knew his father and his forefathers. They used to work on our lands. He held me by the shoulder and pressed it a couple of times. It was as if he was giving me a signal to make me aware what was going on. He said, "His Highness has ordered you come with us to the Prime Ministry."

As usual, a few other people had been asked to go to the Prime Ministry as well, Wazir Saheb, Abdul Rahim Khan, and I.

I told the police officer, "Whenever I am invited to the Prime Ministry a civilian comes to inform us. Why are the police here today?"

He said, "There is no one else there. I was ordered to bring you in."

I agreed to go, and I told him, "Wait for me. I will be back out after I change my clothes."

He said, "No, you're not allowed to go in. Please, follow me."

I turned around and saw another seven or eight armed policemen around my house. In front of my wife and children, with my sick daughter watching from the window, they arrested me and cuffed me with my hands in the back like an ordinary prisoner and took me to the waiting automobile. As we drove away, I could see armed policemen on bicycles or in cars every few hundred yards.

I was brought to the Arg (palace). I asked the police officer, "What is going on?"

He said, "We don't know, and you don't have any right to talk."

We entered the Arg from the big gate on the eastern side. We were stopped just inside the gate. It was very cold, and I did not have warm clothes. I didn't even have socks on my feet because of the abrupt way they brought me in. I was wearing old clothing that looked a little tattered. I only had a flannel cloak around me. I was shivering with cold and was trying hard not to let the police see me do so. I did not want them to think I was shivering because I was cowardly. I realized there must be something very grave going on.

I was alarmed to look toward the southern gate of the Arg and see they had brought in Naib Salar. I could tell it was him because his *imama* (headgear) was discernible, like a crown on his head. He was surrounded by soldiers who took him away somewhere, and I lost contact of him. And then the soldiers came to the car where I was.

They opened the car door. I saw it was Sayed Saleh Khan, the military Commander of the Arg. Another officer came along next to him. I knew Sayed Saleh Khan. He was one of the Sayeds of Kunar, who are called Pachas. He had a cigar in his hand. I was not only accustomed to smoking cigars I was addicted to them. I love cigars. I asked him, "Pacha Saheb, let me have a cigar too."

He gestured me to be quiet. His eyes were tearful, and he said softly, "I'm not allowed to."

We got out and stood next to him. He gestured for me to follow him, along with the other officer. There were more officers behind us.

We walked toward the eastern wall of the palace, and they took us into a very narrow passage, which I had never seen in my life. It was dim and illuminated only by a very low watt light bulb. A couple of soldiers stopped us and went over our clothes, patting us down and touching us all over. They found nothing, except a couple of shaving blades in my pocket.

"Why do you have these?" they asked.

I said, "Because I use them to sharpen the pencils I write with when I am translating the Holy Koran. I had them in my pocket when you came and arrested me."

"You're not to have these," they answered and confiscated the shaving blades.

I understood. It was good they confiscated the blades. Otherwise, I may have tried to take my life because I was new to this degrading journey.

My Cell in the Prison

A door opened for me, and I was asked to go into a room with no floor. When I put my foot forward it sunk into mud. It was lower than the level of the palace, all mud. There was a small window about four meters above me providing the only source of outdoor light. There was also a light bulb high above in the ceiling, but it was dim. There was nothing else in the room, flooring or anything else, except for a small clay pot for holding water.

The soldiers told us, "Please, go ahead."

I told Sayed Saleh Khan Pacha, "You have some guests who are very close to you. Be careful. Stay alert."

He said, "I apologize." His eyes were full of tears.

I tried to find a place to sit in the room. Everywhere I moved my foot, it would go deep in the mud and sludge. I found a spot where the dirt was not wet and sat there quietly. The only noise I could hear was made by the clock tower of the Arg palace. The clock chimed 10 times. It was 10 o'clock. Then it chimed 11 times, then 12 times. It was 12 o'clock. I spread my cloak on the part where the ground was dry, and since I still had wuzu (ablution) I offered the evening prayer and whatever benedictions I could remember, I repeated the benedictions. I was staring death in the eyes. I was thinking fast, and it was hard to concentrate. Maybe there had been an assassination attempt on the King or on Hashim Khan and they thought we were involved in it. Or maybe there had been an unexpected attack on Kabul and they thought we were involved. My thoughts raced in my head, but I could not find any guilt for which I was responsible. I'd totally forgotten the insurrection of Kunar.

A few minutes after I finished my prayers, the door opened, and a guard entered. He wore a woolen coat and woolen socks with leather tops and had Russian galoshes on his feet. He showed no respect or character. I could see only torture and menace in his eyes.

He dropped a piece of bread in front of me and said, "Eat." I picked it up and had no other choice but to eat while he stood there.

He said, "The other one could not swallow this bread." (In our culture, bread and salt are symbols of loyalty and gratitude to the king. To not eat means you are full of shame because you have pierced the trust.)

I realized he was talking about Naib Salar.

"He deserves it. He was very loyal," I said.

The guard ignored my answer. "Do you see this clay pot?" he said. "Whenever you are thirsty, there is water in there for you to drink. The prisoner before you urinated in it."

I said, "Thank you very much. With God's blessing, I may not be thirsty or need water."

Around 2 o'clock I heard noises coming from the narrow passage outside. There were the voices of many soldiers passing through, and something else: Hammers hitting nails? I figured out that the sound must have been the pounding of their feet against the floor, with their metal riding spurs scraping the tiles.

Amongst all this commotion I recognized the voice of Naib Salar. He was talking very loudly, and indirectly I could understand he was trying to calm me down and give me strength. I heard him say, "Go, thank His Highness on my behalf and tell him we appreciate his hospitality. Let him know I'm very happy in my room with the furnishings provided. Let him know I do not agree with him that a commission has been appointed to investigate my work. I thank him for informing me that he has appointed good, honest people to investigate me, but let him also know he doesn't have to. He can appoint anyone, including my enemies, and if he finds anything that points to treason against my religion, against my country or against him, from the day I started working for him until today, he can pass any judgment on me. He should, please, not support us unconditionally and let his good name be dragged with ours." I was shocked listening to his voice. Slowly, the commotion died down.

A gentleman named Haji Aminullah Khan, a Director at the Ministry of Court and the son of Dilawar Khan of Panjsher, entered my room with several soldiers. He did not speak to me, but instead, nodded toward the door, indicating I should go out and stand in the hallway. I did so. He brought a cot into the room, along with bedding and a large water jug with a stone set down in front of it. He was putting other things in there, but I couldn't see. When I tried to look, the soldiers blocked my view and pulled me further down the dark hallway. After a few moments, Haji Aminullah Khan gestured for me to come back in.

When I reentered the room, he announced, "Minister of Court Sardar Ahmad Shah Khan has sent these things for you because of his longstanding friendship with Abdul Rahim Khan (Naib Salar). His Highness, the King, also recommended until the investigation is complete, you should receive every courtesy here."

I saw he had set a strange wooden table in the room with something underneath. I asked, "What is this?"

He answered, "This is a pot for you to use for your needs."

"So we don't have the right to go out to relieve ourselves?" I asked.

"There's no right," he answered. "You will do everything in this room."

I could tell the cot and bedding were from the time of Abdul Rahman Khan. On one side, I saw a large bolt or roll of white textile. With a curious look on my face, I asked, "What is this?"

The Director from the Minister of Court answered, "This is for you to use when you are having meals. Open it up, roll it out, and use it as a drop cloth. You will use a part of it every day and every evening. Once that part is soiled, roll up the soiled part, here, pull out a new strip of clean cloth there."

Looking with alarm at the size of the roll of cloth, I realized that they intended to keep me here for quite some time. I sat down on the bed, and they left, locking the door from the outside.

After an hour or so a man came in and brought food from the kitchen of the Ministry of Court. I was very hungry. He had a big serving tray in which he had a plate of Afghan *pillow* (rice with meat and nuts), a bowl of stew with kabobs, and bread.

The man who brought it in, his name was Ali Ahmad. He was from the Khost province and was working for the prison now, but at one time he had served former Prime Minister Sardar Shah Mahmud Khan Ghazi. He had learned etiquette and fine manners from the household of his respected wife, Qamarul Banat, daughter of Amir Habibullah Khan Seraj.

Ali Ahmad was a softhearted man. He closed the door behind him and told me in a very hushed voice, "Whatever you want, let me know and I will arrange it for you."

I was skeptical, thinking he might be a spy. I replied, "No, thank you. I don't need anything."

"Don't be afraid of me," he said. "I'm also in the service of Abdul Rahim Khan. Besides being responsible for you, I'm also responsible for your uncle, Mohammad Yosuf Khan Safi, who is in the room behind you. He has been in prison for the past 10 years. He has sent his *salam* to you and has asked me to tell you that if you need anything he will definitely send it to you. He admonished you not to be too worried and to stay calm."

I thanked him and did not say a word. I did not send a message back to my uncle, worrying all the time that this could be a setup.

He told me, "Abdul Hadi Khan Dawi is also in prison here. Fourteen years ago, he planted an Afghan *sinjid* tree. It resembles mountain ash and at maturity, bears fruit. Now, he's harvesting the berries and eating them, he has been here for so long."

He told me the names of many other prisoners in the Arg prison. I would listen to him attentively without commenting.

Since it was a very cold winter, he went out and came back with two other people holding a big coal and wood heater and left it in my room along with coal. I was worried if I burned the coal in the small room, it would release toxic gases. I asked him if the coal had been lighted and burned properly. He said, "Don't worry, we have paid attention to each stove for an hour and a half to make sure it's not toxic. The Minister of Court has ordered it be placed in your rooms, and the Arg prison physician has reviewed it. Rest assured it is safe."

Still, after an hour I asked them to take it out of my small room. They removed it, and I fell on my bed.

Prison and Nightmarish Thoughts

What to say about this first night in the prison, and the thoughts racing around in my head! God only knows – why I am here? I was not able to eat properly. All the negative thoughts running in my mind were killing me. My nightmares imprisoned me, weighing on me and shackling me. I knew from experience in the majority of cases, when a person was thrown into the Arg jail as a political prisoner, their families were imprisoned also – their sons, their wives, and their daughters. I was frantic with worry. I knew Sardar Hashim Khan must have sent soldiers to my house where I have a sick young daughter, my young wife, the wife of my older son, Safiullah, who is also young, along with my younger son and also you, little Marie, you were only one year old. You were like a new flower that had just opened up to talking. You were beautiful. I was hallucinating all of you had been taken away and thrown in prison, and my mind ran away with what might be going on with you and what you were being subjected to. Maybe you were being tortured.

I reminisced from the past. The wife and the family of Malik Qais Khogyani were taken to prison; the wife and family of Mir Zamon Khan Kunari were thrown in jail separately; the wife and family of Ghulam Nabi Charkhi were subject to the same fate; the wife and family of Hassan Khan Girdabi Momandi, the same. Many more were victims of this calamity, which struck throughout the families and children and wives of Afghanistan. They were subjected to humiliation and imprisonment without any judicial procedure to address any crime for which they'd been accused. The disastrous treatments were unprecedented. Even at the time of Amir Abdul Rahman Khan, who ruled with an iron fist, the women and children of the accused were not imprisoned except for those women who were accused directly of a crime.

I was obsessed with these thoughts, and the vivid scenes in my head of my wife and children being in jail and subjected to torture. I had a brother named Najibullah Khan who was one year younger than I am, and my youngest brother who was seven years younger than I am. He had lost hearing in both ears and was kind of Darvish (Sufi). He looked enchanted, and both of these brothers were very secluded and very respectful and harmless in their dealings. Both were God-fearing and had a Sufi character. Both worked at the Prime Ministry under strictly controlled atmosphere and were clerks under me. I kept picturing both of them in jail with all their wives and children. I was also imagining Naib Salar's family had been taken and imprisoned. No matter how I tried, these scenes would not leave my mind and continuously haunted me. I would see my wife, my young daughter, my son, his wife, the wives of my brothers and all their children looming in prison rooms without heat or light or furniture. The doors were closed on them, and no one was listening to their screams and pleadings. I imagined my sick daughter, Rabia, was dying, and I could see her body slowly giving up life. These thoughts were my nemesis. I was awake all night. In the morning, I heard the call to prayers from the Arg mosque and other mosques around the Arg in Kabul. The call to prayers gave my heart a little encouragement. I got up and did my wazu (ablutions) and offered morning prayers.

Whatever I ask, I remember
And read in the presence of God
Pleading to God Almighty
Still, I was not satisfied.

These painful imaginations and temptations of doubt

and despair continued to live with me. The nightmarish suggestions were driving me out of my mind. I tossed and turned in bed. Around 8 o'clock in the morning the prison guard came in and brought breakfast. He brought a feast – everything I had never eaten at home for breakfast. He brought in cakes, cookies, milk, black tea, and green tea. I had no appetite, just took the green tea and drank it. The guard asked me to eat something. I told him to leave it I'd eat later. I was anxious, hyperventilating, and worried about what my children were doing and what they were eating. I swear, in the name of God, I was not a prisoner in the Arg prison, but a prisoner of my own sorrow, my anxiety, my despair.

And as Abdul Alah Meirie has said, I was among those prisoners who are blind and prisoners of their own blindness. I was living in prison, but I think the worse kind of prison is the prison of anxiety, the prison of despair, and the prison of hallucination, which is created by man himself.

Fear breeds fear.

My Apprehensions and Hunger Strike

It was noon, and I offered midday prayers. Around 2 o'clock the lunch was served. There was a knock on the door, and they moved out the heater and placed the food on the floor. I ate a couple of morsels just to show the food bearer I was not on a strike. I could tell that the guard was thinking I was trying to commit suicide, and I was starting with hunger strike. He warned, "If you don't eat, the soldiers will come in and hit you with the butt of the gun and force you to eat."

I was kind of intimidated and took a couple of more morsels. I explained, "I'm not feeling well."

To pass the time, I was reciting poetry from my memory under my breath. I asked the prison official if he could bring me a copy of the Holy Koran printed in India. He replied, "You're absolutely not allowed. You are barred from having any book, Holy Koran, or pen."

It was evening and darkness fell. I picked up a few pieces of coal and wrote a poem on the wall of the prison cell. I can't recall now what the poem was. In the morning, when the guard brought my breakfast, as soon as his eyes fell on the wall he said, "Are you trying to have me killed? *May your house be destroyed!* (Afghan saying) Your right to write has been taken away. The investigators will come, and I will be in trouble!"

He wiped my poetry from the wall and cleaned it, despite my pleas to leave it there. "It's only a poem," I said.

He said, "You're not allowed to do that."

I was not paying attention. What kind of walls are these? There wasn't any kind of artwork. The floor underneath the carpet they had dropped on top of the mud was still wet and in many places the carpet had pushed under the mud. I had no choice but to lay down on that dampness. Despite being a young man, my body was in pain from the dampness, and I tried to overcome it. The light from the bulb in the ceiling above was too bright. I couldn't even look around. It was so very sharp and powerful. The rays hit my eyes and felt like daggers going into my pupils. The guard came in, and I told him, "I will go blind. Is it possible for you to turn this light off for a few moments or change the bulb to a lower wattage? Or is there a colored light bulb?"

He answered, "There's no deviation from the prison rules. All prisoners have the same light."

When I insisted he said, "You must be crazy! Do you realize you are a prisoner here? Your wishes are in the wrong place."

I said, "Fine." I did not eat the dinner they brought in. I pushed it aside and did not eat anything the next day either. The guard threatened me several times and may have slapped or punched me to change my mind. He did not curse me or cuss me. I sensed that, emotionally, he understood my pain. Still, I did not eat. I continued my hunger strike. Every time I would see food in front of me, I would see my family, and the women, my sons, and my sick daughter.

My Attempt to Commit Suicide

I remember I kept thinking, "What have I done? What is my crime? I was living at my home with those miserable financial constraints abounding and not even a warm sandal to wear and busy translating and writing the Holy Koran. I had reached the chapter of Surah Nahal when I was thrown in jail."

Those who sell medicine for the ailing heart;
When my turn came, sold torments and persecution.

The guard comprehended my distraught and deteriorating condition. He went out and came back with the prison doctor. The doctor's name was Noor Mohammad Khan. He was from the state of Punjab, India. The doctor was a good friend of Mohammad Hashim Khan. He was also my friend. I had sat with him night after night in social gatherings. He was also a friend of Najibullah Khan, Osman Khan Amir, and friends of my other friends. He was a tall man.

He came into the room and as soon as he saw me he seemed to want to cry and scream; however, he controlled himself and said, "Don't be a coward. Why don't you eat?"

I replied, "You are the coward. I cannot eat, and I'm not going to eat. This food is haram for me (unclean and unlawful from a religious point of view). My wife, my sons, my daughters are in jail, and you expect me to eat? Shame on the food which is being given to me to eat, this is poison for me. Go and tell your friend, the oppressor, Hashim, to oppress as much as he can."

The doctor became very polite and pulled back. He kissed me over my head and face and left. He sent me a bottle of medication. It was a bottle of blue liquid, and there was a label with writing on it and notches so I could see the dosage to take. I was told to take a few notches of liquid every couple of hours. I thought to myself, "I'm not going to drink it."

What I did next was very ignorant and impulsive. I feel bad about it now, and I regret to have done that. These were all satanic impulses. By this time I was far removed from the normal range of thoughts about thankfulness or gratitude or agreement. This was not a brave act, and it was not one of my shining moments. You know what I did? I took the bottle and emptied the liquid into the toilet water bowl and broke the bottle. I took the rope belt at the waist of my sleeping dress out and tied my left wrist tightly and tied the other end to the cot so that my veins showed very clearly. I had seen the doctors prepare to draw blood from a patient like that. I must have read it in a novel this was one way of committing suicide.

I took one of the shards of glass from the broken bottle and cut my veins. Then, I pulled the water pitcher under my arm so it could collect the blood oozing out of my body. I rested against the cot and prayed to the Almighty saying, "You are a witness that I'm committing this suicide and returning your life to you. I cannot live while my sick daughter, my young sons, my wife, the wife of my sons, the wives of my brothers, my brothers, and others lie in dungeons. If I give up my life, they may be spared torture."

In my mind and conviction I was doing this to deliver them from the dungeon. "I am sacrificing my life, Oh God, to you," I kept saying, and I read the Kalimah (the prayers attesting that there is no God but Allah, and Mohammad is the Prophet of Allah). "Allah-o-Akbar, Allah-o-Akbar, Allah-o-Akbar..."

The blood, as the proverb in Kabul goes, ran out of my hand like an arrow through the bow. Gradually, the whole room became pink. I don't know how much time had passed, but I could only see pink and red. Slowly, I passed out.

I felt cold and heard a hideous and dreadful voice and noise like a torrent falling from a mountain. It hit my body with full force. I felt like the whole mountain had fallen on me, and I'm being crushed under it. My eyes opened up, and I saw someone standing over me with a knife. My senses were returning, and I heard someone saying the proverb, *"May your house be destroyed!"*

It was the guard. He said, "You are trying to destroy me and my house, too! What have I done to you? They will kill me now. You will go away without your faith from this world for committing suicide, but I will be killed for nothing! Why have you filled this bowl with your blood?"

He was cutting the rope belt to release my hand. They took the vessel full of blood out of the room and brought in Haji Aminullah Khan, the Director at the Ministry of Court. Some other people, probably detectives so he had witnesses with him, accompanied him. They lifted me up and placed me on the cot and bound my hands on my chest. I was very, very weak, but had sense to realize what was happening.

They brought in the doctor right away. Dr. Khan cussed me and said, "You coward! Why did you do this?"

I replied, "Well, I couldn't kill myself in this attempt, but I will try again. Go and tell Hashim if I have committed any sin or crime, my wife, my children, my family have not done anything to you."

The doctor demanded, "Who has told you that your family is also in jail?"

I said, "That is the custom, and that is what I think. If I live 100 years, I wouldn't mind being in Hashim's jail for all that time, if only you can prove to me my family is not hurt or in jail. But I am certain they have been subjected to this torture. Because of that I will try to kill myself again until I succeed."

I continued to tell the doctor, "I'm not going to leave this world without my faith. This is not a suicide. This is a sacrifice I am willing to make to save my poor sick daughter. And you know she is sick. I'm doing this for the chastity of my family and my principles. I'm doing this for the chastity of my brothers. This is a sacrifice, and God will not count me with those who commit suicide."

The doctor was an intelligent and learned man. He knew these idioms and expressions. His eyes became tearful and he said, "You are right, but be content and patient. Everything will work out, and God will take care of you, I guarantee you that. Just be patient for 24 hours, and I will look into it personally."

I was abject and suddenly taken over by shivering cold. They bandaged my hands. The doctor gave me medication for the blood I had lost. I don't know what it was. They forced me to take all the medicine. I fell back in the bed. The piercing light from the ceiling was still on. I thought, all lights are not to be respected. The light of God is different from the light of Hashim or the light of the prison. There is a big difference. I spent that night in dismay, but now, for the first time in a week, because of the medicine, I surrendered to sleep.

In the morning I woke up for prayers. I could see my left hand was swollen and kind of paralyzed. I performed *wazu* with my right hand and washed the left hand carefully. I offered my prayers, and in a short while the prison official came in and said, "Here! I have brought you good news. Congratulations! *May your eyes see brightly*." (Afghan expression)

I said, "What is the news?"

He answered, "I went personally to your house. Your wife has conveyed her *salam* to you! Every one was in the house. Thank God, all of them are in good health. No one has thrown them in jail. You are worrying without knowing the facts. Here is proof they are all fine. I have brought this from your family."

He handed me a clean set of clothes – a sleeping dress from my wife. I don't know how she managed it, or which tailor she had gone to have these clothes made for me. The textile was close to the canvas normally used for prison. When I changed into the dress, the smell was familiar. It made me think of home.

I was still skeptical, thinking all the time maybe my family was forced to send this. There was a letter from my wife, also. She had written, "All of us are at home. Rest assured. Don't be a coward." Still, I thought maybe she wrote it under duress. This added to my anxiety.

I suddenly realized the smell of cologne was coming out of my new clothes, and when I brought the clothing closer to my nose, I found one part of the shirt smelled stronger of the cologne than the rest. I checked inside the pocket and found a piece of cotton with the same Russian cologne that Annus Khan and Goya Saheb had brought as a gift for me. When I opened up the cotton ball, there was a little slip of paper inside. My wife had written on it, "Be content. We are at home." This put my doubts to rest.

The prison guard came in, closed the door behind him, and said, "I have to give you another piece of news. There is no doubt, and it is true they did not imprison your wife and daughter and family, but they did something worse. Police camps were allowed inside the courtyard of your house to keep an eye on your family. They were there for one day and one night. Your wife and your family were confined behind closed doors."

He continued, "Incidentally, the next day, one of your neighbors, Gen Abdul Ghani Khan Gardezi, Qala Begi, the former Commander of the Arg, came by." Qala Begi and I were next door neighbors, sharing a common wall. "He was passing by the house and talked to one of your men, an elderly man with a gray beard from Panjsher whose name was Omak. He was standing there, and Qala Begi asked him, 'Omak where is Khalilullah Jan?' Omak said he has been arrested and taken to jail. All of them have been taken to the Arg prison.' Qala Begi asked him, 'What can I do for you?' Omak answered, 'For God's sake, we are your neighbors, and we are Muslims. They have brought police in the courtyard to live in a tent against the honor. Why don't you have them removed from there?'"

The prison guard continued his message. "Qala Begi was wearing his uniform, and he asked the policeman, 'Who ordered you to camp out in the courtyard?' The policeman answered, 'My commander from the main police station.' Qala Begi told him, 'Whoever has done that, it's a big mistake. He should not have done it. Get out of this place right away.' The policeman stood firm and said, 'We are part of the police force, and we are not under your command.' Qala Begi lost his temper and slapped or pounded the policeman with his fist and told him, 'Go to your commander and tell him Abdul Ghani ordered you out of the courtyard. I'm standing here. Go and bring all of the police out of the courtyard.' They came out of the courtyard and built their camp on the outside of the property."

The prison guard who told me this story was also from Gardez and was very proud to relay the message to me. I asked the guard if he could bring me a copy of the Holy Koran. He said, "No, you're not allowed to have one."

That night I prayed for Abdul Ghani Khan, and I was satisfied my family was not in danger.

My Inquisition in My Cell

The next day, in the afternoon, Ismael Khan, Governor of Kabul, Haji Amanullah Khan, and one other person came to my cell to investigate why I tried to commit suicide so they could report back to Sardar Mohammad Hashim Khan. He didn't know why a prisoner would try to commit suicide. I had worked for 13 years with him. My father had known him and had helped him in the past. I had done nothing wrong. Because I was trusted by my tribe and the people of Kohdaman and Kohistan, I was subjected to this fate.

Ismael Khan said, "The Prime Minister has sent his *salam* to you and would like to know. Why did you try to commit suicide?"

I told all of the investigators, "The reason I did it, speaks for itself. I am in prison, and I've been thinking that my wife, my daughter, my family are also in prison. I was thinking this because he has done the same to other people in the past."

He answered, "If the wife and family and children are put in protective custody in prison, there is a reason behind it."

I was upset and kept railing, "There is no cause for it. What right do you have to throw families in jail without any proof or provocation?"

Poor Ismael Khan tried to intervene and calm me down. I continued to say everything openly, even though I still had a fever and my hands were tied.

He said, "Tell me what you have to say so when we go back we take your message to Mohammad Hashim Khan."

I said, "I cannot talk about it. I will write it down."

They brought paper and pen. Even though I was not sturdy, still I wrote. I started the letter with a couplet by a poet named Rabiee Foshanjee. Then, I wrote to the Prime Minister:

"Do as much cruelty or injustice as you think your children could bear one day if it is thrust upon them. What right do you have to throw us in jail without any court proceedings or appearing before a judge? Why have you closed the door on life for us and taken away God's gifts from us? I was busy translating the Holy Koran. Just wait, until you witness real hard days ahead. Regards, Khalili"

Ismael Khan read it and said, "This is not right. Don't send this."

I told him, "No, that's what I want my message to be, and that's what I ask you to take back with you."

My Inquisition by Hashim, Daoud and Naim

Three nights later my letter had an effect. Ismael Khan, the Governor of Kabul came along with a military officer and took me away. Let me correct it, I'm sorry, a police officer came in the middle of the night and took me along with him. He threw a blanket over me – one of those woolen shawls, so that I could not see anything. They tied my neck also. I did not know where I was going. I thought they were taking me for execution.

As I passed the cell of Naib Salar, I heard him say, "Be a man and deny!"

I didn't answer him, but I said to myself in my heart, "I don't need to deny or confess to anything. I haven't done anything."

I was forced into a car, and we left for an unknown destination. After a five-minute drive, we reached the destination and got out. When they removed the covering from my eyes, I couldn't see at first because of a very bright light. Then I realized, we were in the Gulkhana (Flower House), that same wretched place where I'd worked every day and wasted 13 years of my life. They tied my hands behind my back. It was probably around 10 or 11 o'clock at night and they asked me to come forward and took me inside.

I saw a team of three people attending this investigation. Hashim Khan sat at the head of the table, and his nephews Daoud and Naim were on his two sides. They had a chair for me toward the end. I sat down. When I did so, Hashim Khan did something he had never done before. He stood in front of me in respect. I was surprised. Was this his chameleon way? Was he doing this as a trick or deceit, so I would calm down and confess to the crime and tell on Abdul Rahim Khan?

I said, "Thank you very much, sir, please, go ahead."

Hashim Khan said, "Khalilullah Khan, did you see what Abdul Rahim Khan has done? Did you know he has been dealt with appropriately for his crime?"

I said, "I have no knowledge of what has he done."

Hashim Khan said, "I have done so much for him. He was the Deputy Prime Minister. While I was sitting in one palace, he was sitting in the other. Did you know that he instigated the insurrection in Kunar?"

I answered, "I have no knowledge of it. I was busy translating the Holy Koran. Abdul Rahim Khan was in Kabul, and you knew that. You knew about his movements. Did he go to Kunar?"

Hashim Khan responded, "No. He started from Kabul. We have found documents supporting it. He was court-martialed and executed today."

In my heart, I said, "May God's wrath be on you!" Instead, I said, "I just came from prison, and I heard his voice."

He said, "If you are a man, deny."

"He was alive a few minutes ago, and you are lying to me right in my face." I continued, "Good? You may think this was a good thing that happened; however, you may repent this someday. Didn't you rush to judgment in this regard? Execute me also? What were these documents which you secured from Abdul Rahim Khan?"

Hashim Khan answered, "Yes, we have documents confiming he started the insurrection in Kunar. There was nothing in writing from him; however, there are people who have confessed to this in writing."

"You acted on the basis of hearsay?" I said. "I swear to you he didn't go to Kunar, not a single day. These confessions by other people may not be right."

"What did he do with the guns he had?" Hashim asked.

For a moment, I thought I should change this strategy. I should use a different approach and get Daoud and Naim involved. I asked the Prime Minister, "What kinds of guns did you find in Abdul Rahim's house?"

He said, "We appropriated 11 guns."

I said, "Abdul Rahim Khan took 400 of the guns that Ambassador Ghulam Nabi Charkhi sent to Herat and wanted to bring them to Kabul. He requested permission from Nadir Shah Shaheed (martyr), and Nadir Shah wanted those guns back. Abdul Rahim Khan had answered that those guns were with the soldiers, and he couldn't return them right away. What happened to those guns?"

Hashim Khan answered, "Oh yeah, you are right." He had forgotten Abdul Rahim Khan had returned the guns to the government weapons depot in Herat, had taken a receipt for them, and had sent the receipt to Kabul. Sardar Hashim Khan had thanked him through a decree. I was the one who wrote the decree for the Prime Minister.

Daoud Khan asked, "What is this story about these guns?"

Hashim Khan responded, "Well, it was something not very important."

I said, "It involved 400 guns, which had crossed into Afghanistan, and since the law of the country did not allow gun smuggling, Abdul Rahim Khan confiscated them and returned them to the government weapons depot in Herat."

Even though Nadir Shah wanted the guns returned to Ghulam Nabi Charkhi, Abdul Rahim Khan cited the law against smuggled arms, and instead, he had the guns stored in the arms depot. Hashim Khan pounced on the opportunity and said, "Maybe these are the guns he sent to Kunar! You're totally right. This is what I was looking for. Now, I found real proof and documents. Now, we can execute him."

What a contradiction of his own stated conviction that Naib Salar had already been executed. Daoud and Naim recognized the truth. I could see the smirks on their faces. I said, "Mr. Prime Minister, you said he had already been dealt with appropriately for his crime. How can you execute him again?"

Instead of acknowledging me, Hashim continued his rant, "We have arrested his son, Abdul Haleem, and he has confessed to everything. We had to force the confession out of them with torture."

"The person you tortured, sir," I said, "Is the same one who brought your brother's dead body from Herat to Kabul. (Abdul Aziz Khan was the father of Daoud and Naim.) Naib Salar had so much respect for him that he drove the hearse himself. And you tortured him."

I could see that Daoud and Naim were reminded of the death of their father and the sight of his coffin arriving in Kabul that day from Herat under the care of Abdul Rahim Khan. Still, they waited this out. Daoud said, "We're not talking about torture or restraint here. Maybe they were not tortured. The Prime Minister is just saying that."

Hashim said, "Go ahead and tell them about the incident of these 400 guns."

I replied, "I have no idea what happened to the 400 guns, why don't you ask Abdul Rahim Khan yourself?"

I was confident Abdul Rahim Khan had returned all the guns to the arms depot and had retained nothing. I thought if he told Hashim this directly, his words would have more weight and Hashim losing respect in front of his nephews, might be shamed into repenting or changing.

I had already told Hashim and his nephews that only 11 guns, three of which were shotguns, were found at his residence and taken away. In Afghanistan, a large family having eight or more guns was not a big surprise. Abdul Rahim Khan was also accused of having a cannon and a machine gun at his residence. What the government spies had actually seen was a power generator from his flour mill, sitting in his courtyard, awaiting repair. It was electrical equipment. There was no document or proof of treason against Abdul Rahim Khan.

Hashim Khan said, "Okay, you go back to jail and remain there for a while. We will have you released later. What difference does it make if you spend a few days in jail?"

I stood up and said, "Mr. Prime Minister, I have two

wishes."

He said, "Go ahead and tell me."

"Even though my hands were tied," I said, "I want to share a story told by the cousin of the Prophet of God, Abdullah ibn Abbas. When he was a young boy, he was curious, and went into the Prophet's room, to see how he passed the night. He said in the middle of the night, he saw the Prophet get up and offer tahajjud (midnight prayers). Abbas related that when the Prophet was done, he saw me also offering that prayer. He passed by me and touched my ears gently and went outside. He looked toward the sky and recited a line from the Holy Koran. Then, he said that in the heavens and in the skies the sign of God is there. He turned his face toward me and said, whenever you see the beauty of the stars, the moon and the skies, always read this ayat (line). Man is a human being, and human beings have a great interest and love to see the beauty of the heaven and sky."

I continued, "You, O Prime Minister, have deprived me from the beauty of the heaven and sky. These nights I do not see the sky. The light is on 24 hours in my face. Is it possible you order them to turn off the light at night, so that through the little skylight I could see the beauty of the heavens and the skies?"

Hashim turned his face toward the left and said something underneath his breath.

I said, "My other wish is this. I have a little daughter, a year old, who I love very much." Marie, I am talking about you here. I told him, "Even though you don't have children, but you love Daoud Khan and Naim Khan, and they are very close to you, you will understand. My child is very poor and destitute. I was her plaything, her puppet. Please, order your men to gouge out my eyes. Kill me and take my eyes in a packet or bag to my little daughter so she can play with my eyeballs and may be busy for a while. She loves me very much. Maybe she will forget me and play for a while."

My tone was very morose and may have been effective at stirring some kind of emotion. When I finished with my request, Sardar Mohammad Naim Khan rose from his chair and said with a heavy voice, "I cannot hear this torment anymore." He left the room without seeking permission from his uncle and closed the door behind him.

Sardar Daoud Khan sat quietly. His face drained of blood out of compassion or anger inside him. I don't know. When he spoke, he said, "I will order you be allowed to leave the prison at night."

Then, I was told to leave. As I left the room, he pressed the call bell on the floor. Captain Jan Mohammad of the Prime Ministry guard came in. Outside the room, I could still hear Daoud telling him, "Keep a close eye on this man. He should have gone crazy in his cell by now. It seems he's still very sane, and he's still talking. Keep him under strict watch."

I couldn't take it anymore. I turned around, stuck my head in the room and said, "Don't be brutal with me. God comes down hard on those who cast merciless eyes on others. *In Shah Allah* (God willing) someday you will be subjected to that force."

Jan Mohammad hit me hard behind my neck and pushed me toward the exit. They threw the blanket over me again, forced me into the car, and drove me back to the Arg prison. Once there, they raised my head and walked me inside. I wanted to inform Naib Salar that I was back. I yelled out, "I was not allowed to talk," and recited the Kalimah. This was my way of letting him know I'd come back in one piece. I walked reluctantly toward my dark and dingy room.

All Men of My Close and Extended Family Are in Jail

A couple of days later we were informed we would be taken before the court. What kind of a system was this? We were not asked anything. We were investigated after we were jailed and all of our lives and our belongings were confiscated. In total, 44 men of our family were behind bars. They jailed my innocent brothers, my cousins, and even far removed family members of Naib Salar. They were all brought from Kohistan and put in jail in Kabul.

Naib Salar's residence was under surveillance and police protection and so was my home. No one was allowed to go in or to go out.

We did not own much in my house. No one could go out and buy anything, and no one could send us money. A few people came to our assistance. One was our neighbor, Allamshahi. He helped us through another friend, Dr. Najmuddin Khan Ansari. There was also one older gentleman from Panjsher, his name was Abdul Rasheed, may God bless his soul. He was from Rahaman Khel of Bazarak. He did not leave us. He could not take money and go outside because they would ask him, "Where did you get it?" Instead, he would bring food and other edibles through Dr. Najmuddin Khan's house. Sometimes, his wife would cook for us and bring it to our house. The wall between our houses was very low. The mother of Dr. Najmuddin Khan would transfer the food to my wife from over the wall, and sometimes, Dr. Najmuddin Khan's mother would cook herself and provide food to my family. It was a very tense situation.

In prison, I was informed the condition of my older daughter, who was sick, was improving. The prison appointed a team of interrogators. Every night a blanket was thrown over my head, and I was taken to the Gulkhana palace to go before the interrogators. We waited in a lighted room, listening to the laughter and sounds of people eating in the next room. I recognized some of the voices. There was Mirza Mohammad Shah Khan, head of intelligence; Commander Khwaja Naim; and Mir Abdul Aziz Khan, the son of Mir Abdul Wahid Khan Saheb, who was the watchmaker of Habibullah Khan Seraj and one of the respected Sayeds of Kabul. I could also hear the voice of Mohammad Ismael Khan Wardhak Mayar, the governor of Kabul. I knew they all were there, laughing, while they made me sit there in cold and crippling winter conditions. I could see some torture equipment in the other room, a whip and other leather artifacts. A young man who appeared to be a soldier came close to me and whispered in my ear, "Don't worry about these things. Strong men have to face these things. I am from Ghazni." He walked away from me, and I was left there to fend myself in this cold and desolate room.

Interrogation, Shackles, and Handcuffs

Marie, I'm talking to you. You are here again on this rainy day, and you are unnerving me by forcing me to continue. Where were we when we stopped yesterday? We were talking about torture.

At night, we were taken to the Gulkhana palace for interrogation. They would throw the blanket over my head with a rope so I wouldn't see anybody outside my cell or on the way. They would take me to the interrogation room. I sat in that room, waiting for these people who were chatting next door, eating what I think was fresh fruit. I could smell tobacco too. When they were done, they asked me to come in. There is no doubt they paid respect to me. They stood up from their places and asked me to sit. I could see they had been writing questions down on some documents. They gave me the documents and asked me to record my answers.

Before I could answer their questions, I started out writing questions of my own:

Why am I summoned to this interrogation room and subjected to an inquisition?

Why am I not called in during the day and presented before a court so I can be prosecuted? Why is a committee from the Department of Justice not appointed to do this? Why have I been thrown in jail before an investigation can take place?

Why am I being put under unbearable conditions in the prison before my crime is proved? Why have I been deprived of the beauty of the sun and stars and moon while also being deprived of due process? Why am I not allowed to have pen and paper and the Holy Koran?

For God's sake I am a Muslim. I am a human being. If I'm going to be executed do it as soon as possible. You can do anything at this time. Today, Mohammad Hashim has all the power concentrated in himself. If he can imprison me, he can kill me. Who is going to question him? Has anybody asked him why I have been thrown in jail this long? Has anybody asked him why he threw Abdul Rahim Khan in jail? Has anybody asked him why he has executed Abdul Rahim Khan?

I wrote these powerful words in beautiful prose and attractive writing because it had been such a long time since I had got hold of a pen. It was like a soldier, picking up a gun in his hands for the first time on the battlefield, ready to avenge his enemies and take out as much frustration as he could. I was like the soldier. I was busy translating the Holy Koran and had reached Surah Nahal when I was separated from it. It was like being separated from my family and friends. Here was a pen, my friend of 40 years, come back to my hand.

They read my answers and responded in writing. This is not a place for poetry, they wrote. You are obligated to answer our questions. If you do not answer our questions, we will be forced to use this equipment of torture on you, even though we don't want to do so.

When I saw the word torture, written in their hand, the hairs on my body rose. I told myself, "Very well, maybe it's time I confess to the crime which I have not committed. It will at least relieve me from the torture of prison and all this subjugation. Being there every moment was a torture." I read the questions. They were asking, "Where is the weaponry of Abdul Rahim Khan?" I wrote my answer, "I'm not the specialist in charge of weapons and responsible to Abdul Rahim Khan. You should ask him yourself where the 400 guns are he took from Ghulam Nabi Charkhi."

When they read my answers, the looks they exchanged seemed to confirm to me they had already talked to Naib Salar, and he had already given them documents proving his innocence regarding the weaponry, adding to the shame of the government for these blanket accusations.

Still, they asked me, "Were you responsible for instigating the people of Kunar and kidnapping some of them?"

I responded, "The people of Kunar, why did they rise and whom did they rise against? Where is Kunar? It is far removed from Kabul, and we are in Kabul."

They continued, "You know where Kunar is and how the people rose up in arms after someone instigated them."

I wrote down, "I know where Kunar is. It's near Jalalabad, and I have no means of contacting those people. Is there any piece of paper or document pointing against this? If so, show it to me. Do we have any witnesses to prove this? I was busy writing the Holy Koran, and Naib Salar was busy in his government duties. He was coming to the prime ministry every day and was here from morning to evening. Even the Chief of Intelligence Mirza Mohammad Shah Khan had him under surveillance and kept a close eye on his activities."

When he read this, Mirza Mohammad Shah Khan smiled and said, "Yes, that's true."

"So when did he have the opportunity to go?" I responded.

They asked me to write whatever I was saying, and then they wrote back to me, saying, "It seems like you're not going to confess."

I responded, "I will never confess to what I haven't done."

They said, "Okay, now we will let you go back to the prison. Go and think about it. You may be subjected to torture in your cell and will lose your dignity."

I said, "I will leave this to God."

I got up from my place. Ismael Khan, the Governor of Kabul held my shoulder and pressed it a little, assuring me that everything would be okay. They again threw a blanket on my face and took me back to the same dungeon from where I came.

The next day, I was taken to the Gulkhana again with my head tied under the blanket. When I entered the interrogation room, I could see they had lined up all the torture equipment on a table. There were also a couple more soldiers standing about the room. They asked me, "Will you confess or not?" This question was not asked by either Ismael Khan the Governor of Kabul or Mir Abdul Aziz Khan who was the head of the personal office of the King. The question was asked by Khwaja Naim Khan, the police commander of Kabul.

I told him, "Never. I'm not ready to confess to a crime I did not commit."

He said, "Well, then we have to use torture to get the confession out of you."

I said, "Okay, write this down on a piece of paper, and I will answer it for you."

They wrote, "If you don't confess, the investigative committee has been authorized to subject you to torture until you tell the truth."

I laughed and said, "That's strange – the investigative committee is putting in writing they are going to torture me!" I wrote down, "Well, when it comes to torture I will write not only that I'm a part of the treason against the nation, I'm also part of all the crimes against the Nadir Shah family, and I will accept taking part of all that happened during the time of Habibullah Kalakani. I cannot stand to take the torture and restraint you are going to impose on me. I'm confessing because of that. And I'm confessing it with pride and honor." I signed the paper "Khalilullah Khalili" and I wrote the date.

When they read the paper, they looked at each other and said, "Your fate has already been sealed." Mirza Mohammad Shah Khan shook his head in disbelief. "Why did you write it?" his eyes said.

My Deliverance by Mohammad Zahir Shah

I don't remember all that happened, but at some point, the living room doors of the Gulkhana were flung open and a young man walked in. He was standing very straight and had his face wrapped up. He was wearing dark glasses. I did not recognize him. He may have been Mohammad Rahim Panjsheri, but his accent did not resemble that of Panjsheri. It might have been somebody else.

He announced, "Are you Khalilullah Khan Khalili?"

I answered, "Yes."

He asked the other people present in the room, "Is he Khalilullah Khan Khalili?"

They answered, "Yes."

He said, "His Highness, the King of Afghanistan, Mohammad Zahir Shah has ordered no one has the right to torture you or threaten you. If there are documents and a trail of paperwork, which implicates that you are involved, and if there are witnesses who can stand up and testify that you are involved in the incident of Kunar, then you will be subjected to punishment. Otherwise torture and threats in the Gulkhana palace, where I sleep at night, is not allowed."

"Has anyone tortured you yet?" he asked.

I was flabbergasted and at a loss for words. One person was saying one thing, and others were saying something totally opposite. I answered, "May God give long life to His Highness the King. So far I have not been tortured. But you see here, the equipment of torture has been made ready to do so." I removed my head gear. "Are they going to torture my feet or other places? I don't know, but they are definitely going to torture me. What you have just said, and the message you have brought from the King of Afghanistan, I'm thankful to God for that. It will save me from this torture. They have asked me questions, and I have answered them. Why don't you read them yourself?"

The young man read the questions and answers and said, "This is not right." He bid goodbye and abruptly left the room.

As soon as this man left the room, Commander Khwaja Naim Khan spoke. "It is very strange that one person, the Prime Minister, has commanded us to torture them, subject them to the toughest inquiry, make their lives miserable, and force them to confess, while His Highness the King of Afghanistan orders that we have no right to torture. Whom should we listen to and whom should we follow? Should we pay attention to the King's words or the Prime Minister's?"

I was encouraged with all this and became a little bold. I said, "Khwaja Saheb, do whatever your heart desires. If your desire is to torture me, then pursue it, and torture me to the point that someday, if I get a chance, I will torture you or my children may torture you. Remember that you should be prepared to take it. These days will pass."

He replied, "God forbid, I don't want to do that. How would I subject you to torture?" His eyes teared up, and he offered me a cigarette. I smoked for the first time in a long time. It was very tasteful. They brought in fruit and offered me oranges and sweet lemons. I did not eat; instead, I requested I be given a copy of Holy Koran so I could read. They replied, "Okay, after this, God willing, you will have everything." I think they wanted to run it by the Prime Minister. I took leave, said goodbye and got up from my place and was again covered by the blanket and taken back.

Governor Ismael Khan came out with me and in a hushed voice said something to the guard who was accompanying me to the prison. I think his name was Mohammad Ali. While I stood there the guard briefly left and came back with something in his scarf. When he opened it there was a small copy of the Holy Koran. "The Governor asked me to get this for you," he said. He added, "If the investigators or other guards come to your room, please keep it discreet."

I responded, "Well, the Holy Koran was hidden from Abu Jahal (the bitterest enemy of Prophet Mohammad PBUH). Now, while there is an Islamic government I should hide the Holy Koran from Muslims? This seems to be a great act. Thank you very much."

I opened it up and saw that it was a small version, containing seven benedictions, including the famous *Duai-ganjul-arsh*. It was one of the thousands of copies printed in India every year. Because of its popularity, this benediction has found its way into the Hadith or sayings of Prophet Mohammad. The popular thought is that whoever reads the *Duai-ganjul-arsh* every day will receive God's reward. If you can't read it every day, at least every Friday night; or if you cannot read it every Friday night, then once every month; or if you cannot read it once every month, then once every year; and if you cannot read it once every year, then at least once in a lifetime.

God's reward from reading *Duai-ganjul-arsh* will be bigger than any performance of Haj; the reward is bigger than many thousands of prayers. If a person reads *Duai-ganjul-arsh,* it is said that he will be safe from the sword and the fire and the curses – nothing will work against him. The hand of the cruel and cruelty will not reach that person. It is a powerful benediction. This benediction is against the Arabic laws. Its name is not Arabic. The word *ganjul* is Persian and the word *arsh* is Arabic. They have been combined to be called *ganjul-arsh (Treasures of Heaven or skies)*. These benedictions are sayings that are not very confirmed. I do not believe that by reading one benediction, a person can receive the reward of a thousand of ghazis (martyrs) or receive the reward of going to Mecca for Haj. I think going to Haj is a separate deed, and Jehad is a separate deed. If receiving God's reward by reciting a benediction is so easy, it gives rise to Islam becoming a commercial thing that pulls Muslims off their guard and keeps them away from business and alms, prayers and fasting, and jihad. This easy reward will push them toward becoming lazy.

Whatever this benediction was, it was good for me and very satisfying to me. I recalled hearing the *Duai-ganjul-arsh* as a youth. My governess, who came from the people of Hazarah Jat, used to recite it every day. My grandmother also recited this benediction in a loud voice every morning after prayers. I remember she also recited a poem in praise of God and his Prophet, PBUH, called *100 Salams*. One of the couplets meant:

Come and listen if you love
the qualities and characteristics of the Prophet.

I used to recite it in appreciation of God and his Prophet, PBUH, while in prison.

I noticed the last three pages of the little booklet the guard had given to me were in very tattered condition. When he came into my cell the next day I told him, in a low voice, I hadn't damaged the booklet, and I didn't want them to seek compensation for the damage from me. He said no, he knew the booklet was already damaged, and there was a story behind it. I asked, "What is the story?"

The Atrocities of the Prison and the Affliction of People

The guard said there was a person named Mir Abdul Aziz who had gone to study in one of the cities in Turkey during the time of Amanullah Khan. He was from the village of Deh Yahya near Kabul and belonged to the family of Mir Najmuddin Khan Ansari. When King Amanullah went to Europe and visited Turkey he had been kind to this young man and had done favors for him. When Amanullah Khan was dethroned, this young man served him well. Amanullah Khan told him to go to Afghanistan and carry some letters and documents on his behalf. This is hearsay, but he was also told if he accomplished this mission, Amanullah Khan would let him marry one of his daughters.

He was supposed to travel to the province of Paktia and carry the documents to the head of the village, the malik of the Niazi tribe. This young man undertook the journey and went through a lot of pain and hard work to get safe passage. He managed to hitchhike through Turkey to India and from there, cross into Afghanistan and reach Paktia. He reached Paktia at night and wanted to go to the house of the head of the village, but he did not have the full address. He had never been to Paktia in his life. He came across a poor peasant on the street and asked for Malik Niazi.

The man answered, "If you pay me, I will guide you to Malik Niazi's house."

The young man told the peasant, "I'll give you 30 rupees."

The man asked him to follow him.

This Malik Niazi, this unfortunate man, I have forgotten his full name. He was one of those people whom King Amanullah Khan had bestowed favors on. The young man reached Malik Niazi's house and took out all those documents he had wrapped around his body and gave them to the Malik. There were three firmans or decrees. Since it was late at night the old peasant requested to sleep there overnight and said he would leave in the morning for his home. While Mir Abdul Aziz and the peasant slept, Malik

Niazi traveled to a location with a telephone. He called Mirza Mohammad Shan Khan and asked him to come and take charge of the decrees, which Amanullah Khan had sent him. He said he had the decrees in his possession and had arrested the man who has brought them.

A caravan of cars and military jeeps were dispatched immediately from Kabul and arrived at the village of Niazi and the house of the Malik. They took possession of the firmans, and the head of the Intelligence Department himself came and arrested poor Mir Abdul Aziz. The young man and the old peasant were thrown in prison. They were shackled and subjected to beatings while being interrogated for their confessions. They were brought to this prison, and they were locked in this room according to this guard. The poor old peasant was put in prison for 30 rupees. After a while Mir Abdul Aziz lost his mental balance and started acting haywire and insane. He went crazy, and finally, he died under the force of the shackles and torture. He was buried in Qole Chakan (a neighborhood in Kabul).

After the guard finished this story, I said "What a pity. He was a young man." I was curious and I asked, "What happened to the old peasant?"

The guard responded, "Don't you hear some voices and noises at night saying 'There is only one God and no other God'?"

I responded, "Yes, I do hear those voices."

He said, "It's the same man who is still in prison. No one is allowed to go near him."

I asked, "I'm not allowed to see him either?"

He said, "That's right. You can never see him. You should remain in this room."

Hearing the history of the former tenant made this room a terrifying place for me. Gradually, I fell ill. Dr. Noor Mohammad Khan came to see me. I asked him if it would be possible to leave this room, which was sinister to me, as if a bad omen was lodged there. I didn't tell him the story. I was saving the guard from any harm. Finally, the commander of the palace guard was informed and after a while he changed my room. After that, I felt that every day things improved a little. The attitude of the officials had also improved.

In the next room, I asked, "Who is in the room next to mine?" I was told it was Abdul Aleem, the son of Naib Salar. I said, "He was brought here, too?"

The guard answered, "Yes, this poor young man has also been put in a prison cell."

I asked him to tell me about the other prisoners, also. He used to tell me about one prisoner each day. He told me about my elderly uncle, Mirza Mohammad Yosuf Khan, with his gray beard, and had been in the prison for 18 years. He had seen the excruciating pain of torture. I asked, "Is Khwaja Mir Najmuddin Khan from Charekar also in this prison?" He said that yes, he was here also. He had fallen ill and was very sick. The prison management tried to send him to the hospital, but they were overruled. He died here, and they took him out of the prison in a coffin.

I asked, "How about Khwaja Mir Alam Khan?"

He said yes, he was also in this prison. He also died here and was taken out from this prison in a coffin.

I asked, "How about Mir Mohammad Saheb Khan of Charekar?" He was one of the esteemed personalities of the northern Afghanistan and had served the ruling family with great honesty. "What happened to him?"

The guard said, yes he also breathed his last in this prison.

"Well," I said, "Anybody else in this prison that you know?"

He said yes, there was one, Sayed Ghulam Haidar Pacha. I knew him. He was one of the Sayeds of Kunar. He was an enlightened, intelligent, and handsome young man. The guard said he was also in this prison. He went through a lot of hard times. He loved his wife very much. His wife died, and they tried to hide the news of her death from him. One day, his young sons came to see him, and they revealed the death of their mother. This man, Ghulam Haidar Pacha, had a panic attack and a nervous breakdown. Even though he had served Sardar Mohammad Hashim Khan in the eastern part of Afghanistan, it did not matter. He pleaded and requested his boys be allowed to stay with him as there was no one at home to take care of them, but he was turned down. He was told it was against the law and the rules. After that, he only lived for a couple of days. He was severely ill, but was not allowed to go to the hospital. He died in the prison.

The guard said Janbaz Khan, Naib Salar who had served relentlessly His Highness the late Nadir Shah (martyr), and was a cousin of Ambassador Ghulam Nabi Khan Charkhi, also died here in the prison. He also saw some very bad days toward the end.

Abdul Hadi Khan Dawi is still here in one of the rooms, the guard said, and at least another 200 different people are imprisoned here. The guard used to come every day and tell me about a new prisoner. He would tell us how they were whipped, tortured, slapped, and slashed.

The prison was making my days, dark and my nights, unbearable. I didn't know what to do. I requested the guard to bring me another book, Hafiz Shirazi's *Mathnavi* (poems including "The Wild Deer"). He said, "Not at all! You're not allowed to. You would be sending me to the gallows!" Almost six months passed in this dilemma. I did not see the sun or the moon during this time, nor did I shower or wash myself. From that little window in the ceiling I could see a part of the sky and noticed spring had arrived. There was a water spout outside the cell where a woodpecker would come and sit and shake his head. I would talk to him, and I would write poetry for him. I would take a piece of coal and write on the wall. The guard would wipe it off whenever it would catch his eyes. One day the guard brought the news that tomorrow would be Maulood Sharif, commemoration of the day of the Prophet's birth and death. I took a piece of coal and wrote 85 lines of poetry; an ode from the beginning of the night until the morning. I titled it, "Midnight."

This ode was pretty long, and I have, unfortunately, forgotten most of it (NOTE: It has been published in the poetry collection of Khalili).

I wrote this on the wall of my cell, and my hands were blackened from the coal. I wiped my face with my hand and offered my morning prayers. I was sitting there and kind of drifting off into sleep when I saw a dream or premonition. I dreamt of good tidings and felt that I would be freed.

The guard came in the cell to bring me the breakfast. When he saw the whole wall blackened with my poetry, he said, "What the hell are you doing? Are you setting me up to be hanged?"

He wanted to clean it up, but I told him, "Don't do it! This is a very sacred ode in appreciation of the Prophet Mohammad, PBUH, in honor of Maulood Sharif today. Your hands will be broken if you do that." The guard was a disciple of Peer Saheb, Naqeb Saheb, Sayed Hassan Gailani.

I said, "For the sake of Sayed Hassan Gailani, don't do it!" Because I asked him in the name of his spiritual guide, he stopped.

He replied, "Since you brought up the name of my sage, I'm not going to clean it." I was surprised he was not willing to keep the ode for the esteem of the Prophet, but was willing to do so now for the sake of his own spiritual guide.

I asked him, "How come?"

He answered, "Well, I'm not going to clean the wall, however, when the investigator comes, I'll make you clean it off yourself."

I told him, "With God's grace, No one will say or do anything."

Mohammad Hashim Khan Resigns

Four to five days later the guard came into my cell unannounced, at an unscheduled time. He looked breathless. I was surprised.

I asked him, "What's going on?"

He closed the door behind him and said, "I've brought some good news for you."

Tentatively, I asked, "What is the good news?" Often they used to bring good news to prisoners as a pretext, so when prisoners were being taken for execution they wouldn't give them any resistance while being transported. I added, "Let me know, and praise be to God, whatever God's will is, I will accept it."

The guard said, "No, no! I really have some good news for you. Sardar Mohammad Hashim Khan has resigned!"

I was afraid he might be trying to entice me to say something.

I said, "No way. It's not possible."

He said, "By the grace of God, he resigned."

I told the guard, "I have a very delicate and expensive (Maur) carpet in my house which is displayed on the wall. If you can prove to me Hashim Khan has resigned, I will give you a marker so you can go to my home and get the carpet as your reward."

He said eagerly, "I'm ready for it." He went out quickly, closed the door, and came back within about half an hour and brought the newspaper *Islah*. I saw the front page, which displayed a photo of Sardar Mohammad Hashim Khan, and read that because of his deteriorating health and overwork, he had presented his resignation to the King Mohammad Zahir Shah, and the King had accepted his resignation. On the other side of the front page, there was a picture of Sardar Shah Mahmud Khan, the younger brother of Mohammad Hashim Khan, who was the Minister of Defense. The newspaper said he has been appointed as the Interim Prime Minister by His Highness and has been asked to name a new Cabinet.

I thanked God. I did not care if Shah Mahmud Khan knew me or not. I did not care if he would help me or not, but what I knew was that, with the grace of God and the resignation of Hashim Khan, many prisoners would be delivered from his dungeons and my fellow countryman would be released back into society. May God give us his blessing so my family and I would be reunited, and my writing be ridden of this nightmare.

I asked the guard, "Did you go and tell Abdul Rahim Khan also?"

"Why should I tell him?" he asked.

I told him to go and discreetly tell him about this. Before he left, he provided me with a small piece of paper and a pen. I wrote a note to my wife saying, "Please give the carpet to the person bringing this note." I predated the note to appear as if I had written it a couple of days earlier so if someone got a hold of it, it would not jeopardize my freedom.

The guard came back the next day and was very happy. He told me that he received the carpet, which was very elegant. I said, "It is yours for bringing such good news."

About a month passed. I was in a better condition and was happier and busy with my thoughts. The guard had gone to my uncle (Yosuf Khan) and brought back the book *Mathnavi* by Hafiz Shirazi for me. This *Mathnavi* was a world for me. I started with the beginning:

Listen to what the flute is saying...

Every day I would read this and the anecdotes of the *Mathnavi* and would take pleasure from it and weep on occasions. The stories reminded me of my boyhood during my father's time. I enjoyed this heavenly book in my prison cell, and I cannot express what an inspiration it was.

Prime Minister Shah Mahmud Khan

After a month, one day I heard the sound of boots and the noise of voices in the hallway. One voice was kind of familiar to me. The door of my cell was opened. Farooq Khan, the Minister of Interior, who was a friend of mine entered the room. He looked at me, and then he turned his face toward the guards and said, "I told you to take me to Khalil Khan, and you brought me to his this *mullah*!"

One of the guards answered, "Sir, this is Khalilullah Khan."

Farooq Khan said, "No way!"

I jumped in and said, "Farooq, look at me! It's me!"

Since we were friends, and he had a sense of humor, we always exchanged good jokes with each other. He said, "You are not Khalil. Go and find a mirror and look into it. You look like an Indian Sikh. Look at the hairs on your face, your head, your beard."

My hair had grown to my shoulders, and my beard ran down to my navel. My hands and feet were swollen because of damp conditions. My back was doubled up because of the chronic pain. I had become a ghostly figure.

I asked him, "Where are you going to take me now? Will you be part of my execution?"

"No, Khalil Jan," he said. "The new Prime Minister has ordered your release."

I forgot to mention something that happened a week prior to Farooq Jan coming to release me. Let me go back and correct myself.

One day, the guard came in and said to me that since he had worked for Sardar Shah Mahmud Khan, if I wanted to write a note to him, he would take it to him.

I said, "Are you crazy? One brother has thrown me in jail. What makes you think the other will release me?"

He answered, "No, this is a different man. He is a good man. He's very compassionate and maybe you may see some good coming out of him. He may release you from this solitary confinement, and we both will be happy."

He went out to find a pen and paper for me. I was wary and thought to myself, this offer to take my request to Shah Mahmud Khan may have been initiated by someone else. When he came back, he had a yellow sheet of paper and a pen and inkpot. I took them in hand and wrote at the top of the paper:

If the storm blows from Baghdad
It is not the fault of the banks of the Arabian Sea.

Then, I continued:

Kunar resurrects and Sardar Mohammad Daoud Khan is defeated and fails in his mission. They take me away from the committee translating the Holy Koran and throw me in jail. It is six months that I am in jail. You have just been appointed as Prime Minister. I will not congratulate you until such time you focus your attention on the prisoners and be compassionate to them. I am not asking you for anything, except to move me from this dark cell to a place with a little more light and air. I am a poet and a writer, and I do not know what sin I have committed. Please show compassion, so God may

302

show compassion to you.

I wrote a very painful and sentimental letter, which would bring tears to any reader's eyes. This guard took my letter and left. He came back next day and said, "You put me in an awkward situation. The Prime Minister was entering his car when I gave him this paper. He read it and pulled out his white handkerchief from his pocket and wiped his tears. He got out of the car again and went inside his house. Then, he came back while still tearful and was very upset. He told me to go and tell you, "Let's see what happens. However, I think you will be released."

I responded, "Let's see what happens, doesn't mean I will be released."

A week after that, Farooq Khan came to my cell.

Change of Prison

A few days later Farooq Khan came to my cell, made fun of my hairs and beard and announced, "His Highness the Prime Minister has ordered you to be moved to the Kabul state prison."

I said, "I don't care where you take me or house me, just take me away from here."

I asked if my uncle was being moved, also, and he said, "No, first we will take you there and then they will allow my uncle to go there too." He used to call the Naib Salar uncle also.

I balked, saying, "This is not appropriate. Leave me here, and we'll stay here together."

He answered, "There is no permission for this. I do not have permission. Do not talk too much."

I was barefoot. My shoes had been lost in the shuffle. I left my room walking on naked feet and saw that two doors after my cell was the cell of Abdul Rahim Khan. His door was ajar, and he was watching out.

Farooq Jan ran toward him and as a sign of respect, kissed his hands. Naib Salar was proudly standing with a face shaven just like any other time and his hairs were in order. When he saw me, he asked Farooq Jan, "Who is this that you have brought to me?"

I said, "It's me," at the same time Farooq Jan said, "Oh, it's Khalilullah."

Naib Salar kissed my face as is customary and asked, "What is happening?"

Farooq Jan told him, "We are taking him to the Kabul state prison."

"I don't want to go there," I told him. "I would rather be with you and Abdul Aleem Khan."

Naib Salar said, "No, my son, it is in our interest that you go out." He pressed my hand a little, and I realized this is what he wanted. I was tearful leaving my uncle in this place.

As we left the hallway I saw in front of me an old man in tattered, poor clothing. He was wearing a waistcoat that was falling apart and had a walking stick or cane in his hand. His beard was long and gray. The glasses he wore on his face were broken.

I asked Farooq Jan, "Who is he?" at the same time that the old man asked Farooq Jan, "Where is he?"

Farooq Jan pointed to me and said, "Here he is."

The old man lunged forward and held me fast, all the while crying and wailing. I tried to see who he was, but couldn't. "I don't recognize you," I admitted.

Farooq Jan shook his head. "You are blind. Don't you see your uncle, Mohammad Yosuf Khan Safi?"

I exclaimed, "God is great!" and fell to his feet.

Yosuf Khan said, "My son, stay here for a minute. I need to do something." He bent to his knees, sat on the ground and thanked God I was delivered from death. He added, "We have lived our lives, and it's okay that we stay here." He asked Farooq Jan if he would allow him to see his friend Naib Salar Saheb.

Farooq Jan said, "Yes, Yosuf Khan, you are allowed only at this time."

I told Farooq Jan, "These two men have been friends a long time. They were together in Russia at one time. I would be so happy to see them together."

We turned around, and I saw this old man with the gray beard, Yosuf Khan, straightening himself up and saying, "I don't want Abdul Rahim to see me bent." The Naib Salar was a little younger than my uncle. They were good friends and joked and had common jokes and common stories.

When Yosuf Khan entered the Naib Salar's cell, Naib Salar turned to Farooq Jan and said, "Today you are bringing all these hermits to me. Who is this you have brought to me now?"

Yosuf Khan said, "I'm not a hermit, my old friend. I am the same Mohammad Yosuf. You don't recognize me?"

I could not watch this desperate reunion. I left the two old men alone together and came to Farooq Jan. I accompanied him out of the prison, into the bright sunlight, and into his car.

Farooq Jan was taking me to the Kabul state prison and turned onto the street where the house of Sardar Mohammad Hashim Khan stood.

I said, "You must be out of your mind! If he comes out and sees me, he will send me back to jail!"

Farooq Jan told the driver to drive a little faster and passed the house quickly.

It was afternoon by the time I was brought to Ismael Khan, the Governor of Kabul. He was overwhelmed and could not believe his eyes. From there I was taken to Khwaja Naim, and finally, to the prison. In Kabul state prison, I later found out, there were 44 members of our family, including my brothers Najibullah Khan and Mohammad Osman Khan. There were others who had never even visited us in a long, long time.

Kabul State Prison

We arrived at Kabul State Prison, where they had prepared a room for me. It had a window with curtains and was located in a place high above the entrance to the prison. I heard a familiar voice. I asked my brother, "Who is this?"

He said, "This is Karim Jan Agha."

I asked, "Which Karim Jan Agha?"

"This is Saheb Zadah Karim Jan, brother of Sher Jan Khan and Attaul Haq Khan Saheb Zadah," he answered.

I asked, "When did they bring him?"

He answered, "The night they took you away to the

palace prison, they were also arrested on the accusation of being friends of Khalilullah."

I sent him a message to let him know I was here. They came right away. We stood up and embraced each other. We said to ourselves, "Let's stay here together." Thus, Karim Jan and I started playing chess. Later, we went downstairs to the room of Sayed Mobashir Tarazi and paid our respects to him.

We came across a very old friend, Torah Sayed Habibullah Farghana. He was one of three refugees from Bokhara. He was a learned man, a man of letters, and his personality was very esteemed among the people. He knew the Holy Koran by heart and was a scholar, a writer, and part of the intelligentsia. He was worth the world.

There was another gentleman named Noor Mohammad Beg, the brother of Sher Mohammad Beg. The Russians considered him a traitor because he was part of the Basmachi movement. But to us, he was a real man of the mujahideen or freedom fighters. He was probably from the Turkman tribe.

These friends became my circle. We used to sit every day together and read the Holy Koran in a loud voice.

We used to learn from these distinguished personalities. It did not feel as if we were in prison. We used to visit Sayed Tarazi quite often. All the prisoners were like children to him. At this time the month of fasting (Ramadan) came. I was anxiously waiting for my friends to visit me. Who was going to give the test of loyalty by visiting one in prison?

A friend is one who holds the hand of a friend
No matter how tired, weary or distressed you are

As I said earlier my room in this prison was above the main entrance door. There was a garden right in front of it and on the other side was the Kabul State Secretariat. Our building was originally owned by Sardar Mohammad Yonus Khan, who rented it to Kabul State Prison. On the other side was the home of Commandant Mohammad Naim Khan.

The first friend whose voice I heard was Sarwar Khan Goya. I heard him calling to me, saying, "Where are you? Where are you?"

Even though the police tried to stop him, he overran them, forced his way in and came upstairs. I saw him trying to reach me, and I pleaded with the police to please allow him in. I was telling them, "He is the King's cousin! Let him come upstairs!" I wasn't lying. Goya was the grandson of Prime Minister Abdul Quddus Khan and Sardar Quddus Khan was a first cousin of the father of Mohammad Hashim Khan.

Goya was coming toward me, crying, and said, "I have brought some very good news for you."

I thought I had been released. I said, "What is the news? Have they permitted me to be released?"

"No," he said, "I have brought news better than that."

I said, "What? Go ahead tell me."

He said, "I read today in the *Islah* and *Anis* newspapers the new Prime Minister Sardar Mohammad Shah Mahmud Ghazi has ordered the shackling of prisoners be stopped. This is to be so, all over Afghanistan."

Goya read a couplet that meant:

Upon seeing your imprisonment mercy spoke,
Not to make any more traps and not to sell any more cages.

I said, "This is really novel for Afghanistan, for someone who is lodged in a prison not to have shackles and chains."

He replied, "You are not the only one without chains and shackles here."

I acknowledged his statement, but memories otherwise were fresh in my mind.

Goya Saheb sat next to me and asked about my time at the Arg prison. I could not speak openly because we were sitting where anyone could hear our conversation. He asked, "What did you do in the prison? What kind of poetry did you write?"

I told him, "Unfortunately, whatever poetry I wrote was on the walls of the prison, which they wiped off. I only have one ode of poetry with me, written as an appreciation of the Prophet PBUH. I named it *Ahe Neema Shaab* ("Wailing in the Middle of the Night").

"Give me that poetry," he asked eagerly. "I want to read it."

He took it and read it with great enthusiasm and affection. I could see that several places in the poem made his eyes glisten with tears. At the end, he said, "God delivered you, and this ode was your deliverance."

Turkish Intervention to Stop the Execution of Abdul Rahim Khan

Soon, I was to learn that it was only with Turkish intervention that Abdul Rahim Khan was saved from execution.

Goya asked, "Do you know what happened after you left the Arg prison?"

I answered, "No."

He said, "They ordered that Abdul Rahim Khan, Naib Salar should be court-martialed in front of other military officers, and then he should be executed by firing squad. They also ordered you should be court-martialed in front of civil servants up to the level of Director General at the Prime Ministry and then be executed by firing squad. Mohammad Hashim Khan said, 'The blood of this contaminated person should not be dropped at the Prime Ministry. He should be court-martialed at the Prime Ministry and executed somewhere else.' It was because he was afraid of being in the same place as a dead body."

God was kind and compassionate and by his grace the Turkish Embassy sent a letter on behalf of Fakhruddin Altai. The Turkish Ambassador presented a letter to the Afghan Foreign Ministry of Affairs. The letter read somewhat like this (paraphrasing):

Since Abdul Rahim Khan Naib Salar has been a servant of the world of Islam, a famous Army General of Afghanistan and a friend of Fakhruddin Altai, the Turkish government herewith expresses deep anguish and requests that if this person has been accused and there is proof against him, he should be tried in an open court, and a witness on behalf of the government of Turkey should be allowed to observe the proceedings. Even if he is found guilty, the government of Turkey still requests the government of Afghanistan, in light of the friendship between the two countries, to reduce the punishment of this person.

I said, "Are you sure of all this?"

Goya answered, "Yes, I have heard this from one of the members of the Royal Family. One of the reasons they stopped from executing you was this letter and the repeated and deep efforts of the Minister of Court, Ahmad Shah Khan, who in earnest was trying to save you. Even though he was a close friend of Naib Salar, his efforts were going nowhere, and Sardar Mohammad Hashim Khan insisted the orders of execution be signed and done with. There was no court proceedings and no due process."

We were still talking when a police officer came up and confronted Mr. Goya. "More than half hour has passed since you've been here," he said. "You have no further right to sit here."

Goya replied, "I've been told this man is free and anyone can come and talk to him."

The police officer said, "There's no such permission."

He started to grab Goya Saheb by the collar to pull him up, but I pleaded with Goya to go. As he left, I requested, if he could, to bring my little daughter Marie and my older son Safiullah back to visit me. "They will not allow my wife or anyone else to come," I said. "But please, try to bring Marie and Safiullah." He said he would try.

I watched from upstairs as Goya left with the police officer. When they reached the garden by the entrance he was still cursing and protesting.

I was very deeply touched. I had seen my dear friend of many years after a long time.

Two and a half hours later I heard the voice of Goya Saheb again. "I'm going to get you and have you arrested!"

he was shouting at the police officer downstairs. "I have official permission to be here!"

I yelled down from upstairs, "It's not the fault of the poor police officer. He's doing what he was told to do. Why don't you just come upstairs?"

Since he was a little overweight, he could not come bounding up the stairs. He said, "I went to so many places, from house to house. Finally, I ended up at Sardar Shah Mahmud Khan's house and saw his wife Qamar-ul-Banat."

Qamar-ul-Banat was the daughter of Amir Habibullah Khan Seraj, and her mother was from Nooristan province. She was a very pious and compassionate lady.

"She called her husband, the Prime Minister, on the phone. After their conversation, she told me there are unfortunate reasons why you may not be released right away because of complications in the family relationship and Mohammad Hashim Khan. She said he's bound not to release Khalilullah Khan in the first round of prisoner releases; however, he may be doing so in the second round. I don't know what was said on the other side of the phone, but after she hung up from talking to her husband, she told me he ordered that any one can go see Khalilullah, and there are no restrictions and please relay my regards to him too."

We were still sitting and talking when the Commandant of the prison, Khwaja Mohammad Naim Khan, approached us. He said, "Mr. Goya, there has been a miscommunication, and I apologize for it. The police did not realize. I understand you went and complained about it."

Goya said, "After a long time, I am here sitting with my friend, and your police officer came and almost tried to pull me away by my collar."

He was a writer and part of the Royal Family, and he really got upset. Goya Saheb was a respected person. Goya said to me, "Now, I will go to your house and carry this good news to your wife, and I will try to bring your daughter Marie Jan to you. I hope she comes today."

I was really looking forward to it. That night we completed the recitation of Holy Koran with Torah

Habibullah as Qari (one who recites the Holy Koran). Karim Jan, myself, and a dozen other people recited the Holy Koran upstairs while Sayed Mobashir Khan Tarazi, along with others, recited the Holy Koran downstairs. The experience of reciting the Koran was very capitulating, like surrender and freedom. It affected us deeply. It seemed as if, with every passage, the chains of injustice were shattered. With every passage, the message of compassion and consolation spread warmly among all the afflicted prisoners. At the same time, it brought a bad omen to the oppressors or anyone who would do injustice.

Marie Visits Me in the Prison

It was around 10 a.m. when I heard the voice of my older son Safiullah. I don't want to repeat his name any more than I must, because he died so young, and repeating his name makes me very sorrowful. Along with him came my adopted brother, Abdul Rasool from Panjsher, whose name I mentioned earlier. Abdul Rasool and Safiullah came upstairs, and then, I saw Marie. She had grown up a little – children grow very fast. Her hair was tousled, and she was kind of wary, as if she didn't recognize me. She hadn't seen me for six or seven months. She stared at me for several minutes, and then suddenly she burst out, "Agha!" (Dad) She ran toward me and threw herself at me.

The night I was taken away to prison, you were so innocent, Marie. That night you also had thrown yourself in my arms. I told you to let go, to leave me, and you kept asking, "Agha! Where are they taking you? Don't go. Stay with me!"

Today, I heard the same voice when you ran and threw yourself in my arms. I kissed you from head to toe, and kissed you again. Abdul Rasool, who was more than a brother to me, sat down with me. My brother Najibullah Khan and Karim Jan were also there. This little child would not leave my side, even though they tried to give her candy from the prison or something else so she could eat. She was clinging to me and kept saying, "Agha, why don't you come home? Agha, are you a prisoner here? Agha, why don't you come home?"

311

I said, "My daughter, I'm not a prisoner here, I am a guest."

She pointed toward Karim Jan and said, "Are you the guest of this uncle?"

I answered, "No, I am a guest of your great uncle, Sardar Hashim Khan, former Prime Minister of Afghanistan."

And thus, continued the passage of time until Marie fell asleep in my arms. It was time for her to go. Abdul Rasool was supposed to take her back. I woke Marie up, but she refused to leave me and go home with others. She held steadfast to me and kept saying, "Agha, I'm not going home! I want to sleep next to you tonight!"

This brought tears to my eyes, and she cried too. I said, "Go," and asked her to go and forced her out. She left crying. I stayed back and broke my fast. Again, I started reading Holy Koran.

Prison and Friends

My friends started coming to the prison to visit. Sayed Shamsuddin Pacha came. Also a good friend of mine, Abdullah Khan came. Abdullah Khan was a Director in the Ministry of Education. He was from Tagao and was from the Safi tribe. Abdullah Khan was the son-in-law of Mirza Mohammad Khan Yaftali. He was a well-groomed man, and he was in college with Ali Mohammad Khan. From the house of Goya Saheb and other friends, we were provided meals every day. All kinds and varieties of exotic Afghan dishes were brought to us. The wife of Karim Jan was sister of Goya Saheb. From the house of Sardars (Royal Family), a very traditional rich and exotic food was sent. We used to invite other prisoners, and the guards to join us.

We invited a guard named Akram Khan and Noor Mohammad Khan Beg, the brother of Sher Mohammad Beg. We invited Abdul Rahman Khan and Mirza Moqeem Khan, who both served Janabe Ali, the King of Bokhara. We would all sit around and exchange stories and listen to each other's memoirs. We used to crack jokes and make fun. Sher Mohammad Beg used to cook a Turkmani dish of rice with nuts and raisins called *qabuli*. It was very delicious. The doorman of the King of Bokhara was also there, and we used to ask him to cook Bokharan dishes for us. This is how we spent the days and passed the nights. In spite of all these stories, life in prison was still difficult. I was separated from my wife and other family. My uncle, Naib Salar, was still in the Arg prison. I did not know what he was going through. No one was allowed inside the Arg prison to bring back news of his welfare. Neither was any news filtered into the prison about us. His other brothers, my uncles, were all in jail too. In fact, 44 members of our family, with whom we shared a blood relation, were in jail. They had no contact with us.

A few more days passed and even the prison Commandant Khwaja Mohammad Naim came and sat with us often. While we sat on the floor, we gave him the only chair we had, since he was wearing military uniform and was the Commandant. He would accept the chair and sit on the end, even though he was younger than I was. In fact, when I was a Director at the Prime Ministry, he was working as a clerk. Now, he was a Commandant, and I was happy to sit on the floor, with him in the chair. Once in a while we would play chess.

One night Khwaja Mohammad Naim Khan dropped in abruptly. He was disheveled and looked teary-eyed. I asked him, "What seems to be the matter?"

He said, "Don't ask. Things are not all right. I have been appointed Commander of Mazar-i-Sharif. This Shah Mahmud Khan is the enemy of his own family." (He forgot that he was talking to me in prison.) "He is the enemy of his family," Khwaja repeated. "He has freed many prisoners and has appointed many of them to government jobs. The family of Amir Habibullah Khan Seraj is all over him. His wife Qamar-ul-Banat (daughter of Habibullah Khan) is his teacher. Whatever foundations were laid by former Prime Minister Mohammad Hashim Khan have all come crashing down. Just beware something big may befall his family."

I answered, "Mr. Commandant, I'm waiting with God's grace that a good fortune will befall for his family, Afghanistan, and for Sardar Shah Mahmud Khan himself.

Whatever he's done so far seems to be a good gesture. He has released prisoners, and he has broken the tradition of shackles and chains on prisoners. He trusts the prisoners, and as you say, he has appointed many to the government. I think all this is good. I don't think Qamar-ul-Banat told him to do all this. He may have received inspiration from God and the Prophet (PBUH)."

I added, "Why are you upset at this? On the contrary, you should be happy. He had appointed you as a Commander of Mazar-i-Sharif. I think you should be happy and celebrate he's not condemning you."

"No, a foundation is being laid for my condemnation," Khwaja disagreed. "That's why I've come to you. Abdul Qayum, this crazy opium addict, he's claiming I took his 100,000 *rupees* (Indian currency; people who used this term usually meant *afghanis*). As God is my witness, I've not taken them. Can you please admonish him?"

I asked, "Where is this Abdul Qayum Khan?"

He said, "He's on the other side of the prison." I asked him how long he has been in prison, even though I knew the answer. He replied, "Probably seven or eight years."

"What was his charge?" I asked him.

"I don't know, but if he's in prison he must have done something," he replied.

I said, "Maybe his sin was he had no sin, just like I am in prison now. Do you think he will listen to me? You say he is crazy and an opium addict. If he's melancholy, will he listen to me? And why?"

Khwaja only repeated, "I ask you, please, talk to him." He became calmer and apologetic and reminisced with me about the days when we were at the Prime Ministry together, and reminded me of his linkage to Khwajas of Arefan and Asheqan (names of places in Afghanistan). He added, "Your father respected my family and my mother's family too. This charge is a big insult for my family. I have not taken anyone's money. Someone must have encouraged him to accuse me."

"Well, I cannot go there to the other side of the prison to talk to him," I said, proposing, "Why don't you send someone to bring this Mr. Aishan to me?" (Aishan is a title given to some Sayeds in Afghanistan that have linkage to the Prophet, PBUH).

He answered, "All right. I will send someone to bring him to you, but I won't be there myself. He curses, cusses, and belittles me. He does not respect anybody."

I said, "Fine. You can go and sit in the other room and wait while I talk to him."

I was flabbergasted at God's turn of events. I looked up to God to acknowledge He certainly does indeed "work in mysterious ways." Even though he is the Commandant and I am the prisoner, Khwaja Mohammad Naim Khan is requesting my help. And I should help him.

Momentarily, I heard the stomping of police boots, followed by the voice of Aishan Abdul Qayum Khan. Seeing me, he called out, "How are you doing my cousin? They have imprisoned you?" And with that we embraced. He was a tall man with heavy bones and a prominent nose. There's no doubt he was addicted to opium.

He was the son of Aishan Abdul Qayum Khan Qadir. He was from Charekar, and his forefathers are prominent in Afghan history. They had fought against the British and thrown them out of Kabul. His father's heroism caused the people to ask him to be their King, but he did not embrace the idea. Instead, he had a silver coin minted in his name. He had this couplet inscription on the coin:

I will mint this coin from gold until I find its owner
I will be melancholy until people are in an uproar at me

Amir Abdul Rahman Khan was crowned King instead, and Aishan Saheb was allowed to live a normal life under his rule. In fact, he was appointed the governor of Jalalabad and died there. Aishan's forefathers owned large tracts of land, and their family had deep roots in Afghanistan. They were from a village near Charekar, named Kofiyan, or Opiyan in Greek literature during the time of Alexander the Great. I do not remember it very well.

There were two Sayed families who used to live in Opiyan. There was a mausoleum with a big dome. A sage by the name of Sayed Jaffar Mojarrad Taba Tabai is buried there. He lived in the time of Zaheeruddin Mohammad Babar Moghul (1483-1530, first King of the Moghul Dynasty, which ruled 400 years), who died around 937 in Hijri-Qamari.

This grave had a beautiful marble stone with writing in Arabic on it. The writing meant, "Here lies one to whom the earth and the sky feel honored." The grave is near the entrance door to the mausoleum. The people of Opiyan believe the grave has been moving gradually closer to the door from its original location. They further believe that once this grave reaches the door, the Day of Judgment will arrive.

The people also believe if someone is bitten by a marauding dog and the victim is brought to the sacred mausoleum of Sayed Jaffar Mojarrad Taba Tabai, by the grace of the sage, the person will be cured after 10 to 15 days.

The other Aishan whose grave is in the mausoleum comes from the other Aishan family in that village, is linked to Aishan Abdul Qayum Khan. They are also linked to the Prophet (PBUH). In recent years, they buried a very pious and sagacious man under this dome by the name of Sayed Jan Malang (whose name means "ecstasy" or "one who has divorced the world"). This happened during the rule of King Zahir Shah. Sayed Jan Malang is a Sayed from Kunar province. Sometimes he used to roam about naked or half-naked wearing a long shirt. He did not follow regular prayers or do all that is required by Islamic law or Shariat. He was always in a frenzy or dominated by madness. But he would never have taken anything from anybody. Sometimes he would curse people, and other times he would be very kind. People considered whatever he said deeply and tried to interpret his gibberish language. He lived in Jabalus Seraj (north of Kabul) and died at the bottom of the fort there. He was buried in the mausoleum of Sayed Jaffar Mojarrad Taba Tabai. I don't think it was called for. After his burial, the mausoleum was repaired. The original design and layout was not replicated. It was more modern and lost its beauty.

Well let's come back to this Aishan Sayed Abdul

Qayum. He called out to me, "You had summoned me."

I said, "Yes. I would have come in person to pay my respects to you, but I was not allowed to do so. I'm thankful you came here. In the name of God, I have something to ask you. First, you have to promise me you will do it. If you promise, it will be good, but if you don't, then it's all right. If what has happened is true, then that's different. But if it's not true, and you said this because you were upset at the moment, then we have to talk."

He said, "What are you talking about?"

I said, "You have filed a complaint against Commandant Khwaja Mohammad Naim Khan."

"Yes, I have filed a complaint," he said angrily. "I am going to smash his brains out."

"Why, Saheb, why?" I asked.

"I've been told he went up to Abdul Rahim Khan's house and took some of his belongings and picked up his hunting gun," he said. "How dare he do that! How dare he hold the gun of that brave man in his dirty hands!"

I said, "I am his nephew, and I am his son-in-law. This is not true. If Khwaja Mohammad Naim Khan has done anything against you or anybody else, I cannot excuse him or pardon him. However, that he held Wazir Saheb's gun or insulted his household is not true. He seems to have a lot of respect for Abdul Rahim Khan. I am in prison, but this man has paid respect to me. Let's think about what great things our forefathers did during their time. They had respect for each other. They would pardon each other if they were asked to do so. Today, I am just a poor prisoner. This Khwaja Mohammad Naim's mother is also from a Sayed family. They are the descendants of Pacha Saheb of Pai Menar."

He replied, "What are you saying?" He meant, "Is that true?"

I said, "Yes, they are the descendants of Pacha Saheb of Pai Menar (a place in Afghanistan). His father is from Arefan and Asheqan (a place in Kabul). He is from your extended family. Khwajas are considered to be very respectful. They have transferred him from here to Mazar-i-Sharif."

"I'm sure you are not going to put down or trample a person when he's down on his luck," I continued. "If I was asking you to pardon him when I was the Minister of Media and Information, or if I had another more important job, and you had turned me down, that would have been fine. I would not have complained or felt bad. Now, I am a prisoner. I am requesting you to do so."

Karim Jan Agha, who was present at that time, was gesturing for me not to say anything. Aishan Saheb was foaming at the mouth. He was very angry at Khwaja Mohammad Naim Khan and the whole establishment.

After listening to me, his ego took over, and he said, "This is just 100,000 *rupees* we're talking about. Even if there were a million *rupees,* because of you, my cousin, I have forgiven him."

"This is very honorable of you, however, you need to do more than verbally forgive him," I advised. "You have to retract the written complaint that is in the works. You should ask them to send the piece of paper back to you and destroy it. Demonstrating you've taken practical steps to forgive him, and not just talked about it, will increase your honor."

He made some obscene gestures about forgiving and said, "I am lingering in prison, and you know why, my cousin? They have confiscated all my land and everything I own. I have not done anything against the government or the state. My only crime is that I am the son of Aishan Abdul Qadir Khan. My father was close to the family of Amir Abdul Rahman Khan, and he served his country patriotically by helping to extricate the British from Afghanistan. The only crime I've committed is that he was my forefather."

He pulled up his trousers and showed the marks and scars of the shackles and chains. He said, "What have I done? Nothing. Did my legs deserve these shackles? They brought me to my knees, and they know that even if they release me, I'll never leave their prison. I was a free man of this country."

I said, "Yes, you are right. There have been a lot of families who have suffered this way. Please forgive give them now."

Tapping hard on my shoulder twice, he said, "Oh, cousin, you have lost your courage!"

I said, "No, actually, this man came and pleaded with me. That's why I'm asking you to forgive him."

Karim Jan Agha was also part of this conversation. We asked for some tea, and Aishan had a cup of tea with us.

I said, "Let us raise our hands to God and pray for the health and delivery of Afghanistan, the success of Shah Mahmud Khan, and thanks on the removal of Sardar Mohammad Hashim Khan."

Aishan uttered whatever came to his mouth. At the end, we escorted him to the stairs, and he went back toward his room.

Soon Khwaja Naim Khan came and I reassured him the application could be retrieved from the Ministry of the Interior, and hopefully, Aishan would not file again. "He's not going to do it again," I told him. "We just decided on this, and we got to this point after a lot of discussion."

Karim Jan Agha said, "Commandant Saheb, may God help you. You will face in your life whatever you have done to other people. And it's not just you who will face it, but the others who have been your cohorts have done it with you. You may have not done much; however, you were under pressure to do it. May God help you. Just agree to this. If this had not been resolved, there would have been many Aishans filing complaints against you. You would not have been able to go to Mazar-i-Sharif."

He concluded, "If you would please listen to my counsel, you should leave Kabul as soon as possible and go to Mazar-i-Sharif and assume your post there. I don't think anybody will follow you there. Expedite your departure to Mazar-i-Sharif, assume your job, and meanwhile, bring the application to us so we can destroy it."

(Karim Jan Saheb spoke in slang Persian and mispronounced a lot of letters.)

Karim Jan Saheb Zadah

Commandant Khwaja Naim Khan said, "Yes, I do agree with all this, but Karim Jan Agha, tonight you are speaking in a strange and different way to me."

Karim Jan answered, "Well, I have a lot of respect for you, but still I would like to ask you why have I been in prison here? I was sitting in my home, and because I am a friend of Khalilullah Khan, was it a crime to be a friend or an acquaintance of him?"

Khwaja said, "I know what Khalilullah Khan has done for me. I'll tell you the whole story."

I said, "You don't have to. I will tell the story."

The story starts when Habibullah Khan Kalakani (1890-1929) requested the hand in marriage of the granddaughter of Amir Dost Mohammad Khan (1793-1863) through Haider Jan, son of Abdul Quddos Khan Etemadul Daulat (a Persian title). The request was accepted, and she was given to him in marriage. At that time, it was said a relationship was established with the prominent people of Kohdaman and Kohistan.

The forefathers of Karim Jan Agha were a prominent family from Kohdaman and Kohistan. He belonged to the family of Khwaja Jan, who was the son of Ghulam Jan Saheb Zadah. Ghulam Jan wrote the *Jang Namah*, which is a national epic of Afghanistan, along the lines of *Shah Namah* by the Persian poet Fardusi. It was published in Kabul during the time of King Zahir Shah. Sher Jan Khan was the son of Khwaja Jan Saheb Zadah. His grandson was executed along with Habibullah Khan Kalakani by a firing squad. His other brother Mohammad Siddiq Khan was a high ranking military general of Afghanistan and had participated in the War of the Freedom of Afghanistan and was a friend of Nadir Shah. He was also executed. Karim Jan escaped to India and stayed there as a refugee for a while.

(This story goes further on, but we will stop here and move on. Karim Jan Saheb was in jail because of his connections to his forefathers and to Habibullah Khan Kalakani.)

Letter of Najibullah Khan to Zahir Shah

Najibullah Khan wrote a letter to His Highness the King, Zahir Shah, in which he said, "If you would like to release Khalilullah Khan and need a bail bond for him, I have two little boys by the names of Waheedullah and Yousuf. You may take both of these boys and put them in the juvenile detention. My wife's name is Sharifa. She is the daughter of Amir Habibullah Khan Seraj. You may put her in the women's jail also. In exchange for these three, please release Khalilullah Khan."

This letter was sent to the King, Zahir Shah, through Shah Mahmud Khan. The King wrote under the application plea, "Whenever Khalilullah Khan is released, this letter will have played a big role in it."

While life continued, I used to receive messages from all over. Sardar Faiz Mohammad Khan also sent me messages. Some of my friends provided monetary help to my household. Mia Jan Agha Hazrat Masoom, may God bless his soul, used to send thirty loaves of baked bread every day to the prison to me through one of his sons. Sometimes, it would be Sabghatullah Jan (who is a mujahideen or freedom fighter now). They would also cook some delicious dishes and send them to the prison along with the bread.

We told them, "We are only two or three people, why are you sending 30 loaves?"

Mia Jan Agha used to say, "You have other prisoners too. Just eat two or three loaves yourselves and distribute the rest to the other wanting prisoners so they will pray for your release."

Mia Jan Agha visited me constantly in the prison. Hashim Shaiq Afandi used to come also and sit and talk. They would empty their hearts and say, "Khalil, you don't deserve to be in prison."

I would answer, "What can I do? This is the destiny."

A young gentleman named Nematullah Pazhwak (later Minister of Education) would send me messages asking if he could be of any service. I would answer, "What can anybody do while I'm in prison?" The people of Kohdaman and Kohistan filed petitions several times for my release. That, too, never materialized.

The surprising thing is I was not left alone in being persecuted, even in jail. The government sent messages to

Mazar-i-Sharif, telling people I was in Mazar-i-Sharif during the time of Habibullah Khan Kalakani and representing him in a high capacity, and if anybody had any complaints against him during that time, then to come forward and file their complaints now. The people responded, "We don't remember Khalilullah Khan from that time, and we have no idea what had happened in Mazar-i-Sharif. No one came forward. Similarly, they asked people from Herat to file complaints against Naib Salar Abdul Rahim Khan because he was working there for the government. These were fishing expeditions by the government. No one from Herat filed any complaints against Abdul Rahim Khan either.

Injustice and the Innocent Prisoners in the State Prison

Shah Mahmud Khan always wanted to release us as soon as possible, but he feared the reaction of Sardar Mohammad Hashim Khan. Even though the former Prime Minister was in retirement, he wielded a great deal of authority. Sardar Shah Mahmud Khan was still his brother.

We used to read and write every day in the prison, but we were conscious to avoid revolutionary subjects, which could become the cause of investigation and delay our freedom.

One day a ruckus started in the prison yard. Khwaja Mohammad Naim Khan was still the Commandant. We were curious to know what happened. We could hear the voice of a young boy, pleading, "Oh, people! Come to my assistance!" I looked out my window and saw a boy, about 10 to 12 years old, being whipped by the police. Khwaja Naim Khan stood nearby, watching and encouraging the person who was whipping the boy to continue.

There was another man who was also yelling and crying. He was bent over in agony. He was yelling, "You're killing him! You're killing him! This was my fault!"

I didn't know if he was the boy's father, but I lost my

patience and yelled angrily out the window from upstairs, "Commandant! Please, for God's sake, stop it!" The whipping continued, and I called out again. "Mr. Commandant, be afraid of God!"

Khwaja Naim Khan yelled back, "This is none of your business! You are a prisoner. Stay there!"

They continued whipping this little boy, and his father was pleading and saying, "Please, forgive him! Please, forgive him, he's just a child!"

I ran down the stairs to the scene. When the Commandant saw me, he asked the man to stop whipping the boy. I saw this little boy up close. His clothes were all dirty, torn, and bloodied.

Khwaja Naim Khan ordered, "Take him right away to Dehmazang (the notorious prison)!"

My heart was so touched by sorrow, I asked, "What has he done?"

The Commandant answered, "I was coming out of the house, and this dirty little bastard had the prayer rug under his arm. He was taking it out of the prison. I happened to note it. He was trying to steal this prayer rug!"

The boy's father pleaded, "Mr. Commandant, please, be afraid of God! He was not stealing anything! This is my prayer rug. I had given it to him to go out to sell and bring me the money."

The Commandant told the man to shut up and ordered the police to hit the man. He was a Qari (one who recites the Holy Koran). He quieted down and said, "Okay, you have the right. You have the power." Under his breath he whispered, "This will be avenged. God will avenge this someday and in some place."

My Release from Prison

Years passed. I was released from prison eventually, and I was appointed Secretary to the Cabinet and then Minister of Press and Information, advisor to the King of Afghanistan and elected a member of the Parliament of Afghanistan. From there I was appointed Afghan Ambassador to Jeddah (Saudi Arabia). I was transferred to the post of Ambassador to Iraq in Baghdad. After a while, the Communists usurped power in Kabul, and I resigned from my post in Baghdad and left for West Germany (1978).

In 1359 (1980) I left West Germany and went to offer Omrah (not the annual Hajj, but a lesser pilgrimage that can be done any time of the year) to the Holy Kaabah (in Mecca, Saudi Arabia, the most sacred site in Islam) and was able to be in service of the Holy Prophet Mohammad PBUH. There were some Bokhara refugees living in Mecca. Most of them had accepted the nationality of Afghanistan. They knew me from the time when I was the ambassador there. They came to me, paid their respects, and showed their love and affection for me. Each one of them would invite me in the evenings for dinner. They would do all kinds of favors for me.

One day, I can't recall if it was at the residence of Shah Elmam Bokharai or someone else's place, there was a gathering of 60 to 70 literary figures and scholars who had come together to show respect to me. Torah Sayed Mahmud, cousin of esteemed Torah Sayed Mobashir Tarzari, was there. Also present was Qari Ibne Yameen, one of the scholars of Bokhara, and some people from Samarqand. The dinner had not been served yet. A man entered the room, and people stood up as a sign of respect to him. A young man in Western dress, with expensive glasses with decorative rims, accompanied him. They came and sat. This Qari did not greet me, and neither did the young man with him. I thought they did not recognize me.

I asked the host, Qari Karamatullah Sabaq Bokhari, who was one of the famous scholars of Bokhara, and also a poet and a writer, "Who are these gentlemen?" He raised his finger to his lips to gesture for me to keep quiet. I was taken aback, but did as he asked. He was a good friend of mine when I was the Ambassador here.

The gentleman suddenly said, in a Bokharai accent, "Mr. Ambassador, I will introduce myself to you." Looking at him, as he stood and started toward me, I began to recollect that he looked familiar. He had a flowing gray beard, was wearing the long Arab *abbai* (clothing), and looked very respected. The young man sitting with him appeared to be learned and knowledgeable. He said, "Before I introduce myself to you, I will pray for all Muslims and you please say Amen." He raised his hands in prayers and said, "Oh God, what are you doing? Oh God, what are you doing? Oh God, we are in your presence, and we are thankful to you. Even though Afghanistan has fallen to the Communists, and Afghanistan is in worse shape today than Bokhara was. All Muslims who are here with me, all refugees who are here with me, join with me in thanking the Almighty."

"Oh, Allah," he said, and the others repeated it. "Thank you that you have brought this Ambassador of Afghanistan, Mr. Khalilullah Khan Khalili, here with us, and we see him in good health. He does not have a country today; neither is he an Ambassador today. I see him in health; however; he has been humbled. He has lost honor." The room erupted in voices. "I said please be quiet! Please be quiet, this is not God's intention."

I was very upset. I said, "Who are you?"

He said, "You didn't recognize me?"

I answered, "No."

He announced, "I am Qari Akram. This young man you see next to me is the same boy years ago whom the Commandant of the Kabul state prison had arrested, accusing him of stealing a prayer rug, and he had him whipped and sent to Dehmazang prison."

"You interceded and stopped the whipping," he continued. "I went through a very bad time. I saw a lot of oppression and injustice. My house was confiscated. Anything I owned was taken away. They had already confiscated my other belongings before, and then they arrested me, accusing me of working for the freedom of Bokhara along with the former King of Bokhara, Janabe Ali. They put me in the same jail where you were, and I was a prisoner. I am the same Qari Akram."

I felt bad, extremely humbled and shameful. I said, "Why are you thanking God that Afghanistan has become worse than Bokhara? The people of Afghanistan didn't do anything to you. It's not their fault."

Other voices joined me in saying the people of

Afghanistan were like brothers to the people of Bokhara. "They opened up their hearts and houses to us," the others said. "They did not hold back anything. They provided us food, water, housing, and land. This Qari Akram who is complaining also has the right. He and his son went through some bad times."

The young man stood up, came to me, and kissed my hands and said, "I remember you yelling from the window for the Commandant to stop whipping me. You interceded and stopped any further damage. Thank you."

More Stories of Crimes Committed in the Arg Prison

This is a story I will remember for a long, long time, and there were many of these stories occurring on a daily basis. At night, in the Arg prison, I used to hear a strange voice repeating the Kalimah (There is no God, but one God) night after night. When I asked the prison guard about this, he said it was the voice of Mir Abdul Aziz of Deh Yahya (a Kabul neighborhood).

They had brought him into the prison, on the orders of Mohammad Hashim Khan, to help them find the home address of a person named Malik Niyazi. However, he ended up in jail himself. It was seven or eight years ago, and he was still in prison. No one was allowed to go to his cell or go near him or talk to him. He wasn't allowed to see the sunlight. No one knew him. He was an illiterate man, a simple man, a man of the desert.

All the hairs in his beard and his head had grown long and gray. His nails had grown long too, and his clothes had become so tattered, they fell off his body. No one was allowed to be in touch with him.

He would sit in a corner of his cell on the damp floor all the time and had a small piece of wood with him. For days and nights he would dig the soft mud out and had almost created a grave for himself. During the wintery nights, he would slip into the hole he'd dug, and he would keep repeating, "There is no God, but one God." He wasn't even able to pronounce the Arabic correctly since he was illiterate.

I asked the prison guard if he would let me see him one day. When Sardar Shah Mahmud Khan took over as Prime Minister, the guard told me, "I will now let you have a glimpse of him." The guard opened my cell door and pulled aside the *kileem* or thin rug that covered the entrance so I could not see out and said, "Stay here, I'll be right back. Keep watching. When the man comes out of his cell to go toward the bathroom, you will be able to see him in the narrow passageway."

I could never believe my eyes when I saw this man. When he came out of his cell, he had a clay water carrier in his hand and was walking in a melancholic way through the passageway. I had never seen a man like him. He was limping on both legs. He still had shackles on his legs and a chain going around his neck. His head and facial hair completely covered his face. When he passed the door of my cell, the stench from his body and the iron in shackles was so strong it was difficult to stand it. I looked at him and kept thanking God in my heart and reciting the Kalimah under my breath; grateful I was not subjected to such oppression.

This week, Dr. Noor Mohammad Khan came to visit me. He looked happy and satisfied. Many of the prisoners had been released. He heard I would be released soon, God willing. When I was in the Arg prison I had told him once, "Doctor, don't worry about me. Here, in my cell block is another sick gentleman. He knows you too. Why don't you go find out about him?" I said in hopes he would go to the cell.

The prison guard wanted to deny him access, but I told the guard, "Be afraid of God! Go and open the door, and let the doctor in to see him."

The doctor was a tall thin man, with a dark complexion and heart disease. He left and went to the man's cell. He was there for about 15 minutes. When he came back, Dr. Noor Mohammad Khan was shaking. He said he was very upset. He told me, "Khalil, may God destroy your house! (an Afghan saying when you don't like someone). I hope you're never released from the prison! Why did you send me to an animal?"

I said, "What is it?"

He said, "I saw a man, hairs all over, and the stench was fetid. Why did you send me to his cell?"

I answered, "I sent you to his room so you could witness his condition. It would be a good deed for you to help this person. Go to Shah Mahmud Khan, and ask that this person be released."

The prison guard also told me a story about this man. He said, "One day, I was coming from the main road toward the south side of the Arg. I was headed inside when I saw an Afghan woman near the footpath. She was wearing a black shawl or *chaderi*. She was wailing and came crying toward me and said, 'For God's sake, I have a son, but I've lost him for years. He belongs to such-and-such village in Paktia (south of Kabul). I've lost him for quite some time. I've never heard his news, dead or alive. I've been told he was brought to Kabul to this white palace, and he's in prison here. I also found out you are from Gardez. Please help me find him.'"

"I asked her, 'What is his name?' She gave me the name, Mir Abdul Aziz. To my surprise, I found out it was the same man who has recited 'There is no God, but one God' all night long. I told her, 'Stay here, I'll go and find out.' She said, 'If you find him for me, I will offer you a gift.'"

"I went inside the prison to this man's cell. He was very thin. He was given half a bread to eat every day and that was it. Once in a while some leftovers were thrown his way. When I went to his cell, I asked him, 'Do you have a mother?' He started crying and said in Pashtu, 'Yes I had a mother. She was alive when they picked me up and brought me to prison.' I asked him, 'Do you have anything I can show her that she will recognize and know you are still alive?'"

"He took off something he was wearing on his neck. It was a long key on a dirty thread. He gave it to me and said, 'This is the key to the room in the barn where we used to lock the straw. It belonged to my mother. Take it, show it to her, she will recognize it.'"

"I took the key back and as soon as she saw it, she started crying and kissing the key and putting it against her eyes. She turned her face toward Mecca and said, 'Thank God he is alive.' She said to me, 'I'll give you a gift.' She looked so poor. I wondered what gift she might have to give. She looked in the pockets of her dress, turning out small bits of no consequence. Finally, she produced a dirty-looking cloth purse and handed me a small container of traditional black mascara with a small utensil used as brush. She said, 'This is the only thing of value I have, you can have it.' I said, 'No, I don't want it.' She said, 'Please, carry it to my son, and give it to him. Maybe he can use this for his eyes.' I took it and gave it to her son."

It had been two days since Dr. Noor Mohammad Khan's visit. On the third day, I heard a little commotion from the narrow passageway. I heard some voices and also the muttering of "There is no God, but one God."

The next day when the guard came, I asked him what had happened. I did not hear the muttering or repetition of "There is no God, but one God" the previous night. The guard said that last night Sardar Shah Mahmud Khan had sent a man to fetch Mir Abdul Aziz. Along with a doctor, they took him to the Aliabad Hospital and removed his chains and shackles. They investigated his case and found he had done nothing wrong and knew nothing and had committed no crime.

When I was released from prison in 1325 (1946) I heard it myself one day from Prime Minister Shah Mahmud Khan that he had given Mir Abdul Aziz 6,000 *rupees* (Afghanis) and allowed him to stay in the hospital until he had fully recuperated. The Prime Minister summoned his mother from the south, asked his mother to pardon him, and then sent them back to their home. This story has always haunted me.

There were many stories like this one.

The Release of the Prisoners

While we were still in the Kabul state prison, every day I would hear some good news. Some days they would announce such-and-such prisoner was released. Some days I would hear prisoners had been released and were appointed to the cabinet or some other high post, such as a governor or administrator. Some who had military background were sent to the Ministry of Defense. Some who belonged to the Ministry of Commerce and Trade were sent there. Some received monetary compensation and some received compensation in the form of land.

My uncle, Mohammad Yosuf Safi, was also released. He was not appointed to a job because he had seen hard labor and tough time in prison and had become very weak. Abdul Hadi Khan Dawi, who had been in prison for 18 years, was released and appointed as Secretary to the Ministry of Court by the King. Mohammad Khan Tata was also appointed somewhere.

We were still in the prison. People would come in droves to meet us and talk with us. We were able to help other prisoners. Our days passed in reading and playing chess. Once in a while Afandi Hashim Shaeq would come, and we would sit and talk about poet Bedil. Betab Saheb would also come and so would Goya Saheb. They would come every three or four days. Annus Khan, since he was very conservative and careful man, would come, but only once a while.

One day Goya Saheb came to visit and brought Annus Khan with him. Karim Jan wanted to play a prank on him. He asked the prison guard, a young military officer, to do him a favor.

He said, "When Annus Khan sits with us for lunch, you come in with paper and pen and announce, 'Today, I have been assigned to write the names of all who are having lunch here. Then, ask Annus Khan, 'What's your name, sir?'"

At lunch and upon our cue, the military officer came and started asking everybody for their names and telling them that he must write their names down and send them to those above him. He asked Annus Khan, "What is your name, sir?"

Annus Khan looked at me, alarmed, and said, "Haven't I told you in the past, so many times, I would not come to visit you? Now what shall I say?"

I said, "Just tell him your name. Let me tell him. His name is Annus Khan. He is the brother of Najibullah Khan, son of Sardar Mohammad Yunis Khan." I added, "He's a famous man and works for the Ministry of Education."

The guard wrote his name down in black ink. I knew the guard was in on this prank. Annus Khan said to the guard, "Just let me finish the lunch with them, and then I will leave, and I will never return here!"

Well, we got him on this prank, and then we all had a good laugh, and we finished our lunch.

I do not remember exactly, but I think I was in this prison for a year, or a year and a half. Compared to other prisons, this was very comfortable. One day Mohammad Assef Khan, the new Commandant of the Kabul state prison, who had replaced Khwaja Naim Khan, came to see us. The prison was readied for his inspection because he was newly appointed. The doors and cells were opened and cleaned. When the Commandant entered the prison yard, he yelled out from downstairs, "Where is my Ustad (teacher)? Where is my Ustad! Where is Khalili Saheb?"

Even though I was not his teacher or Ustad, he had gone to Isteqlal High School during the time of Amanullah Khan. I think he was older than I was. He was doing this to show respect to me. He came up, and he kissed my hand in front of everybody. The people around me were surprised. He was a very nice man with a sense of humor and very kind.

Afterwards, he went to visit Sayed Mobashir Tarazi and others. He talked to the prisoners and asked about their condition. He had his assistant read a decree signed by Sardar Shah Mahmud Khan. Upon the order of the King of Afghanistan, that day, 41 prisoners were released. Some had been in prison for 10 years, some 5 years, some from Herat, some from Kandahar, and some from Mazar-i-Sharif. He announced those prisoners who were from the provinces would be given travel expenses to get to their homes. And if their homes and their lands have been confiscated, he advised they should stay in Kabul and file a petition to the Prime Ministry. All their homes and lands

331

would be returned to them as per the order of the government. This made people very happy, and they lifted their hands to the sky to pray.

The First Visit of King Zahir Shah to the Provinces

I was left in the prison and was not part of this pardon. The Eid time came (the time of sacrifice of lamb and cow after a couple of months of Eidul Fitr; the time of Hajj).

His Highness, the King of Afghanistan had gone on a visit to the Northern provinces. I think he was on a trip to visit Mazar-i-Sharif, Maimana, Herat, Kandahar, and Takharistan. In Mazar-i-Sharif there is a range of mountains called Al Burz. This name has been mentioned in the poet Firdausi's *Shahnamah*.

This was the first time the King of Afghanistan had left the four walls of the Arg and Kabul and his resort of Paghman to travel to the Afghan provinces and meet his subjects. This was the first time the most important prisoner, the King of Afghanistan, was delivered to freedom (he was a "prisoner" figuratively of his uncle, Mohammad Hashim Khan, who wouldn't let him rule).

When His Highness was going to Mazar-i-Sharif on a deer hunting trip, he would go to Al Burz. Sardar Sultan Mohammad Khan, Afghanistan's Ambassador to Moscow, who later became the President of the Parliament and Minister of Foreign Affairs, was also with the King on this deer hunting trip. The weather was good, and it was spring time. Either the King remembered one of my verses of poetry, or someone in his entourage read this for him:

Be happy, oh Al Burz mountain and valley,
Be happy, oh beautiful breeding place of deer.

On hearing this verse, Sardar Sultan Mohammad Khan pointed out to the King, "Your Highness, you are reciting and hearing Khalili's poetry in Al Burz; however, he is languishing in prison."

The King responded, "You know I did not put him in prison."

Sardar Sultan Mohammad Khan said, "Well, you did not imprison him, and you could not stop it. The former Prime Minister, your uncle, imprisoned him. You know it, and he knows it, too. You can release him."

The king replied, "Let an occasion be so I could pardon him."

Sardar Sultan Mohammad Khan said, "There cannot be a greater occasion than this Eid of sacrifice. Normally, Eid is the time you release and pardon convicted prisoners. Would it be possible to release them also?"

The King turned toward his Chief Secretary, Mohammad Omar Khan and ordered him, "Please, call the Prime Minister on the telephone and tell him if there is no other obstacle in the way, to please release such-and-such person from the prison along with his brothers."

My Release from the Prison

I was unaware of all this. One day the son of Mohammed Omar Khan, I think his name was Akbar Jan, visited me in the state prison. He was a nice young man and used to be my student. He came in and said, "Uncle! Let your eyes be brighter! (an Afghan expression used when relaying good news). I have brought some good news for you!"

"What good news have you brought?" I asked him.

He said, "My father called me from Mazar-i-Sharif and said His Highness the King has ordered the Prime Minister to release you from prison. God is great!"

I replied, "Let's see what will happen. God is kind." I thanked the young man, and he left.

I had become used to the prison. How could I separate myself from Torah Saheb (Mobashir Khan)? The worst part, I thought, was they would release me and Karim Jan Agha, who was thrown in jail because of being my acquaintance, would remain here. The brothers of Wazir Saheb, and Wazir Saheb himself, were still in the Arg prison.

Well, the day of Eid came and Mohammad Assef Khan,

the Commandant of the state prison arrived with a vehicle to transport me home. My brothers and I, the three of us, gathered up whatever we had – some books, a few rosaries, a prayer rug, and some clothes – and took them with us. I was looking forward to seeing my wife and my sick daughter Rabia, whom I was going to see after a long, long time. I couldn't believe she was still alive. Mariegak (a term of endearment for Marie), when we arrive at the house, I saw you, too. You were jumping up and down, and I picked you up. It was 1948 (1327 in the Islamic solar calendar).

My friends trickled in one by one to find out about me. Goya Saheb was again the first one to come. Our neighbors, Mr. Alamshahi, may God bless his soul, and Dr. Najmuddin Khan's families prepared food for us for the first night and brought it to us themselves. I talked about my life in prison and told the stories I encountered there.

My wife shared her stories of hard times too. "The worst day of my life," she told me, "Was the day when our elder daughter Rabia was acutely ill, and little Marie was crying and shivering. We had nothing in the house to eat." She mentioned the little store, which could be seen from the window in our house. It was on the corner of Mr. Alamshahi's house. "They would send us fruits and nuts from their store," she said. "This little girl would cry for me to let her go, so that she could buy apples. She would demand some money to do so. One day she slipped out, without money and even the guard on our door did not stop her. She walked slowly with her little steps and reached the store. Since she had no money and the storekeeper was not there, the person working did not recognize her. When she asked for apples, he said, 'Just go away. There are no apples for you.' She came back, knowing that Rabia was waiting for her to see if she would bring some apples. Her face had turned pale, and she was crying vehemently."

My wife continued, "It was heartbreaking and more excruciatingly painful for me than anything else. Finally, the person taking care of the house, Abdul Rashid Panjsheri, whom we used to call out of respect, Uncle, came and said, 'Why are you crying?' I told him, 'My daughter wanted apples and could not get them.' He went out and bought two or three apples right away. When he came back, he only had just his *panjsheri* cap. He had proudly sold his head scarf! He gave these apples to the children. When Mr. Alamshahi came to know about this incident he admonished the storekeeper and almost yelled at him. He told him, 'Whenever they need fruit or anything, don't deny them. I will pay for everything.' However, we did not allow anyone to go to the store, or become that desperate again."

My wife told me of another hard day for her. "It was when they had brought me the news that all three of you – you, my father, and my brother had been ordered to be executed. It was very difficult to take this news, and we turned to one of the sages of Kabul who was your friend. I will not go into detail, but he did not even allow us to enter his house."

It was a rude awakening for me. I said, "Let's not talk about the bad memories." I have never brought the name of this gentleman on my tongue during all these years.

My Exile to Kandahar

The next day, which was the second day of the Eid, I was supposed to go to see Sardar Shah Mahmud Khan, as a tradition, to thank him for his kindness. My two brothers and I made our way slowly toward his office. We hoped we would be allowed in his presence. It was the day when the Prime Minister was supposed to go to his holiday retreat in Reesh Khor, a place close to Kabul. He had finished his meetings and was receiving people that Friday.

We came to his residence and as soon as he saw me, Ghulam Jan Suleman, who knew me from my time at the Prime Ministry and later became Ambassador to Poland, came running toward me and embraced me profusely. He took us directly inside, passing the customary security check. We stood there in the receiving room outside the Prime Minister's private quarters. Ghulam Jan said, "Wait here for the Prime Minister. He will be going to Reesh Khor with his family. You pay your respects right here."

After awhile, the Prime Minister came into the

receiving room and as God is my witness, he showed an aura of bravery, friendliness, and exuberant love. I had never met him. I had only seen him at times from afar and just paid my respects. Whatever dealings we had with the Prime Minister, I had them with Mohammad Hashim Khan.

As soon as Shah Mahmud Khan saw me, he embraced me. I tried to kiss his hand. My brothers also came forward. The first words he said to us were, "Aghai (Mr.) Khalili, you are as clean as a mirror (an Afghan saying, like "clean as a whistle"). Your antagonists tried their best to paint you with a dirty brush, but could not do anything, only fail miserably. His Highness has released you. The orders came from Mazar-i-Sharif."

He continued. "I would congratulate you; however, there is one impediment. In my opinion it is advisable you go to Kandahar for a few days. I will also visit Kandahar for inspection and will meet and greet you there. Just think of it as if you are taking off on a long vacation for three or four months. You understand how difficult it is for me here. We have a family situation and family contact to maintain. I am bound to respect my older brother and sacrifice this for him."

I understood what he was saying, and I replied, "You are right. I would not want to see any conflict engulf your family and create any bad blood."

"I also have a request," I added. "You are respecting your older brother. I also love my younger brothers. I am the one who has been accused. They have nothing to do with this. I will go to Kandahar or leave Afghanistan or go anywhere you want to send me. Your order is most welcome to me. However, my two brothers have had nothing to do with this. They are innocent. They are not even accused. Their only fault is they are my brothers."

He said, "Don't worry. They are pardoned from this very moment. They will not go to Kandahar with you. It's only you who must go."

I thanked him and asked, "What about my wife and my children?"

He said, "Take whomever you like with you. I'm pardoning your brothers. They can stay in Kabul. Whatever salary they were drawing before all this at the Prime Ministry, I will make sure they get it."

We ended our exchange with my greeting, "May God bless you and keep your presence in our nation. And may you have health and dignity."

I tried to assure myself, thinking, what's the difference between living in Kabul or Kandahar? The Prime Minister left for Reesh Khor. The honking of his vehicle and the exhaust from the car mixed with our prayers. We came to our house and thank God, my brothers were relieved of any pressure.

Goya Saheb and other friends came to visit and find out how everything went. I told them, "I have to go to Kandahar."

They all said, "Why don't you wait a few days? Sardar Najibullah Khan is visiting Egypt. He will be back soon and will stop your exile to Kandahar."

I answered, "No, I do not want to put my friend through this inconvenience."

The wife of Najibullah Khan, who was the daughter of Amir Habibullah Khan Seraj, was also eagerly inquiring about my welfare. I received messages from Kohdaman and Kohistan that the people wanted to come and see me. I sent a messenger back, saying, "Not at all. You don't have to come here. It may be damaging to you and me." I did not want Shah Mahmud Khan to have a conflict with his brother, and I did not want people to think I was up to something else.

We had hardly any supplies at home. My wife said, "When you were in prison, some intelligence people came continuously for four or five nights. Somebody sent a report that between your books, you had some damaging documents you had written. Even though your daughter was lying there, sick, and it was winter time, they asked us to move from the warm room to another. Then they would take your books down from the shelf and go through them, page by page. They found nothing."

"These books are becoming my enemy," I said. "Since I'm going to Kandahar, I might as well sell all my books before I leave."

I asked Goya Saheb if he could help me sell my books. He protested. "Why?"

I said, "Please help me to do this. If you don't help me sell them, I will burn them."

Goya Saheb went to the Bank-e-Mille (national bank) to talk to the bank president, Mr. Majid Zabuli. Mr. Zabuli sent a team of appraisers to look at my books and put a price on them. By then, I had only 1,200 to 1,300 books left. The appraisers gave us 3,000 to 4,000 Afghanis and took my books away to Bank-e-Mille. This was the second time my books were taken from my home. The first time, it was my father's library, which was pillaged and destroyed. Now, I was forced to get rid of my books. There's no doubt Mr. Zabuli was very helpful.

It was the month of Qaus (November to December). My younger brother, Mohammad Osman Khan, had a mental disorder and insisted he go with me to Kandahar. No matter how I reasoned with him, he would not accept it. I had no choice but to take him with me.

His daughter was very sick with a childhood disease – chicken pox or measles. I said, "Let's wait for a few days until she recuperates." However, some low ranking official, without the knowledge of Shah Mahmud Khan, insisted we leave right away. They brought a large truck for us and asked us to use it for our family and our belongings to travel to Kandahar. With a heavy heart, I parted from my dearly loved Kabul. I took leave of my beloved friends. The day we left I took my brother's sick daughter in my arms and left for Kandahar. It was the Day of Ashura, the 10th day of Moharram (the day of mourning for the martyrdom of Hussain ibn Ali, the grandson of Mohammad, who was martyred at the Battle of Karbala, 680 A.D.). I said, "Think of the hard times the family of the Prophet, PBUH, had to go through on this day, when they had nothing to drink. And this little beam in my arms may die of this cold. We cannot go against the will of God." We got into the lorry and left for our destination. Mr. Ghulam Haidar Adalat, who later became the Minister of Agriculture, brought a .22 caliber gun as a gift and gave it to me. He belonged to the Mohammed Zai tribe and was from Kohdaman.

We Leave for Exile to Kandahar

We left and continued on our journey. It was a long ride. We reached Ghazni in the evening. The city of King Sultan Mahmood was visible from afar. Some of the houses were dark, and some had shimmering lights.

City of Ghazni is not the same; that I saw in the years past.
What has befallen that this year it has changed?

I was perplexed about where we should spend the night. To whose house should we go? At that time the road passed in front of the Mausoleum of Sanai (Hakim Sanai, the famous Persian Sufi poet from Ghazna, author of the mystical epic *Hadiqat al Haqiqa – The Walled Garden of Truth* – who lived between the 11th and 12th century and died in 1131). The Mausoleum was close to the Ghazni Hotel, which Amanullah Khan had built. There was a gentleman standing in front of it. I thought he was waving at every vehicle coming from Kabul and waved them to stop in front of it. To my alarm, I thought he might be stopping me only, maybe to send us back to Kabul and maybe to jail. Lo and behold, he did stop our truck and waved us to the side. He yelled out, "Is Khalil Khan in this truck?"

I answered, "Yes, please go ahead, I am Khalilullah Khan."

He asked, "Where are you going?"

I said, "I'm trying to find a place to pass the night."

He said, "Qamarul Banat, the wife of Shah Mahmud Khan, the Prime Minister, called us in advance. She has ordered three rooms be reserved for you and your family, and I am responsible for that. We have prepared dinner for you as well as the rooms." He added, "The whole of Ghazni is your home. If this hotel was not available, my house was at your service." I have forgotten his name, but we had found a comfortable place. We were cold and tired.

The hotelier guided the truck to the hotel parking, and we disembarked, the women and children too, and went to the rooms, which had been preheated in the Afghan way.

We had brought two big pots of food with us from Kabul and asked the hotelier to share our food with the others. We distributed one and kept the other pot for ourselves for the journey. The hotel had also prepared good food. Qamarul Banat called from Kabul to confirm we were in the hotel and had reached there safely. The hotelier picked up the phone and assured her that everything was fine, and we were her guests. Qamarul Banat said, "Make sure you tell him that he is my guest." I said to her, "May God bless you, the Prime Minister and your children, and keep you safe in his care."

The Shrine of Hakim Sanai (11th-12th century poet, died 1131)

As soon as I was done eating my dinner I was overcome with the desire to go to the shrine of Hakim Sanai. I performed my ablutions, picked up a flashlight, and started walking to the mausoleum of the sage. I was murmuring to myself, "Let me go to the land of Sanai, to the place of one who has said:

You may have heard repeatedly the attributes of Rome and China;
Get up and come to the land of Sanai and see the beauty for yourself."

I was telling myself,

I'm going to one who has no legs, yet the whole sky is under his feet;
I'm going to one who has no arms, yet the whole world is under his hands.
Throw away your crown and get rid of the throne.
These are the men of God, about whom it is said:
My poem is not just a poem, but it is the world.
My poetry is not just poetry, but a vast teaching.

This was especially true of me, because I looked up to this sage, who was a learned jewel of this land and about whom I wrote a book.

When I reached his Shrine, I could see the lights were on. Mullah Abdul Razaq, who was the caretaker or guardian of the shrine, was sitting there, wearing his old clothing. As soon as he saw me he got up and started weeping and came running toward me and said, "You did the right thing by coming here, my son." I was in the habit, in trying times, of reciting from memory the writings of Hazrat Sheikh Abdul Hassan Shazli (one of the founders of Sufism in Egypt, died 657 AH). Now, I started murmuring about him. I began to feel as if the stones of this shrine were reading to me; the walls and the doors were talking to me. I had some money and presented it as a gift to Mullah Razaq. He said, "It is not possible for me to accept money from you. I will give *you* money. I will give you anything you want. You have the right over the Shrine of Hazrat Sanai. (Hazrat is a title of respect that literally means "Prophet.") The servants of Hakim Sanai are obligated to you."

By the time I was done praying, he had already sent his son out to bring some dry fruits for me. There were a few Ghazni apples also. He wrapped them up in a piece of cloth, which I took from him. I took it back and gave it to my children. We spent the night at Ghazni and in the morning, we left for Kandahar.

What a journey it was! The farther we drove away from Kabul the heavier I felt banishment, poverty, and humbleness closing in on me. I had friends in many cities in Afghanistan. I had friends in Mazar-i-Sharif, in Kataghan, in Herat. I think they knew I might have no contacts in Kandahar, which was why I was being exiled there. I had lived very briefly in Kandahar before this. I did not know more than a couple of people there. Thoughts ran through my head. How am I going to live and socialize in Kandahar? My daughters, my son, and my wife were crying out intermittently, "Where are we headed to?"

We kept traveling, and finally, we reached a place called Qalat. I left the truck and tried to find a place where I could make a phone call from to the Deputy Governor of Kandahar and ask his permission to stay the night somewhere in the city.

I came to a room, opened the door, and there was a man with beard sitting on a cot, trying to stay warm in front of a small stove in which he had built a fire. There was a telephone hanging on the wall. We exchanged greetings, but he was very nonchalant. The room was full of smoke. He asked, "Why are you here this evening?"

I said, "It's not evening yet. It is only mid-afternoon."

He said, "I don't know these things. What I know is that this is not the working hours. I only work until three o'clock. After that, I don't work. In winter, civil servants work until three o'clock only." His way of speaking did not seem to be very literate.

I told him, politely, "I have to talk to the Deputy Governor of Kandahar, if you can, please connect me."

He replied, "Who are you, and why should I connect you to Deputy Governor?"

I tried to avoid answering him directly, but he insisted. Finally, I put my hand in my pocket and took out a few 20 or 30 rupee notes and slipped them under the cushion he was sitting on. He changed his attitude and became friendly and agreed to connect me to Kandahar. I told him to make sure I speak directly to the Deputy Governor. He said, "I cannot do that."

I said, "Okay, can you try to get me the Police Commander, Akbar Khan?"

He knew him and asked the operator to dial Akbar Khan.

When Akbar Khan heard my voice, he recognized me and was very courteous. He connected me right away to Qasim Khan, the Deputy Governor. Qasim Khan was the first cousin of Sardar Mohammad Hashim Khan.

Qasim Khan used to work at the Prime Ministry as the Director of the Second Secretariat Division. We were friends and used to be together from morning to evening. His father was the brother of Sardar Mohammad Osman Khan, a humble, religious, and pious man who avoided being in the presence of Mohammad Hashim Khan. He used to say he abhorred going to the Prime Minister's to eat lunch and felt it was *haram* (prohibitive) to do that.

Osman Khan was a writer and a literary man who appreciated the value of education. He studied poetry and spent his younger days in India. He was handsome and tall; people could recognize him from far away. He was respected by all.

Because he was related to Hashim Khan, Qasim Khan was appointed as Administrator in Jalalabad, the capital of the Nangarhar province. After a few years, he was transferred to Kandahar as Deputy Governor. The position of Deputy Governor of Kandahar was a very important one and was only second to Kabul.

At the present time, I was an exiled man accompanied by my family, trying to talk to him on the phone. I was not sure if he would accommodate me or even return my greeting. I doubted if he would even recognize me in this poor state of affairs. He had an influential job and was surrounded by powerful people who may have changed his attitude.

Anyway, the operator connected me to the police commander who connected me to Qasim Khan, who sounded as if he was emulating the voice of Sardar Mohammed Hashim Khan. He said on the other side, "Who is this?"

I said, "I am Khalilullah."

Even though he recognized me, he said, "Which Khalilullah?"

I said, "I am the same Khalilullah who worked with you at the Prime Ministry and later was imprisoned and now I have been exiled."

Finally, he acknowledged me. He said, "Yes, I know. I've heard you've been exiled. Now, what can I do for you?"

I recited this verse from the poet Kaleem (a respected and renowned poet):

I am like a dove whose feathers have fallen and is seeking refuge;
How long will the tall cedar tree continue to wrestle with me?

I don't know if this verse affected him or not; however, he answered: "I have an empty place here for you. You can come spend the night, but that's it. There's nothing more I can do. In Kandahar, there are no houses available for rent. And the government has not sent me instructions to find a place for you. The government here has no official place in which I could allow you to live. You must try to find a place for yourself." He hung up.

I turned around and saw the operator who had assisted me with the telephone had gotten off the cot and was balancing on crutches in his right and left hands. I could see he only had one leg. He was crying. He said, "My apologies, I did not recognize you!" He ran with his crutches toward me and kissed my hand. He said, "Agha (sir), I am from Haji Peek in Kohdaman, which is near Hussain Kot, the place of your father. I am the nephew of Akhund Mir Azam Shah."

I recognized him. His uncle was my Akhund too (theologian or mullah who teaches religious and prayer rites and the Holy Koran). He used to teach us both. His father and his uncle had lived for a long time at my father's place.

He was surprised and said, "You have been exiled to Kandahar?"

I replied, "Yes, that's what the destiny has brought me, and what God wants."

He pleaded, "Please forgive me, I was not very respectful." He pulled the rupee notes from under the cushion to return them to me.

I insisted he just keep them. He said, "No, I cannot."

He pulled his wallet out of his shirt and added 40 to 50 rupees to the notes and stuck all of it in my pocket, too. He said, "Take it as an offering for you. If I knew that you were coming, I would have had a lamb sacrifice in front of you (Afghan custom of respect for when someone comes to your home)."

I responded, "Don't do anything, just do me a favor. Whenever I need to call Kabul for any reason, help me out there."

He answered, "I have been, and I will be, at your

service."

Section Four

Starting Life in Kandahar

We left the operator's room in Qalat and resumed our journey to Kandahar, which we reached after sunset. The shimmering lights of the City of Ahmad Shah Baba (1722-1772) attracted us from far away. For us, it was a sad picture and a very sorrowful moment for my family. They were already crying and homesick. I was thinking, "Where will I be buried if I die?" I worried about whom I'd be dealing with and what would happen to my family. Will we be going to prison or will we be living with somebody? I worried I would never see my relatives again. I worried I would never see Kabul again. I missed the spring waters of Kohdaman and thought about how I'd been separated from everyone. I am an exile. I have been accused of something. The people will look down at us. We had an older lady with us. She was wailing and lamenting in a loud voice, and my wife and children would follow her. What a dreadful night it was. And Marie, you were next to me.

Finally, we reached entrance to the City of Ahmad Shah Baba. There were a few people standing there who stopped our truck to welcome us with lanterns and gaslights. I learned these people were from Kohdaman and Kohistan who had been exiled before this time in Kandahar. While they were growing up in exile, their fathers died in the local prison, and now they were young men with beards, welcoming us. I talked to them, recognized them, and embraced them. I said, "I have empathy for you, I know what you went through." Unfortunately, you cannot do anything. This class of people is very much oppressed. We walked together and came to a courtyard from the Herat door entrance to Kandahar as per instructions of the Deputy Governor.

I noticed my cousin, Mohammad Islam Khan Maihan, was also there. I asked him, "Where were you?"

He said, "I came here a week ago. I traveled on my bike all the way from Kabul, so I could reach here before you and be here for you when you need me."

346

I also saw a man from a respected and spiritual Sayed family (related to the Prophet). His forefathers were very kind to us. His name was Sayed Mohammad Ayub. He was a God-fearing pious man who had hundreds and hundreds of disciples. His disciples had also come to see us and reached Kandahar before us. People knew him in Kandahar, and he came there to help me.

Finally, we made it to our designated house. It was a disastrous place. I didn't think we would be able to live there. I don't blame the Deputy Governor because in Kandahar at that time it was a difficult to find a place to live. I was very gloomy about this situation. My wife and my children started crying again when they saw the place. It was a house with a big courtyard and two rooms. A little while later, a young man in black dress approached. He was brandishing a gun in his holster. For a moment I thought he would take me to the Kandahar prison. My wife was duly intimidated and upset and said, "If they take you to the prison there's no reason for us to continue to live. We'll sneak some medication so you can kill yourself in prison and try to kill ourselves. Life is not worth living in under these circumstances."

I said, "Let's wait and see."

The man came forward and directly approached me. My heart sank. Instead of saying anything, he caught hold of my hand and kissed it. I was taken aback. I asked, "Who are you?"

He said, "My name is Zikria, and I'm the son of Sayed Khudadaad Agha." God is great! This Sayed Khudadaad Agha belonged to a respected Sayed family of Kabul. He was one of four brothers: Sayed Khudadaad Agha, Sayed Maqsood Agha, Sayed Ahmad Agha, and Sayed Masood Agha. These were people who had participated in the War against the British. They were a learned, literary, and intelligent people. They had left Afghanistan during the time of Sardar Mohammad Ayub Khan and Sardar Mohammad Yaqoob Khan. They had lived in India and returned during the time of Habibullah Khan Seraj. They were highly dignified and respected in the court of Amir Habibullah Khan. This Sayed Khudadaad Agha was a good friend of my father's. Amanullah Khan also had respect for him. He knew my father to the extent that upon the execution of my father, he had exchanged some harsh words with Amanullah Khan. Since people of Afghanistan had a lot of respect for these Sayed families, Amanullah Khan did not condemn him. He was an eloquent speaker and also had a sense of humor. King Zahir Shah respected him.

I asked Sayed Zikria, "What is your designation here?"

He said, "I am *aide de camp* to the Deputy Governor. The Deputy Governor has sent me with his greetings and has also sent some food through his office."

As he spoke, tears rolled down his cheeks, may God bless him. He sat with us while the women and children went to the other room. Slowly, the room filled with those who had come from Kabul to greet us, including Sayed Ayub Khan, Mohammad Islam Khan Maihan, and Abdul Mohammad Khan, my maternal uncle. He was a cousin of my mother and a cousin of Abdul Rahim Khan. There were about 20 to 25 people in the room, and the food brought to us from Deputy Governor's office was sufficient for all of us.

We passed the night and got up early in the morning. We performed ablutions and offered prayers. Abdul Ahad Khan, Administrator in the Arghandab district, was the son of Brigadier Abdul Salaam Khan, my eldest uncle. Abdul Ahad Khan was not just my cousin, but also the husband of my wife's oldest sister, Dilbar (Shah Jan) the eldest daughter of Abdul Rahim Khan. They also came. When we were in prison in Kabul, Mohammad Hashim Khan summoned Abdul Ahad Khan to be brought to Kabul in chains. However Qasim Khan, the Deputy Governor of Kandahar, vouched for him and kept him in Kandahar at his post. It was very strange how he escaped our fate. Abdul Ahad Khan was a very honest man. He was my student. And here, in our first night in Kandahar, he slept in the room and passed the night with us.

The Shrine of the Cloak of Prophet Mohammad

Since I did not know my way around, I woke up Abdul Ahad. It was still dark, and he did not want me to go. He asked, "Where are we going? It's not yet morning."

I said, "I would like to go to the Shrine of the Cloak of the Prophet (*Khirqa Mubarak* or Sacred Cloak) and would like to offer morning prayers there."

He gave in, and we walked to the Shrine and its mosque. There were 300 to 400 people already gathered for early morning prayers. After the prayers, we walked over to the special room, which held the *Khirqa*. There, we prayed, and I put all my trust in the Prophet (PBUH).

This *Khirqa*, the authentic cloak worn by the Prophet of Islam, has a history. The *Khirqa* was passed on from the Prophet Mohammad to Maavia (King of Syria at time of the intra-Islam war). Maavia passed the *Khirqa* to his Companions and from there to the family of Abbasis, and from there, to the Osmania dynasty of Turkish kings, and from there, to Amir Taimur Shah of Khorasan. The Khirqa went from Samarqand to Bokhara, and Ahmad Shah Baba brought it back to Kandahar. When Amad Shah Baba conquered Bokhara he did not take anything from there. He struck a bond of peace with the King of Bokhara and took the *Khirqa* as a gesture of trust, as a gift, and placed it in a silver box.

Today, from Bokhara to Kabul, you can see wherever they had stopped for the night on their journey to bring the *Khirqa* back a shrine has been built. Even the Zulfiqar stone, which is near the Shrine of Sakhi in Kabul, is said to be a place where the *Khirqa* spent the night.

This is a story I have heard. It is a popular belief, but I am not sure about it. When Ahmad Shah Baba wanted to bring the *Khirqa* to Kandahar, he asked one of his ministers, eminent Shah Wali Khan, who was considered to be a scholar, about its authenticity. Ahmad Shah Baba was himself scholar and a learned person. He was a poet in both Persian and Pashto.

Minister Shah Wali Khan sent a message to a man of

letters, a sage, and a great scholar of the time, Mian Faqirullah Shikarpuri, who lived in Shikarpur, Peshawar (a city in the north of Pakistan, bordering Afghanistan). Mian Faqirullah had a collection of rare books. In his collection, he had a book titled "Details about the Cloak" (*Al Burqa-fizikril-Khirqa*), which was written by Jalaluddin Sewati. He also had other books and magazines to support his conviction. He wrote back to Shah Wali Khan "there is no doubt in my mind this is the *Khirqa* of the Prophet (PBUH)."

When Ahmad Shah brought the *Khirqa* to Kandahar he willed that upon his death the *Khirqa* should be placed in a gold holder and hung inside the Dome of his mausoleum. The scholars and religious elite of Kandahar refuted this. They said it wasn't acceptable because a precedent would be set and any future king could will the same for their mausoleum. The sacred *Khirqa* would become a toy in the hands of the kings.

They suggested a separate display place for the *Khirqa*. During his lifetime Ahmad Shah agreed with the scholars and built a separate place for it. Taimur Shah also improved the mausoleum and so did the kings who followed, including the Mohammad Zai kings in the 20th century. There were stanzas from the poetry of Sufi Abdul Hameed Khan Kandahari inscribed all around the dome. The *Khirqa* itself was placed in a box.

After my exile, I visited the *Khirqa Mubarak* in the company of King Zahir Shah to see if for myself. When people see the *Khirqa* they are so influenced by it that some see it as being green, some see it as red, and some see it as purple.

When I talked to the Curator of the place he said it has a camel color, made out of camel wool, and is like a long garment or tunic. On the two sides it has long chalks and is open.

I remember one narration where the Prophet prayed with his hands high above the sky, and it is said that his both sides could be seen, and this *Khirqa* is the kind that would do that while he may have been wearing this.

I have written a beautiful ode in praise of the *Khirqa*

and Kandahar. Dr. Mohammad Iqbal, the famous Urdu and Persian poet, visited Afghanistan during the time of Nader Shah in 1311-1312 (1932 approximately). He visited Kandahar and came to the shrine to pay respect to the *Khirqa*. He also has a poem about it.

Some Challenges of Exile Are Eased, by God's Grace

Finally, we finished our affair and completed our visit to the *Khirqa*. We returned to our abode and from there, left to see the Deputy Governor, with whom I had spent seven to eight years in Kabul. We were stopped outside his office and asked to wait. We sent our message inside and waited for about half an hour. His Excellency invited us inside. When we entered his quarters, he only half-heartedly stood up to shake hands with us, then waved us to sit down at a distance from him.

I could tell he was trying to quickly establish his authority so I would respect him in front of others. This was not the time for me to come in unannounced, to joke, or to relax in front of him, to call him Qasim Jan Agha, or to expect special favors. I should address him as Mr. Deputy Governor and proceed with caution.

We sat down, and he said, "Things happen. Abdul Rahim Khan was at fault, and you are at fault. You were careless. You did not do the right thing. You were taken to prison and, thank God, you came out in one piece."

I bit my tongue while he tried to show his authority and power by admonishing us. I said, "Yes, thanks to God, we came out of the prison unscathed."

I mentioned a similar incident, which happened during the time of Sardar Mohammad Osman Khan when he was Deputy Governor of Kandahar. People were arrested in error, without any proof. They were released, and the Deputy Governor apologized to them.

Qasim Khan was arrogant, replying, "You should be happy you're not being thrown in jail again. You should thank God you're not in prison." Then, he moved away from this, changing the subject. "No matter how much I've tried to find a place for you, I could not," he made excuses. "And a salary of 300 Afghanis has been approved for you from Kabul."

"Only 300 Afghanis?" I asked, stunned by the news. "We are almost 17 to 18 people with my family."

"It's not in my hand," he dismissed me. "This is what Kabul has done, and I cannot discuss it."

We were silent. A lean gentleman entered the room. He had a small pointed beard. I recognized him immediately, but he did not recognize me. The Deputy Governor showed respect and addressed him as, "Hakim Saheb Kalan! (Chief Magistrate) Welcome!"

I recognized him as Sayed Ghulam Rasul, Chief Magistrate of Girishk. He was from among the Sayeds of Kunar, one of the respected Sayed families in Afghanistan. He was the son of Sayed Hussain Pascha, the brother of Sayed Hassan Pascha, a senior military officer who was killed in prison.

He did not recognize me. He told the Deputy Governor, "I have come to see you on my way to Girishk. I wanted to have a few private words with you."

The Deputy Governor said to me, "Khalilullah Khan, please leave so I can talk to the Chief Magistrate of Girishk."

As soon as he heard my name, Sayed Ghulam Rasul abruptly stood up and exclaimed with emotion, "Which Khalilullah is this?"

Qasim Khan shrugged, "Oh, you didn't recognize him. He is the son of Mustufi-ul-Momalik Saheb." (Chief Auditor and Finance Minister during the time of King Habibullah Khan Seraj)

Sayed Ghulam Rasul said, "Oh, may God blind me! (Afghan saying of respect) My eyes must be weakening!" He started crying and wailed in a loud voice.

The Deputy Governor asked, "Why are you crying? You should cry in spite of all my efforts, I could not find a place for Khalili to live."

Sayed Ghulam Rasul replied, "Naib-ul-hikooma Saheb! (referring to the Deputy Governor) Please allow me just one day! I'm not going to go to Girishk today, instead I'll go tomorrow."

Qasim Khan said, "No, you must go today."

Sayed Ghulam Rasul said, "Okay, then give me a half hour! I'll go see what I can do. I'll bring a friend to meet Khalilullah Jan." Even though he was older than me, he was calling me Khalilullah Jan out of respect. He rushed out.

The Deputy Governor had a smirk on his face. "By the grace of God he will find a place for you," Qasim Khan said. "Please have a seat outside until the Chief Magistrate comes back. I need to get ready for work."

We went out and sat in the veranda. The sun was warm. There was a big difference between the climate of Kandahar and Kabul. It was the month of Qaus (November to December), and Kabul was frigid, and even Ghazni had fresh snow. Kandahar was like spring. Previously, I had visited Kandahar in summer and fall, but this was different, bathed in sunshine, gorgeous, lush with pomegranates, grapes, and other fruits. Nothing in this beauty was pleasant for me. If I had come to Kandahar of my own free will, I might have been very happy and enjoyed the fruits and the sun; however, being forced to live in exile made even the bright sun sorrowful and gloomy.

The Chief Magistrate returned approximately an hour and a half later. He saw us on the veranda and was smiling. He went straight to the Deputy Governor, and then, we were asked to come in. He said, "Naib-ul-hikooma Saheb, I have a house I had built in the new part of Kandahar that is close to you. I had rented it out for 2000 Afghanis, and the tenant was supposed to move in today. But just now, I went back and gave him 2500 rupees (Afghanis) and apologized. Even though he'd already moved some of his belongings into the house, he agreed when he heard I wanted to give my house to Khalilullah Jan. He felt sorry for him and returned my house to me. Right in front of you, right here, I want to give this house along with all its furnishings, and even take on the responsibility of paying the electrical bills, to the son of Mustufi-ul Momalik." Tears were rolling down his cheeks as he spoke. "The house is his. He can sell it, or he can give it to anyone he wants."

The Deputy Governor was very happy to hear this. I said, "I thank you very much. May God give you many more, and give you health and wealth and long life." My father had a very close relation with his family. I mentioned to Sayed Ghulam Rasul, "Right in front of the Deputy Governor, I appeal to you that I'm not going to take your furnishings or anything else, I'll only take your house."

God works in mysterious ways. I used to think I had no one to rely on in Kandahar. And now here I am, standing in a beautifully built building made of concrete and cement brick, with separate bedrooms, living rooms, family rooms, dining room, an orchard in the back, a garden in front, running water, electricity, and a small pool filled with colorful fish. I could not have expected any more than what I got for a comfortable living. After the execution of my father, I had never lived in a place so beautiful. I realized how compassionate God can be and how things work out. If I had not come to see the Deputy Governor, I would not have met this noble person, Sayed Ghulam Rasul.

There are so many factors, which could have affected a bad turn of events. If he had gone to Girishk a day before, or if I had come a day later, or the house had been already occupied, I would not have found a place to live.

We prayed right there and went back to our home, thanking God for my good fortune. When we arrived, a meal was sent for us from the Deputy Governor's house. We accepted the food and asked them not to bother any more. We told them the day we left Kabul, Abdul Majid Zabuli and another businessman of Kabul named Sher Ahmad had provided me some monetary help.

Sher Ahmad was a good businessman who liked to talk about politics and dabble in political affairs. Unfortunately, he was illiterate. He had his business during the time of Habibullah Khan Seraj and was striving during the time of Amanullah Khan also. He was a fan of Amanullah Khan. When Habibullah Khan Kalakani came to power and I was appointed the head of the Secretariat, Sher Ahmad sought a *firman* from Habibullah Khan Kalakani to allow him to go to Europe to talk to Nadir Shah and seek his allegiance from him. He left, and I helped him get a decree and papers to travel.

He went and joined Nadir Shah against Habibullah Khan Kalakani. He had in the back of his mind that when Nadir Shah took over Kabul, he would appoint him as the Minister of Commerce or some other high-ranking position. Nadir Shah may have had a good excuse not to, because he was illiterate. He used to stamp his documents and letters instead of signing them and had a clerk who would write his letters for him. He would hold a paper and read it upside down until the clerk would point out to him to hold it the right way. Now, Sher Ahmad has come of age and is well experienced in business. He traded horses and camels to India and had an office in Karachi. When I was leaving Kabul, he was kind enough to help me monetarily. Thus, I did have some money to be on my own and to spend on food for family while in Kandahar.

A couple of days later, an old friend named Sayed Jan Khan Mushavir (Advisor) who belonged to Mohammad Zai tribe, came to our house. He was an advisor at the Prime Ministry, and I had worked with him for seven to eight years there. He was filthy rich. In Qalai Mir Akhor, near Kandahar, he owned thousands and thousands of acres of land. He also had pomegranate orchards, vineyards, villas, and other holdings in Kandahar and other places. He was an educated man, ferociously independent, ambitious, and unruly. He posed as a revolutionary. No one could control him. As soon as he heard about my plight, he came to our house. He was very kind to me and brought seven or eight camel loads of famous Kandahar rice called *maranajani*, flour, oil, and other staples needed for our household.

A few days after another gentleman who had heard of our plight came to visit. His name was Ghulam Farooq Khan Kaku, and he belonged to the Ghilzai tribe of Kandahar and was a member of the Kakar family. He was also a businessman of repute there, along with his two or three brothers. Kandahar businessmen had a good life. They own marvelous places and knew how to live comfortably. This gentleman, Haji Ghulam Kaku, was a friend of my father's. He was a tall, well-built man, very handsome with green eyes. The pupils of his eyes were dilated, as if he was using opium. He took me aside and said, "Why didn't you come to my house?"

I said, "I didn't know about you and your house. I'm an exile here."

He responded, "You're not an exile in Kandahar. You've been exiled by the Durranis. The Ghilzai will give you refuge and keep you in comfort here. We will protect you because your father had done a lot of favors to us. He sent us coal, fuel for burning, rice, chicken, and anything else." Haji Ghulam Kaku's camels arrived, and he brought all these things for us. He said, "I wish all your brothers were here."

I answered, "Don't worry. We may have a lot of guests very soon."

I think I should tell this story too. One day we were sitting idly in our house, and a man approached. He had a beard and was wearing typical Afghan shirt and trousers with a scarf on his shoulders. He belonged to a middle class family of Kandahar. The people of Kandahar are conservative Muslims and particular about their religion. Sometimes, they're very conservative as not to speak Persian either. He looked around wildly and came and sat next to me and asked in Pashtu, "Who is the son of Mustufi-ul Momalik? Where is he?"

I said, "Here I am." We exchanged traditional Afghan greetings.

He said, "You owe me something, which I have come to collect."

At least that's what I understood that he said. I kept thinking someone may have instigated this person's approach to me. I wondered, "Who is he, and what do I owe him?" I had never taken anything from Kandahar. I answered, "Well please, go ahead and let me know."

He introduced himself. He said, "I am the son of the person whose sister was hit by your father's car, and she died."

I became very worried and panicky. I thought he might claim murder charges against me, or maybe he would like to take one of my daughters (the traditional Afghan way of compensation for an accidental death – blood money).

Marie, I'm talking about you. I thought maybe he would take you in return for his father's sister. Almost 30 years had passed since the accident he was talking about. I said, "Well, why don't you tell me what you want?"

He said, "Do you know that your father apologized to my father and extended extreme kindness to him? He awarded my father 30 jeribs of land here in Khodand, near the city of Kandahar." (One jerib is equivalent to 2,000 square meters or 0.494 acre) "The land was owned by the government, and your father paid the state for the land on our behalf. He also gave my father 20,000 rupees (Afghanis) in cash, which was a large amount at that time. At the time, the standard payment for a debt in the case of an accidental death was 7,000 rupees." (Today, according to National Public Radio, Americans are paying thousands of U.S. dollars in blood money to compensate surviving relatives for the deaths of innocent civilians in Iraq and Afghanistan.)

He continued, "Now, we are doing all right and have everything. We have orchards, gardens, and businesses. I receive revenues of 400,000 to 500,000 Afghanis each year from my businesses."

He had confused me by repeating, "You owe me," when really he was trying to explain that he owes us. I asked, "What do you want from me?"

He replied, "All my possessions are at your disposal. My life is at your disposal. My mother has sent me to you. Whatever you need, we are at your service. We can provide you a house, a car, anything else."

I said, "No, thank you. I don't want another house. I don't want another car."

He insisted and brought some supplies. I don't remember very well, but I know he also brought 7,000 to 10,000 rupees. I tried to decline, but he said, "No. Lawfully, this all belongs to you. While you're in Kandahar, I will be giving you this money every year."

Well, I took it. It was a gift from God.

First Automobile in Afghanistan

Let me tell this story too. This is worth listening to.

Amir Habibullah Khan Seraj was the first King of Afghanistan to import an automobile from overseas. The car came with a British driver whose name was Mr. Fennel. He was quartered in Andarabi (a Kabul neighborhood), and he had a wife with him. The people in Kabul called his wife the Maimzan (Lady). Everywhere the Maimzan went the police escorted her. It was a precaution they took, so no one would attack her because of the enmity against the British. Whenever Mr. Fennel completed his duties, he would go straight to his home and close the door. He had an armed guard outside. People in their paranoia would tell Amir Habibullah Khan, "The British have sent this car, and Mr. Fennel to control and kill you."

The first person in Afghanistan who Habibullah Khan appointed to learn how to drive a car was Brigadier Mohammad Azim Khan. He was famous as Ustad Azimo. His family was famous for their involvement in art, culture, engineering, and iron smithing. While the Amir gave Mohammad Azim Khan the military title of Colonel, he was, in fact, illiterate. Yet, he was very smart and sharp and versatile in his profession. He was tall, with a fair complexion, with green eyes, and a small beard. He was very good looking. He had married my father's cousin (father's mother's sister) and that was our relationship and contact with him. He was also our neighbor in Baghban Koocha.

Amir Habibullah Khan told Mr. Fennel, "Colonel Azimo will be your student driver."

Azimo Khan would sit next to Mr. Fennel when he was driving the Amir, and the Amir would sit in the back seat with a couple of other people. At first, the Amir would be upset if the doors of the car were slammed hard. He would tell people, "Go easy on it!" Then, when he was informed that this car needed the doors to be shut hard, he agreed and went along with it.

I remember another small story. One day Mr. Fennel told my father the Maimzan would like to come to his house, see his wife, and observe their life. Since my father was the Minister of Finance and almost the Prime Minister of Afghanistan, he said the Maimzan bought some gifts for his wife. My father agreed to the visit. I remember I was very little, maybe six years old at the time. Traditionally, people had indentured servants, but my father released all of his. We called them uncles and aunts, and the whole household was in their hands. They were empowered.

There was a commotion in our house at the arrival of the Maimzan. The uncles and aunts each wanted to be the person to welcome her. It was decided the wife of Colonel Mohammad Azim, the cousin of my father, should have the honor. The Maimzan was familiar with Colonel Azim's wife because she used to go to his house. She was a very literate lady, well versed in cultural affairs. She knew how to iron clothes, dress up, wear makeup, and do her hair. She was among the enlightened women of Kabul. I think she also knew a little Urdu.

Colonel Azim's wife came to our house and prepared our living room upstairs at the Jahanara Garden (palace). There were gas lanterns placed around the house, along with tables, chairs, and couches, which were covered with a fancy cloth where my mother would sit. I was dressed up in my military uniform, and the American engineer, A.C. Jewett, took a photograph of me wearing it, which was later published in a book compiled from his letters and notes, *An American Engineer in Afghanistan,* in 1948, by Marjorie Jewett Bell.

The cooks prepared a feast for the Maimzan's visit. The lunch included *aashak*-dumplings filled with vegetables, *bolani*-a flat-bread with a vegetable filling, *aash*-a soup with noodles and meat, *qabuli*-a dish of rice with nuts, shredded carrots and raisins, and *naranj palau*-a dish of rice with shredded orange peel, nuts, and lamb. We had a butler named Ali Jan who knew how to arrange these events and arranged the table with western cutlery.

My mother, may God bless her soul, dressed up in traditional clothes and was weighed down with so much jewelry around her neck that she could not stand straight. It was a time when women would cover their faces with a scarf in front of strangers, and there was a discussion as to whether my mother should cover her face even in front of the Maimzan.

The wife of Colonel Mohammad Azim Khan stood at the entrance, ready to welcome the Maimzan. A custom in Kabul at that time was when new guests arrived at your home you sprayed rose water on them. The sprayer containing the rose water looked like a vase with a long neck, about 12 inches long, and a round bowl at the bottom. This was filled with perfume and rose water. My father's rose water sprayer was made of gold with emerald work on the outside. It was said that Bo Bo Jan, the Queen of Afghanistan, famous as Bibi Tajdar, had gifted the rose water sprayer to my father.

As the Maimzan entered, the person in charge of spraying the rose water doused her face with it. Tears welled up in her eyes as the rivulets streaked down her face, carrying her heavy makeup in lines along with it. I remember thinking, "Oh, it looks like little streams of rose water."

The Maimzan looked like she was very upset. There was a large floor-length mirror on one side of the room where she could see herself. She was wearing a long gown. Her waist was very small, and she had a little scarf on her head. Her eyes were green, and she was tall and beautiful.

After she exchanged greetings with my mother she pulled me toward her and sat me down on the couch. I liked her face, and I could smell her perfume. She was being kind to me, and I was enamored with her in the way an innocent child alone can cherish kindness and beauty. Eventually, they went to the dining table for lunch, where I was not invited.

My Father's Automobile

Let me tell you a story about my father's car. After Amir Habibullah Khan, and his sons, the Regent, Amanullah Khan and Inayatullah Khan, I think they had a total of eight to ten cars in the Royal Family. The first person outside of the Royal Family to have a car was my father around 1918. This has been documented in the book based on the notes and letters of A.C. Jewett. The Amir had pressed my father to buy a car, and he did. It was a small Fiat convertible with a canvas top. It could not seat more than four or five people. The car horn was like a small balloon outside of the driver's side, which had to be pressed to honk and warn people. Whenever this car would get as far as the Khairkhana Pass north of Kabul, it could not go across. The driver would be forced to go on foot and bring some water to cool down the engine before proceeding.

My father was very happy to ride in his car. He used to go to Jabalus Seraj and Gul Bahar, a small place north of Kabul (where the first hydroelectric plant was built in Afghanistan) and tour places, inspect the factory of Jabalus Seraj, and meet the people and his family north of Kabul.

Jabalus Seraj had a power plant, and A.C. Jewett, who was an engineer, was the first American to come there to establish a factory. My father was the overseer of the project, while there was a caretaker from the Court who looked after the day-to-day affairs along with Engineer Jewett.

Whenever Jewett would come to Kabul he would stay with us. My teacher would tell me to be rude to him because he was *kafir* (infidel) and being rude to him would be rewarded in the hereafter. Jewett was so much affected by this he wrote about it in his letters and notes. His experiences in Afghanistan were later published in a book, along with my picture. He mentioned me as rude and spoiled.

My father hired a driver from India to drive his car. His name was Edward. People used to call him Edward Khan. I think he was a Christian from Bombay (modern day Mumbai). He was Indian by origin, but became a Christian. The fuel for the car was benzene, which used to come on a cart pulled by oxen via Peshawar from Karachi (currently in Pakistan). It would take up to three and a half hours from Kabul to Jabalus Seraj by car. (Currently, it takes about an hour to drive to Jabalus Seraj and back. The roads have drastically improved.)

When we would drive from Kabul to Jalalabad, we had to spend the night along the way. When my father used to go to Kohdaman and Kohistan, there would be a commotion and chaos among people, who would rush to see the car.

I remember a funny story. One day, an older lady was travelling in the car with us. My mother was in the car as was my uncle, Abdul Rahim Khan. We were going to our retreat in Hussain Kot, north of Kabul. On the way to Hussain Kot, my mother was not feeling well, and we came across an elephant. This old lady said, "Please! Close the eye of the car so he doesn't go crazy and attack the elephant in front of us!"

My Father Has an Accident

One evening during Ramadan (one of the five pillars of Islam, preceding Eid ul fitr) my father was coming home from Chardehi. It was close to Iftar time (breaking of the fast), and the car slipped off the road and hit a poor little girl about eight to nine years old who had a clay water pot in her hand. She was killed. When my father came home, he was very upset and hardly broke his fast with a piece of date and a slice of bread. He turned to us and said, "Why don't you go ahead and break your fast and eat. I am preoccupied with something. I have to tell the Amir Saheb about this accident myself." He was very edgy.

After the evening prayers he had calmed down. He had called Amir Habibullah Khan Seraj. At that time, the telephone was a very privileged possession, and few people had it. We had a telephone at home. My father told Amir Saheb, "Tonight, I have committed a crime. My driver killed a girl by hitting her with the car. You have the right to tell me what to do."

The Amir said, "I will appoint a committee to investigate the incident to establish if the girl had inadvertently run into the road or walked into the path of the car. If that is the case, then you have not committed a crime; neither has your driver."

The investigation established the little girl had strayed into the path of the car. In the report it said that the girl was walking on the right side toward the oncoming car. In Kabul at the time, every major traffic crossing had a tall traffic stand. The stand's lower three meters were black; the upper three meters were red, and at the top was a white iron hand with a finger pointing to the left. The writing on the hand said, "Please walk to your left." If she had been walking on the left, it would have been the fault of the driver.

My father called in the father of the dead girl. He learned the man had been in jail in Kabul for a while as an accomplice to a murder and had been newly released three or four days before. The family was getting ready to move to Kandahar when this unexpected accident occurred. And just as I had mentioned it earlier, my father gave them land, money, comfort, and apology. My father took them to court and had them sign a release from responsibility. They forgave him. Until they agreed to accept his apology, condolences, and forgive him, he was uncomfortable.

The son of the same man met us in different circumstances in Kandahar. He would come once a month to visit and make sure we were comfortable. He was a wealthy businessman and an agriculturalist. He used to bring us fresh fruits and nuts, especially pomegranates, figs, and *shakarpara* (dried apricots). He would invite us at least a couple of times a month to his place for a fish rendezvous.

Kandahar and Its Shrines

Two or three months passed during our stay at Kandahar. I was very restless, bored with no meaningful work to do from morning to evening. Since the city of Kandahar is rich in holy shrines and cultural and historic heritage, I decided I would go exploring and see everything I could.

The ancient city of Kandahar was plundered by the Safavids (1501-1722) whose dynasty united all of Persia and controlled Iran. The Chilzina or the Forty Steps of Kandahar (a rock-cut chamber on the northern side of the old citadel that is accessible by 40 steps) is an historic place, which still has the Persian inscriptions of the Moghul Emperor in the 16th century inscribed on the stones.

The shrine of sage Baba Wali Saheb, a 15th century Sufi saint who also has a town named after him in Pakistan, is also in Kandahar. I do not remember very well, but I think Baba Wali died during the time of Shah Rukh (Turkic conqueror), son of Timur (King) Korgan in 1529. All the Timur Amirs paid a great respect to this sage. On every stone around his shrine, there are inscriptions. It was very difficult for me to read these writings, as they were written during the time of the Timur Kings. This shrine is located on a hilltop or mound, and the new Kandahar hotel had been built close to it. This is really a holy shrine. (It cost millions to reconstruct.)

There are other shrines in Kandahar, too, like Khwaja Chahar Shanba (Wednesday), Khwaja Yak Shanba (Sunday), and Sheenghari Baba. A little further away from Kandahar is a village called Karz and quite a few shrines are located there (Karz is the birthplace of Hamid Karzai, born in 1957, the current President of Afghanistan). I recalled I had a friend in Kabul who was from Karz. His name was Khair Mohammad Khan, famous as Khairo Jan. He was an advisor to Sardar Mohammad Hashim Khan. When Sardar Hashim came to Kandahar during the time of Amir Habibullah Khan, there was an attempt on his life. It was this Khairo Jan who saved him. Later, he was kept in Kabul like an esteemed prisoner at the Prime Ministry. He was with us there. He was a literate person, with a gray beard; very respected, and he knew the Holy Koran by heart.

We went to Karz and visited the shrine. There, we met Mohammad Ali Agha. He was a spiritual and pious man. We also met Abdul Latif Jan Sahebzada, a man who resembled a Darvish (someone following a Sufi Muslim ascetic path, known for extreme poverty and austerity). He had an impressive personality.

There was another Darvish there who would not see anyone. When I sent him a message introducing myself as an exile here from Kabul who would like to visit with him, he accepted and invited me inside the *ziarat* (shrine). He had a special room there, which was well furnished and thick with the fragrance. He himself was very clean, well groomed, and dressed well. He looked mature, like he had attained his age. I tried to hold his hand to kiss it, but he did not allow me. I sat next to him. He appeared to be an intellectual and may have gone through a few years of *riazat* (educational seclusions). He had also performed Hajj (pilgrimage to Mecca). He had taken a vow not to see anyone and not to leave his quarters any more. He had even allocated a grave for himself just outside his room. He was popularly known to the Kandaharis as Ghulam Mohiuddin Agha. There was a custom in Kabul to use the word *Jan* for younger people and *Khan* for people of ripe age. In Kandahar, *Jan* was used for younger people and also with people of ripe age, out of love and respect for them.

Ghulam Mohiuddin Agha prayed for me and for Afghanistan. He said Mohammad Hashim had oppressed many people. "May God give Shah Mahmud the ability to soothe the wounds of the people," he prayed. He talked about my father and the contact he had with him. He said, "Your father sent letters to my father and also gave him gifts of *posteen* (firs)."

Ghulam Mohiuddin Agha gave me a collection of rare incantations or *shazli* (chants and prayers) and also gave me permission to read them (it was customary to give someone a prayer and the permission to read it). He also said that earlier, he had read *Hizbul -Bahr* (*Litany of the Sea*) and had permission to do so from Torah Sayed Mahmood.

From there I went to Khairo Jan's house. It was the time for evening prayers. He sat outside with guards posted. Not everybody was allowed to come in. He was a wealthy man who owned orchards and was very influential. The people in Kandahar trusted him, and he drew a lot of respect. We were allowed to go in.

We went inside and saw Khairo Jan sitting with his long gray beard, down to his navel. His head hairs were all gray and locks of hair lay on his shoulders. He was a handsome man, though it seemed as though he had caught a cold that day. He had about 10 to 12 students around him. He was among the Khans of Kandahar and was not a man of letters or a spiritual title, though he used to teach the Holy Koran to students. He also taught interpretation, and the students listened with rapt attention. I offered my greetings and sat in a corner. He didn't recognize me.

Something I said during the interpretation drew his attention. He looked at me and recognized my voice. We had spent seven or eight years together at the Prime Ministry. The reason he did not recognize me maybe because when I was working in Kabul I used to shave and since being in prison and exile in Kandahar I had let my beard grow up to my chest. My hair had also grown long.

He said, "Are you Khalilullah?"

I said, "Yes."

I could tell he was excited to have me there. He told his students it was time to end that day's lessons, and told them to "pray for this gentleman who is here with us." He said, "Come back tomorrow so we can continue our lesson."

He stood up and embraced me. He ordered tea and Kandahari fruits to be brought in, especially the famous ones: *shandokhani* raisins from Kandahar, green raisins from Karz, and almonds of Kandahar, which had made a name for themselves. All these fruits, along with dried figs, were brought in beautiful fruit platters and bowls and placed on the table. His sons stood in respect as servants to their father. We started to small talk, and he acknowledged he was not sure I was still alive. "It's a miracle from God," he said. "What happened to my friend, Abdul Rahim Khan?"

I replied, "He's still in jail."

Khairo Jan had a few tears in his eyes. He said, "This is what you get for relentless service to Afghanistan." After an hour or so, I took his permission to leave. He took my address, and I had a feeling why he was doing that. A day or two later, just as the custom was, a camel full of supplies of rice, oil, fruits, and a couple of lambs, were brought to our house.

One day the Deputy Governor invited me to his office. When I got there, he asked me to accompany him in his car. He wanted to show me what progress he had made in Kandahar.

The first place he took me was the Kandahar prison project. Sardar Hashim Khan loved to build and establish prisons in all the cities. These prisons were constructed using the same system of principles. This was a system he created. He thought he was omniscient. Sardar Hashim Khan built his prisons so prisoners were isolated and could not contact others. They were strongholds with no way of breaking out. The façades were dressed up, and the inside remained in ancient conditions, based on the darkest of rules, with dim and dingy cells holding the prisoners whom they considered to be the most notorious, dangerous, and prominent.

After inspection of the prison, the Deputy Governor got into the car ahead of me. I told myself, "Why not talk to him and tell him a few things I have on my heart, just like good old days?" I said aloud, "Qasim Jan Agha."

He turned his face toward me with contempt and distain. He snapped, "What do you want?"

I spoke frankly. "You asked me to accompany you to see some projects, and you brought me here first to the prison. I have seen prison in Kabul. I am afraid of it."

He responded, "No, I brought you here so you can witness how we try to comfort prisoners in Kandahar. You have a lot of visitors at your residence. Be careful of your surroundings." With that, he broke into laughter.

I said, "Thank you. God is great, and I'm being careful."

As we were driving, four or five sheep wandered into the middle of the road. A very young shepherd was tending them. The driver pressed the horn several times, but the little boy did not understand. Finally, the driver stopped the car. The police in the escort car behind us also stopped and got out. They walked toward the shepherd boy to admonish him. They got hold of the boy and tried to slap him, telling him, "Why didn't you get out of the road?" The young boy was screaming and crying.

I was very upset. "Tell your men to stop harassing the little boy," I told the Deputy Governor.

He acknowledged what I said and asked his men to stop. I saw an opening and spoke.

"You just showed me the high walls and the strong gate of the prison. I just showed you the tears of oppression. People who go to the prison have no defense against the high walls and have no faith to destroy them. These are the tears that will join together to create a flood of blood, which will destroy the prison."

The Deputy Governor responded, "I will request, Khalilullah Khan, while you are here in Kandahar and while I am here, you hold back your tongue. I love you. You have adversaries. There are a lot of spies around. I don't want you to be subjected to treatment that is uncalled for because you have made yourself vulnerable. And God forbid, I may not be able to save you from it." I thanked him and left for my home.

First Visit of Shah Mahmud Khan to Kandahar (1327 Solar/1948)

A few months later the news came that Sardar and Commander in Chief Shah Mahmud Khan, the Prime Minister, would be coming to Kandahar and Herat on a tour. It was unbelievable how happy the people were at hearing this, especially since he would be inspecting Kandahar projects and would be accessible to anybody. There were no restrictions, and no doors would remain closed. From Rabat-e-Momand to Kandahar is about eight to ten kilometers. All along the way the men, women, and children of Kandahar lined up to welcome him through the gates they had built for this occasion and shouted, "Long live the Father! Long live the Ghazi Commander in Chief!"

The Commander in Chief came, and we went to see him. We were standing in line on one side with the exiles from Kohdaman and Kohistan. The Mohammad Zai family always thought Kandahar to be their home. They were always proud of it. The Prime Minister's motorcade passed by us. I saluted him (*salam*), but he did not recognize me.

After two or three days my wife told me, "It will not reflect well on you, if you don't go to see the Prime Minister who has come here all the way from Kabul. People are going in droves to pay their respects. You may be singled out for being too arrogant, or for not caring about him. Also the salary, which you have is not sufficient enough for us. Why don't you go see him?"

I listened to her words and went to the Prime Minister's residence. There, I saw a friend of mine, Mohammad Anwar Khan, Naib Salar. He belonged to the Noorzai tribe of Farah. He had the assignment of taking people to the Prime Minister and introducing them to him. After greetings I told him, "I would like to see the Prime Minister."

"He's very busy today," said Anwar Khan. "Come back tomorrow."

I left and returned the next day. Again, after a lot of hassle from the guards, I came to the office of the Prime Minister. This time also, I was told by Anwar Khan to come back the next day. I went home and returned again the next day. On the third time, Anwar Khan was very cold in his attitude. He told me, "Don't come back until we invite you." I thought maybe Sardar Shah Mahmud Khan had told him not to allow me to come in.

I went home and was very upset. I had no strength left to fight the authorities. All I had was a pen and a few tears. I picked up my pen and began to write a ballad. Sometimes, the tears fell from my eyes, and sometimes, they fell from the point of my pen. Here are a few lines of the poem I wrote.

Rawaqe Awaragan ("Archway of Exiles")
God knows, I know, and the world knows
I do not need any intuition or witness in this matter
I love every thorn of this country.
Why should the gardener mow the thorn of my body?
All the expanse of this world is God's capital,
From the vast lands of this earth to the high blue
skies...

Rawaqe Awaragan was published in my first or second collection of poetry. I don't remember the full ode except for the couple of quatrains here. This poem was really very beautiful. I liked it myself. There were about 40 to 50 couplets to it. I wrote it, but I did not have the courage to give it to the Prime Minister. I kept trying to think of whom I should give it to, so they could present it to him. There were some clerks who had worked under me, now promoted as directors in the Prime Ministry and were accompanying the Prime Minister on the visit, but even they avoided exchanging greetings with me.

One evening it was raining intermittently, and the weather had turned beautiful. I wanted to go to the Khirqa Mubarak (Shrine of the Holy Cloak) to offer evening prayers there. As I was walking from our house, which was close to the main road, I saw a black sedan pass me, traveling on the road from Kabul. After it passed, the sedan stopped abruptly, and a man came out of it, yelling, "Khalili, Khalili!" When I looked at him, I realized it was Sardar Najibullah Khan. He had just returned from Egypt and was travelling to Kandahar from Kabul at the request of Sardar Shah Mahmud Khan, who liked him very much and wanted to meet with him. Abdul Majid Khan Zabuli was in the sedan with him and also came out. Najibullah Khan started crying.

He asked me, "Where do you live?"

I pointed toward my house. He told Abdul Majid Zabuli to go on with the car and tell the Prime Minister he would follow as soon as he had visited Khalili's house to see his wife and children and have tea with them.

I told him, "Don't do that! You are the Minister of Education. You have come from Egypt and have not yet seen the Prime Minister. It's not good for me, and it's not good for both of us. You will become responsible for this."

He replied, "I don't care about those things. I am the same Najeebi, and you are the same Khalilullah Khan Khani that we were then, and we still are the same. Let's go and walk toward your house."

He came to my house. He saw my sparsely furnished home with the little *sandali* (heater) in the middle of the room. He saw I was wearing an old faded jacket purchased from the secondhand American market (Kanuiland Kandahar had used clothing markets where people would buy trousers, jackets, and shirts) because I couldn't afford anything else. He saw my wife, who was the daughter of Abdul Rahim Khan, Naib Salar, in her outdated clothes. He saw my children in the same condition. He could not hold back his tears and continued to cry.

He said, "Bring me some tea, for I have come a long way." He wanted to drink tea with us, no matter how poor the conditions. The tea was brought in. He asked me, "Did you see the Prime Minister?"

I replied, "I went there three times, but I couldn't see him."

"Who told you that he would not see you?" he asked.

I explained, "Mohammad Anwar Khan, Naib Salar did not say the Prime Minister wouldn't see me, but he told me to come back tomorrow and then again the next day, and then again the next day. Eventually, he told me not to come until they asked me to. Thus, I deduced from that the Prime Minister does not want to see me." I tried to make little of it. "I don't need to see him," I added. "Why should I? My wife had insisted; otherwise, I would not have gone."

"The Prime Minister thinks highly of you, especially his wife Qamarul Banat," Najibullah Khan said, asking, "Have you written anything new recently?"

I pulled the paper from underneath the *sandali* and gave him the new poem I had written, *Rawaqe Awaragan*. He started reading it. Najibullah was a poet himself – a rather good one – and a writer of beautiful prose. He was an eloquent speaker and well versed in French and English, and knew Arabic and Persian. He read and read, shed some tears and said, "I will take this poem to the Prime Minister."

My wife hesitated. "This may hurt us," she said. "He may not like it and will further put us in jeopardy."

Najibullah said, "No, he cannot hurt me and nor you all. I know very well." He left the room, and I came out with him to the door to say goodbye.

The next day, around 10 o'clock in the morning, a car was sent for me, and I was told that the Prime Minister wanted to see me. When we got there, Mohammad Anwar Khan was pacing up and down with his hands behind his back. As soon as he saw me, he smiled and said, "It wasn't my fault. His schedule was very tight, and there was no time to send you in. I wanted to send you in at a good time."

I said, "Well, it doesn't matter." Anwar Khan was a good man, and I liked him very much. He was my friend.

We went inside the living quarters of the Deputy Governor and sat there. Najibullah Khan came running when he saw me, followed by Ateeq Khan. Abdul Majid Khan Zabuli also came because of Najibullah Khan. The sun shone brightly, and we all were sitting outside. The Prime Minister came, and we all got up and lunged toward him to exchange greetings. He was cold to me. He was embracing the others in the Afghan custom of kissing on the cheek three times, but he did not embrace or kiss me. He sat down and turned his face toward me and said, "Aghai (Mr.) Khalili, what harm have I done to you?"

I was flabbergasted. I said, "I have no complaint against you, Your Highness."

He said, "This ballad you have sent me is an insult to me. From beginning to end, it's an insult to me. Is there more insult than this? You have written you came to my door and no one allowed you inside. Who didn't allow you inside?"

The Prime Minister turned to Anwar Khan and said, "If Khalili falls on the ground and becomes dirt or dust, still he would not come to see you. He had come to see me. Why didn't you allow him to come inside? Thus, it's not Khalili's fault." He turned to me and said, "Why don't you come and let me kiss your face?" I stood up and ran toward him. He kissed my forehead. I kissed his hand. He was older than me and was my elder.

Anwar Khan said, "Saheb, may I have the poem so I could read it, too?"

The Prime Minister responded, "Now, you want to insult me too?"

Najibullah Khan laughed, and said, "No, let me read it aloud, so everybody can throw insults!" It was just a joke. He read the poem aloud for everyone to hear.

"This is beautiful! This is great!" said Shah Mahmud Khan, expressing his appreciation for my poem.

A gentleman came in. He had a salt and pepper beard, and his dress was very Darvishi. He was acting like a Darvish Sufi, very *qalandari* (like someone who is crazy).

He was none other than Sayed Shamsuddin Kabarzani. This Sayed Shamsuddin belonged to the Sayed families of Zoori who lived in Kabarzon, a village three to four kilometers from Herat. When I was in Herat at the time of Abdul Rahim Khan Naib Salar, we used to visit them. This Sayed had a habit of donating most of his belongings every year to the needy. People would be invited to his house and were told that Agha Saheb ordered anyone could enter the house and take whatever they like – carpets, *kileems,* prayer rugs, books, etc. This was his routine every year.

Sayed Shamsuddin was also hard of hearing and always talked very loud. The Prime Minister respected him very much and offered him a seat at the head of the gathering. The Prime Minister asked about Herat and about the weather there.

Shamsuddin Agha said, "I'm here on behalf of the people of Herat to invite you to come to Herat and not to go back to Kabul from Kandahar. We want you to see the people of Herat, see your own people, and see Herat. We want you to witness the affinity of the people toward you."

The Prime Minister answered, "Oh, yes, I will definitely be coming to Herat. I have decided that, and also His Highness, the King, has asked me to visit Herat, also."

Shamsuddin Agha continued. "Further," he said, "When you come to Herat, I have a request you please visit the house of this Darvish."

The Prime Minister said, "Very well, I shake my hand with you, and I will definitely come to your home."

And as the Darvishs are, Shamsuddin candidly and very informally held the Prime Minister's hand and said, "I'm holding your hand and shaking with you. All these people are witness to you coming to my house." Everybody acknowledged they were witnesses to the Prime Minister's promise.

Shamsuddin Agha further said, "I am not acquainted with some of these witnesses here. Please introduce them to me." He looked at me first and shouted, "I do recognize this man. Are you Khalilullah Jan?" He recited the *kalima* loudly. "Sweet memories of good old days," he declared, "And sweet memories of those friends and loyals. You are

373

Khalilullah Jan!"

Shamsuddin Agha turned to the Prime Minister and demanded, "Prime Minister Saheb, who imprisons Khalilullah Jan? Who throws Khalilullah Jan in jail?"

The Prime Minister said, "I did not do that. The elder Prime Minister had done so."

I interjected and said, "The destiny had imprisoned me."

Shamsuddin Agha asked, "What did you do with Abdul Rahim Khan? Where is the sincere servant of Afghanistan? What did you do with the servant of Herat? Is he still in prison?"

I told him, "He's still in the prison."

"The people of Herat will ask you, what did you do with our father figure?" said Shamsuddin Agha. "He was the father of Herat."

The Prime Minister assured him, "I promise you, when I go back, I will present this to His Highness, the King. And I hope he will be released."

Shamsuddin Agha again questioned the Prime Minister, "Why did you send Khalilullah Jan to Kandahar? Why didn't you send him to Herat where I would have sacrificed my house, my property, and my life for him?"

The Prime Minister responded, "May God willing, we will send him to Herat also."

Witnessing all this was a very well dressed and handsome young gentleman, who looked like a young Sayed Jamaladdin, got up and came to me and kissed my hand. I said, "Young man, I don't recognize you."

He said, "I am Sahebzadah Abdullah Jan from Deh Khwaja." Deh Khwaja is a place near Kandahar with a large family of Naqshbandis (particular followers of a sect of Islam).

I knew who he was. I said, "Are you the son of Omar Jan Sahebzadah?"

"Yes," he answered. His father, Omar Jan Sahebzadah, had a large mosque and a *Khaneqah* (monastery). From the time the mosque and *Khaneqah* was established, it was used only for reading Holy Koran, praying and talking about God (*zikr*). No one talked about worldly things there.

These were all men of letters and erudite people. The people of Kandahar hold them in great esteem, especially the Ghiljaiz. This young man, Abdullah Jan, was a scholar and an intellectual. I had heard about him from others.

"I was not here when you arrived in Kandahar, or I would have come to see you," Abdullah Jan explained. "I had gone to visit Quetta and Baluchistan. When I came back, I heard about your presence in Kandahar, but by then the Prime Minister's visit was taking place, and I was unable to come and see you." The meeting ended here.

Accounting Department at the Sugar Corporation (1327 Solar/1948)

The next day or the day after, Sardar Najibullah Khan invited me to the Prime Minister's again, and told me, "The Prime Minister has recommended two positions for you. He is offering to appoint you as Accountant General of Kandahar (Mustufi), or he will make you the director of the sugar corporation."

I thought to myself it would not be a good omen to become the Accountant General (Mustufi). I told Najibullah, "You know my father was Mustufi Momalik, the Accountant General of Afghanistan. He wielded a great deal of respect and power, and yet, he was killed without due process. After he was murdered, all his possessions were confiscated. You know this very well. You and I have lived as neighbors in Kabul."

Najibullah Khan reminded me about my position as Mustufi during the time of Habibullah Khan Kalakani; however, being in that position had led to so many obstacles for me. This was the third time I was being offered the same title. I decided not to do that again. I told Najibullah Khan, "The Deputy Governor who is in charge will not let me operate freely."

Najibullah Khan said, "Okay, why don't you join one of the corporations?"

I replied, "Fine, I'll do that." I agreed, even though I abhor working under business people. I had to accept those terms.

Najibullah Khan left me and went inside. He came back after half an hour. He said, "The Prime Minister says he would have been more pleased if you had accepted the job of Accountant General. He would have called you Mustufi Saheb. This would have reminded us of your father. Since you didn't accept that position, he is appointing you the head of the accounting department at the Kandahar Sugar Corporation. Please go and take charge of the department."

Since the small amount of sugar produced in Afghanistan in the factories installed by Amanullah Khan in Jalalabad and Pule Khomari was not sufficient for the whole country, the majority of the sugar and sugar products were imported. In order to control the distribution, in every city – Kandahar, Herat, Mazar-i-Sharif, etc. – a sugar import corporation was established. Tons of sugar and related products were imported and distributed through these centers at a predetermined price. There was a lot of underhandedness and black marketing of the product. A large tonnage of it was sometimes purchased and sold outside of Afghanistan.

Thus, the sugar-manufacturing corporation was not manufacturing any sugar in Kandahar. It was a shell organization, which held a monopoly over the import of sugar and related products. No one was allowed to import sugar into the country except for this corporation, which a few businessmen owned.

I was officially appointed, and the next day I went to assume my job. The corporation was located in a big building near a cemetery. I could see lines of people, men and women with applications in their hands, waiting for the director to approve distribution of some sugar to them. A three-day supply was the usual approved amount. My job was to determine how much sugar came that day, how much was sold, and how much money was sent to the bank.

Also, I was required to know how much sugar was in storage, the quality of the sugar being brought in, and the control of the amounts sent to other cities. The president of this corporation was a businessman named Abdul Khaliq Niazi. Sometimes, he worked in Kandahar, and sometimes he visited Herat. When I was in Herat years ago, I had met him. He would come to see me in those days and was always trying to flatter us. Now, he was the president of the company, and I was working under him. It was tough on me, but I accepted it.

I reported for work and went to one of the directors, a man named Ahmad Shah. I knew him from Kabul. As soon as he saw me and read the paper announcing my appointment, he became very agitated. He angrily asked one of the peons to bring a desk and a chair, and place it in the outside entrance to the room. He said, "This is the Accountant Khalilullah. He will be sitting there. If I need anything, you will ask him to come in."

Turning to me, he said, "Why don't you go and sit there. We will call you when we need you."

I was taken aback, but did not say anything.

In his colloquial pronunciation, Ahmad Shah added, "Don't interfere in any of the proceedings. Do as I tell you. I will give you the facts and figures. You just work on them."

I answered, "Fine, I will do that."

I left Ahmad Shah's office and went to see Najibullah Khan, who was in the building where the Deputy Governor worked. I told Najibullah Khan, "I would like to pass on this opportunity. I don't want to be Mustufi or an accountant in the sugar corporation. When I went to the sugar corporation, Ahmad Shah told me to 'work on the numbers I give you and work on them the way I tell you to.' In all my life, I've never taken a bribe or fixed numbers or been part of any corruption. I cannot do this. He made me sit in a hallway. It is difficult to work with this man."

Najibullah Khan went inside to see the Prime Minister. He came back out and invited me inside and also brought in Abdul Majid Khan Zabuli.

Najibullah Khan said, "There has been a big misunderstanding. I did not say you should be appointed as a clerk in the accounting department. We wanted you to be the director of the corporation. You are appointed to control the whole business with its dealings in sugar, sugar import, benzene gas, kerosene oil, and clothing. These are all imported through the depot, and you should oversee all these five departments."

I said, "I hope I can manage and measure up to this task."

Najibullah Khan said, "Don't talk any further." He returned to his office and wrote a decree, and it was signed. I was given the letter of appointment. Mohammad Anwar Khan also signed it. I was feeling kind of embarrassed about how to approach Ahmad Shah, the son of Karim Khan. He was younger than I and may feel snubbed because he was very rude with me. I had no choice but to move forward.

I went back to see Ahmad Shah. He was sitting in his office. As soon as he saw me he said, "I was looking for you! I had wanted you to come in, and you were not there."

I said, "Mr. Director, unfortunately I had to take care of some business. I may not be able to work with you any further. Please, I would like to talk to you in private if it is possible, and then I will be leaving."

He said, "Why don't you want to talk in front of these other people?"

I told him, "It is kind of private, and I should talk to you." I didn't want him to feel embarrassed. Well, he asked the people sitting around to leave. I closed the door and presented him the letter of appointment. He opened the letter, read it, and I could see his demeanor changing as I was standing and watching. He got up from his chair and apologized to me.

I told him, "I have not come here to insult you or harass you. I have been appointed here, and I have no other choice. If you need anything, God willing, I will help you."

I left the room, and to the people who were standing outside the building in line to purchase the products, men and women, I said, "Oh sisters and brothers! I have a request for you. I have brought a message from the Prime Minister of Afghanistan. Please leave today, and give me some time, until the day after tomorrow and then come back. I have been appointed as the head of this corporation. I will try to change the process of distribution. Instead of you coming to the main depot, I will find a way to bring the supplies closer to your neighborhoods. You will be able to purchase sugar according to your needs by paying for it. Just do not hoard any sugar or any other products. Please buy according to your needs. I will be very strict regarding the black market, and I promise you, I will keep an eye on it." They were very happy to hear it and agreed to leave.

There were a large number of officials in the building. Over the next few days, I called all of them in. Khairo Jan also sent his son to me, Sayed Jan Khan, who was one of the advisors. Ghulam Dastagir Jan, who was also a friend of mine, came. He was a Sardar from Sarpozah, the son of Sardar Atta Mohammad Khan. They all offered their volunteer services to improve the lot of the people of Kandahar. Together, we were able to visit the city, find locations for distribution centers, and execute good plans in the interest of the people. We opened approximately 60 to 70 outlets in Kandahar and obtained monetary guarantees from the people who would operate them. We made the announcement of the opening of the neighborhood distribution centers in the newspapers and at the markets.

When I went to see the Prime Minister, he said, "Khalilullah Khan, hopefully when I come back to Kandahar on my way to Kabul, with God on your side, we may not see these lines of people formed in front of the sugar corporation building."

I told him, "With your blessings, we have already worked on it, and you may not find people lined up even now."

I remained in the job for a while. The poet whose poetry was sweeter than sugar became the servant of the sugar trader.

While I was unable to continue to do what I liked most, I was able to seek out the many Kandahari literary people in the trade circles and find satisfaction among these writers and erudite men. There was Maulavi Sharfuddin Khan, Maulavi Abdullah Jan, Aghai Khalis, and Aghai Aishi. Of these exiles who had come to Kandahar, Abdul Khaliq Khan later became the Deputy Mayor of Kabul. He was the son of Lalah Abdu Qadir, who was exiled in Kandahar. I also became friends with Aghai Mohammad Ghaus Reshad Logari. He was a gentleman.

Sardar Shah Mahmud Khan, after inspecting the functioning of the government in Kandahar and tying up loose ends in the financial, agricultural, and educational fields, left Kandahar for Farah and Herat. We got busy with our work. My job paid me well. Not only did the corporation compensate me for my work, but also the corporation paid travel expenses. I had never made that much money in my life. This showed me the clear difference between entrepreneurship and officialdom. For example, a government official working in a certain position might be making 300 *afghanis* per month, while a person working for a corporation in the same position would bring home more than 2,000 *afghanis* per month. This was not a very healthy balance. This is what laid the groundwork for a future Communist revolution in Afghanistan.

It was not in my power to change this or tell them not to give me a salary higher than a government official for the same work. On my part, I did talk to Sardar Najibullah Khan about the meager compensation paid to the government workers. He raised the matter with the Prime Minister who said, "Government budgets have constraints." It was true; the budgets were very tight. With these low salaries, the government officials were either forced to cross legal boundaries to accept bribes or forced to leave their jobs to join private corporations.

My Involvement with Kandahar's Schools and Literary Circle

Besides my regular job at the corporation, I became involved in the schools. Sardar Najibullah Khan, who was the Minister of Education, gave his approval for the Kandahar School Board to use my expertise. I was appointed as a teacher at the Ahmad Shah Baba and Mirwais High Schools.

Besides teaching history and literature, I wanted to create a special program to show the very conservative Pashtu speaking people of Kandahar, and Dari speaking people, the commonality between their two cultures and languages. The best example was Ahmad Shah Baba himself, who is a source of pride for Afghanistan and the people of Kandahar, who adored him. He was a poet in both Pashtu and Dari. My intention was not to force them to choose one culture and language over the other, but to open their minds to both. I selected lesson subjects and stories that were in the spirit of cultural unity. I would teach about prominent personalities in Islam who advocated unity, such as Sanai (11th – 12th century Persian Sufi poet), Nasser Khusrov (Persian theologian and philosopher, 1003-1088), the prose of Khwaja Abdullah Ansari (the Sage of Herat, 11th century Persian Sufi poet), and the ballads of Sheikh Saadi (one of the greatest classical Sufi authors of the 13th century).

Among my friends who would visit my home there was the Momand family of Akbar Khan Lalpuri. Akbar Khan Lalpuri was an elder of the Momand tribe, and his son, Zafar Khan, was a prominent Afghan who wielded a lot of respect. During the time of Amanullah Khan, he was appointed as Commandant of the Police of Kandahar. He was very polite and respectful to the people of Kandahar. When he retired from work he was elevated as an elder of Kandahar. His family was regarded in high esteem.

Zafar Khan's sons lived in Kandahar. I remember the names of some of them: Mohammad Nasser, Mohammad Nadir, and Mohammad Kabir. They were educated and scholarly people who were considered to be the elite of Kandahar. His second son, Nadir Jan, became my friend. He used to read and understood poetry well. He introduced me to some high Kandahar personalities. I can never forget them. One was Haji Atta Mohammad Kandahari. He was famously called Haji Akhund. He was followed and admired by the Kandhari younger generation. He was between 60 and 70 years old. He possessed many books and also had a book trade, with many rare manuscripts in Arabic and Persian. I used to read his books all the time. He was a mystic who followed Shah Abdul Khair Mojaddadi Dehlavi. He acquainted me with the writings of Hakim Attaullah Iskandarani. I had not read anything of his up to that time. Also, through him, I read the writings of Sayed Abdul Wahab Shahrani and also of Abul Shah Mojaddadi. Haji Akhund was a teacher of Nadir Jan. He would not take disciples and did not consider himself a sheikh (intellectual). He had no claims to sagehood. But whenever he entered a gathering and talked, one could see he was well versed in philosophy and Sufism. Haji Akhund would visit me often, and we would sit late in the nights and talk. With his talk he would soothe me and give me satisfaction in exile in Kandahar.

My exile was comparative. I was exiled from Kabul yet being in Kandahar was not considered to be in exile. The real exile is when one is forced to leave his country: away from your home, away from your land, and also away from Kandahar.

Some prominent families of Kandahar sent their young men to me so I could teach them Dari, and they could learn how to read, write, and compose. I had seven or eight students with various schedules. They would come and sit in the outside living room and study Dari. One of them was Abdullah Karzai, the son of Khair Mohammad Khan Karzai, about whom I have talked earlier. There was a son of the Lodin family; his name was Nasrullah Jan. There was a son of one of the Sayeds of Kandahar who were traders, but I don't recall his name right now. All these would surround me like hovering moths. They were very devoted to their learning. They were very attentive when I taught them. They took over all the chores of my house. I was happy I was training some young men. More than that, I wanted these young men to be at the service of (11th century Persian Sufi poets) Hazrat Abdul Majid Majdood Sanai and Hazrat Khwaja Abdullah Ansari, as well as (13th century Persian poets) Hazrat Maulana Jalaluddin Mohammad Balkhi Rumi (1207 – 1273), and Sheikh Saadi Shirazi (13th century). I wanted them to learn Islamic culture from these erudite personalities. Sometimes, I would also teach them Jalali Dawani (philosopher and theologian, born in 1426, author of *Akhlaq-e-Jalali* or Jalalean Ethics). Occasionally, Haji Akhund would sneak in and sit in a corner, and assist me as I needed. He would recite some Dari poetry and some Pashtu poetry for the students. This would warm up our meeting.

The Booksellers Market

I was fortunate to learn about a treasure of information regarding the sale of books. I was told that every Tuesday in the Shikarpur Bazar, the students brought books from all around Kandahar, such as Nawzad, Girishk, Mir Bazar, etc., and would sit on the side of the street hawking the books. One could find rare books here. When I found out, I committed myself to going there every Tuesday after noon prayers.

There used to be eight or ten different people selling books on the street. They would lay the books on a white sheet on ground and sell them. These were not their schoolbooks. They would go around to villages, close and far, and buy books to sell them here. They had heard the foreigners would buy the manuscripts at high prices. Hearing this made me uncomfortable. This meant these rare manuscripts were going out of the country. I did not like this, yet I myself purchased a few of these handwritten books from there.

One day, when I was at this bazaar, I saw a book from afar. I was drawn to it because of the beautiful dark blue captivating binding (the color of lapis lazuli) and golden writing. At first, I thought it was the Holy Koran or Hadiths (sayings of Prophet Mohammad) or maybe an interpretation of the Holy Koran. I went to the seller picked up the book. It was thick. When I opened it up, to my shock, it was in Dari. It was fancifully hand written with little golden circles at the end of every sentence. These little circles are normally used in the Holy Koran. The footnotes in this book resembled the writing of the Holy Koran. The golden ink was used in many places.

When I focused my attention on the writing, I could see it was the *Kimiyai Saadat* (*The Alchemy of Happiness*) by Hazrat Imam Ghazali (famous Muslim writer, philosopher and poet -1058-1111, who wrote more than 70 books on Islamic sciences, philosophy and Sufism).

The book was complete, and on the last page, I do not

remember correctly, but I think this book was written between 20 to 40 years after the death of Imam Ghazali. The writing was very, very florid and embellished. The letters appeared to be raised when you ran a finger over it. It was written with all the power and beauty of an author. Right now, I'm forgetting the full name of the book. (*Kimiyai Saadat* was a brief version, in Persian, of Ghazali's major work, *Ihya Ulumiddin*, or *The Revival of Religious Sciences*).

I asked the student, "How much is this book?"

I think he said it was 300 *afghanis*. I was thrilled, but did not show my eagerness (300 *afghanis* was about five dollars back then). I did not have the money on me or at home. I sent the driver of the car to my office, and he brought 300 to 400 *afghanis* back. I realized the book was worth much more, and 300 *afghanis* was an injustice to the seller because he did not know the value of the book. But if I told him the value, I was concerned he would raise the price so high, it would jump out of my reach, and then he would keep the book to sell to a foreigner or to a Kandahari trader who sell books outside of Afghanistan. I told him that while 300 *afghanis* was expensive I would give it to him. In addition, I took his name and the place where he lived.

Mullah Akhtar Mohammadi was a bookseller in one of the Kandahar bazaars. I would always visit his shop to purchase books, and Haji Akhund and I would sometimes sit in his shop. Some people even commented to me, "Why do you go and sit in this bookshop? You're the director of a corporation."

I went to Mullah Mohammadi and showed him the book I had purchased and told him the name of the seller and where he lived. I asked him if he would go to the weekly bazaar and buy a few books from this person at more than the asking price to compensate him for selling this book to me so cheap. I also gave him 300 more *rupees* to give to this young man in the name of this book. Mullah Mohammadi agreed. I cannot vouch he did this, but I did my duty and actually purchased this book for 600 *rupees*.

I admired and loved this book. It was one of my prized

possessions. I donated it to the Royal Library for safekeeping. It was the safest place in my mind. I recall that before my appointment to Ambassadorship of Afghanistan to Saudi Arabia, I visited the Royal Library and saw the book there. I remember coming back after that, when visiting Kabul from Saudi Arabia, it was still there. I don't know now what may have happened to it over the years. It may still be there, or it may have fallen into the hands of the Russians, or it has been destroyed.

Bost Fort

Mr. Shamsuddin Majrooh visited me from Kabul. He had been appointed by Abdul Majid Khan Zabuli to work at the bank during this time and was assigned to audit the financial institutions in Kandahar. It was a blessing in disguise for me.

I suggested to him, "When you are auditing the institutions in Kandahar, why don't we go and check the petrol depot at Girishk?"

Since I was restricted to Kandahar, I had to seek special permission from Mohammad Qasim Khan, the Deputy Governor. We sent a note asking for his approval to allow me to accompany Pascha Saheb (Majrooh) on his trip to Girishk, which was granted. We also took the Deputy Governor's brother, Karim Jan. He used to work at the Prime Ministry with me at one time and was a good friend of mine. He was an upstanding and noble man.

We loaded a car and headed for our auditing rendezvous. This was one of our best travels. The reader may think, "What is good about auditing a petrol depot?" The real story is, I had been told by many people in Kandahar, including Haji Akhund, that the fort at Bost near Girishk is located in the midst of archeological sites from the Ghaznavid time (11th century). This is what I had on my mind, to visit the archeological sites. The excuse was Sayed Shamsuddin's visit and the auditing of the petrol depot. We wanted to go to Lashkari Bazar and Bost Fort. We had also taken with us some hunting guns and hunting paraphernalia. We were loaded with food we prepared that could last in travel, and flasks filled with hot tea.

We reached Girishk first and spent the night there. We went to the petrol depot and checked the operation. From there, we drove to the ruins of Lashkari Bazar (an 11th century city on the east side of the Helmud river in southwest Afghanistan). It was breathtakingly beautiful. We crossed the desert, the fields, and the land. The Bost Fort had not been repaired yet. We finally reached our destination. The people of Kandahar normally called it "Beest Fort," but in the geography books it has been referred to as Bost Fort (the remnants of the Fortress of Alexander the Great 356 BC- 323 BC).

I read in a book that the name given to this place may be a misnomer. *Boston* means a garden and *bastan* is the plural of the garden; that is, two gardens. But, this is not right. There are further explanations I have read somewhere about the naming of this fort.

Before we reached the Bost Fort, there was a place on our way called Sarkar. A mystic by the name of Faiz Jan Agha lived there. I do not remember his proper name. He was sitting in a small wooden enclosure, hardly bigger than a wooden crate, called a *capah*. It had branches and some thorns all around it. The roof was laced with mud, thorns, and leaves so in winter it was insulated, and the snow would not melt and seep inside. It was so small not even a single man could easily lie down in it.

In this place, Faiz Jan Agha lived as a Darvish. Sayed Shamsuddin Khan did not believe in mystics and Darvish. Shamsuddin Khan stayed outside while I bent myself to squeeze inside this *capah* with difficulty. When I went in I saw a man whose hairs from his head and beard were all one. His white beard was in his lap. He looked very mystic and enlightened. Your eyes would not allow you to gaze at him for long. I paid my respects and talked softly to him in Pashtu.

He welcomed me and said, "Bring that gentleman inside."

When Pascha Saheb came in, the Darvish stood up from his place and shook his hand. He addressed him as, "Agha Saheb!" I was taken aback. The Darvish returned to a pensive mood. How he knew Agha Saheb's name is a

386

mystery to me. He gave his blessing and prayed for us. We offered some money to him. Karim Jan also offered some money. The Darvish turned all this down. He did not like us offering him money.

We left the hermit and started our journey toward the fort. I was reading the poetry of Farrukhi (Royal poet of the Ghazavids, 10th and 11th century). I had his collection with me. I also had a book of Baihaqi (Islamic scholar, 994-1066, who authored many volumes of history). Reading these poems and writings had a mystical effect on us as we traveled.

Finally, we reached our destination, arriving at the time of evening prayers, as the sun was moving toward setting. This fort was located on a high hill with a bridge. As we got out of the car and slowly walked over to the remnants of the fort, I recalled a ballad from Farrukhi. The ballad goes something like this:

Suddenly I heard the cry of the gushing waters of the Helmand River...

It is here the Helmand River rushes down and passes underneath the fort with all its power and glory, roaring until it bifurcates under the bridge to create two waters.

One could see the sunset in a panoramic view stretching into infinity. As far as the human eye could see, there was no obstruction as we watched the sun drown into a bloody red horizon.

Around the fort a wall has been erected. Inside the fort, the arch of Bost rose magnificently, resembling a huge bow. It dates back to the Saffarid dynasty (861-1002). Unfortunately, the inscriptions on the arch are no longer readable. There is some artwork and tile work, which is still visible, made of glass and ceramic. All the living quarters are empty and unlivable. There is no noise or voice of any kind there. It is serene with a pin drop silence broken only by a perching owl or a flying bird.

We were told you could find wild game, wolves, and coyotes. I picked up the hunting gun to be on the safe side from the attack of a hungry wolf or coyote.

We went up the fort and peered toward the bottom and saw a building had been built with most of it underneath the ground. There were at least four floors, and it was very large. You could see the Helmand River from there. All around this building looked like a big bowl, about 50 meters in diameter. It was shaped like a cup, and around it was living quarters with verandas in front of the rooms. Since it was getting dark we could not go down into the remnants. We found a couple of elderly people walking, and they explained the history to us. One of them said this whole town was a prison. Other people mentioned some other historical places.

I recall seeing something like this in India. Because the weather in Bost is hot, maybe the building was constructed underground to keep it cooler in hot weather. Maybe rulers and other leaders of the regime spent their summer days here getting away from the sun. I am convinced of this, and I believe some of the buildings and architecture also support my theory.

We sat there until the burning sun went down. The men we met there brought us a few coins from the time of the Ghoric and Ghaznavid eras (In mid-12th century, Ghor, a province in central Afghanistan, expressed its independence from the Ghaznavid Empire). Some of the coins were very dark; others were silver. We bought the coins from them. Later in the evening we went to stay at the house of Sardar Mohammad Naim Khan, who welcomed and respected us. He was a scholarly man and very well versed in the history of the area. His father was a friend of my father. He had a big house, a big courtyard, with servants and orderlies. The inside was well furnished with Afghan and Iranian carpets. I observed very ancient china in his house, and other antique and expensive china. This place was far away from being pillaged or destroyed. All their possessions were maintained through the generations. They were always hospitable to travelers. They had an Iranian *chehlem* (hookah) like Muzaffaruddin Shah used (1896-1907). The Sardar himself smoked *chehlem*.

The next morning the Sardar said he would take us to a place called Lashkargah. We again rode in the car to Lashkargah. It seemed we were the first people to visit

Lashkargah and bring back the news to Kabul. Lashkargah had ancient buildings, homes, and some forts. Some of them had collapsed roofs; other roofs were still in place, though the colors faded. The doors to the forts and homes were still visible.

There were very high entrances to the places. I have read that the rulers of the time and the Ghaznavids used to build very high and mighty entrances to their forts. One of the reasons was that they entered these forts and courtyards on their elephants. The elephants were saddled with platforms where people sat and carried the rulers' standards or flags. It was a bad omen if the standard was lowered while entering the fort. The doors and gates were constructed very high so the national flags could pass through without being lowered.

Lashkargah is a place, which is vividly mentioned in the history of Baihaqi. According to Baihaqi, Sultan Masood laid its foundation. We went around the remnants trying to read and see every part of it. This is the way of the world. Nothing remains forever. Neither the elephants remained, nor the mark of the sultans. There were no armies left and no people. There were no aromas of exotic foods cooking in the sultans' kitchens. There were no lights, no torches, and no smoke rising. This was not one of those majestic and thriving civilizations, no bustling or hurrying people. We spent a day there. In the evening, we went back to Sardar Naim's house. Since the brother of Deputy Governor was also with us, Sardar Naim insisted we spend the night again at his place.

The next day we went to Girishk Bazar and stayed at the Hotel Girishk. The hotel was built during the time of Amanullah Khan. It was a comparatively good hotel and well managed. We took showers there and left for Kandahar the next day. Pascha Saheb remained in Kandahar for a few days and then went back to Kabul.

I wrote a full report and presented it to Sardar Najibullah Khan. A few days after my report was received, Aghai (Mr.) Kohzad – that is Ustad Ahmad Ali Kohzad – who was an archeologist, was hurriedly dispatched from Kabul, along with another French archeologist. They came by car to Kandahar and asked me to accompany them back to Lashkargah. We drove back to Lashkargah and stayed there a while, camping out. They brought me back to Kandahar and went back to Kabul. Mr. Ali Kohzad wrote a book about Lashkargah, but did not mention me. I asked him why, and he told me, "I was afraid that if I mentioned your name, you might be questioned about why you went to Lashkargah with us. I did not want any repercussions for you." I replied, "Well, if you did it with your best intentions, it's fine with me." So, I'm not hurt.

Popularity of Shah Mahmud Khan among the People

Shah Mahmud Khan, upon his return from Herat, stopped in Kandahar again, and the people of Kandahar lined up on the streets for him. Since his first visit, many of them filed complaints against Mohammad Qasim Khan, the Deputy Governor. The complaints ranged in nature, but in fact, the underlying truth was they were complaining against Sardar Hashim Khan. Qasim Khan himself was not a bad man and was not complacent. However, over the span of Mohammad Hashim's rule, 16 or 17 years, the people had not been treated well, and they were unhappy. They never saw the Prime Minister during those 17 years. They had not set eyes on the king's face. For 17 years, no one heard their complaints. For 17 years, many of them had been prisoners in Kabul.

Abdul Aziz Khan, the Director of Communications and Press in Kandahar, used to work at the Ministry of Foreign Affairs in Kabul. He was from Kandahar. He was an intellectual and a scholarly man. He was arrested and thrown in jail for quite some time. Sardar Shah Mahmud Khan released him when he came to power. He was appointed as Mayor of Kandahar. Abdul Rahman Lodin, who was from Kandahar, was taken to Kabul and appointed Mayor of Kabul during the time of Nadir Shah. He was later executed. Similarly, there are other elite and prominent Kandahari personalities who were placed under house arrest in Kabul. Let me mention a few: Khairo Jan;

Sayed Jan Khan, advisor; Mohammad Anwar Khan Achakzai, Naib Salar, and more.

With Shah Mahmud Khan's coming to power a new ray of hope brightened the people. Shah Mahmud Khan sat with the people, talked with the people, and listened to their complaints. He embraced them and showed them kindness. People were encouraged to bring forth their grievances and present them to the Prime Minister. He told people right then and there, "I hear all of you. I have empathy for you. I will look closely at your grievances. I will remove Mohammad Qasim Khan from his post as Deputy Governor, and I will send a new Deputy Governor as soon as I get back to Kabul."

Let me mention here that I had another friend in Kandahar by the name of Qazi Ghulam Aishan. He was from Qarabagh of Kohdaman (north of Kabul). Qazi Aishan was the judge of the primary court of Kandahar. He was a graduate of the Sharia (religious law) school; a progressive young man who learned French on his own and was well read. He also liked hunting. Being from Kohdaman, he was my friend. He used to come to my home often, and we would read Arabic books together. He was good at Arabic literature and knew Dari very well. He was a judge with a clean conscience and clean hands. The people of Kandahar respected him. Later, I learned the Communists had murdered him during their rule in Kabul.

Qazi Aishan was not very happy with the Deputy Governor. When he heard about his replacement, he came to our house to give me the good news.

The Prime Minister finally left Kandahar, and we remained busy with our lives. There was a man named Sayed Jalal Agha. He was the son of Sayed Mohammad Hassan Agha, who was one of the old *mustofis* of Afghanistan and had worked with my father. Sayed Jalal was a prominent citizen of Kandahar with many followers. I recalled he used to dye his beard. He worked in the government and was considered Deputy Mayor of Kandahar. He encouraged people to raise their voices against the Deputy Governor. He was kind of an older revolutionary man, may God bless him. He was also a good friend of mine and used to come to my place.

The Deputy Governor heard about my contact with Sayed Jalal, and at first thought I was in cahoots with Sayed Jalal to plot against him. He realized Sayed Jalal was working on his own to agitate people. The Deputy Governor summoned me, and when I went to his office, I could see he was not the same man whom I had met before. He had gone back to his old demeanor of the Director in the Prime Ministry. He was much kinder and seemed to have got off his mighty horse.

Addressing me, he said, "Please admonish Sayed Jalal not to spread rumors against me. This is not a good thing."

I answered, "If Sayed Jalal listens to me, I will talk to him right away."

I went back and asked Sayed Jalal not to spread people's hatred against the Deputy Governor. "He's already been suspended and will be leaving soon," I explained. "It seems uncalled for to instigate people at this time against someone who has fallen."

Sayed Jalal accepted my plea. Later, he went to the Deputy Governor and told him, "You have asked Khalilullah to contain me. Since he is a guest of Kandahar and in exile here, I have listened to his advice and will not do anything against you." This pleased the Deputy Governor.

Change of Local Government in Kandahar

One night we were sitting with the Deputy Governor in his office. We were listening to a radio broadcast from Kabul. The announcer reading the news mentioned, "Sardar Qasim Khan, the Deputy Governor of Kandahar has been relieved of his duties. In his place, Sardar Mohammad Younis Khan has been appointed the new Deputy Governor of Kandahar."

Mohammad Younis Khan was the son of Brigadier Mohammad Ali Khan, who was himself the son of Sardar Sultan Mohammad Khan Tillai (Golden). Younis Khan's father was also the uncle of Sardar Mohammad Yosuf Khan, who was in turn the father of Nadir Shah. Younis Khan's mother belonged to the Barakzai tribe and was the sister of Ulia Hazrat, Queen mother of Amanullah Khan. Sardar Mohammad Hashim Khan was not very fond of Younis Khan because he was a cousin of Amanullah Khan. However, since Hashim Khan was also related to him, he had to be nice to Younis Khan.

Mohammad Younis Khan was young man who had graduated school and excelled at architecture. Previously, he headed the Department of Building Construction in Kabul and had no other experience in civil service.

In Kabul, I used to teach Mohammad Younis Khan. When he studied with me, he would bring his book, *Ayam-e Mahbas* (*The Days of Imprisonment*) a collection of political articles by Ali Dashti (Iranian nationalist, 1894-1982). I would help him read and understand it, but I used to tell him, "You cannot learn grammar from these articles. You must read textbooks for grammar." He would protest, "No, I like this book, and I want to read it."

I was happy to hear Mohammad Younis Khan was coming. A few days after the news, the society of Kandahar was again bustling with activity. The poor people of Kandahar were all subject to the rule of the government and government officers. The word was out that the new Deputy Governor is coming. To demonstrate their enthusiasm, people went up to Qalat and Moqor to welcome him (small towns leading to Kandahar that the Deputy Governor would reach first in his journey from Kabul). They carried with them gifts and other offerings for him. Meanwhile, the traders went and built entrance gates to Kandahar.

Qazi Aishan came to me and said, "We should also go and welcome the Deputy Governor to avoid any misunderstanding or give him an excuse for not being good to us." He asked me to accompany him and added, "You know him."

I said, "Yes, I *used* to know him."

Qazi Aishan pleaded, "I know that you know him well. Why don't you accompany me to welcome him?"

I tried to get out of it, but he insisted and since he was a friend too, I gave in. I knew he was more concerned for himself since he was a judge and would not take bribes from anybody. He was afraid he would have adversaries who would get to the Deputy Governor before he could reach him. People who are judged always criticize judgments, no matter how right they are.

I went to my wife and told her how I had agreed to accompany Qazi Aishan on this trip. I sought her counsel. She said, "What if you go there and the new Deputy Governor is not courteous to you? He may not be the same Younis Jan who you knew when you were in Kabul. He is Deputy Governor now."

I asked, "How do I get out of this without hurting Qazi Saheb's feelings?"

My wife and I agreed that Qazi Saheb and I should not venture out beyond Kandahar, but stay within the city limits. That way, we would not be seen as going out of our way to approach him. Also, she reminded me, because I was in exile, I may not be allowed to go any further out of city limits anyway.

I left the house to go and talk with some of my friends, including Nadir Jan Agha and others. They also agreed, "Since Qazi Saheb insists, you should go, but stay within city limits of Kandahar." Nadir Jan Agha joined us also. We found a car to carry us all with our hunting guns. Qazi Saheb was fond of hunting. He was famous for it. He especially loved to hunt pheasants.

We reached Qalat, which is within the city limits of Kandahar and were told the Deputy Governor had arrived. Many people had come to greet him, and there was no room in the hotel.

A large orchard and vast garden had been prepared for the Deputy Govenor's reception. He sat on the ground, surrounded by hundreds of people. As we walked in, he was admonishing them for having come so far to welcome him. When I heard his annoyance, I was a little intimidated about going forward. But since we were already there, my friends insisted on moving toward him. I, for one, was not very convinced because I had been in jail until recently and was still in exile. As we moved closer the Deputy Governor looked up toward us. Spotting me, he stood up from his place and shouted in front of all the people. "I have to go, my teacher is here! This is a good man!"

He came forward and pulled me near him, and in front of all the people he kissed my hand as a teacher. As tradition goes, I kissed his face. We were almost the same in age. I held Qazi Saheb's hand and said, "I did not come to you. This man, who is a good friend of mine, brought me to you. He is the judge of the primary court."

Younus Khan showed kindness toward Qazi Aishan and was very courteous. I also introduced Nadir Jan Agha to him. Nadir Jan Agha was a magistrate (*hakim*) in one of the districts, I think Arghandab, and was the son of Mohammad Zafar Khan Lala. Younis Jan acknowledged, "Yes, I have heard your name."

Younis Jan made us sit next to him, and tea was brought in. He ordered his assistants to prepare the continuing journey to Kandahar and asked me to accompany him back.

I whispered softly in his ear. "Why don't you go ahead since you have your *mustofi* with you and your military commander and your police commander? We will follow you and stop on our way for some hunting." I knew the Deputy Governor was also an avid hunter. However, today he had to hold back his enthusiasm of hunting and accompany the entourage toward Kandahar.

The Deputy Governor's aide was a man named Sayed Mirza Khan. He was from Guldara (north of Kabul). He knew me well. He took me to the side and said, "*Bibi* (the Lady) wants to see you." The wife of Sardar Mohammad Younis Khan was the daughter of Sardar Abdul Quddus Khan, the Prime Minister. She was very smart and intelligent.

I asked him, "Do you mean the ladies there with head coverings? (Head scarves and *hijabs* were strictly enforced at that time.)

Sayed Mirza Khan said, "No, why don't you come with me? She's standing near the car. She'll be heading to Kandahar. She's waiting for you."

I went with him. She removed her veil and spoke to me very kindly. She said, "I had to greet you. You are just like my brother. My father used to consider your father as his son." Her eyes filled with tears. "Don't you ever think that because Younis is Deputy Governor and you are in exile that will make any difference to us. You are not in exile here. You are the same teacher to Younis who used to guide him in Kabul. You have a right over him (Afghan saying). Younis is your servant, and I'm also here to be of service to you. My children are at your service. Consider yourself to be the Deputy Governor here."

I became very emotional too. I said, "May God give you a long life. You really come from a long linkage of nobility. You are very gracious."

We exchanged these greetings and parted to begin heading our way to Kandahar. When the Kandaharis witnessed the wife of the Deputy Governor paying so much respect to me, it increased my respect in their eyes. They all became kinder to me. Finally, the entourage left, and we waited for the dust to settle. Qazi Saheb and I came to our car and started back. We found a flock of pheasants on our way and had a good hunting. We finally reached Kandahar. I narrated my epic to my wife, which made her comfortable and content. Nadir Jan and Qazi Saheb were also happy with me for introducing them to the new Deputy Governor.

When I reached home I saw Haji Akhund sitting and waiting for me with a book under his arm. I asked him, "Is everything okay?"

He answered, "I've brought a new book for you." He showed me the book. It was a beautifully written manuscript. "I hear you went to welcome the Deputy Governor," he continued. "In my opinion, it wasn't the right thing. The Deputy Governor should have come to you. Why did you do that? You should not be going to their doors. What else can they do to you? You were jailed, you were exiled, and you are living without any material comforts."

I responded, "These two people, the Qazi and my friend Nadir Jan, dragged me out there."

He nodded, "Yes, I know. Nadir made you go because

he was afraid the bribes he took during his time may come back to haunt him. This way he's now acquainted with the Deputy Governor."

I said, "Well, I will admonish him not to take any bribes in the future. Why don't you take a few of these pheasants we brought home?"

He shook his head. "No," he said. "I'm not going to take your birds."

Nadir Jan interjected, "I have prepared dinner at my place. The weather is very nice. I request you come to my home. You all are invited as well." Finally, we all agreed and went to his place.

My Friends from Kabul

My friends used to come from Kabul to see me in Kandahar: Shah Abdullah Khan, Dr. Anas Khan, Goya Saheb, etc. They used to come in groups sometimes and enjoy the beautiful weather of Kandahar. We used to sit around and talk. Mohammad Younis Khan always tried to make sure I was comfortable in my exile. He held back nothing and acted like a brother. He would tell the people of Kandahar that, "Khalilullah is my teacher." However, inside myself, in the hollow of my surroundings and in my heart, I always considered myself a prisoner, a prisoner of circumstances. I used to miss Kabul and my memories from there, from Kohdaman, and from Kohistan.

My mountain, my kaaba (holy place, Mecca), and my country
The garden of my heaven, my Kohdaman
Waves of my tears pour out in torrents in your memory
Only my eyes know, my nights know and myself know.

The people of Kandahar had a habit of getting together in specific places like recreation centers on the weekends, during springtime. The people of Herat did the same. We called these gatherings *melaa* (fair). Most of these recreation centers were in and around cemeteries, since there were no other designated places.

The favorite food of the people of Kandahar during

melaa was lettuce with a dip of *sikanjabeen* (a mixture of vinegar, sugar, and ginger).

They would go to Baba Wali Saheb, Sheenghari Baba, or Sher Surkhwali. Sometimes, they would go to Khwaja Yakshanba (Sunday or the first day of the week). I would avoid these places. I would mostly be with Abdul Aziz Khan Kandahari, who was the mayor of Kandahar and a writer and scholar himself. At one time, he was also in jail for quite a while. Lala Zafar Khan Momand's family was also close to us. Qazi Saheb Ghulam Aishan always tried to make sure I was not left alone. On weekends and holidays we would go hunting or visit historical relics of Kandahar.

Whenever I heard about a writing or a book, I would go after it. At the grave of Baba Wali, I remember spending all day trying to figure out the writing on the tombstone. Reading it was very difficult and required a lot of attention. I left no stone unturned in trying to figure out writings on historical monuments and relics, especially what Baihaqi had pointed out in his history. I visited Lashkargah a few more times.

Cracks Begin to Show in the Ruling Family

Abdul Majid Khan Zabuli was the business magnet at the time. He represented the capitalists of Afghanistan. He was all-powerful. The corporations he controlled were all involved in government affairs and contracts. Sardar Mohammad Younis Khan was a very honest man who trusted them. Abdul Majid Khan gradually increased his influence in the government, thus controlling the social politics of Afghanistan and leading to the establishment of an organization called Waish Zalmiyan (a leftist political movement) in 1947. Afghan youth were encouraged to come together and form a party. What was the reason behind it? Up front it appeared to be an innocent organization for youth; however, behind the scenes the real objective was unclear. It didn't pass the smell test.

Kandahar was a fertile breeding ground for this political movement because Abdul Majid Khan considered himself to be from and close to Kandahar. He sowed the seeds of discord between Dari and Pashtu. At the same time a contradictory action was taken, and the Americans were allowed to develop the Hermand Valley following an expansive agricultural plan for Afghanistan. Now, we know that the assistance of the Americans was confined to this Hermand plan. They were not allowed to exploit the petroleum reserves in Herat or work on the oil and gas reserves in the north. Similarly, they were not allowed to improve and build the highway to the north. They did not allow the Americans to work on roads from Kabul to Jalalabad. All these places were left in the hands of the Russians, who gradually implemented their long-term goals.

During this time the issue of Pashtunistan (Pakhtoonistan) rose to prominence. (Pashtunistan is an historical area populated by indigenous people reaching back to the first millennium. Since it was divided between British India and Afghanistan in 1893 – Amir Adur Rahman Khan -- it has been a place of contention.)

Sardar Mohammad Daoud Khan and Sardar Mohammad Naim Khan, who had recently risen to power, (Daoud Khan became Prime Minister 1953-1963 and later first President of Afghanistan, 1973-1978) were not very happy that their uncle, Shah Mahmud Khan, was Prime Minister. In their opinion, Sardar Mohammad Hashim Khan was the rightful Prime Minister. They considered themselves, and no one else, to be heirs of Hashim Khan's legacy. They also held the view that the descendants of Mohammad Yosuf Khan should rule Afghanistan in a bifurcation of power. The sons of one mother, Mohammad Nadir Khan, Shah Wali Khan, and Shah Mahmud Khan, should be content with the rulers of the crown. Thus Mohammad Zahir Shah, the son of Mohammad Nadir Shah, became the king after the death of his father (1933). The owners of the crown and the son of the other wife, who were the sons of Mohammad Aziz Khan, should take executive power of the country. In their thinking, the Prime Ministry should also be inherited.

Abdul Majid Khan exploited this window of

opportunity and inflamed the issue. Shah Mahmud Khan, it appeared, had become conscious of this; yet he did not want any bad blood to run in the family. It is significant in that the family of Nadir Shah was famous for family unity from the time they came to power in Afghanistan (that is, from the time of Amir Abdur Rahman Khan), until the time Sardar Shah Mahmud Khan became the Prime Minister. Their family, including men and women, would get together once a week to discuss the domestic and foreign affairs of Afghanistan and exchange opinions. They would try not to execute anything until they had time to discuss it in a family meeting. They never allowed any obstructionist to interrupt their bond. In spite of that, the obstruction gradually wedged its way in. If this kind of interference had improved the plight of the people it would have been welcome; however, it caused their downfall and damaged the interest of Afghanistan.

Looking back in history, the downfall of the family of Ghaznavids (975 to 1187) came about because of the opposition of the eldest son of Mahmood Ghaznavi, Mohammad, and his second son Masoud, who had an adversarial relation, causing the overthrow of the empire. Similarly, the family of Ghorids (12th and 13th century) met the same fate of opposition and destruction, and so did the Kings of Khwarizm (12th and 13th century), who were destroyed by the internal conflict between the queen and her oldest son, Khwarizm Shah (1150-1206).

Ghengis Khan (1162-1227) exploited the disunity, and the Islamic world fell to him in blood and dust. Not too far back in history the family of descendants of Mirwais Khan (1673-1715) fought and killed each other and destroyed the country. The family of Ahmad Shah (1722-1773) after Taimur Shah (1748-1793) forcibly blinded anyone who could have a claim to throne and killed them, adding to the affliction of Afghanistan. The Mohammad Zai family, brothers of Amir Sher Ali Khan, used internal insurrections to fight against him. In the family of Amir Abdur Rahman Khan (1840-1901) there is no doubt that Amanullah Khan had a falling out with his father, Habibullah Khan Seraj and his uncle Sardar Nasrullah Khan. This paved the way for the fall of their government (1929) and the ascension of Habibullah Khan Kalakani (1890-1929). Family discord caused the downfall of Amanullah Khan. I know the intricate details about it, how it happened, and how messages were exchanged between Habibullah Khan Kalakani and those supporting him who were close to Amir Amanullah Khan. This is not the place to discuss this further.

When Nadir Shah came to power as king, his brother became Prime Minster, and a third brother became the Minister of Defense and so on and so forth, it was welcomed as a great unified step forward by the people. They believed Afghanistan would flourish under this unity, and they would leave the days of affliction behind. However, this kind of rule was against the time. The times for monarchy and family rule were changing. In this sense, the strict family rule may have led to the future destruction.

Sardar Mohammad Daoud and Sardar Mohammad Naim Khan reinvigorated the issue of Pashtunistan. It was said the brothers wanted popular support and a solid stage for themselves by having a document, which would prove to the people of Afghanistan that they cared about them. Nadir Shah, Shah Mahmud Khan, and Shah Wali Khan had documented proof, along with medals and honors to show the people that they were part of the fight for the independence of Afghanistan. They were recognized as the victors of the battle of Thal Fort (a British fort at the entrance of the Khurram Valley that was besieged by the Afghan Army during the third Anglo-Afghan War in 1919). They claimed they delivered Afghanistan from the hands of Amir Habibullah Khan Kalakani. However, Sardar Mohammad Hashim Khan, Mohammad Daoud Khan, and Mohammad Naim Khan played no part in the war of freedom, or the battle of Thal or the victory against Amir Habibullah Khan Kalakani. Mohammad Daoud and Mohammad Naim were very young at the time.

Here, with the issue of Pashtunistan, they tried to justify their political and military prowess. They wanted medals and their names on certificates. They may even have had the idea of a victory arch and obelisks for themselves to match the gates built for Amanullah Khan for his participation in the War of Independence and also for Nadir Shah. Since Mohammad Nadir Shah and his brothers Sardar Shah Mahmud Khan and Sardar Shah Wali Khan had deep and great influence in southern Afghanistan, Mohammad Daoud and Mohammad Naim also wanted to replicate it for themselves.

The Issue of Pashtunistan

The easiest issue Mohammad Daoud Khan and Mohammad Naim Khan found to exploit and invigorate was the Pashtunistan situation. When India was being partitioned (1947) into two countries as India and Pakistan they vehemently raised this issue. Afghanistan did not recognize Pakistan officially in the first days. The Afghan representative at the United Nations declined to support. They did not come forward and candidly say the land of Pashtunistan is part of Afghanistan. They raised a different issue. They took the high road and said Afghanistan supported the statement that Pakistan had been created and was free. They said Afghanistan supported the idea that the people of Pashtunistan should have the right of self-determination and the right to create their own country between Afghanistan and Pakistan. Pakistan did not accept it, and this issue became a bone of contention, which continues today.

The spiritual and religious leaders of Afghanistan, like Janab Nourul Mashaekh and the Hazrat of Charbagh, were against this. The people divided into two clear factions, and the Waish Zalmiyan created by Abdul Majid Khan supported the concept of Pashtunistan. The leaders of Pashtunistan like Abdul Ghaffar Khan and others were welcomed in Kabul like heads of state and were accorded great honor.

Mohammad Daoud Khan oversaw the whole creation, invigoration, and flourishing of the Pashtunistan issue. A new department was established under the name Tribal Affairs. A small unit for Tribal Affairs existed before. Sayed Shamsuddin Majrooh, a prominent personality of Afghanistan, headed this new department. The work for

402

Pashtunistan took off with all its energy. Radio Kabul was part of the propaganda. Every day, morning and evening, the national anthem of Pashtunistan was sung.

Long live Pashtunistan
Long live the gardens and flowers...

A good portion of the country's revenue was spent on this propaganda and part of it was sent to support Pashtunistan. For example, sugar purchased for local consumption was often diverted toward Pashtunistan instead of the Afghan people receiving it. The people did not even get half of it. The same was true for flour, fuel, and other consumer goods. A large portion of the assistance provided by Americans and other countries was spent on Pashtunistan.

Waish Zalmiyan was the force behind pushing the issue of Pashtunistan to the forefront. The irony of the whole thing, and what surprises me most, is that Noor Mohammad Taraki (1917-1979; became first Communist president of Afghanistan in 1978 and was killed in 1979); that cursed Taraki who was the chauffeur of Abdul Majid Khan Zabuli and later became his aide de camp, had a prominent role in this Waish Zalmiyan. Abdul Rauf Benawa Kandahari, who belonged to an elite intellectual family of Kandahar, also had a part in this. Noor Mohammad Siyah, son of Abdul Sattar Khan, one of the industrialists of Kandahar also had a share in it. Others, like Babrak Karmal (1929-1996, of Parcham party, General Secretary of the Central Committee of the People's Democratic Party), who became Communist later, were a part of this. Some people, such as Abdul Hadi Khan Dawi, one of the elders of Afghanistan, who joined Waish Zalmiyan were innocent bystanders, who did not realize or recognize the main objective of this party. Waish Zalmiyan produced a publication by the same name, *Waish Zalmiyan*. Abdul Majid Khan was the architect and founder of this movement.

Arrival of Hazrat Shor Bazar in Kandahar

When I was still in exile, things took an unexpected turn when Hazrat of Shor Bazar came to visit Kandahar from Kabul. Deputy Governor Mohammad Younis Khan avoided his visit by touring Girishk. While he was gone, the Deputy Governor's wife called me and sought my advice on how to proceed with Hazrat Saheb's visit.

"Pay your respects to him and honor him," I advised her. "He's Hazrat Saheb. He was a friend of your father and a friend of Abdul Quddos Khan, the Prime Minister. He was the friend of your family, and he is a stalwart of Afghanistan."

"What you are saying is true," she agreed. "However, instructions from Kabul are on the contrary. We are being encouraged to disgrace him."

I asked her, "Can you do that? Can you disgrace Hazrat Saheb?"

She answered, "No. I cannot. My husband could not stand following the instructions either."

I asked her, "Where is the Deputy Governor?"

"He has hidden himself by visiting Girishk," she admitted.

"Then the best course is for you not to interfere," I advised. "Since the Deputy Governor is not present, you should not encourage people against Hazrat Saheb."

The wife of Deputy Governor continued, "What do I do? Hazrat Saheb called me last night and said he will come to visit me tonight."

"That's not very difficult," I answered. "Since the Deputy Governor is not here you should arrange a room for Hazrat Saheb at the hotel and provide him with hospitality."

I personally did not want Hazrat Saheb to be insulted or disgraced. The wife of the Deputy Governor agreed.

The Hazrat Saheb came and checked into the hotel, but his benefactors, supporters, and loyal disciples came to the hotel and took him to their homes. The people of Kandahar visited him in droves, offering their respect and courtesy.

Hazrat Saheb sent out his greetings in the form of a pamphlet or flyer that included a few lines of poetry by Hafiz Sherazi, which translated something like this:

The ball of prosperity and success
is lying in the middle of the field;
No one dares to retrieve it. Oh the brave riders!
Where are you?

The pamphlet he was distributing called on people to wake up to what the Hindus were doing to the Muslims in India: killing, pillaging, and destroying their property. "They have slain the daughters of Islam!" the pamphlet declared. It was an intense pamphlet with language calling for unity and calling for a *jihad*, making it mandatory for the Muslims. The fighting between the Hindus and Muslims was ongoing.

Mohammad Alam Khani was from Logar and was the Military Commander of Kandahar. When he heard about all this, he sent a few of his plainclothes henchmen to mingle with the crowd and create commotion for Hazrat Saheb. They would listen to him and then curse him, making fun of his name. His name was Sher Agha (sher means lion), but they would call him Feel Agha (*feel* means elephant). Finally, they succeeded in removing Hazrat Saheb from Kandahar. After experiencing this disrespect and pushback from people, he left.

As far as I know, there were many, many young men from Kandahar, from the east of Afghanistan, from the south of Afghanistan, and even from Kohdaman and Kohistan and central Afghanistan who took up arms, left their homes and without the blessings or permission of the government, joined the Pakistani army to fight against the Indians. They fought bravely and many of them were killed. This led to a total break in the relationship between Hazrat Saheb and the Royal Family. Sardar Shah Mahmud Khan was at a loss for words or actions. He tried to keep Hazrat Saheb from being upset; however, Hazrat Saheb was very offended. There was no way to compromise or reach compensation. Hazrat Saheb was under surveillance

in Kabul. Secret police were appointed to follow him there.

The Visit of Sardar Naim Khan to Kandahar

When Sardar Naim Khan came to Kandahar, the people welcomed him warmly. This poor soul (Khalili) also went and stood in line; I didn't know what else to do. If I didn't go and welcome him, and he comes and knows I am here, he may hurt me. If I go to welcome him, he could insult me in front of people. I was of two minds. With an anxious heart, I decided to go. Goya Saheb, Annus Khan, and Shah Abdullah had also come from Kabul. Goya Saheb and Shah Abdullah stood next to me. Annus Khan, the way he always did, was very timid and stood further away from us. He had been visiting Kandahar to check education affairs and thus had an excuse to stand closer to the incoming guest. When Sardar Naim Khan arrived unexpectedly, he was very nice and kind to me in front of the people of Kandahar.

They all went to the Deputy Governor's place with Sardar Naim Khan. He turned to Annus Khan and asked, "Where is Khalili?"

Annus Khan answered, nervously, "I have no idea."

Goya Saheb spoke up. "Annus Khan knows where he is. Every night Annus is with Khalili at his house. Khalili has gone back to his home."

"I am aware of this," Naim Khan said, looking at Annus Khan. "No one has stopped you from going to Khalili's house. I'm sure you are having a good literary discourse while you are together. Tell me, has he written any new poetry?"

Goya Saheb answered. "These days he has reduced his poetry writing, but he's busy researching Kandahar's history. Anywhere he finds a stone or a grave he studies it and writes about it. He has turned his face away from the living and is pursuing the dead."

By saying this, Goya Saheb was informing Mohammad Naim Khan of his concern for me.

Afterwards Sardar Najibullah Khan came to Kandahar and headed the delegation to Pakistan from there. He returned very happy. He reported, "I have been working hard on an understanding between Afghanistan and Pakistan, and Pakistan has accepted an internal self-determination for the people of Pashtunistan. The people of Baluchistan (north of Pakistan and a hot spot for political strife) and Pashtunistan have also agreed to this. This is in the interest of Afghanistan, and the area will be quelled from the heat of insurrection."

He announced all of this on his return, but later was shut out from talking about it anymore. The opposition to Sardar Najibullah Khan was obvious, and he was depicted as pro Pakistan.

Next came Sardar Faiz Mohammad Khan, who was on his way to Turkey. He came to my house. He was a very good friend of mine and was thoughtful and considerate of me. We sat and talked and cried together.

I asked him, "How do you think the future looks for our country?"

He responded, "Afghanistan is being destroyed. They did not listen to me. I'm going to Turkey. Why don't you come with me?"

I shook my head. "How can I go?" I asked.

"I will take you with me in my car and cross you over the border. No one can turn you back."

"What about my wife and children?" I asked.

He said, "Leave your family here."

"No," I said. "It's not possible for me to leave them."

We talked, and when the conversation lightened, we laughed together. He was my guest for another night and as usual he was very, very courteous and friendly. He was a great man, a learned man and understood the pulse of politics. He foresaw what would happen to Afghanistan. I can vouch and witness in front of God that Sardar Faiz Mohammad Khan and Sardar Najibullah Khan were against the new political developments in Afghanistan and had predicted the outcome.

The Iranian Delegation Reaches Kandahar from Kabul

Najibullah Khan called me from Kabul, informing me the Iranian delegation was on its way from Kandahar to Kabul. He asked me to be on guard and said, "Do not reveal you are in exile there. Instead, welcome them as your host, and tell them you're on vacation in Kandahar."

He had already spoken to the Deputy Governor, Younis Jan, who confirmed to him I would be the host. I asked him, "Who is in this delegation?"

He answered, "The Iranian Minister of Education, Dr. Ali Asghar Hikmat, and a couple of other people by the names of Mr. Ragh and Dr. Bayani."

"I don't think it's possible for me to whitewash the truth and tell them I'm here just on vacation," I told him. "They may even know the reason of my presence here."

"They have no idea. Watch out," he warned. "If you don't, it may hurt your chances."

"Thank you very much for your kindness," I told him.

The delegation arrived and I went to welcome it. It was the first time I had met Mr. Hikmat, and the first time I was a host to foreigners. I accompanied them to Sardah Gardens and the famous Forty Steps (that lead to the *Chilzina – 40 steps*, a rock-cut chamber) and saw the inscriptions with writings of the Moghul Kings. We also went to see the Holy *Khirgah*, the mausoleum of Ahmed Shah and many other libraries.

Dr. Bayani was an intellectual and a scholar. He was very well versed in books. When he saw my copy of *Kimiya-e-Saadat* (*The Alchemy of Eternal Bliss* by Imam Al Ghazzali (1055-1111) first translation published in 1910) he said excitedly, "Sir, this is an authentic first edition and one of the oldest manuscripts. It has no comparison and no mistakes. Why don't you give it to me and I will have it reprinted."

I answered, "This is the property of Afghanistan, and I do not want it to become a source of tension." Thus, I excused myself and did not give him the book. They presented me with a certificate of appreciation, which all three of them had signed.

It was time for evening prayer, and we were at the Babai Hotel having tea together. The discussion turned to Hafez Sherazi (Persian lyric poet, 1325-1390). I asked Dr. Ali Asghar Hikmat, "What has caused Hafez to become so famous in the world? In Afghanistan, in most families' homes, you will find a collection of his Persian poetry (*Divan*). There is no one young or old, man or woman, who does not recognize Hafez. Even illiterate people can recite his poetry by heart. Traditionally, before they would start any project or do any work, they would consult Hafez. They open the book and whatever it says, they follow it as a superstition. They consider his poetry as a prophecy. They swear an oath on his poetry."

Dr. Hikmat replied, "It is the unique style of Hafez, which has captured the hearts and minds of the people."

I said, "Maybe there is something more to it."

Dr. Hikmat asked, "What is that?"

I explained, "Hafez knew the Holy Koran by heart and may have drawn his inspiration and his conclusions from it."

Tears suddenly welled in the Minister's eyes, and he said, "It never occurred to me the youth in Afghanistan would perceive this side of the poet. I did not mention this side of Hafez to you. Now I can tell you, I truly believe Hafez's poetry was inspired by the Holy Koran. In fact, I have written an essay under the headline, *The Effect of the Clarity and Eloquency of the Holy Koran in Hafez's Poetry*. It has not been published yet."

Amid a stream of his tears, the Minister added, "We are also Muslims, and we believe in the Holy Koran. In fact, I have read an interpretation of Holy Koran printed in Kabul. I saw the first volume was written in a very eloquent prose. In the second volume; however, the style of writing had changed. It was a good style, but why was there such a deep difference between the two volumes? What do you think?" He insisted on hearing my answer.

I answered, "Maybe the second volume was translated by someone else."

He continued to press. "I heard the first volume was

written by Khalili."

I answered, "They may be correct."

He said, "Then why wasn't your name included in the introduction and foreword written to this interpretation of the Holy Koran?"

I answered, "Maybe they did not want to write anybody's name, so that God will reward me more this way."

Dr. Ali Hikmat abruptly asked me, "What are you doing in Kandahar? Why are you not in Kabul? You could be very helpful there."

I explained, "I'm just visiting here."

He broke into laughter and said, "We have information you were released from prison and are exiled here. I went to Istalef and saw the beautiful Gulbahar and Paghman with its mild weather. No one would be visiting Kandahar in this heat, when the climate of Istalef, north of Kabul, is so pleasant."

He continued, "I know everything about you and what you have gone through. Why are you hiding that from me?"

I answered, in resignation, "What benefit will it bring to narrate my story to you? I am here, and I am thankful. My destiny is in the hands of God. He may have wanted it this way."

The Minister said, "I'm aware of the whole story. While talking to your friend, Sardar Najibullah Khan, I insisted he talk about you. He would not. He also hid it from me. But some of your other friends did tell me, including my host in Kabul."

I didn't know who his host in Kabul was. The minister announced, "When I return to my office in Iran, I will write a letter regarding your translation and interpretation of the Holy Koran. I will request permission to allow you to be our guest in Iran for a while."

I told the Minister, "I beg of you not to do that. This may create more obstacles for me."

He said, "Alright, sir. I would like to print the work of Khwaja Abdullah Ansari in Iran. We have the first volume of his works, but it is not well written and may have some errors. I had tried to find a better version of this book in

Afghanistan, but I could not."

I did have a copy of a much better version; in fact, it was an original of Khwaja Abdullah Ansari that I'd purchased from a village in Ghor. This is the village where the mausoleums of the Khwajas of Chisht are there. The manuscript was with me in Kandahar.

I told the Minister, "I have an original copy at home, and I will show it to you."

When I brought the book to him, he was flabbergasted. "What a sacred thing to do," he said. "If you can part with it, I will offer to purchase it at any price."

"I will never sell this sacred work at any price," I answered. "It would be like selling the Holy Koran. However, I have two conditions, and if you meet them, I will lend it to you."

"First," I said, "When you publish a reprint of this book, you will please mention you brought this book from Afghanistan."

He picked up the pen and speedily wrote that, "This complete and beautiful work belongs to Mr. Khalili, which I have brought from Afghanistan. I have borrowed it from him, and I promise on the Holy Koran that when I print this, I will mention and thank Afghanistan and you."

I said, "There's one more thing you have to do. Once you have printed the book, please return my original copy."

He wrote it down in the letter, "As soon as the book is printed, I will return the copy, which belongs to Khalili to him."

I said, "Good. Now, I will guide you to another place where you can find more volumes of this book. When you go to Herat, you should go to Gazar Gah Sharif and go to the library of Hazrat Khwaja Abdullah Ansari. Mr. Mir Ghulam Haidar Khan, the curator of the Khwaja Abdullah Ansari mausoleum, will help you find the volumes you seek."

Dr. Ali Asghar Hikmat, the Iranian Minister of Education, answered, "Definitely, I will do so, and I am headed there."

I added, "I will write a letter addressing Mr. Mir Saheb to please present you with a copy. Show him my book

411

also."

The Minister replied, "Very well."

I wrote the letter to Mr. Mir Saheb and a few days later the delegation left Kandahar, bound for Herat. In Herat, I heard Mir Saheb gave the rest of the volumes to Dr. Hikmat to take back to Iran for reprinting. However, almost a year passed by, and I thought my book was lost.

One day, I received the new book, which the Minister had published in Iran, and also my original book I had lent to him. I noticed right away that in the introduction he had kept his promise. I was very happy to get my book back. This book remained in my library until it was plundered by the Communist and Russian forces. They took away the irreplaceable book. I have no idea where it is now or who is in possession of it.

I remained in Kandahar and was very happy with Sardar Mohammad Younis Khan. The people of Kandahar were also kind to me and had given me the title of Director of Sugar. At times when some of the noble and respected families in Kandahar had a falling out, instead of going to the judicial system, they sought my counsel. They would also seek my counsel through the Deputy Governor's office by appealing to them to appoint me as an arbitrator. I would go and help them to reach compromise.

Gradually, I became a Kandahari. I used to visit Khak Rez, where the tomb of Hazrat Shah Masood resides. He had been mentioned in a book by the name of *Turfah-ul-Akram*. This book was published in India in three volumes. It gives a profile of Hazrat Shah Masood. He was from the Sayeds of Sabzwar of Iran and had come to Afghanistan during the time of the Safavids (1502-1736). He was a noble Sayed for whom the people had a great respect. They called him Shah Saheb. He had taken residence at the foot of Ghumdan Mountain, and his tomb attracts lovers. His personal belongings, books, furnishings, utensils, and pots are kept in the storage there. His other belongings are still in Khak Rez Kandahar. They date back 500 to 600 years. There's a mosque there near it is a semiprecious stone mine of Shah Masood, which people sometimes in error call Shah Maqsood. The mine was eventually shut down or maybe it ran out of precious stones. The popular saying there is the precious stones hid themselves because the government was not very kind to people and the mines lost their preciousness. The famous rosary, the Shah Masood stone (Maqsood), comes from the Ghumdan Mountain from near the tomb of Hazrat Shah.

One day, I was at the tomb of Shah Saheb. It used to take almost an eight-hour drive from Kandahar to this place, and there was a mountain pass to cross on the way. While I was there, I received news via telephone from Kabul to Kandahar that I was blessed with a son. My wife had gone to Kabul to visit her family. The government had allowed her to go. When I heard the news, I named my son right then and there as Masood. I named my son who was born in my absence as a respect to the tomb of Shah Masood.

As you will recall, I was in the Arg prison in Kabul when I received similar news that a son, Nejatullah, had been born to me. At that time, Sardar Shah Mahmud Khan had newly assumed the post of the Prime Ministry, and I was allowed to receive the Hafez collection of poetry, *Divan*. Upon the news of Nejatullah's birth, I opened up the *Divan* as a good omen to see what page it opened up to. My eyes fell on this couplet:

Yesterday at dawn I was released from my sorrow
In the darkness of the night, I received a drink from the
fountain of youth.

Mohammad Hashim Khan's Anger over My Return to Kabul

Sardar Najibullah Khan and Sardar Younis Khan, the Deputy Governor of Kandahar, both appealed to the King of Afghanistan through Sardar Shah Mahmud Khan. Somehow they were able to secure permission from His Majesty for me to travel to Kabul. I was allowed to visit Kabul for a month or two and then return to my family and my job in Kandahar. I was happy at this turn of events. Whenever I traveled toward Kabul I would be on the

413

Seventh Sky. My Kandahari friends would always accompany me to the edge of Kandahar. After leaving Kandahar, I normally stopped in Ghazni to visit the sacred grave of Hakim Sanai before continuing on to Kabul. The first time I traveled to Kabul, I went to the King's Court. Still, my lionhearted uncle Abdul Rahim Khan lingered in the Kabul jail.

I was granted an audience with the king. Hashim Khan was still alive and heard I had come to Kabul. I heard he was talking about me, and saying, "How come this man is still alive? Shah Mahmud Khan is a simple man. He does not know Khalili incited people in Kandahar and is ringing them around himself. Today or tomorrow he will literally light a fire there (Kandahar). I have information about it." Even Shah Mahmud Khan had told Najibullah Khan to tell "a certain person" to leave Kabul soon "because my brother is not very happy."

I stayed in Kabul 15 to 20 days and then said goodbye and went back to Kandahar. I remained in Kandahar another five to six months, when I received a full pardon. All exiles in Kandahar were pardoned except for the people from Kohdaman and Kohistan. Some of those exiles were still in jail in Kandahar. Their families were allowed to live in Kandahar, but they had to panhandle sometimes to make ends meet. Those who were sent to Herat as exiles were in the Herat prison, and their families were panhandling in Herat to feed themselves. Similarly, the same fate fell to the people who were exiled to Mazar-i-Sharif. One of these exiles was the first wife of Amir Habibullah Khan Kalakani. She was in jail along with her two or three daughters in Mazar-i-Sharif. Her daughters grew up there.

My Appointment as Deputy Vice Chancellor of Kabul University

We left Kandahar for Kabul. Najibullah Khan and my other friends came out to greet us and welcome us to the city. Sardar Mohammad Annus Khan also came by. I went to live in my humble house in Kabul in Karte Char. A few days later Najibullah Khan recommended I be appointed as

Deputy Vice Chancellor of Kabul University, as an assistant to Sardar Mohammad Annus Khan. I pleaded with both of them, "I do not know any foreign language, and I'm not versed in modern education."

Najibullah Khan replied, "The Prime Minister has signed the order. You do not have any other job at this time. You should assume this post."

I realized the Prime Minister did not want me to work close to Abdul Majid Khan Zabuli. I also did not want to be part of their circle.

I sought permission from the Prime Minister to visit Kohdaman occasionally. The Prime Minister happily obliged me. However, he murmured to me, "Be careful. His Highness, the former Prime Minister Mohammad Hashim Khan, sometimes visits his landholdings in Kohdaman. Try to avoid the days when he's traveling there." I submitted to the will of God.

I also came to know informers had provided information to the Prime Minister Shah Mahmud Khan. They reported to him, "The people of Kandahar are coalescing around 'a certain person' and may be plotting against the state. The presence of this person in Kandahar may hurt the interests of the government." Since Sardar Shah Mahmud Khan was a very honest and pious man he did not give heed to these conspiracy theories. In fact, to safeguard my interests, and myself, he brought me from Kandahar to Kabul.

From the southside window of the Arg one can see the Kabul River. A bridge used to cross this place. During the time of Amir Habibullah Khan Seraj, this bridge was called One Paisa Bridge, or Penny Bridge, because whoever crossed it would be charged one penny to cover the expenses of building and maintaining the bridge.

The bridge connected to Chahar Bagh where the dome of Mahmud Shah (the son of Ahmed Shah Baba) is located. Mahmud Shah and his brother Shah Shuja-u-Mulk (1785-1842, fifth King of Afghanistan) are both buried there. When Amanullah Khan became the king, the Chahar Bagh (Four Gardens) was renamed Baghe Omoomi (Public Garden).

Every evening people used to gather there to enjoy the weather and listen to recordings about news developments on a gramophone (a record player), which was installed there to inform the people, because there was no radio at the time. Slowly, restaurants were opening up and people were becoming used to them. Sometimes bands of music would come together there and play.

This is where the University offices were housed, in a two-story building in the Baghe Omoomi of Kabul.

I worked as Deputy Vice Chancellor of the University for five or six months along with Mohammad Annus Khan. I worked sincerely and earnestly in that position. I respected him and did my utmost to be professional while working with him. But since we had been friends for so long – always very informal and exchanging humorous tidbits – it was difficult to put all that aside and work in an office sitting with him as my direct supervisor. In fact, we shared an office instead of two adjoining ones, to avoid the scenario where he would call out to me and I would have to come and stand in front of the desk of my friend.

That would have been difficult and totally against my nature. Annus Khan also was not comfortable having an assistant like me who knew him so closely. I decided to quit my job, but retain my friendship. I placed my resignation letter on Annus Khan's desk, citing a very minor excuse or pretense, and left the office.

My Visit to Kohdaman after My Freedom from Exile

It was wintertime. His Highness Shah Mahmud Khan had gone on an inspection visit to Mazar-i-Sharif and Kataghan (the name of an estate). Sardar Najibullah Khan was also out of town, so I took advantage of it. Without permission, I loaded my family and my belongings into a vehicle and left for Qarabagh (north of Kabul), where I planned to spend the winter at my paternal estate. We passed the severe winter smoothly there. I even welcomed my friends who visited me, though I was careful not to have too many people around me. I became convinced the time of informers and spies was behind us, that no conspiracy would be successful, and if witnesses reported anything wrong on my part, that Shah Mahmud Khan would not believe them. Leaving Kabul and going to Qarabagh was not a crime. My resignation was not a strike against me either. I had confidence and trust in Shah Mahmud Khan.

It was hunting season, and I used to go out tracking game. Pheasant was my favorite. There was a place, an acre or two, in an area full of water (large pond) where people would leave decoys so the real ones flying by would come down to refresh themselves, and we would shoot them. We hid in the bushes with our guns and had a good time. Sometimes, we would catch a wounded bird, still alive. We would take care of the bird while it recuperated, then set it in the pond as a decoy. This type of pond, called *noor,* was popular in both Kohistan and Kohdaman. Unfortunately, this type of hunting, to me, was very cruel. I eventually gave it up because I saw how it would harden people's hearts and make them very mean.

I was in Kohdaman until the month of April. In April, the brother of Najibullah Khan came from Kabul, bearing an urgent message from Ali Mohammad Khan, the Deputy Prime Minister, asking me to come to Kabul right away.

His Highness Shah Mahmud Khan had also returned to Kabul from Mazar-i-Sharif. I was partly afraid and partly content as I left my house after goodbyes and proceeded to Kabul. The next morning, I went to visit Ali Mohammad Khan at his residence. He was a very good friend and a kind person. He held two portfolios: Foreign Affairs and Deputy Vice President.

I asked him, "Is everything okay? You summoned me to come to Kabul."

He answered, "You made a mistake when you left Kabul without permission and went to Kohdaman. People gathered around you there, and your friends from Kabul also visited you. Even some people who are out of favor met with you there."

I responded, "Well, if going to Kohdaman is a crime

and friends visiting me is a crime, then whatever punishment it requires, I understand. I am here."

He continued. "Why did you resign as Deputy Vice Chancellor of Kabul University?"

I answered, "I could not continue to be an assistant to a very close friend like Annus Khan. Because we are friends, there is no formality between us. Trying to change from being close to being formal is a difficult task."

He broke into a big laugh like he used to and said, "Now, the Commander in Chief wants to see you. I've been asked to appoint you as Chief of Intelligence for the Prime Ministry."

I was kind of taken aback. Mirza Mohammad Shah, who was the Chief of Intelligence, had just died.

Being the Chief of Intelligence was a very delicate and important position where you had your hand on the pulse of the state. I had been a prisoner. I was considered a criminal. I was close to gallows. How come today I am being considered for this Chief of Intelligence job? I needed time to think.

I respectfully asked Ali Mohammad Khan, "Will you please allow me to think about it tonight and seek some counsel on it? Tomorrow, I will give you my answer."

He said, "Fine, but don't go back to Kohdaman. Do not seek advice there. Don't tell anybody about this."

I said, "I'm not going to tell anyone. I'll keep it to myself and mull it over."

Let all the musical instruments break
So that I hear something from the heart

Ali Mohammad Khan was a man of letters, a politician, and a man who would recognize talent. He was intelligent, eloquent, a highly civilized man and had beautiful handwriting. I may have said this before, but he was one of the top students in his class from Habibiya High School. He was originally from Badakhshan. He was tall and handsome and when he would talk and elucidate a point, he impressed the people around him. When he gave a lecture or a talk, the audience would be mesmerized. He was an ardent follower of Mirza Abdul Qadir Bedil (1814-1873) and always selected and read *Ghazals* (poems). He copied over the *Ghazals* of Bedil in his own handwriting. It was a beautiful collection of his poems. I don't know what happened to them.

I went home. That night I visited Goya Saheb, may God bless his soul. I did not tell him why I was there. Among our friends, we always hid our important secrets from him because he could not keep a secret. He could not hold back, but would blurt it out. By one excuse or another he would always reveal it. I kept thinking and analyzing the offer made for job of Chief of Intelligence.

As much as I thought about it, I said to myself, "This is just a job for listening and spying. I don't have any mysterious knowledge. Spies and informers are sometimes people who have weaknesses. People sometimes lie to get to a means. Some informers and spies have destroyed families for their short sightedness for very small amount of money. I will have to prepare reports based on their supply of intelligence and will have to keep abreast Sardar Shah Mahmud Khan. I may create some unwanted ripples."

I told myself I should not accept this position. I may die of hunger. I may go to prison again. But, I decided not to accept this position.

My Appointment as Secretary to the Cabinet

The next day I went to see Ali Mohammad Khan at the Prime Ministry. When I entered his office, he saw my face and thought I had accepted the offer. I was smiling and happy, but I was happy because I had made my decision not to accept the job.

As soon as he was alone he turned to me and said, "So what did you decide?"

I told him, "I'm not going to accept this job on any terms. I would earnestly plead you to extend your helping hand to me just as you have done in the past as my teacher, as my friend, as my benefactor, and mentor. Please do something so that the Commander in Chief, Sepah Salar, is not offended by my turning down the position. I'm not going to accept it."

He said, "Is this your final answer?"

I said, "Yes, this is my final answer."

He replied, "God willing, this may be a good decision by you. I will go right away and inform the Prime Minister because they are waiting for your answer."

He left and went to the Prime Minister's office. He was there for a while and came back and said, "The Prime Minister was very kind and respects your decision for not agreeing to take the job. However, he has another offer for you so you're not without a job and may continue to serve your country. This job is forced upon you, and you have to accept it."

I asked, "What is it?"

He said, "You have been appointed as Secretary to the Cabinet. Since the Chief of Intelligence used to hold both of these positions, you will only be Secretary to the Cabinet."

I said, "I'll be most happy to accept this position and serve in my best capacity. The cabinet is the cabinet of our nation. The ministers belong to Afghanistan. We are all from this land. There will be no higher honor for me than to assume this position under Prime Minister Shah Mahmud Khan, who is responsible for the release and freedom of thousands of prisoners."

I repeated again, "Yes, I accept this position."

Ali Mohammad Khan replied, "Now go to the Prime Minister's office, he wants to see you."

I went to Shah Mahmud Khan's office. He was sitting with all his glory behind a desk. I paid my respects. He did not offer me a seat, so I kept standing.

He was kind of irritated at the time. Addressing me, he said, "Khalili, don't think for a minute I'm afraid of you. By God, I'm not afraid of anybody but God. However, I have compassion. I am always very worried about you. I always remember the hard times you have gone through – hard times that not too many people have seen; the hard times your father saw; the hard times your uncle saw and your family saw and your other uncle saw. It is because of this I do not want people to conspire against you again, make you afflicted, and make us put you through that again. I have trust in you, and this is why I want to appoint you in a very difficult and sensitive position. You did not accept the Chief of Intelligence position. It was a very good assignment. Yet, you may have done the right thing. I will find someone else for that post. However, you are now the Secretary to the Cabinet. You will be present at all Cabinet meetings. You will not have the right to vote. Your job will be to write down all the proceedings and whatever is said there."

When he finished, I said, "It will be an honor and a pleasure to do this. I did not ask for the right to vote."

He said, "Go and write your own Firman (edict). Your position and compensation will be equal to the President General, and you also have the right to an automobile. You can have the one Mirza Ali Mohammad Shah used to have. As of tomorrow, start your duties."

I kissed his hand, paid my respects, and prayed along with him. I asked God to give me strength to perform the job.

I came home and sent my brother to Kohdaman to bring back my family, my wife and children. No one would believe this. He even asked me to write my own Firman. I wrote my own Firman and when it was signed, it was published in the *Islah-Anis* newspaper. All my friends and even some of my enemies came to celebrate for me. They were surprised at the developments and congratulated me. They were especially flabbergasted on my appointment to Secretary of the Cabinet. I told them, "I don't know if it's right or wrong, but I never betrayed Mohammad Hashim Khan or Afghanistan or Sardar Shah Mahmud Khan. I am well qualified to do the job, and I'm just as qualified as the people who performed the job before me."

Everyone congratulated me.

I Am Handed My Own File Condemning Me

The first day when I assumed my duties, surprisingly

enough my own files were presented to me by a man named Mirza Mohammad Hassan Khan. He lived in the Shewaki neighborhood of Kabul, and he was the son of Lala Amir Mohammad, a political refugee in India during the time of Sardar Mohammad Ayub Khan (1857-1914). Hassan Khan's father was close to the family of Nadir Shah. Hassan Khan was a Director of the Department of Documents in the Prime Ministry.

He brought a stack of files to me, and the first or second file was my own. He may have done so intentionally, if so, I think his motive was to indirectly inform me I had been dealt with very kindly by being appointed to this job, in spite of what was written in my file. Then again, maybe he made a mistake and gave me my file unintentionally.

Opening the file, I read a portion of a document. It said because Abdul Rahim Khan had a hand in the insurrection against the government by the people of Kunar, a province in Afghanistan, therefore the cabinet endorses Abdul Rahim Khan should be executed by firing squad. I read that Khalilullah Khalili, who is part of this instigation, should be condemned by all the heads of the departments of the Prime Ministry, and he should be hanged at the Prime Ministry. I read that Abdul Haleem Khan, the son of Abdul Rahim Khan, should also be hanged. The paper said their other close relatives should be exiled within Afghanistan and their possessions be confiscated.

This document was signed by each of the cabinet members. Mohammad Hashim Khan had added his signature, signing underneath, in English, in red ink. Then, it was sent to the court to be signed by the king, yet Mohammad Zahir Shah did not endorse it.

I'm convinced Mohammad Zahir Shah did not want to sign it. There is no document proving or supporting my theory, yet it is possible Sardar Ahmed Shah Khan, the Minister of Court, may have interceded. Sardar Shah Mahmud Khan may have played a role as well.

Whatever transpired at the time, I was able to read the document with my own eyes. I told the Director, "This is from the grace of God." The irony, I was now standing in the same office where the order for my execution was written. I was now the head of the department, which condemned me. The file that could have decided my fate was now in my hand.

"What should I do with all these documents?" Mirza Mohammad Hassan Khan asked me.

I said, "I will write a note on the side, saying the file should go to safekeeping. Please do not destroy it. Keep it in our office."

I wrote the note on the side of the file. It was my first official act as Secretary of the Cabinet.

A few days later, my first cabinet meeting took place. In summer, cabinet meetings were held at the first palace of the Prime Ministry; in winter they were held at the Gulkhana, which was toward the north side of the Prime Ministry. The meeting room had a big round table. All the ministers sat around it. Some of the faces drew my attention, like Mir Sayed Qasim Khan, who was accused of having a hand in the assassination of Nadir Shah and had been in prison for 16 to 17 years. He had also been in prison during the time of Amir Habibullah Khan Seraj. And now, he was Minister of Justice.

Mir Atta Mohammad Khan Herati, a member of the intelligentsia of Herat and a Sayed family, a good writer and researcher, was at the table as President of the Elders and head of the Senate. I may be mistaken regarding Sayed Qasim Khan. He probably held some other portfolio than Justice.

Fazal Ahmad Khan Mojadadi also was part of the Senate and present. Others around the table included Mirza Mohammad Khan, Minister of State; Ali Mohammad Khan, Deputy Prime Minister and Minister of Foreign Affairs; Sardar Mohammad Daoud Khan, Minister of Defense; Sardar Assad Khan, son of Amir Habibullah Khan Seraj, as Minister of the Interior; Mir Haider Khan Husseni, son of Qazi Atta Mohammad Khan, as Minister of Finance; Abdul Majid Khan Zabuli, Minister of Commerce. Zabuli was the head of the capitalists of Afghanistan, founder of Waish Zalmayan (the socialist movement), groomer of Noor Mohammad Taraki (first Communist President of Afghanistan 1978-1979/ belonged to Khalq wing of the

Afghan Communist party), and a benefactor of Abdur Rauf Benawa. Sayed Shamsuddin Majrooh, head of Tribal Affairs and Mohammad Hashim Maiwandwal (1919-1973), (who later became the Prime Minister of Afghanistan and was executed by the Communists in 1973), Minister of Information and Press, were also there, as well as Engineer Akram Khan, Minister of Public Works, who was later assassinated by the Communists, and also Dr. Majid Khan, as Minister of Education.

I am writing this from memory and may have mixed up or missed a few names and portfolios here. I think Fazal Ahmad Khan Mojadadi was the Minister of Public Works. Akram Khan had not become the Minister yet.

I entered the room and sat toward the end of the table right in front of the Prime Minister. All of the dignitaries present congratulated me. According to the set protocol, the Ministers would give me their briefs, and I would read each one of them aloud to the cabinet. The cabinet would then discuss each one and take appropriate action. Whatever discussion took place, I would summarize on the side of the brief. As a headline, I would write, "the cabinet has decided thus and so...." At the end, the Ministers would sign the piece of paper, and it would be placed in the file.

The very first day I made one fundamental change. I used more modern wording, and this drew attention from the Ministers. Prime Minister Shah Mahmud Khan, since he was well educated and a literary man who even wrote poetry, liked the changes I brought to the language of the cabinet. The first day went really well.

During the second cabinet meeting a misunderstanding took place.

The cabinet decided on the budget for mapping the Helmand River and digging two canals. I wrote this down, and the cabinet endorsed it. However, when the time came for each Minister to sign the paper, Kabir Khan Lodin arbitrarily put a line through my words and restricted the project to mapping only.

Mir Haidar Khan noticed what he was doing from across the table. I also noticed it. My generosity took over my better judgment. There was a competitive spirit between Mir Haidar Khan and Kabir Khan Lodin. Both were brilliant, educated men. When the time came for Mir Haidar Khan to sign, he said, "This has been altered. It's not right. It should be initialed by the Prime Minister." Turning toward me, he added, "Did you alter this?"

I kept quiet. I did not want to cause embarrassment to Kabir Khan Lodin. After all, he had been my student, and his father was a friend of my father who had worked with him at Qalai Murad Beg.

The Prime Minister also noticed and pushing the paper toward me, he looked at it, but did not initial it.

I offered, "I will correct it next time."

The rest of the papers were signed, but I held back not telling the others what had transpired. The meeting broke up. As I organized the papers and documents, and the Ministers talked among themselves, Kabir Khan Lodin kept quiet about the whole thing.

It was customary for the cabinet secretary, as a sign of respect, to stand in the hallway to let the Prime Minister leave before moving on. Also, if he had any last minute instructions, he could tell me then. After the meeting broke up, Mir Haider Khan may have told the Prime Minister what the real story was.

As I was leaving the room and headed into the hallway the Prime Minister dashed toward me and said, "Mr. Khalili, everything has its place. Your feelings, as a Kohdamani, also have a place. Kabir altered the document, and yet you took the fall for it and were quiet. I directed my anger toward you. I apologize for that. I take back my anger. And, I'm going to censor Kabir next Monday."

I replied, "Saheb, please move beyond censure. I will correct the paper and present it to you on Monday."

What happened the next Monday was one of the shining moments of Sardar Shah Mahmud Khan's administration. He did not bring it up.

As the days went by, the authority and strength of Abdul Majid Khan Zabuli increased. One realized he had established a rapport with Sardar Mohammad Daoud Khan and wanted to exploit Daoud's arrogance, inexperience, and hubris. During the cabinet meetings, there were lots of words exchanged between Shah Mahmud Khan and Sardar Daoud Khan, and always Shah Mahmud Khan showed patience and dignity. Daoud was an impatient man, and Abdul Majid Khan Zabuli tried to fuel the fire. It reached to the point where it spilled beyond the cabinet and became a source of family tension. The unity and understanding of years between the families started falling apart, which did not serve the interests of Afghanistan.

One of the points of contention was the establishment of the National Club. The founders of the National Club were Abdul Majid Khan Zabuli and Sardar Daoud Khan. They acquired a building in the Shahre Nau (new city) neighborhood of Kabul. At first they brought in the Afghan students who had gone for higher education to France. Gradually, they attracted other youth. Since they could not use the Waish Zalmayan (the socialist movement) to their interests, they started this new organization.

I went to the National Club. I thought that it would serve the interests of Afghanistan and help with the unity of the people. Messers Mahmudi, Ghobar, and Ulfat did not join us. They said, "We will never be part of it."

I told them, "If we join this organization together, we can recommend proposals for improvements to the government and the Royal Family. If they accept our proposals for the benefit of Afghanistan, it will be a good thing. If they do not, then we can still help to bring changes for the reforms ourselves. But if you continue to be worried about the organization, the country will never be on the path of reforms. We may lose it." I added, "Shah Mahmud Khan is the kind of man who likes to hear every proposal and pay attention to it."

I did my best, but Messers. Mahmudi, Ghobar, and Ulfat did not accept my advice. However, I soon realized there was more to the National Club than met the eye.

The discussion centered on education. They brought in students and created a student organization or federation. They brought this organization to Shah Mahmud Khan and presented him the title, "Father of Democracy." All this had the appearance of being fueled from beyond the borders. Every act of benevolence of Shah Mahmud Khan appeared to be a negative against him. The movement came to a boiling point when the Habibiya High School was set on fire. The Paghman Cinema, west of Kabul, was burned. An American tourist was killed in Maimana province, creating an embarrassing international situation. Many other acts of defiance took place.

Whenever Shah Mahmud Khan informed His Highness, the King, would pay more heed to his cousin than to his elderly uncle and would say, "My Agha Lala (older brother) would never do anything to jeopardize the interests of the country. Whatever they do is correct; they are the youth."

My Appointment as Minister of Public Information

I continued to be the Secretary to the Cabinet, but gradually a change occurred in the cabinet, and my additional appointment as Minister of Public Information was one of them. Initially, it was very difficult to argue and fight my way through every document. Every difference of opinion was considered as against the youth of Afghanistan. Any opposition to the non-Islamic ideology was a position against the youth of Afghanistan. Opposition to the Communists was opposition to the youth of Afghanistan. Opposition to those who were against the freedom and independence of Afghanistan was opposition to the youth of Afghanistan. It created situations, which were instantly riotous. The members of the Royal Family fanned these volatile situations. We were clearly seeing many of these movements were inspired and conspired by the Communists. In cabinet meetings and at the meetings of the Ministry of Public Information, we would recommend they stop or censor their publications, but the next day a voice would be raised to free the publication, and there was no one to prove whether the government had a hand in it.

Many of the unfortunate things started from here and took a life of their own. We received information that the Russian embassy was distributing books, newspapers, and magazines. Noor Mohammad Taraki was responsible for distributing much of this propaganda. Many people observed Taraki going to Abdul Majid Khan Zabuli's place, but no one said anything about it. If Taraki was on a mission from the government, there was no one to prove it.

Many of the youth in the Royal Family were also duped into this. They would think, "We can play the Communists and deceive them." They did not realize deceiving the Communists was not an easy task. Instead, they were deceived.

Today, Ghobar is dead. He was a very good friend of mine. Mahmudi is dead, and I will soon die. I swear by God's name that Mahmudi was one of the most patriotic young men of Afghanistan. He was a faithful Muslim and would have never opted for the leftist ideology. He was against the government for being too inclined to not take action. (Abdul Rahman Mahmudi was a fighter for movement in the late 1940s/early 1950s. He was imprisoned until shortly before his death in 1963). No one ever asked, "What was the crime of Mahmudi?" He was never brought to the court or given a chance to explain.

One day these groups demonstrated and came toward the Prime Ministry. The next day eight to 10 of those people were put in jail, including Mir Ghulam Mohammad Khan Ghobar, Mahmudi, and Hatifi. There were even some among them from the Royal Family. A few of the names were Dr. Qayum Rasool and Abdul Hai Khan, son of Abdul Hossain Khan Wazir. He was a cousin of Sardar Hashim Khan.

None of them were leftists. They were against the leftist movement and wanted the government to listen to them. No one listened. They all were sent to jail. Thus, the whole political front was left for Noor Mohammad Taraki. And if *noor* means light, then the front was left for this dark light. The political front was left for Babrak Karmal and those who wanted to bring in the Communists. They pushed back the young men who opposed them. The moment any spiritual leader or scholar raised a voice, they were accused of being an opportunist and a reactionary living in darkness and accused of keeping Afghanistan backwards. They were swiftly imprisoned and left there.

They got to all of the pulpits and corrupted them too. As soon as religious leaders spoke openly or criticized, they were be branded as reactionaries and told they did not have the right to talk except to collect charity, pray five times, fast, and not to discuss social justice.

They brought a few scholars from Herat and threw them in jail. The same thing happened to the scholars of Kandahar. No one knew their fate. The youth of Afghanistan went one way, and the scholars went the other way. The political front was clear for the Communists. It was a known fact the Communists at night were either at Daoud Khan's place or Abdul Majid Khan Zabuli's home.

The effort continued to weaken Sardar Shah Mahmud Khan's government. There was a person named Hakim Jan in the Cabinet who was appointed as Minister of Public Works. He had been the Afghanistan ambassador in Moscow for years. When the Russian army came into Afghanistan, he was given a very high status till his death. No one knew this son of Mullah Qandi was a Communist while he was even the ambassador in Moscow. He was the son of a religious person and a trusted person of the Royal Family. Sardar Mohammad Daoud Khan trusted him fully. Yet he was sending delicate information and proceedings of the cabinet to the Russians. He worked on weakening Shah Mahmud Khan and would brand any youth of Afghanistan who was in favor of real democracy as a Communist and pushed to send them to jail. Thus Ghobar, Mahmudi, Abdul Hai, and Dr. Qayum Rasool were all in prison, yet Hakim Jan remained free and well. No one lifted a finger against Noor Mohammad Taraki, Babrak Karmal, or even Abdur Rauf Benawa, who turned out to be a leading Communist (Khalq and Parcham), which no one knew about him.

Efforts to Further Weaken Shah Mahmud Khan's Government

My country and my countrymen suffered from our own doings. All the attention of the people was targeted toward the Pakistan situation and the enmity within. If a person spoke to a Pakistani, he went to jail.

Sayed Ahmad Khan was one of the most revered and respected men of Kohdaman. He was the grandson of Mir Bacha Khan Ghazi, a representative of Kohdaman in the Afghan Parliament for many years. Surprisingly enough, Mohammad Daoud Khan named the governorate of Kohdaman after Mir Bacha Khan Ghazi. Sayed Ahmed Khan was thrown in jail for a very minor incident. He was travelling to or from Kohdaman on a rental lorry and had a few passengers with him. When they stopped for evening prayers near Badam Bagh, they asked a Pakistani gentleman who was traveling with them, and who appeared to be an Islamic scholar or mullah, to lead the prayers. He accepted. The rest of the people stood behind him and after prayers were over they followed him in the prayers. Mohammad Rasul, son of Mohammad Ghaus Khan, Naib Salar who was the Chief of Intelligence of Mohammad Daoud Khan, had a bone to pick with Sayed Ahmed. Upon receiving this intelligence he had Sayed Ahmed arrested and brought to jail. For three months his family had no knowledge of his whereabouts. After three months it was revealed he was in solitary confinement in Kabul. Sayed Ahmed Khan was a member of the parliament, and yet with no legal proceedings, he remained in jail for three years before being released. His family had served the Afghan nation. His forefathers were freedom fighters. They would arrest anybody who became popular and well known or had any following. An excuse would be created, and they would go to jail. They would make the government look bad and also Sardar Daoud Khan look bad. People hated these actions.

Still the government of Sardar Shah Mahmud Khan wasn't weak enough in their eyes. They came up with another scheme. They bundled the Ministries into various groups. The Ministry of Defense and the Ministry of the Interior were bundled together and given to Mohammad Daoud Khan. The Ministry of Education and the Ministry of Public Health were bundled and given to Sardar Faiz Mohammad Khan. The Ministry of Commerce and the Ministry of Finance were bundled and given to Abdul Majid Khan Zabuli. There was no apparent reason, only the excuse that Shah Mahmud Khan was old and could not control his affairs.

Abdul Majid Khan Zabuli continued to rocket his power. Mohammad Daoud Khan took over two powerful ministries. Daoud Khan was not able to get hold of the affairs of two powerful Ministries; although, he thought he was on top of things. He tried the methods used by his uncle, Sardar Shah Mahmud Khan; one of them being an open court at the Ministry of Interior where people could bring their grievances in the form of applications. He would sit there and try to look dignified and serious just like his uncle used to do. He would take people's applications, read them and write the answers or sometimes give them to the secretaries to answer them back.

One day, a gentleman from Kohdaman who had been subjected to many atrocities and much injustice, and who had taken his application to various departments but all his efforts were in vain and no one would acknowledge him, finally appeared in front of Sardar Daoud Khan. He presented his grievances three or four times and got the approval of Sardar Daoud Khan on his applications. The custom was that once the grievance was presented, a note on the application would instruct the petitioner to take the application back to the governorate for follow up. The governor was then obligated to read the application and take care of the situation. Sometimes, if they were kind enough, they would add "Please report back to the Minister of Interior of your action."

For example, the Ministry of Justice was asked to review the application and send their findings to the Ministry of Interior. So here we have the Ministry of Justice, an entity in itself, being asked by another equal entity to provide answers to it! The Ministry of Justice dealt in judicial affairs while the Ministry of Interior dealt with internal security. The Ministry of Interior did not have a right to undermine Ministry of Justice, but since they were lumped together and the orders came from Sardar Mohammad Daoud Khan, his orders were to be obeyed.

This person who had already taken recommendations and approval from Daoud Khan in the past was not being heard. He came back again to Daoud Khan, asking him to interfere on his behalf. Daoud Khan said, "You are a rude man, and you're interfering in my work. You come here every day."

This man had premeditated his actions. When Daoud Khan turned around and asked his assistants to not allow him to enter the premises anymore, he pulled out a can of gasoline and poured it over himself. He said, "If they don't allow me to come to the Ministry of Interior and have my voice heard, I'm not going to live in this world anymore, and I'll immolate myself." He then pulled out a matchbox, lit a match, and turned it on himself.

He may have thought people would run and save him from himself, or maybe he really meant it. He burnt like a candle in front of Sardar Daoud Khan. There was nothing left of him except some flesh and bone. He was rushed to the hospital. Even his mother, when she came, did not recognize him.

I think I have strayed, however let me add this. The informers had provided baseless intelligence that this person had a connection with Khalili and Khalili put him up to it. As God is my witness, I had no knowledge of it. There is no doubt this man was from Kohdaman and had come to me with his application. However, all Kohdamanis whenever they needed anything would come to me first. Some I would admonish, and some I would speak to incessantly, telling them not to do anything wrong. I never instigated any one. But since this was Sardar Daoud Khan, he would accept anything from others, which was against me. He accepted this, and his anger was further inflamed against me. He wanted revenge, and even went to the King of Afghanistan and told him so. Yet Sardar Shah Mahmud Khan stood with me and by me. He talked him down, and put this situation to rest with his reasonable arguments.

Days and nights passed. The work of the nation was left untended, and more energy was wasted on these petty differences. The people who had a vested interest played on the differences between the uncle and his nephew and fanned the flames. Unfortunately, the king himself was arbitrary, just like the poet says:

The cupbearer gives the cup full,
Sometimes to the right, sometimes to the left.

He could not stand up, neither to his uncle, or his cousin. He did not want to make his uncle feel bad and could not stop his cousin. He would say yes to both of them. He would attest to the arguments of each of them. The cabinet meetings also carried this dysfunction into its operation. Abdul Majid Khan Zabuli appointed some members of the Royal Family to important posts in his corporations. He appointed Mohammad Omar Khan, son-in-law of King Nadir Shah, who had no knowledge of finance, as president of a bank. There was a gentleman named Karim Jan, who was also related to Habibullah Khan Seraj. He was also appointed as President of the Royal Bank. With these actions, he would indirectly control them. He appointed Mohammad Naim Khan, the younger brother of Mohammad Daoud Khan and one time Minister of Foreign Affairs of Afghanistan, as an honorary president of many of his financial institutions. Whichever Minister would listen to him and follow his advice, he would contribute big chunks of money to him and shower him with gifts and cars.

At this time a chamber of direct control over all businesses was created – kind of a "Department of Monopoly," and Abdul Majid Khan Zabuli was in control of it. For example, if vehicles were imported, they would come through this department, and Majid Khan Zabuli approved the sale to anyone he wanted. Whoever he approved would be obliged to him. Anywhere he established a corporation he would appoint one person who was highly connected to the Royal Family, to be the head of that corporation. Thus, he was controlling the destiny of a lot of people. No one knew what was actually going on.

Ironically, Sardar Daoud Khan and Sardar Naim Khan were staunch supporters of Majid Khan Zabuli. It was surprising, also, that a person of the caliber of Ali Mohammad Khan, who was a very intelligent, smart, and cautious man, was supportive of Abdul Majid Khan Zabuli.

The only person who would not back Majid Khan Zabuli was Shah Mahmud Khan himself, along with Mirza Mohammad Khan Yaftali and Hazrat Fazl Ahmad Khan Mojadadi of Herat. They were openly opposed to Majid Khan Zabuli and would sarcastically say, "So, we have come to the point that the leadership of Afghanistan should be handed over to Majid Khan Zabuli? This will someday bring shame and repentance to all."

Zabuli's Ill Treatment of Shah Mahmud Khan in Cabinet Meeting

It was the springtime and flowers bloomed all over the Prime Ministry. The tensions and quarrels that had been behind the scenes were transformed into quarrels and tensions in the open. In the evening, the road was full of flowers under the stars as the Ministers gathered in the Gulkhana on the north side of the Arg for a Cabinet meeting. Sardar Shah Mahmud Khan had not arrived yet. Mohammad Daoud Khan called me and said he was sick and would not be able to attend the meeting. I do not know if he was really sick or if it was an excuse.

The other Ministers came, and the meeting was held in the absence of Shah Mahmud Khan. The meeting was called to discuss the expenses of the Afghan hajis (pilgrims to Mecca). The Ministers decided to limit the number of hajis to go to Mecca that year and reduced the amount of money to be given to each haji. The discussion had not ended yet when Shah Mahmud Khan suddenly arrived. Normally, he had a habit of kissing the face of every Minister (the Afghan custom of kissing on the cheek three times). Then every Minister would kiss his hand. That night when he entered the meeting, he looked very angry and upset and did not kiss anybody. There were furrows of worry on his forehead. He sat down in his chair and without greetings, asked, "What were you doing?"

Ali Mohammad Khan said, "We were not doing much, just talking about the foreign exchange that should be given to the Afghan hajis."

He said, "Good. I remember something." He turned

toward Majid Khan Zabuli and said, "Abdul Majid!" He
did not address him as Khan or Minister. He never used to
do that. He would always say, "Wazir Saheb."

"Abdul Majid," he repeated, "I asked you to give one
thousand dollars to Rahim Khan, the Deputy Mayor of
Kabul, who is going to Europe and America on his medical
leave. Why did you turn down my Firman? You have a lot
of nerve."

Emboldened, Abdul Majid Khan Zabuli answered, "I
did the right thing by turning down your Firman. "He
continued, "Actually I didn't turn it down, the Board of
Directors at the Bank turned it down."

The Board of Directors of the Bank approved new
regulations and giving money to Rahim Khan was against
the new regulations.

The Prime Minister said, "Why weren't these
regulations of the Board of Directors of the Bank explained
to me so I would not have given the order? And why were
not these regulations sent to the Prime Ministry for
approval and for authentication by the government?"

Abdul Majid Khan Zabuli said, "Not everything is
under the control of the government or under your
authority."

Shah Mahmud Khan angrily replied, "You send money
every month to your wife in the United States. Do you have
the right to do that? You keep sending large amounts of
foreign exchange, and I, who give a thousand dollars to an
Afghan, my Firman is not good anymore? The doctors have
attested he is sick. Why do you send money to your wife?"

Majid Khan Zabuli answered, "Why do you send
money to Zalmai, your son?"

Shah Mahmud Khan countered, "My son has gone
overseas to study."

Majid Khan Zabuli shouted, "I also have the right to
send money to my wife. Don't mention my wife anymore
and keep quiet!"

Shah Mahmud Khan was enraged and in his typical
accent, addressed Majid Khan Zabuli, who in turn, made
fun of his accent. It got to the point where Shah Mahmud
Khan called in the guards to throw him out.

In this meeting of the Cabinet, Assadullah Khan, son of Amir Habibullah Khan Seraj, nephew of Shah Mahmud Khan, was present. Sardar Ghulam Farooq Khan, who later became Minister of Interior, was there, as was Ali Mohammad Khan, Faiz Mohammad Khan, Qazi Mir Atta Mohammad Khan, and Mir Haider Khan. No one moved. Mohammad Hashim Maiwandal (1919-1973, who later became Prime Minister), and Sayed Shamsuddin Pacha were sitting next to me. I realized that now things may get out of hand. The soldiers will come in, pull Abdul Majid Khan away by force and rebuke him for being rude to Shah Mahmud Khan, who in turn may order the soldiers to beat Majid Khan right then and there, in front of everybody. This would give a proof to Sardar Mohammad Daoud Khan he should have this simple hearted and noble man, Shah Mahmud Khan, removed from his job.

I got up from my seat, went to Majid Khan, put my arms around him and said, "Leave the meeting now."

He was shaking out of fear or anger. He turned to me and said, "Show me the way." I brought him outside, gave him back his hat, and he got in his car and left. I returned to the meeting.

The room was silent. I broke the silence and addressed the Prime Minister. "Sadr-e-Azam Saheb, you have always said 'a man's patience is a powerful weapon. Always use patience.' Why did you lose your patience tonight? Please allow me to read the briefings to you."

He reacted angrily and threw a pencil he had in his hand toward me. "You want me to be dishonored and still remain in office," he said. "I do not accept this, and I do not want to remain Prime Minister after this. I piss on it!" He stood up to leave and added, "I'm going to go right now and end this thing, once and for all. I will confront the backers of Abdul Majid. I am a soldier, not a Prime Minister."

He left the room. I ran out and had his car brought up to the door. He got in it and left for his house. I came back to the meeting and sat down. Everybody asked, "Has Shah Mahmud Khan left? He may throw Abdul Majid in jail or order his execution."

The night passed. The next morning the Prime Minister did not come to work. Around noontime I went to his house, wary that he may have been upset at me for pulling Abdul Majid away from the meeting, or that I confronted him about his lack of patience. It was the time of *hejab*, and the women and men were separate in the house. I was invited inside. Sardar Assadullah Khan was sitting with the Prime Minister. As soon as they saw me they got up. The Prime Minister sat me next to him and said, "I'm very happy. What a nice thing you did. May God keep you in his protection. I'm thankful to you."

I was flabbergasted. I said, "Saheb, what happened?"

He said, "Sit down and let me explain. Last night when I came home, I had not prayed the evening prayers. I started my *asha* (late evening prayers). When I was bowing and repeating 'God is great' I realized I'm a humble human being. And when I went into full prostration toward God (the ritual of prayer) and said 'Praise be to God' I realized I am a very modest, humble, and self-effacing human being of God. I finished my prayers. Before I prayed, I had all these vengeful ideas running through my mind, that I'll have Abdul Majid brought in here and shoot him myself, because I know where he's coming from. I wish he was getting inspired by my nephew, yet I'm sure he's got connections somewhere else."

I interjected, "Saheb, then what happened?"

He said, "I went to the palace and met his Highness, the King. I noticed His Highness was very concerned. I guessed Abdul Majid had gone to see Mohammad Daoud Khan, who took Abdul Majid with him to the palace and had hidden him there so that I may not lay my hands on him."

"When I went to the palace, the king got up, kissed my hand as an older and kind uncle, and said the kind words he always says. He said, 'I've been told that Abdul Majid showed great hubris tonight. You can avenge that or take your revenge with me. You should punish me. Please do not be upset. You can curse me, you can punish me, and do whatever you want to me. I am right here in front of you. I'm at your service.'"

"I said. 'I'm not going to punish anybody. I have forgiven Abdul Majid. Since Abdul Majid abused me and was disrespectful to me tonight, I have forgiven him. Yet, I want to let you know, your Highness, King of Afghanistan, that by allowing this kind of brazen disrespectful attitude, Afghanistan will suffer. Afghanistan will be lost. You will lose your throne, and I will also be destroyed. If you and I are removed from the scene, it's not as precarious as losing Afghanistan. This black spot will always remain as a scar for our family. It would be in the best interest of all if I resign from my post tonight. Thus, I leave the state of affairs in your hands, and you don't have to play any games.'"

"His Highness was moved by my words, and I could see tears rolling from his eyes. He kissed my hand again and swore on the soul of his father and on God and insisted I continue my work. He said, 'We will do anything and everything you say. I have never played a game with you, and I will not start now. I promise in the name of God I will stick to your words.' I thought to myself, what else can he say? He said everything.' I recall the bloody face of his father (when Nadir Shah was assassinated by a high school student). I recalled him lying on the grass at Gulkhana palace. I remember his pale face upon seeing his father killed. I decided to forgo this incident and came back to my house. Tomorrow, I will come to work at the Prime Ministry as usual. I prayed to God for his success."

The next day, he came to work as usual. Abdul Majid did not report to work for a few days. He was heard saying he was so ashamed of what happened that he felt so dishonored. He didn't know how to face the Prime Minister. Actually, he was intimidated, afraid, and ashamed of the one who incited the whole incident.

While meeting other people during this time, Abdul Majid would brag, "I do not want to work anymore until the Prime Minister asks me himself to do so and apologizes. I will not go to work. He sent word to tell the Prime Minister he feels so shamed he will not face him. Finally, on the day of Eid-e-Qorban (the Eid of Sacrifice, the Muslim festival for Haj,) Abdul Majid was presented to the Prime Minister. He immediately kissed the hands of the Prime Minister and celebrated the Eid with him. The Prime Minister forgave him.

Shah Mahmud Khan Visits Kandahar Again

During the time I was Secretary to the Cabinet and had not yet been appointed as Minister of Public Information, I accompanied Shah Mahmud Khan on an official visit to Kandahar. It was the first time I would be traveling by airplane. I admit I was afraid, but since the orders came from the Prime Minister I had to comply.

We drove from Kabul to Kandahar by car and flew from Kandahar to Girishk by airplane. We spent one night in Ghazni, and the people welcomed us with open arms. In Kandahar, a crowd gathered forming lines on two sides of the road to greet us warmly and enthusiastically. They would call out, "Ghazi Baba! (Islamic tradition states that if you survive a jihad, like Shah Mahmud Khan survived the war of freedom, you are called Ghazi. If you are killed, you are a martyr.) The Prime Minister got out of the car and mingled with the people and embraced them, greeting each and every one of them. He stayed in Kandahar for a few days. There, I pleaded the case of those who had been exiled in Kandahar from Kohdaman and Kohistan. He pardoned them and told them, "You are free to go to Kabul."

The people of Kandahar came together at the military base and offered Shah Mahmud Khan a special scarf for his shoulders, a special head cap and a *chapan* (an Afghan lightweight coat, green and white striped, which is open in the front and not buttoned). They helped him into the *chapan,* the scarf and the cap, and gave him the official title of Ghazi Baba. Shah Mahmud Khan accepted with grace and told them, "Oh, people of Kandahar, you have given me this title, and this scarf and cap and *chapan,* and I have accepted them as a servant of the country. I am a servant of the King of Afghanistan. I'm honored to serve the Afghan nation. I have served in the court of the King of

Afghanistan, which you people have regarded with respect. You have made me very proud. I accept your gift as precious wealth."

I wrote down all these developments and sent them to the Ministry of Public Information in Kabul, which published my articles in the newspaper and announced them on the radio. I noticed whatever I wrote they would make certain changes or edit parts of it and would publish it according to their own taste.

The official visit ended, and we returned to Kabul. The Prime Minister told me, "You and I are both very unfortunate. Do you know what happened in your absence?"

I said, "No."

He answered, "When the people of Kandahar bestowed their respect upon me in the form of the scarf, the cap, and the *chapan,* the informants brought news to the king that Shah Mahmud Khan is lying in wait for the succession to become king. They reminded the king that this is the way the people of Kandahar honored Ahmad Shah Baba (1722-1773, a guard of Nader Shah who became king)."

He continued, "Back then, they told Ahmad Shah Baba, you are the king. And now the people of Kandahar have given the same treatment to Shah Mahmud Khan that they gave to Ahmad Shah Baba. They told the king, this may have been done at the behest of Khalilullah Khalili, because Khalili is the one who sent news reports from Kandahar to be published in Kabul. If I had not been here (Shah Mahmud Khan), I'm afraid they would have definitely done harm to your poor soul."

I kissed his hand and said, "Saheb, you can order me to jail, but neither you nor I had anything to do with this."

During this visit we also had gone to Girishk where he reviewed the work of an American company. This company was in Girishk, away from everybody's eyes, possibly to avoid letting the Afghan people know about the cooperation and assistance of the Americans. The land they gave the Americans to work on was not fertile and would take at least four or five years to show any return. Propaganda railed against the Americans' lack of success.

The Americans toiled away while the prominent, sensitive, and important developmental projects, such as the construction of the Salang Tunnel, which connects northern provinces to Kabul, or the Darunta Dam, or the rich and fertile agricultural lands in Jalalabad, were given to the Russians whose tanks rolled in after December 1979. Like the oil reserves of the north, these obvious, sensitive, and important jobs were given to the Russians so they could prove their success to the people and win their hearts and minds for the future.

While visiting the Bost Fort, Lash Kargah, and Helmand, the Prime Minister had some time available at night. Our entourage included Mirza Mahmud Khan, the Minister of State; Engineer Akram Khan, the Minister of Public Works; Mohammad Anwar Khan, Naib Salar; and myself. We stayed at the Hotel Girishk, and the Prime Minister sent Mohammad Anwar Khan on an errand, and then shared a secret with Mirza Mahmud Khan, Akram Jan, and me.

He said, "It seems to me that Abdul Majid Khan has given the Helmand Valley project to the Americans as a political move, so the people of Afghanistan may not know of the cooperation and assistance of Americans to them. This project does not seem to be very beneficial to the Afghan nation. Even if it comes to fruition, it is in a remote area, away from the population and away from the center of people's attention. And, he has given the most beneficial projects to the Russians. No matter how much I have tried to talk to His Highness about this, I am unable to convince him."

Time passed, and I became the Minister of Public Information and continued to hold my position as Secretary to the Cabinet. Mohammad Daoud Khan and Naim Khan resigned their posts and left. Hashim Khan was at his residence and meeting a large number of people every day. His Highness, the King, wanted to make his uncle happy and gave him the Shahrara palace to live in. He also gave Hashim Khan the state guesthouse.

The state guesthouse has quite a history. Nadir Shah built it on the premises of the Arg in a corner for high profile state guests like presidents or kings who would visit Afghanistan. When his son got married, Nardir Shah gave it to his son Zahir Shah. Zahir Shah turned around and one day gave the house to Naim Khan. Naim Khan in turn, sold it back to the government for an exorbitant price. The government turned around and gave the state guesthouse as a free gift to Sardar Hashim Khan for his services. He gave it back to Naim Khan, and his nephew lived there throughout his life.

Shahrara Palace and Signing the Agreement with the British

The Shahrara palace was built during the time of Amir Abdul Rahman Khan. It has a high tower and is located near the main road connecting Kabul to the north. When Abdul Rahman Khan was signing the agreement for the British to leave Kabul, Amir Abdul Rahman Khan's camp was located near this tower. It wasn't a significant tower at that time. It was just a mound of dirt and was known as the Mound of Snakes. The British camp was located where the main road is. When the agreement was signed and the British pulled their troops out of Afghanistan, Amir Abdul Rahman Khan in order to memorialize that day, ordered a palace be built right where this camp was. Thus, the Shahrara palace was built. He also ordered that where the British camp was, a main road should pass through it and that's where the main road was built so the land where the British camped would always be under the foot of the Afghans. Later, Amanullah Khan turned the Shahrara palace into Habibiya High School. All this was inscribed on a stone installed inside the palace.

It remained like this until Nadir Shah came and conquered Kabul against Habibullah Khan Kalakani. During that time the palace was burned down and the story says the people who burned the Bala Hissar Fort were behind the burning down of the Shahrara palace. Both symbolized opposition to the British. These were not repaired for a long time and remained burned shells both by Bala Hissar Fort and Shahrara palace.

When Sardar Hashim Khan resigned, the king granted the palace to Sardar Hashim Khan in lieu of his services to Afghanistan. He decided to turn it into a hospital with paying services, but before this could happen, Hashim Khan died.

Pashtunistan Continues to Occupy Center Stage

The issue of Pashtunistan took the center stage. There was an unbreachable difference in the cabinet meetings. Nothing of significance was achieved. Only minor things were being decided. The more substantial issues were sent to the king for his decision.

On one hand, I wrote down the proceedings of the cabinet on minor issues and on the other, I would write a satiric poem every week about the dysfunction in the cabinet, in public language that was easily understood by everybody. I called it, "The Monday Letter." These satiric poems were copied by Maiwandwal and Sayed Bahauddin Majrooh and distributed to people. When Maiwandwal left the cabinet meeting, only Majrooh was there, and he would copy my Monday Letter and give it to people. I have lost those poems in moving. I don't have them with me. Copies were in my library; however, the enemies of civilization and humanity destroyed my library and must have taken those writings too.

Here is a poem as an example of the issues discussed in the cabinet that were so insignificant:

One day I saw a mouse that went to a sugar shop.
He ate and ate as much as he could.
What do the ministers think about this issue?

Or, there was a long poem I wrote about a conversation between a despotic minister and a tyrannical Sardar like Mohammad Daoud Khan:

The Sardar would say,
"Minister, the air is red like snow.

The earth is cold as fire."
And his Minister would answer,
"Yes sir, yes sir, yes sir, Bale Saheb."

I must have written more than 100 of these satirical poems. Eventually, they found their way to Sardar Daoud Khan. When Shah Mahmud Khan resigned, I was subjected to an inquisition about these poems. Sardar Daoud Khan summoned me to his residence. I'll talk about that in detail later. I had mimicked his accent in my poetry. For example, when Sardar Daoud Khan would call someone "Brother," he would say, "Beyather," pronouncing it as "Bee-ath-er." They were funny poems because they were word plays on the sound of his accent and his pronunciation of words. (The translation of these words into English may not convey the same message.)

The last days of the rule of the Prime Minister Shah Mahmud Khan were spent in humility. Gradually, I loosened the control of the Ministry of Public Information and made the decision to let people write what they wanted to in the newspaper. But, I banned the distribution of the night letters, *Shab Nama*.

I used to publish a weekly paper by the name of *Neelab*. Mohammad Firoz Salek Salangi, who later became a member of parliament, was its editor. I wrote the articles and published *Neelab* with my own money. I used satire and criticism in the same sentence. I told Shah Mahmud Khan that this was my weekly. It also carried some poems, and 1,000 copies were distributed in Kabul. I had a collection of them in my library. They fell into the hands of the pillagers and plunderers.

People were thrown in jail because of their political leanings. A protest rally was held in Kabul that Mahmudi and Ghobar orchestrated. The rally was nothing of significance. God is witness that Shah Mahmud Khan did not want to do this. The governor of Kabul was a man named Hakim who was also working temporarily as Minister of Interior. He came and said, "Afghanistan will be destroyed if these people are not stopped and arrested. They will go directly to the Arg and attack it. His Highness, the King, has directed me that I should immediately arrest them."

Shah Mahmud Khan said, "Well, I will seek His Highness, the King's, permission before embarking on this."

When Shah Mahmud Khan left for the Arg to see the king, Hakim sent the police force to arrest participants in the rally. About 15 or 16 young men were arrested and thrown in jail. This was significant because a group of enlightened youth was arrested and thrown in jail. This was a bad omen for the future of Afghanistan.

Shah Mahmud Khan lost his popularity. The enlightened youth who were in jail did not know who had them imprisoned. Maybe, the king also did not realize. There was no doubt the Communists had a hand in this action, and Hakim was a big part of it.

This was a time when the Iranian academia delegation visited Afghanistan. Sayed Nafisi was part of it. It was the first time we could talk openly and frankly to a foreign delegation. The only delegation we were prohibited from talking to was the friendly Pakistani delegation. Sayed Nafisi met with the king and told him, "Your Highness, because of these agreements you signed with your northern neighbor; one day, they will demand something in return. I have come to your country as an historian and writer. If your northern neighbor demands something in the future, what would your answer be?"

The king said, "This is government business. We will answer about tomorrow, tomorrow."

Sayed Nafisi wanted to meet Sardar Daoud Khan, but Daoud declined. Sayed Nafisi talked to many people and separated facts from fiction, analyzing for himself the issue of Pashtunistan.

This disorganization could be seen in the operation of the government. I opened a large library as part of the Ministry of Public information. Shah Mahmud Khan came and opened it officially. After that, many news magazines issued monthly became dailies. Slowly, the freedom of writing and freedom of print came into existence. We created and organized a framework for public information.

The only way to stop the spread of Communist ideology in Afghanistan was to use the training we received 1300 years ago from our religion of Islam. There was nothing else available to fight the propaganda. Islam is rooted deep in the people of Afghanistan. Here, it would have been effective to have a congregational mosque in every village, a contact with the Ministry of Public Information, a religious magazine to counter the propaganda, and access to foreign radio.

We compiled a list of congregation mosques and mosques in the outlying areas of the country, especially in the northern provinces. We created a magazine called *Payame-Haq* to attract scholars and intellectuals. We purchased small radios at low prices and ordered radios from overseas to give the villagers access to foreign radio stations. We planned to expand our education plan into the Uzbeki and Turkmani languages. We were determined to move forward with our plans.

The Sapling Planting Day (Green Day)

Besides other developments in Kabul that took place during the time Shah Mahmud Khan was Prime Minister, there was a case of Sayed Ismael Bel Khabi and Khwaja Mohammad Naim, former commander of the main police center (Kotwali), who had been arrested by the government.

Every year on the day of Nawroz, a tradition since the time of Amanullah Khan, it was customary for people, especially from the countryside, to come together to plant saplings. The villagers poured into Kabul bringing their beasts of burden and other domesticated animals for an exhibition. The high-ranking government officials and ministers put on traditional clothing and headgear to attend. The king also attended this gathering while Nadir Shah was alive. After that, the Prime Minister took over the role of opening the agricultural fair.

During the time of Nadir Shah this festival was held at Babur Shah Gardens. Amanullah Khan also held these gatherings there. One Nawroz day at the Babur Shah Gardens, the weather was very pleasant in Kabul. Some clouds floated in the skies, looking like white sheets, and the sun played hide and seek. It was as if the white sheet-like clouds were cleaning the sky. People gathered and Nadir Shah, with his typical majesty, drove through Kabul toward the veranda of the Babur Shah Gardens. This veranda had been constructed during the time of Amir Abdur Rahman Khan (Amir of Afghanistan, 1880-1901). Chairs were arranged for the seating of the entire court. Nadir Shah arrived in his black limousine, which always had two flags on both sides of the car. One of them was the Afghan flag with the pulpit or *mehrab and member*; the other flag was embellished with the Royal Court seal. Nadir Shah exited his car. As he entered the veranda, the detail of soldiers assigned to him gave a salute.

The famous singer Ustad Qasim was singing. People stood and enjoyed the fine weather, the majestic arrival of the king, and the music in the air. As soon as Nadir Shah sat down, Ustad Qasim, who always recognized the occasion and sang accordingly, started a ballad of Shaikh Ajal Saadi, the famous 13th century Persian poet.

The cloud, the wind, the moon, the sun and the sky are all active at your service,
so that you can work hard to earn your bread and not become lazy.
All these are at your service and are in waiting for you.
It is not wise or justifiable if you do not take advantage of this.

Qasim sang this poem repeatedly and so beautifully that Nadir Shah could not hold back his tears. The power of the poetry got the better of the majesty of the crown. The tears from his eyes dripped from underneath his glasses. Nadir Shah was moved. He ordered that all the gathered villagers should be invited into the veranda and come near the court of the king. The elderly came closer and sat and listened to the music and ate at the king's *sufrah* (the large cloth that is placed on the floor for the meal). All of the villagers came forward from Chardehi and Kohdaman in their traditional dresses and sat on the floor. When they were settled, Ustad

Qasim sang poetry.

My love and your majesty are in unison.
This is a new tradition; that the king and the pauper are
together.

The Friday prayers were offered right then and there, on Nawroz, under the shining sun, after a day of beautiful weather at the residing place of the Monarch Mohammad Zaheeruddin Babur (1483-1530, descendant of Timur and founder of the Mughal Dynasty). Later, a swimming pool was built in this place, which I think took away part of the beauty of these gardens. The imam for these Friday prayers, for Eid, in the presence of the king, was assigned to a Sayed family who was descended from Mir Waiz. Amir Abdur Rahman Khan had once married a daughter of this family by the name of Bibi Tajdar (alias Bobo Jan). The imam or *khatib* was a noble old man with a flowing white beard. Unfortunately, during his *khutba* (address) to the gathering, in which the name of the king in power is by tradition mentioned, he mentioned the name of the former king, Amanullah Khan, instead of Nadir Shah. It was a time when the family of Amanullah Khan and the family of Nadir Shah were at daggers drawn. As soon the name of Amanullah Khan left his lips, people were taken aback, especially Sardar Hashim Khan, whose reaction was like a wounded snake. Prayers ended, but Nadir Shah was brave enough to ignore what the imam had said, and invited the imam to dinner with him.

After this, the location of the traditional gathering was changed to Sakhi Maidan, the place in Kabul where the mausoleum of Sakhi, called Panjai Sakhi Shah Maidan, is located on the southwest side of Asmai Mountain. The mausoleum has a large dome and inside the dome is a black stone with the imprint of the palm of a hand on it. This has not been carved into the stone, but seems to be an imprint. One can see the lines of the hand in it. It is people's belief that Hazrat Shah Wilaetmaab (Hazrat Ali or Prophet Ali the fourth Caliph of Islam, both Sias and Sunnis revere him) came here and put his hand on the stone. Outside the dome there is another big stone. This stone has a crack in it. It is said Hazrat Shah Wilaetmaab or Hazrat Ali cracked the stone. There is another belief about this stone that Ahmad Shah Baba, on his way to Kandahar, bringing the cloak of The Prophet Mohammad (PBUH) with him from Badakhshan, stopped here for the night and laid the cloak on the stone.

It was decreed the Nawroz gathering should be held at the Ziarat (mausoleum of Sakhi). One reason was because it had a vast field large enough to accommodate many, many people. Every year the Prime Minister opened these fairs. All the dignitaries and foreign ambassadors attended it. People came from all parts of Afghanistan, including the people of Kabul and adjoining states.

Recently, the King of Afghanistan went to Europe for an eye ailment. This was his first official journey to Europe. He returned coming back through Iran and was the guest of the King of Iran.

It was Monday, four days before the day of Nawroz. Sardah Shah Mahmud Khan broke from tradition and announced he would not be able to open the agricultural fair or even attend it because of a prior engagement.

People complained to me the location of the fair was a cemetery with the mausoleum and the Ziarat inside it.

"People come there and trample on the graves, and I don't want to be part of this desecration," they said.

Amiruddin Shansab was the Minister of Agriculture. The fair fell under his jurisdiction. He was educated in France and was a simple man who did not realize what was going on around him. He insisted that His Highness, the Prime Minister, should attend, and he continued with his arrangements. Shah Mahmud Khan tried to excuse himself by saying his health did not permit him, and he was not going to attend. He elucidated further, saying, "If any of the Ministers want to attend, they have the right to do so. But, I will not be a part of it."

Mirza Mohammad Khan, the Minister of State, and a couple of other ministers also declined the invitation. I debated what the real issue was.

Plot against Shah Mahmud Khan

In the middle of the night, on the eve of Nawroz day, a man named Mir Khairuddin arrived at my home in Karte Char from Kohdaman. He was a scholarly man with a turban and a beard. I had a small guest room inside the courtyard. Whenever my acquaintances and friends from Kohdaman and Kohistan visited me, they stayed there.

The next day I got up early and after the morning prayers, I went out into the street and enjoyed the early morning breeze on this Narwoz day. It was Friday, and I had plans to have my official car brought later so I could take a drive to Kohdaman maybe, or Istalif, a beautiful place north of Kabul.

I waited for my friend Sayed Shamsuddin Pacha. The sun had just come up. It was a beautiful day. Qazi Abdul Hussain Khan Qara Baghi was also with me. He said, "Mir Khairuddin arrived last night, and he seems very worried. He was so worried that even last night, he did not want to come out of the room he is in, and now he's confined there. He confided in me and said "Please, do not tell anybody I am here, and if anyone asks about me, please hide me."

I sent for him quickly and asked him to come outside into the street. He came out sheepishly, and I could see he was pale in the face. I said, "Mir Khairuddin, what is the matter? Is everything okay? Is somebody sick?"

He said, "I will whisper it to you, in your ear." He came closer and said, "Something has happened, which I think I should not hide from you. An insurrection was planned, and they had tried to pull me into it too. I escaped last night and came to your house to inform you the insurrection failed. Please, for God's sake, give me sanctuary."

I said, "You wretched one! Go back to the room and stay there. You should have discussed it with me before you got involved with this!"

As we were talking, Mohammad Kabir Khan Ghorbandi, who represented Ghorband in the parliament, came by in a horse-drawn carriage. He was my friend. He took me to the side and said, "Today, there was a plot to arrest Shah Mahmud Khan and all the ministers. The conspirators brought in a battalion of soldiers and stationed them near Asmai Mountain. The plan was to break into Dehmazang Prison, give arms to the prisoners, and start an insurrection. However, Sardar Shah Mahmud Khan got wind of it and has had all of the leaders arrested and thrown in jail."

I said, "Who were they?"

He said, "One of them, I know, was Khwaja Naim, the Commander. The others were Mr. Bel Khabi, son of Gow Savar (bull rider) Hazarah and another from the Harzarah tribe. These were the few people that I knew."

I said, "You're not part of it?"

He said, "No, thank God, I was not. I came here to make sure you were also not part of it."

I said, "Not at all. I am very sincere to Shah Mahmud Khan and my country. I consider this impertinent at this time. There is no reason for anybody to go against Shah Mahmud Khan."

As we walked back to my house I saw police walking around the outside, and a few of them were in the courtyard. I realized now that Mir Khairuddin could create a problem for me.

A few minutes later, the telephone rang. I went inside and Sardar Shah Mahmud Khan was at the other end of the line. He asked me to come to the Prime Ministry urgently. We used to joke and poke fun with each other, but this was no joke. He said, "Make sure you bring a change of clothes, because you may be here for a while and may not go back to your home." I thought I was going to jail.

I went to the Prime Ministry to see Shah Mahmud Khan as soon as possible. He was sitting in the Gul Khana Palace and looked very gloomy.

Raising his head, he said, "See? You see what happened?"

I said, "Saheb, what happened?"

"They brought me the intelligence report," he explained. "Sayed Ismael Bel Khabi, who is one of the scholars from Mazar-i-Sharif and son of Gow Savar (bull rider) Hazarah and wretched Khwaja Mohammad Naim, former commander of Kotwali formed a clique. They convinced the Turkman commander of a battalion to be on their side and go to Asmai Mountain and use arson to burn down 13 buildings in Kabul. One of those buildings was the Jawad Khana Fort where Hazrat Saheb Noorul Mashaeq resides. Also, the house of Abdul Ghani Khan Qala Begi and some other houses."

He asked me a direct question: "Mr. Khalili, you were not part of it?"

I said, "You should investigate if I was part of it. If you inflict a wound on me without cause, I will consider it a salve. Even if you give me poison without a cause, I will consider it a drug. You have released hundreds of people from prison. I will not hold it against you, if you imprison me again without cause."

I added, "There is an incident that happened a few nights ago I should tell you about. The sons of Haji Abdur Rahman Khan Kohdamani invited me to their house. They also invited Khwaja Naim. I didn't go there."

He said, "Yes, I am aware that you did not go. They wanted to bring you there that night to fill you in on the plan and have you put your hand on the Holy Koran and swear you in with them. You were smart not to go there."

I said, "I did not know that. I did not go because I was not feeling well."

He detailed the plan further, mentioning some other names, a few of the people from Kohistan like Khwaja Ikram and others who were also part of it. "They were all arrested," he said. "Nothing untoward happened, and the big upheaval in Kabul city had been avoided."

I said, "Who informed you?"

He mentioned the name of a person from Wardak who informed him. "One evening I was playing billiards at my home, and he asked to speak to me directly, in private. He did not want to talk in front of my wife or my aide. When we were alone, this man told me what was happening. He has continued to provide me intelligence."

The Prime Minister mentioned a couple of other names of people who were supplying him with information. He said, "Now that this has taken place, I want you to go and write a firman to appoint yourself as my aide, and to appoint a couple of other people as part of a commission to look into this matter."

I said, "Saheb, if you really want to get to the bottom of this, and if you really want this to be an unbiased report, don't appoint me."

He asked, "Why?"

I said, "Because you know very well when we were thrown in jail Khwaja Naim had a very unpleasant attitude toward us. People know of his actions against us. If we find him guilty, they will definitely think I am avenging those actions. Then the real intentions of this whole plot will get shoved under the rug, and it will become a personal vendetta."

He thought for a moment. "You have the last word," I added.

He said, "You are absolutely right. Good. Very well."

It raced through my mind that I should not be part of a commission to investigate an intellectual and scholar like Mr. Sayed Ismael Bel Khabi. He was my friend. I did not think it appropriate to investigate this spiritual man and scholar who hailed from the Shia sect of the population.

Mirza Ghulam Mustafa Khan from the Prime Ministry was appointed as the head of the investigative commission. The Prime Minister also appointed his aide de camp and a few other people. The Firman was written, and he signed it. The investigation started and without any torture, it was completed at a rapid pace. I heard from Mirza Ghulam Mustafa Khan, who was a good friend of mine that Khwaja Naim denied the whole affair and cried profusely. He said he was part of it. He said he was supposed to collect all this intelligence and take it back to the Prime Minister.

On the other hand, according to Mirza Ghulam Mustafa Khan, Sayed Ismael Bel Khabi did not deny his involvement. Instead, he confessed his intention was to reform the government of Afghanistan. "The state of affairs has gone astray," he told the commission. "The government has lost focus and has no knowledge of what is happening around it, in the country, or in the Islamic world. The change I wanted to bring was either by force or through bloodless revolution. No one is to be blamed. I am the one who started this."

The investigators asked him if he was willing to write this, and he said, "Yes." In his own handwriting he confessed, "I was working on this change in the interest of Islam and in the interest of Afghanistan."

Thus, investigating others became immaterial and all intelligence was gathered through him.

There was another misgiving in this whole affair, and the issue was raised in the cabinet meeting. The cabinet decided Khwaja Naim should be executed. When the king returned from his trip overseas to Iran, their decision was presented to him. The day the cabinet approved the execution of Khwaja Naim, Sardar Mohammad Daoud Khan did not agree to sign.

He said, "I will present my reasons directly to the king."

People were skeptical. Later on, it was revealed when Khwaja Naim came from Mazar-i-Sharif, he was seen in and out of the house of Sardar Mohammad Daoud Khan, who was also the Minister of the Interior. It is said, even though it is hearsay, that Khwaja Naim, according to himself, was offered the post of the head of intelligence if the coup was successful. The family feud was alive and well in this case. The king suspended the execution of Khwaja Naim at the behest of his cousin (Sardar Mohammad Daoud Khan).

The cabinet and Sardar Shah Mahmud Khan reached the consensus that since Sayed Ismael Bel Khabi was a brave and intelligent man, and had confessed bravely, then he should not be executed. Instead, they decided he would be imprisoned until further investigation was completed.

Because of those incidents and until the time I was the Minister of Public Information, I endeavored to establish contacts with the mosques and create circle of scholarly people to improve people's literacy. We selected some enlightened scholars of Afghanistan to oversee this network and guide them to improving people's lot. These scholars included people like Janab Maulana Mansur Ansari, Maulana Saifi, Maulana Abdul Hai Panjsheri, Maulavi Ghulam Nabi Kamavi, and Maulavi Amanullah, who was as famous as Khan Maulavi of Qarabagh. We appointed Maulavi Shah Mohammad Irshad of Kohistan as assistant to this commission. The *Nilab* magazine was also printed. We changed its name to *Payam Haq* (which means "Rightful Message" or "Just Message"). We provided a budget for printing it and made it an official organ. We also worked on getting radios. We requested scholars from around the country introduce young men at every mosque as liaisons for every village. We, also, with the approval of the elder of each area, worked to provide people trained in First Aid, so they could meet the basic medical needs of the wounded or sick until they could get to a hospital. We also got permission to empower the heads of the mosques to have the right to work with district magistrates and governors of their districts and provinces to meet the needs of the people.

The Ministry of Public Information used to send the world news and news of Afghanistan to all the areas. The goal was to propagate the national unity of Afghanistan, to spread talk about the respected religion of Islam, and to make people aware of the ills of corruption, bribery, and oppression. We let them talk freely about whatever difficulty they faced and encouraged them to inform the government center in Kabul. We proposed the telephone system be extended to be at their disposal, so they could call the center freely. But just as I had mentioned earlier, as soon as Sardar Mohammad Daoud Khan became Prime Minister, he abolished all of this, which did not prove to be wise for the future.

The Resignation of Shah Mahmud Khan

Shah Mahmud Khan resigned. His resignation was a beautiful story. One day he called me in. I went to see him.

He said, "Do you know what rumors are prevailing in Kabul?"

I said, "Yes, there's talk among people you would like to resign, and that His Highness, the King has said, 'If my uncle does not resign, I'm going to abdicate the throne, and I will proceed to Saudi Arabia to perform haj and will live there.' I don't know what the truth is, but this is the rumor. When people ask me, I tell them his is all lies, has no basis. This is a rumor spread by the rumor mill."

He said, "What should I do? All these rumors are being spread by Hakim, the son of Quandi and those around Daoud Jan."

I answered, "This is a harbinger of the destruction of Afghanistan. The fire is burning in your own house. We people cannot extinguish this fire."

He said, "I receive telephone calls every night. My children receive telephone calls. My friends receive calls, all saying they have heard I have resigned. I think it will be a good idea if I publish an announcement and relieve people from this tension and rumor."

I said, "Very well."

I summoned Mr. Roshan, who was educated in the United States and was the editor of *Anees* newspaper. I asked him to interview the Prime Minister. He went, interviewed the Prime Minister, and drafted an article in which he quoted Shah Mahmud Khan as clarifying he had not resigned and had not presented his resignation to His Highness, the King and neither had His Highness, the King said he will abdicate the throne.

"These are all rumors," he said in the article. "I am a devoted servant of Afghanistan, and I'm always ready to serve the country. I am sincere to the King of Afghanistan, and I will serve him in the military or the public sector. I am always sincere and loyal. All these rumors are just rumors."

The interview was brought to me. I made some minor corrections to the article and showed it to the Prime Minister. He asked me to add this couplet of Hafiz, the famous Persian poet:

Until I die and I am in the shroud
Until that point, I'm not going to let you go, or leave you
alone.

I said, "Saheb, this has perfect timing. And the couplet is very meaningful here." The gist of his interview and the couplet was that until he dies and is buried, Shah Mahmud Khan will not shy away from serving his country, either as Prime Minister or as an ordinary person while living at home.

The article was published in the *Anees* newspaper. The people took the interview the wrong way. They thought Sardar Shah Mahmud Khan wanted to be the Prime Minister until death.

Sardar Sultan Ahmad Khan, who was the foreign minister at that time, was an artless, simple man. People said he was in with the Communists, though I do not believe it. Dr. Khushbeen even wrote about this in his book, but I still do not believe it. Sardar Sultan Ahmad Khan took a copy of the newspaper with the interview about Shah Mahmud Khan and went to Paghman outside Kabul where His Highness, the King was in retreat.

He had the ear of His Highness and showed him the newspaper, saying, "See what the Prime Minister has written?"

Sardar Mohammad Daoud Khan and Sardar Mohammad Naim Khan also brought this to the attention of His Highness, which fanned the fire. The king was not very happy and returned to Kabul. The adversaries of Shah Mahmud Khan became bold. They knew Shah Mahmud Khan would not do anything against His Highness, the King. They knew no one would have done what Shah Mahmud Khan did at the time when Nadir Shah was assassinated, and the people wanted Shah Mahmud Khan to become king, yet he declined and left the crown for Zahir Shah. At that time Zahir Shah did not accept this, and Shah Mahmud Khan insisted and kissed Zahir Shah's hand as a sign of obedience and submission. He always stood as a loyal subject. Whatever they did to him, he never complained. His adversaries were saying he had become old and could not shoulder the responsibility of the government and Zahir Shah said, "Who should I fall back on except my two cousins, Mohammad Daoud Khan and Mohammad Naim Khan?" Zahir Shah had said this many times before.

At night, during a meeting, the king asked Sardar Shah

Wali Khan (1888-1977), brother of Shah Mahmud Khan and uncle of the king, "Please go to Sardar Shah Mahmud Khan and give him this newspaper and tell him I have lost patience. Tell him he has no choice but to resign."

Sardar Shah Wali Khan took the assignment. There was a little tension already between the two brothers. The reason being the daughter of the king, Princess Bilqees, was engaged to the son of Sardar Shah Mahmud Khan. However, the son of Shah Wali Khan, Sardar Abdul Wali, married her. The king was present during both engagements. This created a little tension between the two brothers. Both of them were good men.

Shah Wali Khan came to see his brother Shah Mahmud Khan and said, "You wrote this article in the newspaper, and now you are daring to oppose your own nephew, the son of His Highness, the King Nadir Shah Shaheed (martyr)."

As soon as he heard the name of His Highness Shaheed, Sardar Shah Mahmud Khan, had tears rolling from his eyes. He said, "I will sacrifice my life for him, but you are witness that someday, you all will repent. Let's go and see His Highness, the King." The two brothers left together for the meeting.

The next morning, I went to the Prime Ministry. This is very interesting. It's an historical time. The fate of Afghanistan took a turn right here. I saw Ali Mohammad Khan sitting there with Hakim, the son of Quandi, along with Mir Haidar Khan Hossaini. It was said Hakim was a handsome young man and was well liked by Ali Mohammad Khan. In the past, whenever I visited Ali Mohammad Khan, he would have a very warm attitude and would stand up and respect me and shake my hand and insist I sit near him. Today, he was nonchalant and had a very cool attitude. Hakim did not even move from his place.

Mir Haidar Khan was my friend, the noble son of Qazi Mir Ata Mohammad Khan, who was a Sayed and a scholar from Herat. I knew his father well. He gestured to me as soon as I tried to sit. Ali Mohammad Khan said, "Khalil Jan, are you aware of the Prime Ministry? Why don't you go and find out?"

Normally, he used to say "His Highness Ghazi Prime Minister Saheb." That's what he used to say. Today, strikingly, he was saying "Prime Ministry." I thought either the Prime Minister was wounded or had been killed, or something had happened. I said, "No, I have no information. What has happened?"

I didn't wait for an answer. I left the room. The Prime Minister's office was in the same building on the second floor. I entered his office without permission. There were a few members of Parliament sitting there with him. When he saw me, he was happy and told them, "The Minister of Public Information has brought some work for me which needs attention. I will say goodbye to you, and we will see you in the future." The members of Parliament left.

The Prime Minister looked very worried and distressed. I said, "Saheb, is everything all right?"

He said, "Did you see what His Highness, the King did?"

I said, "What happened?"

He said, "The newspaper was brought to his attention. You are a witness, and God is my witness that my intentions are not ill. When I wrote the couplet of Hafiz that 'I'm not going to let go until I die,' I meant I will serve Afghanistan and the King of Afghanistan in any capacity, either as Prime Minister or as an ordinary man sitting at home. I don't mean that being Prime Minister is not important. If the king wants me to walk out right now, he should call me."

I said, "If the king calls me and asks me to come, I will go right away to his Palace, and I will explain everything to him. I am his Minister, and I am willing to give my deposition."

The Prime Minister picked up the telephone and dialed the number for His Highness, the King. When the king answered he handed the phone to me.

I said, "Your Highness, God is my witness that I love my country and swear on my motherland your uncle did not mean what has been said about the article in the newspaper and the couplet of Hafiz. What he meant with this couplet

459

is that while he is alive and until he pulls up the shroud and turns to dust, he is not going to hold back serving Afghanistan and serving the King of Afghanistan very sincerely."

"I gave him this couplet of Hafiz," I said. "He did not even remember it. I reminded him of it before he wrote it."

On the other end of the phone the king responded the way he used to respond all the time. "Yes, this is true," he said. "I also understand it this way. There's nothing to it. Nothing is going on. In the family, these things happen, and we will resolve it among ourselves."

What he meant is, "It is none of your business."

The Prime Minister took the telephone from my hand and continued the conversation, "Whatever was said to you was correct except for one thing. I do remember the couplet of Hafiz, and I wrote the couplet myself. Khalilullah Khan has nothing to do with it." And then he hung up. Turning to me, he said, "Do you realize they will get you for what you just admitted to, even though you did not?"

I said, "If I will be admonished, I will accept it with a smiling face."

I continued, "What are you going to do now?"

The Prime Minister answered, "I will resign."

"Saheb, that's not right," I interrupted. I knew what would befall him after he resigned. I further said, "Saheb, you should invite all your ministers to come together and make an announcement. After all, they have served under you. Tell them you are getting older and weaker and cannot continue with the responsibilities of the Prime Minister. Tell them anything you would like to say."

He shook his head. "I cannot hide behind old age. I am strong. I am healthy."

I said, "Well, use some other reason for resigning. Say you have reached a point where you do not want to continue. You may even find some other ministers who will resign with you. Take your resignation, and the resignations of the others and give them to the king."

He answered, "No, my son. This may give way to some other misunderstanding and misfortune."

I said, "Well, there you have it. It's your call."

I left the Prime Ministry and went home, thinking about what would happen. I have seen his adversaries bold enough to distribute *Shabnamah* (Night Letters), which cursed him and accused him of every wrong. They held nothing back. A new Prime Minister would have to be someone who is a charismatic leader and knows how to play on people's emotions. I'm not saying a person should be corrupt or a traitor to the country, but he should have a very emotional quality of inciting people. The person should be ambitious and an opportunist, so that those qualities can be exploited for their own end.

As I mentioned, they were using abusive language. I do remember when I established the Paghman movie theater, I had a small hotel built next to it and invited the Prime Minister himself to visit. They knew he was going to be there. They had written graffiti on the wall of the movie theatre, rude remarks, such as "why don't you leave so your young nephew can come in and become the Prime Minister," only with cuss words. The Prime Minister saw the graffiti and so did Hakim, who was standing with him. The Prime Minister said, "They can cuss all they want, I never said no to my young nephews. They can always take over." These occurrences had become very common.

I was at home. It was around 6 or 7 o'clock in the evening when my telephone rang. My heart pounded. I was sure it was the Prime Minister.

"Hello," I answered the phone.

"Mr. Khalili?" It was the Prime Minister.

I said, "Bale Saheb (Yes, sir)."

He answered with a beautiful couplet:

"The heart is not like a pigeon who can fly away ;
and then come back to sit
against a corner of the roof
Once you fly, you're gone. "

I said, "What did you do?"

He answered, "I went and tendered my resignation. The king was sitting at his desk, and I put it in front of him. Shah Wali Khan was there, and so was Mohammad Daoud

461

Khan, Mohammad Naim Khan, and the Queen. I told the king, 'this is you and your crown and your work. Right here, right now, this night, in front of your desk, remember this: I will not commit treason to you or to Afghanistan. If I don't want to leave my post, no one can throw me out. I'm popular with the Afghan army and the people of Afghanistan. The facts and God are on my side. Just because you are the son of Nadir Shah, I will resign. You will be happy I'm not on the scene. Please keep my words in your memory. The day will come when you will really repent.'"

Daoud Khan interrupted me, saying, "What do I have to regret?"

I answered, "You will regret your actions." After I said that, I got up from my seat and said, "May God be with you."

The king walked with me up to the stairs. I kissed his face and came back to my home. And here, my son, after this I have no job."

I responded, "Well, may God be with you. What should I do?"

He said, "Watch what happens to you tomorrow."

Mohammad Daoud Khan Becomes Prime Minister (1953-1963)

I knew in my heart that this man might have ill intentions against me. My enemies had made Sardar Mohammad Daoud Khan very angry with me. As the proverb goes, he was ready to do anything at a moment's notice. My adversaries enticed someone to file a claim against the estate of my father for an orchard and garden, which he owned in Kohdaman. There was another very unchivalrous act, which was done against me, which I'm not going to mention here. Besides the land claim, they also found a couple of people to accuse me of accepting bribe as part of my job as Minister of Public Information. God is my witness I have never known or had any contact with these people. They never crossed my path. I was certain Hakim had instigated them, hoping I would be provoked into reacting irrationally and getting into a fight with them so I would be arrested. I told them to go ahead and file a claim against me, and I would see them in court.

The next morning I received a call from Sardar Mohammad Daoud Khan. Instead of any greetings, he barked into the phone, "I have told the other ministers, and I'm telling you, to go and wait for instructions at the Ministry of Public Information until you are replaced by someone else. It might take four to five days, but during that time, whatever transpires in the Ministry of Public Information, you will be personally responsible to me."

I told him, "Your uncle has resigned. I was part of his cabinet, and now I have resigned too. I cannot work for a single moment now."

He yelled, "I am ordering you and putting you on notice. You know me very well."

I responded, "Bale Saheb (yes, sir), I know you very well."

He hung up, and an official car from the Ministry arrived at my home. I got in and went to the Ministry. Abdul Sabur Naseemi was my assistant. He was the nephew of Qazi Abdur Rahman Khan, the head of the Supreme Court who was murdered by Amanullah Khan, on the issue of veil (hejab). He was a scholar and a very learned man from Paghman. I saw him at the Ministry, and he seemed very gloomy. Some of the very brave and honest employees of the Ministry came to see me. They asked me if I was going to resign.

"If you resign, we will resign too," they said.

I told them, "I'm not going to resign because I have been fired. The cabinet has fallen."

It was difficult for me to publish all the Firmans and statements. These were the worst five days of my life. Shah Mahmud Khan sat at his home, while I continued publicity and promoting Mohammad Daoud Khan. "What can be worse than this?" I kept wondering. By stroke of luck and God's mercy, these Firmans did not come through as fast as I had expected. I was supposed to go and inspect the government printing press where 300 to 400 people worked. The press was inside the courtyard of the Arg. The director of the press was Mirza Sher Ahmad Khan.

Working with Sardar Mohammad Daoud Khan is an Uphill Task

Mirza Sher Ahmad Khan was from Kabul. He called me on the phone and said, "The press workers want to come see you and thank you for all you have done. This would also take the form of protest, endorsing your status, and demanding you continue your work. They are very happy with you," he said.

If Sardar Mohammad Daoud Khan comes to know about this, he will conclude I conspired it, I thought.

I said, "I will not accept this and do not recommend you do this."

I took the transport and headed toward the Arg courtyard. I went to see the press workers. They were very poor and underpaid employees, and I had helped them in the past. I had increased their salaries, added incentives, and added overtime to their pay. I had also built rooms for them so they had a place to sleep there because some of them came from far-flung places and in winter it was difficult to travel. I made arrangements so they had heat in their rooms, and at night, when they used to work, I made sure they had food and other facilities. As soon as I arrived at the press, they flocked around me like moths around a candle. I said goodbye to them and told them, "Here I have come myself to you, you don't need to come to the Ministry."

They answered, "No, we will go to the house of Sardar Saheb, and we will talk to him about you continuing in your position."

I said, "No. Never do that. If you go to Sardar Saheb's residence, I should head to the gallows myself."

They laughed, and the issue was put to rest.

Stopping the Publication of Defamatory Article in Payame Haq against Shah Mahmud Khan

After the gathering dispersed and I was alone with Mirza Sher Ahmad Khan, he said, "Maulana Shah Mohammad Reshad has brought an article and wants it to be published in *Payam Haq*."

I was the founder of the magazine. In his article he tried to condemn Sardar Shah Mahmud Khan as much as possible and used very poor language. He even called him a hypocrite in the article. At the same time he welcomed Sardar Mohammad Daoud Khan. I was deeply touched by his negative writing. Until yesterday, when Sardar Shah Mahmud Khan was the Prime Minister, this man from Kohistan was at his beck and call. And today, he had totally turned around. I went and sat in the office of the head of the press, and I asked him if the article had been printed.

He said, "No it's still in process."

I asked him to bring me the article. He did, and I read it. It really contained derogatory remarks against the former Prime Minister.

I told the director of the press, "May God bless you for doing this noble act of making me aware of this article."

Sardar Mohammad Daoud Khan would have definitely come down hard on me for this. He could not and would not find anything of which he could accuse me, yet publishing this article would have led to my punishment, and Sardar Shah Mahmud Khan would have also been upset with me for turning my back on him. It would have been a very cheap and degrading action, that in the last five days of my service, I should be remembered for publishing something like this writing against this great man who was in service of Afghanistan.

Mr. Reshad, who had a limp in his leg, came to the office. His father was my teacher and friend, by the name of Mullah Ghulam Mohammad. He was a good man.

Mr. Reshad came in and without even any greeting demanded, "Who has suspended my article?"

He addressed the head of the printing press who

responded the article had been suspended by the Minister of Public Information. Reshad in the same breath said, "The Minister of Public Information has no right to do this because he does not have a job."

I interrupted in the conversation. I said, "What you are saying is not right. Sardar Shah Mahmud Khan was the Prime Minister of Afghanistan. One of his nephews is the King of Afghanistan. The other nephew is the new Prime Minister of Afghanistan. He, himself, holds the title of Commander in Chief, even as he sits at his home. This is not in your interest to use these words about him. Until yesterday you were playing a different tune for Shah Mahmud Khan, and today, you are completely changing the tune. He's a scholar and a learned man. You don't have any right to write against him like this."

Mr. Reshad became infuriated, and I got upset also. We entered into a scuffle, and he left the room in anger and went down the stairs complaining. Within half an hour of this conversation, I received a telephone call from Sardar Mohammad Daoud Khan, who very rudely asked me to come to his office right away. I knew in my heart it was because of the incident, which had just happened here. I called the director of the printing press and told him I was leaving, and I may not be coming back, and to please let my family know I had gone. I felt like I was headed to prison. I could not control my emotions. On my way out, I took a copy of the article with me.

I went to Sardar Mohammad Daoud Khan. He was still at his home because he had not yet assumed the office of the Prime Minister. He was waiting to complete his cabinet. He was also working on further plans for Afghanistan and wanted to have a copy of his plan with him when he took office. Every day his friends, such as Hakim, Mr. Adalat and many others, came to his house and met like an inner cabinet, to plan for the future. The most trusted lieutenant he had was this Hakim Khan who later on became Communist and his activities are well known. Also, it was Mr. Adalat who later became the Minister of Public Works and then, bless his soul, died. The other person I remember who was close to Sardar Mohammad Daoud Khan was Mr.

Mir Mohammad Yosuf Khan, who later became Minister of Agriculture. They were acquainted with Daoud Khan in Paris.

I went to him at his house. He was taking a leisurely walk with Mr. Abdullah Malik Yar, who had come from Lashkargah where he was the President of the Hermand Project. He had come to Kabul to congratulate Daoud Khan. I joked with Malik Yar when I saw him saying, "So, you have reached here, too?"

Sardar Daoud Khan heard my comment to Malik Yar. Turning his face toward Malik Yar he said, "Why don't you leave? I have to talk to this man, and then I will give you a call and ask you to come in."

Mr. Malik Yar looked at me with kindness or pity in his eyes, as if I was the sacrificial lamb. He did not say anything and slowly walked away. I felt he wanted to turn back and put in a good word for me, but thank God he did not.

The Sardar and I both went toward his house and sat in a room. Without any small talk he angrily turned to me and said, "What right do you have to push around a director of a department and cuss him out? When you are cussing someone and breaking his head open, what should I do? Should I start killing? What should the king do?"

I answered, "You can kill people, and the king also can kill people. And you can break people's heads. Yet, I did not break Reshad's head or hurt him. He walks with a limp and while leaving the room abruptly in anger he hit his head on the frame of the door and hurt himself. His head was injured, and he came running to you to file a complaint. I'm sure you remember the famous proverb, "Every one has seen the injured and bleeding head of the slave, but no one has seen the bleeding heart of the lady of the house (an Afghan proverb)." Please ask him, why did I pull the article from publication? Ask him the reason, please."

Instead, he asked me, "Tell me, why did you do so?"

I pulled out the copy of the unpublished article I had brought with me and asked him to read it. He read it, and appeared to be disgusted by the time he reached the end. I

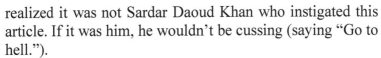

realized it was not Sardar Daoud Khan who instigated this article. If it was him, he wouldn't be cussing (saying "Go to hell.").

He asked, "Who wrote this article?"

I answered, "The same director you are talking about who came to you, and you are censuring me for him." I added, "If this article had come out, the infighting of your family, which you have the right to do among and between yourselves, this would have affected the whole house of the nation of Afghanistan. We have been destroyed for years from these infightings and always the nation has been suffering. I did not allow the printing of this article. Your uncle, Sardar Shah Mahmud Khan, would have read this article. What would he have said to you? What would he have said to the king? Your adversaries would have used it against you. I stopped this article from being published. Reshad cussed and cursed, and so did I. Now, you have the right to do whatever you want. The doors of your prison are always open. I will go there again."

Daoud Khan said, "Whoever condemns you for this article is himself condemned. However, I have another bone to pick with you."

I was surprised. I asked, "What is that, sir?"

"Why did you not kill him?" Daoud said. "You should have taken a revolver and shot him."

I replied, "Sir, his head hit the wall, and he bled a little, and you summoned me to censor me. If I had killed him, what would you have done to me? Besides, I don't want blood on my hands."

Sardar Daoud Khan said, "Well, you are free to go. Your presence is very helpful. Please go back to your job, and this man is suspended as of now from his job. Please have them stop his stipend. Also, he should pay one month's salary back to the state as penalty."

I said, "Okay," and started to leave his room. Before I left, I turned back again and said, "I have a request. If you would be kind enough, please let me go to my home. Incidents like this will continue to happen. It's better for me not to even work the rest of the five days."

He said, "I would like you to work, but if you don't

want to, it's your call."

I said, "Thank you." I went home and returned the official car, closed my doors and stayed back.

Later that same day, Sardar Shah Mahmud Khan called me and said, "Come to my place."

I said, "I have no transport, Sir. I will leave my house now and walk to your place."

He said, "No, I will send you my car and driver."

When the transport came, I went to him. He said, "Did you know the enemies have instigated some people to sue you on certain things?"

I said, "Yes, sir, I'm aware of it. People have been told I took bribes while constructing the building. I'm glad you know the facts that for days and nights I have gone hungry. You know I have requested an advance on my pay so many times from you. You also know I have fought against the people who used to bribe."

He said, "Yes, I know everything, and I have told his Highness, the King about you. I have mentioned to him if he wants me to be happy then he should not listen to what Daoud Jan says about Khalili. I have told him do not listen to anybody about him." He added, "Do whatever his Highness, the King says, and you will be fine."

I said, "Thank you."

My Meeting with Zahir Shah, King of Afghanistan

I went home, and a day later a car was sent from the Ministry of Court to fetch me to the Arg palace. The driver said, "His Highness, the King of Afghanistan, would like to see you at his residence." This was an honor and a source of pride. This was not available to everyone.

I went to see His Highness, the King. He stood from his place and welcomed me very warmly, with a great deal of respect. I, too, held his hand and sat down next to him. I could see in his eyes kindness and admiration for me. He paused for a few seconds, and then broke the silence, saying, "If a gardener, for example, of this palace garden where we are sitting, picks a flower and puts it in his lapel, does anyone have the right to stop him from doing so? I asked you to come here because you are a poet and a writer, and I had this question on my mind, and I wanted to ask you about it."

I answered, "Your Highness, you are being very generous. This is a case of justice and jurisprudence, and it is a legal question. If the gardener is also the owner of the garden, then he has owner's rights in the garden, and no one can say anything against him. However, if the garden is owned by someone else, the gardener does not have the right to pick a flower and place it in his lapel."

The king explained his purpose. "Now, I am considered to be the owner of this garden and also the King of Afghanistan, I would like to take these flowers from the garden of literature of Afghanistan and place them on my desk. Those flowers are your writings and your books. I would like to appoint you as the head of my Secretariat. You should accept it. God has given me this wisdom with a little delay, however."

I got up from my place and kissed the hand of His Highness, the King and said, "I am honored and proud and respectful toward your words, Your Highness. I would like to thank you for this. Since this is the start of a new era, with all due respect, your cousin, Prince Sardar Mohammad Daoud Khan is young and hot under the collar. Also, at this time, your very beloved uncle, Sardar Shah Mahmud Khan, who provided great service to Afghanistan, is a little depressed. Any word written in your Firmans or in the memos, which may not be liked will be associated with me, because I am your Chief Secretary. Maybe this will again create an atmosphere of mistrust and misunderstanding for you. I would appreciate something lower or lesser in responsibility at this time. I would be more than glad to shoulder that responsibility, whatever it is. I even know how to garden. I am from Kohdaman. It is better for me if I do not shoulder this greater responsibility."

The king responded, "Please, go home and think about it and come back tomorrow."

I went home and discussed this with my wife. She said, "You did the right thing."

The Commander in Chief Shah Mahmud Khan called that night and asked, "Why didn't you accept the offer?"

I explained to him my reasoning. He said, "What you're saying makes sense. I will talk to His Highness, the King, and maybe we will come up with another responsibility. But, make sure you accept this time because there are people out there would like to hurt you."

The next day, when I wanted to leave my house, my friend Mohammad Annus Khan came to me and said, "His Highness, the King is going to see you. Whatever he's offering just accept it. Whatever he's ordering, do it. Sardar Mohammad Daoud Khan is not going to stand in your way. He does not want to hurt you. He has a lot of respect for his uncle (Shah Mahmud Khan) and also the people of Afghanistan. You have not done anything wrong. There are other people around Sardar Mohammad Daoud Khan. He spoke in my ear, saying there are Communists around him. If you stay at your home, they will definitely get back to you. It is good for you to accept what the king has offered."

I realized Sardar Shah Mahmud Khan might have put Annus Khan up to talking to me.

My Appointment as Media Advisor to the King

I went to the Arg palace again. I was sent directly to His Highness, the King. He was very polite and courteous as usual. Upon seeing me, he said, "I have found a job for you."

I responded, "Your Highness, you are very kind."

He said, "I will appoint you to my court as my Media Advisor."

I responded again, "This is good news, and there will be nothing better than this. However, I hope controlling the media may not be my responsibility."

He answered, "No, not at all. That is the job of the government."

I said, "Will I be here with your Highness?"

He said, "Yes," and added, "I have one more responsibility for you. I would like you to be my teacher and teach me Persian literature."

"Your Highness, you are the teacher of all," I answered. "Whatever I know, I will definitely impart it to you. I will try my best to make you familiar with the literature of Persian language. And through this, I will introduce you to the Persian (Dari) poets. I know you have been away from your country for a while."

He said, "This is what I want from you. Please go and write your own Firman."

Hafez Nur Mohammad Khan Kohgadai wrote the Firman. He was the Chief Secretary of the king. He was also my friend. He came from Nahrain. Kohgadai had a slight streak of envy and jealousy. He was afraid that I might become the Chief Secretary. While he was writing the Firman, he wrote the date as the 13th of Safar (a month that migrates in the lunar calendar), which is considered to be a bad omen. The king did not notice it, and I just let it go.

I went to work as the Media Advisor to the king. I was informed Sardar Mohammad Hashim Khan was not very happy when he came to know about my appointment. Even though he was sick, he began turning and tossing in his bed like a curling snake. This was mentioned to me by Dr. Zahir Khan who became the Speaker of the Parliament (and later Prime Minister) and was a very good friend of mine. At that time, he was Deputy Minister of Health and was the attending physician for Sardar Mohammad Hashim Khan. He said, "As soon as Hashim Khan heard about your appointment, he was very upset, and his blood pressure went up. You should have waited for a few days. He was leaving for overseas."

I said, "It is not my business, and I do not care about it. I have been appointed to this job."

The Death of Hashim Khan (1953)

Not even a week had passed. It was time of evening prayer, and I was at my home. Mohammad Annus Khan came to the house and said, "Come with me, I need to talk to you." He was a very careful man. He took me to a secluded place where the Ghazi High School now stands. It was a wooded then. There were some old trees there, and he looked around to make sure no one was listening.

I said, "What's the word?"

"Something big has happened," he said. "I just want to make sure no one is around."

"Are you okay?" I asked him. I thought something extraordinary had gone down.

He said, "It is very big news. Today, Sadre Azam Saheb Kalan (the Great Prime Minister), His Highness Mohammad Hashim Khan, has died."

"I think you are trying to tell me this to calm me down," I said. "Yet I will never be happy upon his death. Is this correct?"

He confirmed, "Yes, he has died."

I recited the traditional line from the Holy Koran, "We are all from God, and we return to God." I did not say, "May God bless him."

"You are most welcome to come in," I said. Annus Khan came into the house, and we talked and talked for quite some time. My other friend, Sayed Shamsuddin Majrooh also came. Hazrat Saheb and Mia Jan came by. They were happy about my appointment as Media Advisor to the King of Afghanistan. Some other friends also came to my house. This story of Hashim Khan's death was repeated from one mouth to the other. Dr. Zahir Khan called me and said, "Rest assured. He's not coming back."

Sardar Hashim Khan's Funeral

The next day we went to the funeral of Sardar Hashim Khan. His body was placed in a coffin in front of Dilkusha Palace in Kabul for viewing by mourners. They used chunam (an Indian plaster made from shell-lime and sand), then marked white lines in front of it for the high VIPs to stand, with others standing in line behind them. The first line was marked for cabinet ministers; the second line or row was for foreign ambassadors from Islamic countries. The third row was for the parliamentarians, and the fourth was for intellectuals and scholars. The fifth and final row was for family, friends, and others close to Hashim Khan. All this was written down.

I did not find a place for myself among the king's advisors, so I stood to the side, in a corner. Abdul Malik Khan, the new Minister of Finance for Daoud Khan, handled most of the arrangements. He was a very active, sincere, and organized man. He approached me, unaware I had been appointed as an advisor to the king. The announcement had not yet been published in the newspaper. He wasn't very friendly to me. He said, "You're also here? Why don't you go and stand in the area marked for general public?"

I replied, "I wish I had been allowed to stand with the general public. However, I am here on duty."

The Chief Secretary of the King interjected, "Yes, he's the new Media Advisor to the King."

Abdul Malik Khan's comment was an old Afghan proverb: *Murabbi daree, murabba bokhur*," which means, "Now that you have a mentor, so eat jam." He meant that since Shah Mahmud Khan was my mentor, I had found favor with the king.

Funeral prayers were offered, and the funeral took place at Eid Gah (the congregational mosque). Sardar Hashim Khan was laid to rest near his brothers and his uncles and was left there to answer to The Almighty.

Working in the Royal Library

With the passage of time, I saw change and improvement in the attitude of His Highness toward me. We started reading and studying books together. What I did first was to bring to him Saadi's famous *Gulistan* and *Bostan* from the Royal Library. (Sheikh Mushharrafuddin Muslehuddin Saadi (1184-1291) traveled extensively in the Muslim world and incorporated his rich experiences in these two books, which were translated into many languages and used as basic texts to teach generations).

The Royal Library was an excellent repository of books, with many rare manuscripts, which were given to the king as gifts from different intellectuals and scholars. The king himself had acquired many of them also. The king loved beautiful handwriting. He also liked painting and was well familiar with miniature art.

He liked my commentary on Sheikh Saadi. The Bostan of Saadi had been printed in Kabul by Mir Amad during the time of Amir Habibullah Khan Seraj. We talked about Mir Amad and started reading the *Gulistan*. We discussed the characters of the kings in Saddi's book. I said, "Your Highness, please do not think I have selected these stories of the kings because you are the king. That is how it is in the book. It depends on you which chapter we start with."

He responded, "I will not go past the characters of the kings. We will start from here." And so, we read and discussed his poetry, such as:

What is the use of being a powerful ruler?
It is better to die than to oppress your subjects.

Saadi's powerful lines of poetry are still very capitulating.

Slowly, the king became more open and relaxed. One day, he told me he would undertake a hunting trip to Darrai Ashraf (Ashraf Valley). I had heard of Darrai Ashraf and knew it was a beautiful place in the center of the Hindu Kush Mountains, close to Kahmard and Serghan north of Kabul. It is secluded, off the beaten path, and away from the main road, but still accessible by automobile. There were plenty of partridges, trout, and deer. I accompanied the King of Afghanistan to this beautiful place. The spotted fish, or trout as the Westerners say, are delicious and wonderful. Strangely enough, trout is only found on the northern side of the Hindu Kush Mountains in our country. As we traveled farther north and went higher, the water became cleaner and colder, and you could find trout in increasing numbers. The spots on their bodies are reddish, and as you go further north the taste of the fish becomes better.

Afghanistan has different varieties of deer also. There is a kind of deer called the snake eater. There is a story (mentioned in the "Animal Kingdom") behind this name. It is said once this type of deer eats a snake, its body is poisoned and for 40 days it should not drink water. If it drinks water, the deer dies. However after 40 days, if the

475

deer comes to water and drinks, then the poison has no effect. There is Arabic poetry mentioning this snake-eating deer also.

When you travel to Darrai Ashraf, one can see the ancient remains of buildings. It has been said in the books that King Timur (1772-1793) fell sick there. I have forgotten the exact name of this place in the hunting valley at this time.

The name of Darrai Shikari had also appeared in books, and it is said the Ghori kings (Ghorid Dynasty was 1148-1215) stockpiled their military equipment and other supplies here when Genghis Khan's army attacked them (1162-1227).

We spent three to four days there, and then came back to Kabul with the king. We did not interfere in the political affairs of the country. We started reading books, and with the permission of the king, we went in the Royal Library, and I began to catalogue the Library's handwritten manuscripts and rare books. I catalogued three hundred of them. Mr. Humanyoun Etemadi, the Royal librarian, worked with me. He was a very talented miniaturist.

These rare books had some strange things in them. They had traveled from the libraries of one king to another and finally landed in the Royal Library of King Zahir Shah. Many of these books had the seal of the Moghul Emperors. All the books were inventoried once a year or every two years to make sure they were still there. The person doing the inventory had to sign and press his seal to ensure that the inventory was attested. Some of the attested inventories were signed by Annus Khan, Amanat Khan, or Mullah Muwajah.

I took the responsibility of finding out who Mullah Muwajah and Amanat Khan were. Who is this Amanat the librarian? I did the research and found these people and made them part of the catalogue, matching the person to the seal. I asked Humanyoun Jan to copy and transcribe them. One of the rare books that drew my attention was an anthology of Hazrat Sheikh Saadi (1184-1283). I don't think the anthology is still there. The anthology was written in the Nasakh style of writing on yellowish colored paper with an ordinary handwriting. The poetry of Hazrat Sheikh Saadi had not yet been alphabetized. The books or titles were mostly not under *Gulistan* (The Rose Garden) or *Bostan* (The Orchard), but Saadi Namah.

Precious Books in the Royal Library

When I compared the *Gulistan* of Saadi with the *Gulistan* of Farrughi, I found many variations in the two publications. I noted them carefully and corrected more than 100 words in Farrughi's book. I wrote them down and entered them into the catalogue. The original *Gulistan* of Saadi was written by Mohammad Bin Mohammad Shirazi, alias Dawar, in Shiraz, the present day Iran. In my opinion, this book was brought to Afghanistan after the Afghans invaded Iran. The book must have fallen into the hands of the army of Ahmad Shah Khan or Shah Ashraf, reached Afghanistan in this way, and was kept in Herat. Someone from Herat presented the book to the King of Afghanistan as a gift. Since the book was very simply written, with no miniature art of gold columns, it was shelved in the library of the king as an ordinary book. I found it accidentally because it attracted my attention.

There was a book of illustration and references of Ibne-Sina (Persian philosopher, 980-1037, author of more than 240 surviving texts on a range of subjects, including *The Book of Healing* and *The Canon of Medicine*). I don't recall the details, and I could not find the author of it during that time. There was a delicately put together work of (Persian mystical poet) Hafiz (1325-1389).

The catalogs I put together covered almost 800 pages. In those days we did not have photocopy facilities, and I could not find anyone to transcribe the pages for me. I did transcribe one copy for my personal library and left one copy at the Royal Library. From my own copy, I rewrote almost half of it separately for an Indian historian named Tara Chand. He had written many books. Abdurrauf Benawa took that from me and gave it to Tara Chand. He promised he would publish it under my name; however, I never heard back from him and have no way to know if he ever published it. Since almost all my library was

477

confiscated, my books destroyed and my papers scattered, my copy of the catalog may have been lost too. During the time of the Russian occupation, the Royal Library was looted. I don't know what happened to the catalog list or the valuable manuscripts in the Royal Library.

There were albums, art books, and books of pictures; there was the artwork of Behzad (1450-1535, Afghan painter) and a copy of the Holy Koran from the time of Sheikh Ahmad-e Jam (1048-1141), which had been presented to the King of Afghanistan as a gift, and the king had placed it in his Royal Library. That was also lost. There were so many other items dating back thousands of years that must have been looted and trampled.

One day, we were informed that the government wanted to renovate the basements of Burj palace. While digging through, they came across a big box full of rare handwritten books and tablets. Famous scholars and writers had written these works in large handwriting. The works were done in beautiful writing in Herat and brought to the palace of Amir Abdul Rahman Khan by Hafiz Noor, who lost a few of the works along the way; however, the rest survived and were kept in the Royal Library.

I took time to write some books. I wrote *Nai Namah*, the *Story of the Flute*. I also wrote *Zamarrude Khooneen*, the *Bloody Emerald*. The magazine *Faiz Quddus* was also written there. I had quite a few reference books available to me. There was a copy of the poetic work of Mirza Abdul Qadir Bedil (1642-1720), which was copied while he was alive. The only other copy I've ever seen was in a library in Paris. I had written a few articles regarding that. Besides numerous articles and books written from ancient times, the Royal Library also housed the sacred stone from the mausoleum of Hazrat Ali at Mazar-i-Sharif. All these things were in the Royal Library, and all of them were looted. Afghanistan's rare manuscripts and historical documents were plundered, burned, or destroyed. When I recall all those books and documents, my eyes well with tears. This was the historical treasure of Afghanistan, the treasure of our people, the pride of our nation.

The King of Afghanistan decided the Royal Library

should be transferred to the library of the Ministry of Education. I was the bearer of this news to Dr. Majid Khan, the Minister of Education. He was happy to receive the news. He said, "Our shelving in the ministry library is not ready yet. It will take some time, so keep the books there. Once the shelving in our stacks is ready and the chemicals required to maintain and prolong the life of these books is available, we will shift the books." This gradually gave me peace of mind. I went to the Ministry of Court, thought upon this, did my work, and tried not to intervene in any other affairs.

In a reorganization of the Ministry of Court, Hafiz Noor Mohammad, who was acting Chief Secretary, became the Chief Secretary. He attained a high title and elevated position. Being a Darvish, I did not want to say anything about this man until I was working at the Ministry of Court. I wrote a poem and presented it to the king. It went something like this:

A camel one day complained to God saying,
"I have carried a lot of burdens,
I have traveled the deserts and the mountain,
I have eaten a lot of thorns,
And yet I have one request:
When you present your animals,
Don't tie my leash to the tail of a donkey."

In other words, "Please allow me to stay at home, to retire in my humble abode." A Firman was instantly written, and I was promoted as Minister without Portfolio, or a Minister Advisor. This allowed me to accept foreign invitations to travel overseas.

I Am Invited to Visit Iran

This was the time when the Hermand River Project became a bone of contention between Afghanistan and Iran and brought the two countries to the brink of war. Iranian writers produced propaganda against the Afghan nation, insulting our nation and our history. Afghan youth also picked up the pen and answered those baseless accusations by writing against Iran. The enemy who did not want the two nations to live as brothers fueled the fire. The Iranian ambassador to Afghanistan one day told me – I don't remember his name – the conditions are worsening. He told me, "Awake and stop these accusations, and the cursing between the two nations."

I answered, "Your nation is more to be blamed for it. It is not the fault of the people of Afghanistan. I cannot do anything about it. It is the Iranian writers who have started this."

He talked to his government, and I received an invitation to visit Iran on behalf of Dr. Mehran, the Iranian Minister of Education. It was a friendly overture. I took this friendly invitation to the King of Afghanistan. The king said, "We will run it by the government." He talked to his cousin. God softened his heart, and Daoud Khan approved my travel. I went to Iran. For the first time, I saw Tehran. It was the first time I had this sacred mission on my shoulders, which was to remove the seeds of contention and fire between the two brotherly nations and not allow water to turn into blood.

I went to Tehran and met the writers and intellectual scholars of Iran. I met the scholar Farozanfar and Dr. Rezazadeh Shafaq. I met Ali Dashti. They all came around me like moths to a candle. A large reception was thrown in my honor in the halls of the Ministry of Education. Almost a thousand people came together. They took me there, and I read my famous *Mathnavi* (couplet poem) *My Salams to the Intellectuals of Iran*. It was warmly welcomed. From there I was taken to Shiraz and visited the famous mausoleum of Hafiz Sherazi.

The Memoirs end here abruptly. Prof. Khalili was unable to complete the last chapter before his death in Pakistan on May 4, 1987. He was re-buried on May 23, 2013 at the Kabul University campus after his remains were brought from Peshawar, Pakistan.

Appendix

Paradise on Fire

By: Khalilullah Khalili
English Translation By: Afzal Nasiri

Introduction

The diminution of the myth of the Soviet Union's military optimism on the total victory through a quick surgical strike in Afghanistan has persuaded or forced – through unsound reasoning – their military high command in consonance with local communist lackeys – into massacring the innocent population in vengeance.

The recent bombardment (second week of October 1983) of the small, but exceptionally beautiful valley town of Istalif (p.p. 35,000 approx.), 25 miles north of Kabul, is one more example of the Soviet genocide in Afghanistan.

The Soviet Mig-23s, Su-7 and helicopter gunships swooped on the town emptying their heavy loads on innocent people, killing, injuring, and displacing thousands of men, women, and children. To underline the heart piercing, cruel, and lamentable act of the Soviet invaders here is the translation of extracts from a threnody written by the former politician, diplomat, poet, and scholar of Afghanistan, the eminent Professor Khalilullah Khalili, dedicated to the martyrs of Istalif.

About Professor Khalili, he has authored more than 70 books and booklets on history, philosophy, and literature, including four volumes of his poetic collections – in Persian and Arabic languages, some printed in the U.S. He lives in the United States as a refugee, in oblivion, in the small town of Maywood, New Jersey, coming here after resigning his last post as Ambassador of Afghanistan to Iraq, Kuwait, and Arab Emirates in the aftermath of the Soviet sponsored bloody communist coup d'état in his motherland.

Now 78, Professor Khalili has devoted his life to freedom of his country through his inspiring pen. He has immensely contributed towards striking a bond of unity and

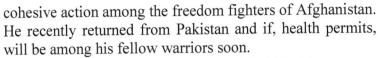

cohesive action among the freedom fighters of Afghanistan. He recently returned from Pakistan and if, health permits, will be among his fellow warriors soon.

Afzal Nasiri
November 1983
Maywood,   New

Jersey

In the name of God,
the just, the powerful.
If Afghanistan, as has been said, be the heart of Asia,
the city of Kabul is the center of that heart
and Istalif is a piece of emerald shining at its side.

Just like the old plane trees with their abundant branches
rooted deep down into the hearts of the mountain,
its history too is deeply rooted into the hearts of time.

According to some philologists,
Istalif and "Istafeel" have the same origin,
meaning vineyard.

It is said that when Alexander's (son of Philip) army
came across the slopes of the Hindukush mountain range,
face-to-face with the luxuriant and green valley of Istalif,

Glimpsing the grapes – like studded chandeliers hanging
from every branch,
some luminous like a shining star, some glowing like a
black pearl
and some delicate as a rose petal.

Spontaneously, this pleasant valley was named "Istafeel,"
later came to be known
by the Persian speaking people as Istalif.

Yes, the genealogy of words,
like the genealogy of human beings,
is full of such scattered stories.

Sultan Abu Sayeed Koragani,
used to call Istalif,
the Samarqand of Khorasan

Because he found the fruit of Istalif
as sugary as the fruit of Samarqand –
unaware of the fact that one day

The fate of the innocent people of Istalif
will surpass the bitterness
of the bloody adventure against the Moslems of
Samarqand.

Mohammad Zaheeruddin Babur, the founder of the Moghul
dynasty
in the sub-continent and Jehangir, his great-grandson, both
monarchs,
men of letters and attainment – have praised the valley of
Istalif.

The former eulogizing the beauty of this valley
and the latter, praising the wholesomeness of its fruits,
spanning into one chapter.

I very well remember the day when the late Professor
Arnold Toynbee,
contemporary historian and philosopher,
was our state guest in Istalif.

He was running frantically up and down the trees
sometimes casting sight on the green valley
of Kohdaman, Parwan and ruins of ancient city of Bagram
and sometimes gazing at the small town of Istalif,
muttering to himself.

At the sunset that day when the hosts informed him about
the departure to Kabul,
he declined to go saying, "Today, I have seen your blue
skies, snow covered hilltops
and green prosperous valleys from the two sides of Istalif

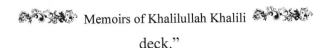

deck."

He continued, "I see the road, at the bottom of my
viewpoint,
through which we have traversed the cavalcades of kings
during the consecutive centuries."

"What a civilization, what a culture,
have existed here
and what a treasure is buried in the heart of this land.

On the other side, I see the small town of Istalif,
where, like the honey-bee comb, the houses are built
one on top of the other."

"From a distance, I kiss each and every leaf
of those green gardens
draped in colors and aromas.

While standing in solitude at the holy shrine
of that spiritual Gnostic I imagined to have broken from
this world
of materialism and darkness and to have joined the other
world."

"Today I saw a group of holy men whose foreheads
glittered with the sign of faith and whose eyes
flashed freedom and generosity."

"I saw in the other part of the town a pottery plant
with self-created designs, shapes and colors.
In the workshop of Istalif potters,

I understood the real meaning of Omar Khayyam's poetry,
translated by Fitzgerald,
which I had read in my youth."

I went to a pottery plant last night
I saw two thousand pots, some expressive, some quiet;
One pot asking the other pot. Where is the potter, the

buyer, the seller?

The philosopher Toynbee further said:
"Until I do not spend part of this night here,
I will not return to Kabul."

"Tonight I will whisper to the stars.
I will touch them from the high branches
of the aged plane tree."

"Let me listen to the music of the cheerful running
of the river, hymns of the leaves of the trees
and the voice of the nightingale."

"Your Istalif by day is a paradise of blossoms, butterflies,
flowers and colors, and by night is the manifestation of
stars,
moon and light of the beautiful town."

Alas! That land of believers, that land of the free,
that paradise of innocence was bloodied, burnt and raised to
the ground
by the blood-thirsty invaders.

The bereaved mother, who had witnessed the killing
of her young daughter and son, had a message.
What a painful message!

A message whose every word was colored with
the blood of a beautiful virgin girl and whose every line
was soaked in tears of the bereaved mother.

It was a message of death of the youth,
cry of shackles of the prisoners, moaning of the wounded,
mourning of the defenseless, gusting of the winds –

All coupled with smoke and smell of the half burned bodies
of human beings and tumultuous cries of Takbeer by the
freedom fighters,
of the nation of Tawheed, (monotheism),

Mixed with the deafening deadly thunder
of the enemy bombardment.
Yes, this was the message of the people of Istalif.

Where, in one day, on the crime of believing in God and
freedom,
the bloodthirsty communist soldiers suddenly, attacked
from land and air,
using modern weaponry against defenseless people of the
defenseless town.

The invaders bombarded them, burnt their farms,
destroyed the trees and flowers,
polluted the air with –

Chemicals and different poisons, eliminated all edibles and
livestock
they could lay their hands upon, demolished places of
worship
and wiped out signs of life and civilization.

Consequently, hundreds of mothers were hanged to trees –
with their breasts and thousands of children were thrown in
fire
and smoke and in burnt and demolished houses.

In this adventurous attack,
more than 10,000 men, women and children
were martyred.

Where in the spring, silvery stars fell from flowers,
where in fall, leaves fell like colored stars, and where
history, beauty, and desire of the people were fervent –

All was raised to the ground in blood and fire.
What is left? Just a few words which became eternal part
of the history of our country, that is –

Curse be on the Oppressive Power of the time

which is the enemy of the independent nations of the world and is also the Plunderer of right and justice.

Note: British historian Arnold Toynbee (1889-1975) wrote *A Study of History, 1934-1961,* which examined world history and the rise and fall of civilizations.

The Cry of the Statue

By: Khalilullah Khalili
English Translation By: Afzal Nasiri

Introduction

The Statue of Liberty glorifies the United States. Its majestic torch has shown light over the years to the deprived masses around the world, many of whom have found the love of mother in its wide open arms.

Poets and writers have eulogized it often but Prof. Khalili's approach is unique. Unique in a sense that he feels the pain, the pain of the symbol of freedom, the pain of the mother hidden under the iron and steel face of the statue.

A mother who is hurt at the upheavals, the bloodshed, the massacres, and annihilation of its children all over the world.

According to Prof. Khalili the symbol of freedom is losing its phenomenon. Small nations are being trampled. Trampled under the feet of monstrous, ungodly, unreligious powers in the world.

Prof. Khalili calls attention, in this brief work, of the United States to revive the phenomenon of freedom represented by the Statue of Liberty.

This Masterpiece is part of his long line of poetic collections and other works on history, philosophy and literature. He wrote it on the eve of the departure to the U.S. from Germany in 1978.

I have tried my level best to retain the context of the original Persian written by him. However, no perseverance on my part can give the same flow, beauty, and meaning to the English translation, of this Afghan poet and philosopher's works, which are in Persian and Arabic only.

> December 10, 1983
> Afzal Nasiri
> Maywood,   New
> Jersey

It is midnight. Darkness and indignation have filled the air.
I am rolling from side to side, burning in the fire
of the tragic events of my country.

My memory is awake but my speech is silent.
My eyes are closed but my heart watches.

Slowly the darkness rules supreme over me.
My eyelids become heavy with sleep.

Sleep is a strange phenomenon.
It has yet to be explained by science.
Our terrestrial body remains on earth
and our soul wanders around the stars.

We are in the present
but our thoughts travel far in the past
and see the unseen future.

Sleep gave my thoughts
wings and feathers like a pigeon.

I reached a land where the creations
of its palatial buildings kissed the skies.
The people of this land had sunk the flag
of wisdom on the moon, the land where everything
was the manifestation of power and technology.

Something which attracted my attention most
was a statue sculpted out of steel – the Statue of the
Mother.
The passage of years had covered her tresses with dust.
Her eyes were still. She held a torch in her hand.
A torch in the name of freedom.

The sculpture, in spite of all proficiency and versatility,
could not give the face of the statue the mien of a mother,
because the expressions on the face of the mother
are created by the Great Artist – The Master Creator – The
God.

In the book of this world there is nothing more beautiful
and attractive than mother. The heart of the mother
holds infinite love of God and mysteries of his solitude.
In the eyes of mother is the light of God.
Her fingers hold the pen to destiny
and her fist holds the key to the endless treasures.
On her lips is the bliss of life.........

A voice is coming from a distance.
Behold! Whose voice is this in the middle of the night,
piercing deep into my heart?
I am perplexed! Oh God! As if the steel statue has come to
life.
Its words are as ardent as fire; and as bright as light.
It was complaining. Complaining of the deeds of the man
of this age:

"It is the age of power; it is the age of insanity.
The people who have conquered the moon
do not know they are caught in chains themselves."

"What is its usefulness? Its technology has touched the
skies
but under its feet flow streams of tears and blood."
"Free and God-loving people have installed me on this vast
land
and have given the torch of freedom in my hand."

"Not just freedom of America, but freedom of all the
nations of the world.
Freedom of every human being; every human being who
nurtures hope."
"Now I shed tears on the death of freedom."
"Where are those men and women who would light this
torch of freedom?
Or, take it away from me and forget it as symbol of
freedom
of all nations whose blood has been spilt
and whose freedom usurped by the ungodly mights?"

Yes! Freedom is a gift of God, and the right of humanity.

Photos

Figure 1. Professor Khalilullah Khalili

Figure 2. Professor Khalili with daughter Marie in Saudi Arabia, where he was Ambassador of Afghanistan

Figure 3. Khalilullah Jan, "Sweet Friend of God," the eldest son of the Mustofi, at his father's house in Hussain Kot, near Kabul.

Figure 4. Mirza Mohammad Hussain, Khalili's father, he was the Chief Accountant (Mustofi-ul-Momalik) of Afghanistan at the time of King Habibullah Khan Seraj

Figure 5. Naib Salar Abdurahim Khan Safi, Prof. Khalili's Uncle

494

Figure 6. Professor Khalili with grandson, Khalil Nasiri (Marie's eldest son)

Figure 7. King Zaher Shah with Professor Khalili with participants of Al Beruni Conference in Kabul in 1973.

Figure 8. Khalili with Pope John Paul at the Vatican.

Figure 9. Professor Khalili with King Zaher Shah

*Figure 10. President Daoud with Prof. Khalili in Baghdad, Iraq.
Khalili was Ambassador of Afghanistan to Iraq & Kuwait.*

Figure 11. Marie and Afzal (son-in-law) with Prof. Khalili

Figure 12. King Zaher Shah and President Karzai celebrating Khalili's anniversary.

Figure 13. King Zaher Shah, President Karzai with Masood Khalili, son of Khalili (and the current Ambassador of Afghanistan to Spain on the right) in Kabul.

Figure 14. Najibullah Khan (Khalili's brother)

Figure 15. Amir Habibullah Seraj, father of King Amanullah Khan during his visit to India.

Figure 16. King Amanullah Khan

Figure 17. Amir Habibullah Khan Kalakani (1929)

Figure 18. Amir Habibullah Khan Kalakani (in white) and followers

Figure 19. King Nader Shah, father of Zaher Shah

Figure 20. King of Bokhara Sayed Alem Shah (Janabe Aali)

Figure 21. Khalili with King Hussain of Jordan

Figure 22. Khalili with King Faisal of Saudi Arabia

Figure 23. Khalili with Mao (of China)

Figure 24. Professor Khalili's Uncle, Mohammad Yousuf Khan

Figure 25. Prof. Khalili in philosophical mind

Figure 26. Professor Khalili was reburied with honor on May 23ʳᵈ, 2012 in Kabul at the Kabul University grounds.

Glossary

Term	Meaning
Alif ba	Persian ABC's
Aqrab	October
Arg	Fort
Assad	July
Bache Saqqa	Son of a water carrier
Chalam	Small, funnel looking clay pot
Chapar khots	Cots or beds
Chapra ghat	Powerful and strong man
Dastar	Headband
Dilkusha	Palace
Durban	Door keeper
Farahbad	Happy place (name of city)
Firmans	Decrees
Frangi	Foreigner
Ghazal	Poem
Ghulam Bacha Aam	General servants
Ghulam Bachas	Court servants
Ghulam Bache-Khas	Main servants
Ghulor sheer	Milke
Ghulor tursh	Sour
Gunbud	Dome
Hadis	Sayings
Hakim	District Magistrates
Hakeem	Local medicine practitioner (greek)
Hamam	Public bath
Hookah	Water pipe
Iftar	Breaking of fast at sundown
Jaddi	December
Jan	Mister, form of respect
Jashen	Independence Day
Jashen Isteqlal	Month of Assad
Jehad	Holy War
Jerib	a unit to measure land, less than acre
Jirga	Elder tribal assembly

Kafir	Infidel
Kaftarkhana	Pigeon homes
Kandak	Battalion
Khan	Noble
Khirgah	Tents
Khutba	Speech
Kilems	Special kind of floor cloth, like a Indian dari
Kulong	Pheasant
Kurk	100 % woolen cloth, used to make robes (Chapan)
Lorries	Trucks
Lunghi	Head covering
Maghreb	Sunset
Maidan	Fields
Maila	Festival
Masoom	Innocent
mehrab and member	Arch and pulpit
Mujahideen	Freedom Fighters
Mujahed	Singular of Mujahideen
Mujavir	Caretaker
Mullah	Religious teacher
Munji	Savior
Munshis	Secretaries
Nai	Flute
Naib-Salar	Commander
Naibul Sultana	Representative of the crown
Naji	Saved
Nizamnamas	Ruling documents
Parsi	Farsi or Persian
Pista	Pistachio
Qanavez	Silk cloth produced in Heart
Qazi	Judge
Rakaats	Number of Prayers
Ramadan	Month of Fasting
Robab	Short-necked lute made of wood
Rubaiyats	Couplets
Rukoo	Bending in prayer, up to the knees

Saher	Start of fasting at sunrise
Salamkana	Greeting room
Sarai	Hotel
Saur	2nd month of Spring (April-May)
Sayed	a title, lineage from Prophet Mohammad
Seekh	Spit, for fires
Siahbad	Dark wind
Soor cap	Black cap
Sunbula	September
Takbeer	Call to Prayer
Tambour	Long necked lute
Ustad	Professor
Zedoary	Perennial herbs

Index

Haji Ismail Siyah, 35

Haji Mohammad, 118

Haji Nawab, 105, 118, 206

Hakim, 23, 24, 25, 28, 33, 64, 65, 71, 72, 73, 90, 96, 98, 99, 110, 155, 157, 163, 178, 179, 180, 196, 231, 310, 311, 349, 378, 392, 406, 407, 417, 419, 422, 423, 427

Hakim Sanai, 96, 163

Hameedullah, 58

Haqiqat, 121

Haram Sarai, 19, 77, 98

Harbia, 11, 136

Hashim Shaiq Afandi, 163, 164, 166, 167, 172, 189, 294

Hassan Gailani, 273

Hassan Khan Girdabi Momandi, 248

Hassan Khan Shamilo, 133

Hassan Pakravan, 142

Hayatullah, 15, 213

Hazrat Allama Mohammad Siddiq Khan Qazi, 147

Hazrat Imam Ghazali, 350

Hazrat Mojaddadi, 46, 57

Hazrat Pasha, 134

Hazrat Shah Wilaetmaab, 410

Hazrat Sheikh Bedil, 151

Helmand River, 354

Henry McMahon, 126, 135

Hermand Project, 427

Hermand River Project, 439

Hindu Kush Mountains, 435

History of Abul Feda, 156

History of Farishta, 156

History of the Ghaznavid Period, 220

Hizbul -Bahr, 334

Holy *Khirgah*, 373

Hotel Ghazni, 152

Hukumat-e-Alas, 32

Hussain Afandi, 139

Hussain Kot, 11, 12, 30, 34, 38, 44, 52, 54, 61, 153, 220, 315, 330

Hussein Razamjo, 82

Ibrahim Beg, 70, 71, 79

Ibrahim Khalil, 59

Ibrahim Khan, 153, 154, 158

Iftar, 19, 87, 331

Imam Abu Ismail, 29

154, 174, 175, 183, 184,
194, 199, 200, 262, 265,
266, 270, 271, 286, 382,
385, 386, 387, 397, 411

Mirza Mohammad
Hussain Khan, 9

Mirza Mohammad Khan
Murshid, 154

Mirza Mohammad Khan
Yaftali, 73, 286, 397

Mirza Mohammad
Qasim Khan, 62, 64, 70,
75, 80

Mirza Mohammad
Yosuf, 62, 90, 95, 271

Mirza Qasim, 63, 71

Mirza Qasim Khan, 63

Mobashir Tarazi, 205,
206, 209, 279, 303

Mobashir Tarzari, 296

Mohammad Abdou, 236

Mohammad Afzal, 25,
28, 81

Mohammad Alam
Khani, 370

Mohammad Alam
Kohistani, 17

Mohammad Aman
Khan, 22

Mohammad Amin Khan,
122

Mohammad Annus, 239

Mohammad Anwar, 337,
339

Mohammad Anwar
Bismil, 122

Mohammad Anwar
Khan, 40, 130, 345, 403

Mohammad Assef, 305

Mohammad Attiq, 115,
116

Mohammad Ayub, 317

Mohammad Azim, 78,
212, 327, 328

Mohammad Bin
Mohammad Maroof, 221

Mohammad Bin
Mohammad Shirazi, 436

Mohammad Daoud, 6,
103, 109, 114, 122, 133,
139, 153, 158, 162, 178,
202, 215, 216, 229, 276,
365, 366, 367, 368, 387,
389, 392, 393, 394, 395,
396, 397, 399, 400, 404,
406, 415, 416, 418, 422,
423, 424, 425, 426, 430,
431

Mohammad Ghaus, 59,
75, 76, 91, 347, 393

Mohammad Ghaus Khan
Barekzai, 59

Mohammad Gul Khan
Momand, 95

Mohammad Hashim, 39,
90, 96, 103, 110, 111,
112, 113, 114, 119, 120,
128, 152, 153, 154, 159,
161, 174, 176, 178, 180,
181, 183, 184, 185, 188,

192, 193, 195, 196, 198,
199, 202, 208, 209, 211,
212, 215, 216, 217, 222,
228, 230, 231, 232, 233,
234, 236, 237, 238, 251,
255, 256, 263, 272, 273,
274, 279, 280, 282, 283,
287, 292, 295, 298, 304,
307, 313, 314, 318, 333,
357, 359, 365, 367, 378,
379, 385, 386, 387, 399,
432, 433

Mohammad Hassan
Agha, 358

Mohammad Hassan
Khan, 18, 168, 385, 386

Mohammad Hassan
Siyah, 170

Mohammad Hayat, 11,
140

Mohammad Ibrahim
Alamshahi, 122

Mohammad Ibrahim
Khan, 59, 111, 153

Mohammad Ibrahim
Safa, 122

Mohammad Islam Khan
Maihan, 316

Mohammad Kabir, 39,
348, 412

Mohammad Karim
Khan, 38, 91, 117

Mohammad Khan Tata,
302

Mohammad Nadir, 4, 14,
16, 17, 38, 102, 103,

112, 114, 120, 153, 158,
178, 183, 184, 199, 218,
348, 365, 367

Mohammad Naim, 122,
139, 158, 162, 193, 215,
216, 217, 218, 219, 221,
222, 223, 226, 228, 261,
280, 284, 286, 288, 290,
291, 295, 355, 365, 366,
367, 372, 396, 408, 413,
418, 422

Mohammad Omar, 80,
181, 305, 396

Mohammad Osman, 309

Mohammad Qasim, 352,
356

Mohammad Qasim
Sharifee, 132

Mohammad Rafiq, 86,
103

Mohammad Sadiq
Mojaddadi, 46

Mohammad Sayeed
Khan, 79

Mohammad Usman
Khan Amir, 128

Mohammad Wali, 37,
38, 39, 49, 213, 214

Mohammad Yosuf, 49,
61, 62, 73, 91, 246, 278,
279, 302, 359, 365, 427

Mohammad Yosuf Khan
Safi, 246, 278

Mohammad Younis,

527

About the Authors

Marie Khalili Nasiri and Afzal Nasiri

Marie Khalili Nasiri is the daughter of Khalilullah Khalili. She was born in Kabul, Afghanistan and had her early education at the Rabia Balkhi High School.

Later she studied Arabic language in Jeddah during the time her father was Ambassador to Saudi Arabia.

She was later hired by the Ministry of Information and Culture and appointed reporter at *THE KABUL TIMES* (English) daily newspaper. She was in charge of the Women's page at the paper.

In 1975 she was appointed as Secretary of the Afghan Women's Organization to celebrate the United Nation's "Year of the Women".

She is married to Afzal Nasiri, who also worked at *THE KABUL TIMES* as a journalist. They met and married in 1975 in Baghdad, Iraq, where her father was the Ambassador of Afghanistan at that time.

Marie and Afzal moved to the USA after the Soviet invasion of Afghanistan in 1979. Marie worked diligently towards the cause of women in Afghanistan after the Taliban control in 1996 to 2001. She traveled to different places in the USA to fight against the " Plight of Afghan women," delivering lectures and talking to various influential groups, raising awareness to Afghan women cause.

Marie and Afzal live in Manassas, VA with their two sons.

Afzal Nasiri holds a Masters in Political Science from a reputable university in India. He also has journalism training and courses. He graduated High School from Roman Catholic School in India.

In Afghanistan Afzal worked at *THE KABUL TIMES* Editorial Board from 1973 to 1980 before he left his country for the US after the Soviet invasion. He has written many articles in Afghanistan, India and also articles and op-eds in local papers in New York and New Jersey. Afzal's father hailed from the Farza (Kohdaman), North of Kabul and was a political refugee in India from childhood.

Al Nasiri can be reached at afzal.nasiri@gmail.com or 703-447-1656. Please visit our website at: http://memoirsofkhalili.com

Made in the USA
San Bernardino, CA
17 October 2015